MW00715398

ITALIAN COOKING

First reprint March 2009

Italian Cooking
was created and produced by McRae Books Srl
Via del Salviatino, 1 – Fiesole (Florence), Italy
info@mcraebooks.com
Publishers: Anne McRae and Marco Nardi

Project Director: Anne McRae
Design: Marco Nardi
Edited by Carla Bardi
Photography: Lorenzo Borri, Keeho Casati, Mauro Corsi, Walter Mericchi, Leonardo Pasquinelli, Gianni Petronio, Studio Marco Lanza
Home Economist: Benedetto Rillo
Layouts: Laura Ottina
Repro: Fotolito RAF, Florence

ISBN 978-88-6098-086-1

Printed and bound in China

General Information

The level of difficulty of the recipes in this book is expressed as a number from 1 (simple) to 3 (difficult).

Carla Bardi

ITALIAN COOKING

McRae Books

CONTENTS

STARTERS

BRUSCHETTA

Toast the bread until golden brown on both sides. • Rub half a garlic clove evenly over each slice. The crisp toast works like a grater. • Drizzle with the oil and season with salt and pepper. • Serve warm.

Serves: 4

Preparation: 5 min.

Cooking: 5 min.

Level of difficulty: 1

- 4–8 slices day-old, firm-textured bread
- 2–4 cloves garlic, peeled
- 4–8 tbsp high-quality extra-virgin olive oil
- Salt and freshly ground black pepper

TUSCAN-STYLE CROSTINI

Serves: 6–8

Preparation: 35 min.

Cooking: 30 min.

Level of difficulty: 1

- **14 oz (400 g) chicken livers**
- **4 salt-cured anchovy fillets**
- **1 tbsp salt-cured capers, rinsed**
- **3 tbsp butter**
- **1 onion, finely chopped**
- **$^1/_2$ cup (125 ml) dry white wine**
- **$^1/_4$ cup (60 ml) extra-virgin olive oil**
- **Salt and freshly ground black pepper**
- **$^1/_2$ cup (125 ml) Beef Stock (see page 946)**
- **1 French loaf, sliced and toasted**

Trim any connective tissue and discolored parts from the chicken livers and chop into small pieces. • Finely chop the anchovy fillets and capers together. • Melt two-thirds of the butter in a frying pan over medium heat. Add the onion and sauté until tender. • Add the chicken livers and simmer for 5 minutes, stirring frequently. • Season with salt and pepper. Add the wine and simmer for 15 minutes, stirring frequently. If the mixture dries out, moisten with the stock. • Remove the pan from the heat and set aside to cool a little. • Place the liver mixture on a chopping board and chop finely. • Heat the oil in the pan over medium heat and add the liver mixture, anchovies, and capers. Stir well, add the remaining butter, and simmer for 3–4 minutes. • Spread the mixture on the toast and keep warm in the oven until just before serving.

NEAPOLITAN CROSTINI

Preheat the oven to 350°F (180°C/gas 4).
• Spread the slices of bread with a generous helping of butter then cut them in half. • Place a slice of mozzarella on each slice of bread and top with a slice of tomato and some pieces of anchovy. • Season with salt, pepper, and oregano. • Bake in the oven until the bread is pale golden brown and the mozzarella has melted, about 10 minutes. • Serve hot.

Serves: 6–8

Preparation: 15 min.

Cooking: 10 min.

Level of difficulty: 1

- **10 slices sandwich bread**
- **¹/₂ cup (125 g) butter**
- **8 oz (250 g) mozzarella cheese, sliced**
- **3 large ripe tomatoes, thinly sliced**
- **6–8 anchovy fillets, chopped**
- **Salt and freshly ground black pepper**
- **1 tsp dried oregano**

CROSTINI WITH MUSHROOMS

Heat the oil in a large frying pan over medium heat. Sauté the garlic for 2–3 minutes, then add the mushrooms, bay leaf, cloves, and peppercorns. • Cook over high heat for a few minutes, then add the wine, lemon juice, and salt. Cover the pan and simmer over low heat until the mushrooms are tender. • Spread the mushrooms on the toast and serve warm.

Serves: 4–6

Preparation: 10 min.

Cooking: 15 min.

Level of difficulty: 1

- $1/2$ cup (125 ml) extra-virgin olive oil
- 4 cloves garlic, finely chopped
- 1 lb (500 g) white mushrooms, peeled and thinly sliced
- 1 bay leaf
- 2 cloves
- 10 black peppercorns
- $1/3$ cup (90 ml) dry white wine
- Salt
- Freshly squeezed juice of 1 lemon
- 1 French loaf, sliced and toasted

SEAFOOD BRUSCHETTE

Serves: 4–6

Preparation: 30 min.
+ 1 hr. to soak the
shellfish

Cooking: 20 min.

Level of difficulty: 2

- 8 oz (250 g)
  mussels,
  in shell
- 8 oz (250 g) clams,
  in shell
- 2 tbsp extra-virgin
  olive oil
- 2 cloves garlic
- 2 tbsp finely
  chopped fresh
  parsley
- 1 cup (250 ml) dry
  white wine
- 8 oz (250 g) shrimp
- 1 red bell pepper
  (capsicum)
- 1 scallion (green
  onion), finely
  chopped
- $1/2$ tbsp butter
- 1 tsp saffron,
  dissolved in $1/2$
  cup (125 ml)
  lukewarm milk
- Salt and freshly
  ground black
  pepper
- 8–12 thick slices
  toast, rubbed with
  garlic

Soak the mussels and clams in a large bowl of cold water for 1 hour. • Pull any beards off the mussels and scrub well. Rinse under cold running water. Drain well. • Sauté 1 tablespoon of the oil, with the garlic and parsley in a large frying pan for 2–3 minutes. • Add the mussels and clams and pour in half the wine. • Cover the pan and place over medium-high heat for 5–10 minutes. Shake the pan often until the shells are all open. • Strain the liquid the shellfish produce and set aside. Discard any shells that haven't opened. • Detach the mussels and clams from their shells and set aside. • Shell the shrimp and devein. Chop off the heads and rinse thoroughly in cold running water. • Carefully wash the bell pepper, cut in half, remove the seeds and core, and dice. • Sauté the scallion in a frying pan with the butter and remaining oil. Add the bell pepper and sauté briefly, stirring continuously with a wooden spoon. • Add the remaining wine and simmer over high heat. • When the wine has evaporated, add the mussel liquid and the saffron and milk. Season with salt and pepper. • Cook over high heat for a few minutes until the sauce has reduced. Add the mussels, clams, and shrimp and cook for 3 minutes more, stirring often. • Sprinkle with the remaining parsley. • Spoon the seafood over the toast (bruschette) and serve hot.

SICILIAN-STYLE CROSTINI

Cut the slices of bread in half and remove the crusts. • Heat the oil in a large, deep-sided frying pan until very hot and fry the bread until golden brown on both sides. • Drain on paper towels. • Place the vinegar, sugar, and water in a small saucepan over medium heat and bring to a boil. Add the capers, pine nuts, raisins, candied lemon peel, and tomatoes. Simmer for 5 minutes, stirring gently. • Spread the fried bread with this mixture and serve hot.

Serves: 4

Preparation: 10 min.

Cooking: 10 min.

Level of difficulty: 1

- **4–8 slices firm-textured bread**
- **1 cup (250 ml) extra-virgin olive oil, for frying**
- **2 tbsp vinegar**
- **1 tsp sugar**
- **2 tbsp water**
- **1 tsp salt-cured capers, rinsed**
- **2 tsp pine nuts**
- **2 tsp raisins**
- **2 tsp candied lemon peel, diced**
- **2 ripe tomatoes, diced**

PROSCIUTTO WITH CANTALOUPE

Slice the cantaloupe into 8–12 wedges and remove the skin. • Place the slices of melon on a large serving dish. Arrange the prosciutto around them and serve.

Serves: 4–6

Preparation: 10 min.

Level of difficulty: 1

- **5 oz (150 g) prosciutto (preferably top-quality Parma ham), thinly sliced**
- **1 medium cantaloupe (rock melon)**

PIQUANT GREEN OLIVES

Serves: 8–10

Preparation: 10 min.
+ 2 hr. to rest

Level of difficulty: 1

- **60 large green olives, pitted**
- **4 cloves garlic, finely chopped**
- **1 tbsp finely chopped parsley**
- **1 tbsp coarsely chopped fresh mint**
- **Pinch of dried oregano**
- **1 tsp red pepper flakes**
- **$1/4$ cup (60 ml) extra-virgin olive oil**

Rinse the olives in cold water and pat dry with paper towels. • Lightly crush the olives with a meat-pounding mallet. • Place the olives and garlic in a serving dish. Add the parsley, mint, oregano, pepper flakes, and oil. Mix well and cover. • Set aside in a cool place (not the refrigerator) for 2 hours before serving.

MINI SAUSAGE ROLLS

Serves: 4–6

Preparation: 25 min.

Cooking: 15 min.

Level of difficulty: 1

- **10 oz (300 g) frozen puff pastry, thawed**
- **6–8 long thin sausages**
- **1 large egg yolk, beaten**

Preheat the oven to 400°F (200°C/gas 6). • Lightly oil a baking sheet. • Roll the pastry out on a lightly floured work surface to about ¼ inch (5 mm) thick. • Cut the pastry into rectangles the same length as the sausages and wide enough to wrap them. Place a sausage on each piece of pastry and wrap it. • Using a sharp knife, cut each roll into three pieces. Place the sausage rolls on the prepared baking sheet, seam side down. Brush the tops of each one with egg yolk. • Bake until the pastry is puffed and golden brown, about 15 minutes. • Serve hot or at room temperature.

QUICK MINI PIZZAS

Preheat the oven to 400°F (200°C/gas 6).
• Lightly oil 2 baking sheets. • Roll the pastry out on a lightly floured work surface to about ¼ inch (3-mm) thick. Use a cookie cutter or glass to cut out disks of pastry. Re-roll the scraps of pastry and continue cutting out rounds until all the pastry is used. • Place the pastry on the prepared baking sheets. Prick each one a few times with a fork to stop them puffing up too much during cooking.
• Place the tomatoes in a bowl and stir in the anchovies and oregano. Season with salt and pepper. • Spoon a little of the tomato mixture on each pizza, spreading it evenly with the back of the spoon. Sprinkle a little of the mozzarella cheese on each pizza. Drizzle each one lightly with oil. • Bake until the pastry is puffed and golden brown and the mozzarella is melted, about 15 minutes. • Serve hot or at room temperature.

Serves: 6–8

Preparation: 15 min.

Cooking: 15 min.

Level of difficulty: 1

- 14 oz (400 g) frozen puff pastry, thawed
- 1 (14-oz/400-g) can tomatoes, chopped, partially drained
- 4 anchovy fillets, chopped
- 1 tsp oregano
- Salt and freshly ground black pepper
- 5 oz (150 g) mozzarella cheese, cut in small cubes
- 2–3 tbsp extra-virgin olive oil

FRIED MOZZARELLA

Break the eggs into a shallow bowl. Season lightly with salt and beat well with a fork.
• Place the flour in a second shallow bowl and the bread crumbs in a third. • Heat the oil in a deep-fryer or deep frying pan over medium heat. • Dredge the slices of mozzarella in the flour then dip them in the egg. Place in the bowl with the bread crumbs, turning over to coat well. Shake gently to remove excess. • Fry in the oil in small batches until golden brown on both sides. • Remove with a slotted spoon and drain on paper towels. Season with salt to taste. Continue frying the mozzarella is all cooked. • Serve hot.

Serves: 4–6

Preparation: 10 min.

Cooking: 25 min.

Level of difficulty: 1

- **2 large eggs**
- **Salt**
- **$^1/_2$ cup (75 g) all-purpose (plain) flour**
- **$1^1/_2$ cups (200 g) fine dry bread crumbs**
- **2 cups (500 ml) olive oil, for frying**
- **12 oz (350 g) mozzarella cheese, sliced about $^1/_2$-inch (5-mm) thick**
- **1 tsp dried oregano**

BAKED CHEESE AND POLENTA BALLS

Bring the water and salt to a boil in a large saucepan or polenta pan. Pour in the polenta and stir until it is thick and coming away from the sides of the pan as you stir, about 50 minutes. (This dish can also be made with precooked polenta that will be ready in 10–15 minutes). • Stir the nutmeg and garlic into the polenta. • Spread the polenta out on a marble bench top or polenta board and let cool. • Preheat the oven to 400°F (200°C/gas 6). • Butter a large baking dish. • Shape tablespoons of the polenta into balls the size of a golf ball and use your index finger to press 2–3 pieces of cheese into each one. • Place in the baking dish and sprinkle with the Parmesan. • Bake for 10–15 minutes, or until the Parmesan is browned and the cheese inside the balls is melted. • Serve hot.

Serves: 6–8

Preparation: 30 min.

Cooking: 60–70 min.

Level of difficulty: 2

- **2 quarts (2 liters) cold water**
- **1 tsp salt**
- **1 lb (500 g) polenta (yellow cornmeal)**
- **$^1/_2$ tsp ground nutmeg**
- **1 clove garlic, finely chopped**
- **10 oz (300 g) Fontina cheese, cut in small cubes**
- **4 tbsp freshly grated Parmesan cheese**

SAVORY PASTRY FRITTERS

Serves: 8–10

Preparation: 40 min.
+ 1 hr. to rise

Cooking: 20 min.

Level of difficulty: 2

- 1^1/$_2$ oz **(45 g) fresh yeast or 3 (^{1}/$_4$-oz/ 7-g) packages active dry yeast**
- **1 cup (250 ml) warm water**
- **3^1/$_3$ cups (500 g) all-purpose (plain) flour**
- **1 teaspoon salt**
- **4 tbsp melted lard**
- **2 cups (500 ml) oil, for frying**

Dissolve the yeast in the water and set aside to rest for 15 minutes. • Mix the flour and salt in a medium bowl. Make a well in the center and pour in the lard and yeast mixture. Stir with a fork, gradually working in the flour. • Transfer the dough to a floured work surface and knead until smooth, about 10 minutes. Shape into a ball and leave to rise in the bowl for about 1 hour. • Roll out the dough into a sheet ^{1}/$_8$ inch (3 mm) thick. Cut into lozenges or rectangles about 2 inches (5 cm) long. • Heat the oil in a deep-fryer or deep frying pan over medium heat. • Fry the fritters in batches until golden brown all over. • Drain on paper towels and serve hot.

FRIED POLENTA WITH PEAS, MUSHROOMS, AND CHEESE

Heat the oil in a large frying pan over medium heat. Add the mushrooms and peas. Mix well and simmer for 10 minutes. • Add the capers, salt, and pepper. Cook for 5–10 minutes more, or until the vegetables are soft, stirring occasionally.

• Lightly flour the polenta slices, dip them into the egg, and then into a bowl containing the bread crumbs. • Preheat the oven to 400°F (200°C/ gas 6) • Heat the frying oil in a deep-fryer or deep frying pan until very hot. Fry the slices of polenta in small batches until golden brown on both sides.

• Drain on paper towels and arrange in a buttered baking dish. • Cover each slice with a spoonful of peas and mushrooms, and a slice of mozzarella.

• Bake for 10 minutes, or until the mozzarella is melted and golden. • Remove from the oven, sprinkle with the basil, and serve immediately.

Serves: 4

Preparation: 25 min.

Cooking: 30 min.

Level of difficulty: 1

- **2 tbsp extra-virgin olive oil**
- **8 oz (250 g) white mushrooms, sliced**
- **8 oz (250 g) fresh or frozen peas**
- **1 tbsp salt-cured capers, rinsed**
- **Salt and freshly ground black pepper**
- **4 tbsp all-purpose (plain) flour**
- **8 large slices cold polenta (see page 237)**
- **1 large egg, beaten**
- **1 cup (150 g) fine dry bread crumbs**
- **2 cups (500 ml) oil, for frying**
- **4 oz (125 g) mozzarella cheese, sliced**
- **4 tbsp finely chopped basil**

FRIED PANINI WITH PARMESAN, PROSCIUTTO, AND TOMATO

Serves: 4–6

Preparation: 10 min.

Cooking: 10 min.

Level of difficulty: 2

- **16 slices white sandwich bread**
- **3 oz (90 g) prosciutto (Parma ham), thinly sliced**
- **3 oz (90 g) Parmesan cheese, cut into flakes**
- **2 large ripe tomatoes, thinly sliced**
- **Salt and freshly ground black pepper**
- **Leaves from 2 sprigs of basil**
- **$1/3$ cup (90 ml) milk**
- **4 large eggs**
- **1 cup (150 g) fine dry bread crumbs**
- **$1/4$ cup (60 g) butter**

Cut the bread into 3 inch (8 cm) disks using a cookie cutter. Arrange the prosciutto on half the disks of bread. Top these with the Parmesan and a slice or two of tomato. Season with salt and pepper. Add a basil leaf to each one and then cover them with the remaining disks of bread. Press together very firmly. • Put the milk in a bowl. Break the eggs into another bowl and beat well. Put the bread crumbs into a third bowl. Dip the panini in the milk and then in the egg. Finally dip them in the bread crumbs, ensuring that they are evenly coated all over. • Melt the butter in a large frying pan over medium heat. Add the panini and sauté for 3–5 minutes, until golden brown. Turn and sauté for 3–5 minutes, or until golden brown and crisp all over. • Drain on paper towels.
• Serve warm.

RICE SUPPLÌ

Serves: 4–6

Preparation: 45 min.

Cooking: 45 min.

Level of difficulty: 3

Bring the water to a boil in a large saucepan over medium heat. Add the tomatoes, ¼ cup (60 g) of the butter, and ½ teaspoon of salt. Add the rice and cook for 12–15 minutes, or until tender. Drain and let cool. • Add the Parmesan and 1 of the eggs. Mix well. • Heat the remaining 2 tablespoons of butter in a large frying pan over medium heat. Add the onion and sauté for 3–4 minutes, until transparent. Add the prosciutto, beef, and chicken livers. Sauté for 2 minutes, or until the meat is lightly browned. Add the mushrooms, tomato concentrate, and water. Season with salt and pepper and lower the heat. Cover and simmer for 20 minutes, stirring from time to time. • Shape about 3 tablespoons of the rice mixture into a ball using your hands. Make a hole in the center of the ball and fill it with some of the meat sauce and a piece of mozzarella. Cover with a little more rice and press together to seal. Repeat until all the rice, meat sauce, and mozzarella are used. • Dip the rice balls in the remaining egg then roll them in the bread crumbs, ensuring that they are evenly coated. • Heat the oil in a large frying pan over medium heat and fry the supplì in small batches until golden brown all over, 5–7 minutes per batch. Scoop out with a slotted spoon and drain on paper towels. • Serve hot.

- 4 cups (1 liter) water
- ³/₄ cup (180 g) chopped peeled tomatoes
- ¹/₃ cup (90 g) butter
- Salt
- 1¹/₂ cups (300 g) short-grain rice
- ¹/₂ cup (50 g) freshly grated Parmesan cheese
- 2 large eggs, lightly beaten
- 1 small onion, finely chopped
- 2 oz (60 g) prosciutto (Parma ham), chopped
- 4 oz (125 g) lean ground (minced) beef
- 2 chicken livers, finely chopped
- 1 oz (30 g) dried mushrooms, soaked in warm water for 15 minutes, drained and chopped
- 2 tablespoons tomato concentrate
- 3 tablespoons water
- Freshly ground black pepper
- 3 oz (90 g) mozzarella, cut into small cubes
- ¹/₂ cup (75 g) fine dry bread crumbs
- 4 cups (1 liter) olive oil, for frying

MUSSEL FRITTERS

Serves: 4–6

Preparation: 30 min.
+ 1 hr. to soak the
mussels

Cooking: 30 min.

Level of difficulty: 2

- 1¹/₂ lb (750 g) mussels, in shell
- ¹/₂ cup (125 ml) dry white wine
- ³/₄ cup (180 ml) cold water
- 2 tbsp butter
- ¹/₄ teaspoon salt
- 1 cup (150 g) all-purpose (plain) flour
- 4 large eggs
- 2 tbsp finely chopped parsley
- 4 tablespoons freshly grated Parmesan cheese
- 2 cups (500 ml) oil, for frying

Soak the mussels in a large bowl of water for 1 hour. Pull off any beards, scrub, and rinse well in cold water. • Put the mussels in a large frying pan over high heat, sprinkle with the wine, and cover the pan. • When all the shells are open (discard any that do not open), pick the mussels out of their shells. • Bring the water, butter, and salt to a boil in a small pot, add the flour, and remove from the heat. Beat with a wooden spoon until thick and well mixed. • Return to low heat and stir until the mixture sticks to the sides and bottom of the pot. Let cool. • Stir in the eggs one by one, and add the parsley, Parmesan, and mussels.
• Heat the oil in a deep-fryer or deep frying pan to very hot. Drop tablespoons of the mussel batter into the oil. Fry until puffed and golden brown.
• Drain on paper towels, sprinkle with salt, and serve at once.

Serves: 4–6

Preparation: 5 min.

Cooking: 10 min.

Level of difficulty: 1

FRIED HERBS

- ²/₃ cup (100 g) all-purpose (plain) flour
- ¹/₃ cup (90 ml) sparkling mineral water
- 1 cup (250 ml) sunflower oil, for frying
- 24 sage leaves
- 24 sprigs flat-leaf parsley
- 24 large basil leaves
- Salt

Place the flour in a medium bowl and add the water. Beat with a whisk to make a smooth batter. • Heat the oil in a small, deep frying pan over medium heat. • Dip the herbs in the batter and then drop them in the oil. Fry until golden brown, 2–3 minutes. • Transfer to a layer of paper towels using a slotted spoon and let drain. • Arrange the fried herbs on a serving dish and sprinkle with salt. • Serve hot.

DEEP-FRIED CALAMARI WITH ALMONDS

P lace the flour, salt, and pepper in a bowl. Put the eggs in another bowl, and mix the bread crumbs and almonds in a third bowl. • Roll the calamari in the flour, shaking off any excess. Dip in the egg then roll in the bread crumbs and almonds. • Heat the oil in a deep-fryer or deep frying pan until hot and fry the calamari in batches. Remove with a slotted spoon as they turn golden brown (about 5 minutes) and drain on paper towels. Do not cook for longer or the calamari will become tough. • Garnish with the parsley and lemon and serve hot.

36

Serves: 4–6

Preparation: 15 min.

Cooking: 20 min.

Level of difficulty: 2

- $1/2$ cup (75 g) all-purpose (plain) flour
- Salt and freshly ground black pepper
- 2 large eggs, beaten
- 2 cups (300 g) fine dry bread crumbs
- $1/2$ cup (60 g) almonds, finely chopped
- 4 cups (1 liter) oil, for frying
- 14 oz (400 g) calamari bodies, sliced in rings
- 8 sprigs parsley, to garnish
- 1 lemon, sliced, to garnish

FRIED ONION RINGS

Mix the flour and salt in a bowl. Make a hollow in the center and add the egg yolk and oil. • Use a whisk to stir the mixture as you add enough water to form a thick, fluid batter with no lumps. Set aside for 30 minutes to rest. • Just before frying, beat the egg whites until stiff and fold into the batter. The water can be replaced with milk, which will make a soft sweet batter, or beer, which puffs up during frying and is crisper. • Separate the onion rings and place on a clean cloth to dry. • Heat the oil in a deep-fryer or frying pan to very hot. • Dip the rings in the batter, shake off any excess, and fry in batches until golden brown. Turn once or twice during cooking with tongs or a fork. • Scoop out with a slotted spoon and drain on paper towels. Season with salt and serve hot.

Serves: 4–6

Preparation: 20 min. + 30 min. to rest batter

Cooking: 20 min.

Level of difficulty: 1

- **1 cup (150 g) all-purpose (plain) flour**
- **$^1/_4$ teaspoon salt**
- **1 large egg, separated + 2 large egg whites, beaten to stiff peaks**
- **1 tbsp extra-virgin olive oil**
- **Cold water**
- **6 medium red or white onions, peeled, and sliced into thin rings**
- **2 cups (500 ml) oil, for frying**
- **Salt**

CHEESE APPETIZERS

Preheat the oven to 400°F (200°C/gas 6). • Mix the Fontina, parsley, Parmesan, eggs, and pepper together in a large bowl. • Roll the puff pastry out until very thin then cut into squares about 4 inches (10 cm) wide. • Brush with half the melted butter. • In the center of each pastry square, place one tablespoon of the cheese mixture and fold the dough over it to form a triangle. Pinch the edges to seal well. • Place on a greased baking sheet. • Brush with the remaining butter and bake for about 30 minutes, or until golden brown. Serve hot.

Serves: 6–8

Preparation: 15 min.

Cooking: 30 min.

Level of difficulty: 1

- **5 oz (150 g) Fontina cheese, cut in small cubes**
- **1 tbsp finely chopped fresh parsley**
- **3 oz (90 g) freshly grated Parmesan cheese**
- **3 large eggs, lightly beaten**
- **Freshly ground black pepper**
- **1 lb (500 g) puff pastry**
- **2 oz (60 g) butter, melted**

CREAMY GORGONZOLA WITH CELERY

Serves: 2–4

Preparation: 10 min.

Level of difficulty: 1

- **8 stalks celery**
- **2 oz (60 g) creamy Gorgonzola cheese**

Clean the stalks of celery, removing any tough fibers. Wash thoroughly and dry. • Fill the stalks with the Gorgonzola (kept at room temperature for 1–2 hours).

EGG AND ARUGULA TARTLETS

Serves: 4–8

Preparation: 45 min.

Cooking: 15–20 min.

Level of difficulty: 1

- **14 oz (400 g) frozen shortcrust pastry, thawed or 1 recipe Shortcrust Pastry (see page 959)**
- **5 large eggs**
- **1/2 cup (125 ml) milk**
- **5 oz (150 g) freshly grated Fontina cheese**
- **2 tbsp butter**
- **1 onion, finely chopped**
- **1 clove garlic, finely chopped**
- **3 tbsp pine nuts**
- **1 bunch arugula (rocket), chopped**

Preheat the oven to 375°F (190°C/gas 5). Butter 8 small tartlet pans. • Roll the pastry out on a lightly floured work surface to 1/4-inch (3-mm) thick. Cut into rounds large enough to line the bottoms and sides of the tartlet pans. • Bake in the oven for 10 minutes. • Melt the butter in a medium frying pan and sauté the onion and garlic until transparent, 2–3 minutes. • Beat the eggs and milk in a medium bowl until frothy. • Remove the tartlet cases from the oven and spoon a little of the onion mixture into each one. Sprinkle each tartlet with some of the cheese. Divide the milk mixture among the tartlet cases. • Bake until the filling is set, 15–20 minutes. • Toast the pine nuts in a frying pan. • Sprinkle the hot tartlets with arugula and pine nuts and serve hot.

CHEESE, PEAR, AND WALNUT MOLDS

C ombine the cheeses in a bowl, mix, then add the walnuts, pepper, and brandy. • Carefully stir the pear pulp into the cheese mixture. • Butter 6–8 small molds and fill with the mixture. Chill in the refrigerator for at least 1 hour. • Invert the molds onto serving plates, garnish with the chives, and serve.

Serves: 6–8

Preparation: 15 min. + 1 hr. to chill

Level of difficulty: 2

- 6 oz (180 g) ricotta cheese, drained
- 8 oz (250 g) mascarpone cheese
- 8 oz (250 g) Gorgonzola cheese
- 2 cups (250 g) finely chopped walnuts
- Freshly ground black pepper
- 2 tbsp brandy
- 4 large sweet pears, peeled, cored, and finely chopped
- 1 tbsp butter
- 2 tbsp finely chopped chives

QUICK GORGONZOLA FOCACCIA

Serves: 4–6

Preparation: 15 min.

Cooking: 25–30 min.

Level of difficulty: 1

- **2 tbsp butter**
- **14 oz (400 g) frozen puff pastry, thawed**
- **6 oz (180 g) Gorgonzola cheese, cut in small cubes**
- **1 large egg, lightly beaten**

Preheat the oven to 375°F (190°C/gas 5). • Butter a 10-inch (26-cm) round baking pan. • Divide the pastry into two pieces the same size. Roll one piece of pastry out on a lightly floured work surface so that it is large enough to cover the bottom and part-way up the sides of the pan. • Place the pastry in the pan. Prick the surface well with a fork so that it doesn't puff up too much during cooking. • Sprinkle the Gorgonzola over the pastry, leaving a ½-inch (5-mm) border free of cheese around the edges. • Brush the border with the egg. • Roll the second piece of pastry out so that it is large enough to cover the pan. • Place the pastry in the pan over the cheese, pressing down gently around the edges to seal. Prick in several places with a fork. • Bake until puffed and golden brown, 25–30 minutes. • Serve hot.

CHEESE FONDUE

Let the cheese rest in the milk for 2–3 hours. • Transfer the cheese and milk to a fondue pot and place it in another pan filled with boiling water. • Add the cream and salt and mix well. • Remove the fondue pot from the larger pan of water and place it over the flame on its fondue stand in the center of the table. Do not let the fondue boil. • Arrange the diced bread on a platter. Each diner uses their fondue fork to dip dices of bread into the fondue.

Serves: 6

*Preparation: 15 min.
 + 2–3 hr. to rest*

Cooking: 15 min.

Level of difficulty: 2

- **1 lb (500 g) Fontina cheese, diced**
- **1 cup (250 ml) full cream milk**
- **1 cup (250 ml) heavy (double) cream**
- **Salt**
- **Day-old bread, diced, to serve**

PARMESAN "ICE CREAM"

Serves: 6–8

*Preparation: 10 min.
+ time to churn or
freeze ice cream*

Level of difficulty: 1

- 1 lb (500 g) freshly grated Parmesan cheese
- 4 cups (1 liter) heavy (double) cream
- Salt and freshly ground white pepper
- 5 oz (150 g) prosciutto (Parma ham), thinly sliced

Melt the cheese and cream in a double boiler over barely simmering water. Do not let the mixture boil. Season with salt and pepper. Set aside to cool. • Pass through a sieve and transfer to an ice-cream maker, following the directions for traditional ice-cream. If you don't have an ice-cream maker, pour the mixture into a freezerproof container and freeze, stirring at intervals as the mixture thickens. • After 3 hours, transfer to a food processor and blend until smooth. • Return to the freezer and repeat after another 3 hours.
• Serve the "ice cream" with the prosciutto.

BUCKWHEAT PANCAKES WITH VEGETABLES

Buckwheat Pancakes: Place the milk and ¼ cup (60 g) of the butter in a medium saucepan over medium-low heat and stir until the butter has melted and the milk is just simmering. Remove from the heat and set aside for 10 minutes to cool. • Stir the yeast into the milk and butter and set aside until frothy, 10–15 minutes. • Place both flours and the salt in a medium bowl. Pour in the yeast mixture and stir until well combined. • Cover the bowl with a clean cloth and set aside in a warm place until the dough has almost doubled in bulk and the surface is bubbly. • Stir the eggs into the batter. • Melt 1 tablespoon of butter in a medium frying pan over medium heat. Add enough of the pancake batter to cover the bottom of the pan. Cook until golden brown on the bottom and bubbly on top. Flip and cook the other side. • Stack the cooked pancakes in a warm oven while you cook the remaining batter. • Preheat the oven to 400°F (200°C/gas 6). • Vegetable Filling: Heat the oil in a large frying pan over medium-high heat. Add the vegetables and sauté until just tender, 7–10 minutes. • Season with salt and remove from the heat. • Fill each pancake with spoonfuls of the vegetable mixture. Fold in half and place in a baking dish. • Sprinkle the pancakes with the cheese. • Bake in the oven until the cheese is melted and bubbling, about 10 minutes. • Serve hot.

Serves: 4–6

Preparation: 45 min.

Cooking: 45 min.

Level of difficulty: 2

Buckwheat Pancakes
- 1¹/₂ cups (375 ml) milk
- ¹/₂ cup (125 g) butter
- ¹/₂ oz (15 g) fresh yeast or 1 (¹/₄-oz/ 7-g) package active dry yeast
- 1 cup (150 g) buckwheat flour
- ¹/₃ cup (50 g) all-purpose (plain) flour
- ¹/₂ tsp salt
- 2 large eggs, beaten

Vegetable Filling
- 2 tbsp extra-virgin olive oil
- 1 large leek, thinly sliced
- 1 large white onion, finely chopped
- 2 zucchini (courgettes), diced
- 2 medium carrots, diced
- Salt

VEGETABLE MOLD

Serves: 4–6

Preparation: 45 min.

Cooking: 1 h

Level of difficulty: 2

- 5 oz (150 g) butter
- 1¹/₂ lb (750 g) Swiss chard (silverbeet), coarsely chopped
- Salt and freshly ground black pepper
- Freshly grated nutmeg
- ²/₃ cup (100 g) all-purpose (plain) flour
- 3 cups (750 ml) milk
- 1 cup (125 g) freshly grated Parmesan cheese
- 4 large eggs, beaten
- ¹/₂ cup (75 g) fine dry bread crumbs
- 1 recipe Meat Sauce (see page 951), optional

Place ¼ cup (60 g) of butter in a large, heavy saucepan over medium heat. Add the Swiss chard and sauté until just tender, 5–10 minutes. Season with salt, pepper, and nutmeg. • Transfer the vegetables to a food mill or food processor and chop until smooth. Place in a large bowl. • Heat 5 tablespoons (75 g) of butter in a medium saucepan over medium heat and stir in the flour. When smooth remove from the heat and add all the milk at once, stirring constantly. • Return to low heat and stir constantly until thickened, 7–10 minutes. • Remove from the heat and season with salt, pepper, and nutmeg. • Stir the sauce into the vegetable purée until smooth and well mixed. • Stir in the cheese then add the eggs, mixing well. • Butter a 2-quart (2-liter) ring mold. Sprinkle with the bread crumbs, making sure that they stick to the sides of the mold. • Carefully spoon the vegetable mixture into the mold, smoothing it into an even layer. • Immerge the ring mold in a large saucepan of barely simmering water and simmer for 45 minutes. • Preheat the oven to 400°F (200°C/gas 6). • Remove the ring mold from the pan of water and bake in the oven until a toothpick inserted into the center comes out clean, 15–20 minutes. • Serve hot, with the meat sauce spoon into the center, if liked.

POTATO TART

Preheat the oven to 375 (190°C/gas 5).
• Butter a 9-inch (23-cm) tart pan. • Bring a
medium pan of water to a boil. Add the potatoes
and boil for 2–3 minutes. Drain well. • Place a layer
of potatoes in the pan and sprinkle with cheese.
Season lightly with salt and pepper and top with
pieces of butter. Repeat this layering process until
all the ingredients are in the pan. • Bake in the
oven until the potatoes are tender and the cheese
topping is golden brown, 25–30 minutes.
• Serve hot or at room temperature.

Serves: 4–6

Preparation: 45 min.

Cooking: 45 min.

Level of difficulty: 1

- **2 lb (1 kg) potatoes, peeled and thinly sliced**
- **8 oz (250 g) freshly grated Parmesan cheese**
- **$1/2$ cup (125 g) butter**
- **Salt and freshly ground black pepper**

STARTERS

SPINACH AND POTATO APPETIZERS

Preheat the oven at 400°F (200°C/gas 6).
• Boil the potatoes in their skins for about 25 minutes. • Drain, slip off the skins, and mash until smooth. • Place the potato purée in a saucepan and add two-thirds of the butter, the salt, pepper, nutmeg, and milk. Place over low heat and, stirring constantly, dry out excess moisture. Set aside to cool. • Cook the spinach in a pot of salted, boiling water until tender. Drain well and squeeze out excess moisture. Chop finely. • Beat the egg and one yolk together and mix well with the potato purée. • Divide the potato purée in two and mix the spinach and a dash of salt into one half. If the mixture is too moist, stir over low heat to dry. • Grease a baking sheet, spoon the potato mixture into a pastry bag, and squeeze out into walnut-sized rosettes. Repeat with the spinach mixture. • Beat the remaining egg yolk and brush the rosettes with it. • Bake for 20 minutes.
• Scoop the rosettes off the sheet with a spatula and serve hot.

Serves: 6–8

Preparation: 30 min.

Cooking: 1 hr.

Level of difficulty: 2

• 2 lb (1 kg) boiling potatoes
• $1/2$ cup (125 g) butter
• Salt and freshly ground black pepper
• Dash of nutmeg
• 1 cup (250 ml) milk
• 1 lb (500 g) fresh or frozen spinach
• 1 large egg + 2 large egg yolks

OCTOPUS SALAD

Place the octopus in a large pot of cold water with the vinegar, carrot, celery, onion, garlic, parsley, and salt. Cover and bring to a boil over high heat. Lower the heat and simmer for 1 hour. • Remove from the heat and leave to cool for at least 2 hours in the cooking water. This cooling time is very important because it makes the octopus meat tender. • Skin the octopus (it will come away easily together with the suckers – a few of the latter can be added to the salad). Cut the body in rings and the tentacles in small pieces. • Transfer to a serving dish and season with oil, lemon juice, salt, pepper, and pepper flakes. • Toss well and serve.

Serves: 6

*Preparation: 30 min.
+ 2 hr. to soften*

Cooking: 1 h

Level of difficulty: 2

- **2 lb (1 kg) octopus**
- **1 cup (250 ml) white wine vinegar**
- **1 carrot**
- **1 stalk celery**
- **1 small onion**
- **1 clove garlic**
- **5 sprigs parsley**
- **Salt and freshly ground black pepper**
- **$^1/_4$ cup (60 ml) extra-virgin olive oil**
- **Juice of 1 lemon**
- **$^1/_2$ tsp crushed red pepper flakes**

TUSCAN BREAD SALAD (PANZANELLA)

Serves: 4

Preparation: 5 min. + 30 min. to soak and chill

Level of difficulty: 1

- 1 lb (500 g) dense-grain, day-old bread
- 5 medium tomatoes
- 2 red onions
- 1 cucumber
- 12 leaves fresh basil, torn
- Salt and freshly ground black pepper
- $^1/_3$ cup (90 ml) extra-virgin olive oil
- 1 tbsp red wine vinegar

Soak the bread in a bowl of cold water for 15 minutes. • Squeeze out as much water as possible, then crumble the almost dry bread into a large salad bowl. • Slice the tomatoes and squeeze out as many seeds as possible. Peel the onions and cucumber and slice thinly. • Combine the tomatoes, cucumber, basil, and onions in the bowl with the bread. Season with salt, pepper, and $^1/_4$ cup (60 ml) of oil. Toss briefly. • Chill in the refrigerator for 15 minutes. • Just before serving, add the vinegar and remaining oil and toss again.

CAPRESE SALAD

Place the tomatoes and mozzarella in a large salad bowl. Add the basil and garlic. • Season with salt and pepper and drizzle with the oil. Toss gently and serve. • If liked, drizzle with the balsamic vinegar.

Serves: 4–6

Preparation: 10 min.

Level of difficulty: 1

- **2 lb (1 kg) cherry tomatoes, cut in half**
- **1 lb (500 g) fresh mozzarella cheese, cut in cubes**
- **Fresh basil leaves, torn**
- **1–2 cloves garlic, finely chopped**
- **Salt and freshly ground black pepper**
- **$1/4$ cup (60 ml) extra-virgin olive oil**
- **2 tbsp balsamic vinegar (optional)**

TOMATOES WITH TUNA AND MAYONNAISE

Serves: 4–6

*Preparation: 20 min.
+ 1 hr. to chill*

Level of difficulty: 1

- 8 round ripe tomatoes
- Salt and freshly ground black pepper
- 4 hard-boiled eggs
- 6 anchovy fillets, finely chopped
- 2 tbsp salt-cured capers (half finely chopped, half left whole)
- 12 oz (350 g) tuna, crumbled with a fork
- 2 tbsp finely chopped parsley
- 1 cup (250 ml) mayonnaise
- 16 fresh basil leaves, torn

Rinse the tomatoes under cold running water. Slice the top off each tomato. Use a teaspoon to remove the pulp, taking care not to break the skin. Place the tomatoes upside down in a colander to drain for 10 minutes. • Season the insides with salt and pepper. • In a bowl, mash the egg yolks with a fork and add the anchovies, chopped capers, tuna, and parsley. Stir in almost all the mayonnaise. • Chop the egg whites and add them to the mixture. Season with pepper. • Fill the tomatoes with the mixture. Top each tomato with a teaspoon of mayonnaise. Garnish with the remaining whole capers and the basil. • Chill in the refrigerator for 1 hour before serving.

61

MARINATED ANCHOVIES

Serves: 6–8

Preparation: 25 min.
+ 4 hr. to marinate
+ 2 hr. to stand

Level of difficulty: 2

- 1 lb (500 g) fresh anchovies, cleaned
- 2 cups (500 ml) white wine vinegar
- $1/3$ cup (90 ml) water
- Salt
- 1 tablespoon black peppercorns
- 2 cloves garlic, sliced
- 4 bay leaves
- 2 dried red chilies, crumbled
- $1/2$ cup (125 ml) extra-virgin olive oil

Arrange the anchovies in 1–2 layers in a deep, rectangular dish and cover with the vinegar and water. Season with salt and set aside to marinate in the refrigerator for 4 hours. The anchovies will "cook" in the vinegar and turn white. • Drain the anchovies thoroughly and rinse out the dish. • Arrange the anchovies in the dish again. Sprinkle with the peppercorns, garlic, bay leaves, chilies, and salt to taste. Drizzle with the oil. • Set aside for 2 hours at room temperature before serving.

STUFFED MUSSELS

Soak the mussels in cold water for 1 hour. Pull off any beards and rinse well. • Preheat the oven to 400°F (200°C/gas 6). • Open the mussels with a short, strong knife. Remove and discard the empty half of each shell. • Arrange the prepared mussels on an oiled baking sheet. • Blanch the tomatoes in boiling water for 2 minutes. Drain and slip off the skins. Chop the tomatoes. • Heat half the oil in a large frying pan over medium heat. Add the tomatoes and sauté for 2–3 minutes, or until they begin to break down. • Add the bread crumbs, garlic, parsley, and cheese. Season with salt and pepper and mix well. • Spoon a little of the filling into each of the mussel shells. Drizzle with the remaining oil and bake for 10–15 minutes, or until the are mussels cooked through. • Garnish with parsley and serve hot or at room temperature.

Serves: 4
Preparation: 20 min.
Cooking: 15–20 min.
Level of difficulty: 1

- 2 lb (1 kg) mussels, in shell
- 3 large ripe tomatoes
- 1/2 cup (125 ml) extra-virgin olive oil
- 2 cups (120 g) fresh bread crumbs
- 2 cloves garlic, finely chopped
- 3 tbsp finely chopped fresh parsley + extra sprigs, to garnish
- 1/3 cup (50 g) freshly grated pecorino or Parmesan cheese
- Salt and freshly ground black pepper

VENETIAN-STYLE SCALLOPS

Serves: 6

Preparation: 10 min.

Cooking: 10–15 min.

Level of difficulty: 1

- ¼ cup (60 ml) extra-virgin olive oil
- 24 sea scallops
- 2 tbsp finely chopped fresh parsley
- 1 clove garlic, finely chopped
- Salt and freshly ground black pepper
- Freshly squeezed juice of ½ lemon

Heat the oil in a large frying pan over medium-high heat. Add the scallops, parsley, and garlic and sauté for 2–3 minutes, or until the scallops are cooked through. Do not overcook the scallops. Season with salt and pepper. • Spoon the mixture into six scallop shells or individual serving dishes. Drizzle with the lemon juice and serve.

BREAD &
FOCACCIA

WHOLE-WHEAT LOAVES

To prepare the yeast, place the yeast and sugar in a small bowl and pour in half the water. Stir until the yeast has dissolved then set aside to rest for 10 minutes. • Put both flours in a large bowl with the yeast mixture, salt, and remaining water and stir until well mixed. Transfer to a lightly floured work surface and knead for about 10 minutes. • Place the dough in an oiled bowl, cover the bowl with a cloth, and set aside to rise until doubled in bulk, about 2 hours. • When the rising time has elapsed, transfer the dough to a lightly floured work surface and knead for 5 minutes. • Divide the dough into two equal portions and shape each one into a long loaf. Sprinkle with flour and use a serrated knife to cut diagonal slashes about ¼ inch (5 mm) deep along the top of each loaf. Repeat, making slashes in the other direction to create a grid pattern. • Cover with a cloth and leave to rise for 1 hour. • Preheat the oven to 400°F (200°C/gas 6). • Bake the bread until risen and golden brown, 30–40 minutes.

Makes: about 2 lb (1 kg) bread

Preparation: 30 min.

Rising time: 3 hr.

Cooking: 40 min.

Level of difficulty: 2

- 1 oz (30 g) fresh yeast or 2 (^{1}/$_4$-oz/ 7-g) packages active dry yeast
- 1 tsp sugar
- 1^1/$_4$ cups (300 ml) warm water
- 3^1/$_3$ cups (500 g) whole-wheat (wholemeal) flour
- 2 cups (300 g) all-purpose (plain) flour
- 1–2 tsp salt

HERB AND WALNUT LOAVES

Makes: about 2 lb (1 kg) bread

Preparation: 40 min.

Rising time: 90 min.

Cooking: 45 min.

Level of difficulty: 2

- 1 oz (30 g) fresh yeast or 2 (¹/₄-oz/ 7-g) packages active dry yeast
- ¹/₂ cup (125 ml) warm milk
- 3 cups (450 g) all-purpose (plain) flour
- 1 tsp salt
- 1 large egg
- Freshly ground black pepper
- 1 tbsp finely chopped fresh sage
- 1 tbsp finely chopped fresh rosemary
- ¹/₄ cup (60 g) butter
- About ¹/₂ cup (125 ml) warm water
- ¹/₂ cup (75 g) finely chopped walnuts

Place the yeast in a small bowl with the milk. Stir well and let rest for 10 minutes. • Place the flour and salt in a large bowl. • Beat the egg in a small bowl until frothy. Season with pepper and beat in the sage, rosemary, and butter. • Gradually stir the yeast mixture into the dry ingredients. Add the egg mixture and stir well. Add enough warm water to make a fairly soft dough. • Transfer to a lightly floured work surface and knead for 5–10 minutes, or until smooth and elastic. • Shape into a ball and place in an oiled bowl. Cover with a cloth and place in a warm place to rise until doubled in bulk, about 90 minutes. • Preheat the oven to 350°F (180°C/gas 4). • Oil two 9 x 5-inch (23 x 13-cm) loaf pans. • Punch the dough down. Place on a lightly floured surface and knead in the walnuts. • Divide the dough evenly between the pans and bake for about 45 minutes, or until well-risen and golden brown.

HERB BREAD

To prepare the yeast, place the yeast and sugar in a small bowl and pour in half the water. Stir until the yeast has dissolved then set aside to rest for 10 minutes. • Put both flours in a large bowl with the yeast mixture, herbs, salt, and remaining water and stir until well mixed. Transfer to a lightly floured work surface and knead for about 10 minutes. • Place the dough in an oiled bowl, cover the bowl with a cloth, and set aside to rise until doubled in bulk, about 90 minutes. • When the rising time has elapsed, transfer the dough to a lightly floured work surface. Knead for several minutes. • Divide the dough into 4–6 equal portions and shape each into a loaf about 14 inches (35 cm) long. • Place the loaves on two oiled baking sheets. Pull the ends of each loaf around and join them to make circular loaves, or leave them straight, as preferred. • Use a serrated knife to make a ¼-inch (5-mm) deep incision along the top of each loaf. • Cover with a cloth and let rise for 30 minutes. • Preheat the oven to 400°F (200°C/gas 6). • Bake until risen and golden brown, about 30 minutes.

Makes: about 2 lb (1 kg) bread

Preparation: 30 min.

Rising time: 2 hr.

Cooking: 35 min.

Level of difficulty: 2

- 1 oz (30 g) fresh yeast or 2 (¼-oz/ 7-g) packages active dry yeast
- 1 tsp sugar
- 1¼ cups (300 ml) lukewarm water
- 4 cups (600 g) whole-wheat (wholemeal) flour
- 1 cup (150 g) all-purpose (plain) flour
- 1 tbsp finely chopped fresh oregano
- 1 tbsp finely chopped fresh marjoram
- 2–3 tbsp salt

POLENTA ROLLS

Place the water and oil in a small bowl and stir in the yeast. Set aside for 10 minutes. • Put the flour, polenta, and salt in a large bowl. • Add the yeast mixture and stir until smooth. • Knead on a lightly floured work surface for 10 minutes. Place in an oiled bowl and let rise for 1 hour. • Turn the dough out onto a lightly floured surface and knead for 5 minutes. • Divide into 16 portions and shape into bread rolls. • Arrange the rolls on a baking sheet lined with waxed paper. • Make slashes in the top of each roll using a sharp knife. • Cover and let rise for 30 minutes, or until doubled in bulk. • Preheat the oven to 350°F (180°C/gas 4). • Sprinkle the rolls with a little water to keep them soft and bake for 35 minutes, or until golden brown.

Makes: 16 bread rolls

Preparation: 20 min.

Rising time: 90 min.

Cooking: 35 min.

Level of difficulty: 2

- **Scant 1 cup (220 ml) warm water**
- **1 tbsp extra virgin olive oil**
- **1 oz (30 g) fresh yeast or 2 ($^{1}/_{4}$-oz/ 7-g) packages active dry yeast**
- **2$^{1}/_{3}$ cups (350 g) all-purpose (plain) flour**
- **$^{2}/_{3}$ cup (100 g) polenta (yellow cornmeal)**
- **$^{1}/_{2}$ tsp salt**

SPICED BREAD ROLLS

Makes: 8 bread rolls

Preparation: 20 min.

Rising time: 30 min.

Cooking: 30 min.

Level of difficulty: 2

- 1 oz (30 g) fresh yeast or 2 (^{1}/4-oz/ 7-g) packages active dry yeast
- ^{1}/4 cup (60 ml) warm water
- 2^1/3 cups (350 g) all-purpose (plain) flour
- 1 cup (150 g) rye flour
- ^{1}/4 tsp salt
- 1 tsp ground cinnamon
- ^{1}/2 tsp ground ginger
- ^{1}/4 tsp ground cloves
- ^{1}/4 tsp freshly grated nutmeg
- 3 large egg yolks
- 3 tbsp butter, softened
- 3 tbsp honey
- ^{1}/3 cup (90 ml) milk
- 1 large egg, lightly beaten
- 1 tbsp aniseeds

Place the water in a small bowl and stir in the yeast. Set aside for 10 minutes. • Put both flours, salt, cinnamon, ginger, cloves, and nutmeg in a large bowl. Mix well. • Add the egg yolks, butter, honey, milk, and yeast mixture. Mix well to make a smooth dough. • Turn the mixture out onto a lightly floured surface and knead for 10 minutes. • Divide the dough into 8 portions and shape them into rolls. • Arrange the rolls on an oiled baking sheet. Cover and let rise for 30 minutes. • Preheat the oven to 350°F (180°C/gas 4). • Brush the rolls with the beaten egg and sprinkle with aniseed. • Bake for 30 minutes, or until golden brown.

HAZELNUT ROLLS

To prepare the yeast, place the yeast and sugar in a small bowl and pour in half the water. Stir until the yeast has dissolved then set aside to rest for 10 minutes. • Put both flours, the hazelnuts, and salt in a large bowl and mix well. Pour in the yeast mixture, 3 tablespoons of the oil, and the remaining water and stir until well mixed. Transfer to a lightly floured work surface and knead for about 10 minutes. • Place the dough in an oiled bowl, cover the bowl with a cloth, and set aside to rise until doubled in bulk, about 90 minutes. • When the rising time has elapsed, transfer the dough to a lightly floured work surface and knead for 2–3 minutes. • Divide the dough into 14–18 equal portions and shape into rolls. • Transfer to two oiled baking sheets, keeping the rolls well spaced (they will double in size as they rise). Cover with a cloth and leave to rise for 1 hour. • Preheat the oven to 400°F (200°C/gas 6). • Bake until risen and golden brown, about 20 minutes.

Makes: 14–18 rolls

Preparation: 30 min.

Rising time: 2 hr. 30 min.

Cooking: 20 min.

Level of difficulty: 2

- 1 oz (30 g) fresh yeast or 2 ($1/4$-oz/ 7-g) packages active dry yeast
- 1 tsp sugar
- $1^1/4$ cups (300 ml) warm water
- 2 cups (300 g) whole-wheat (wholemeal) flour
- 3 cups (450 g) all-purpose (plain) flour
- 1 cup (120 g) roasted hazelnuts, coarsely chopped
- 1–2 tsp salt
- $1/4$ cup (60 ml) extra-virgin olive oil

BRAIDED HERB LOAF

Makes: about 1 1/2 lb
(750 g) bread

Preparation: 40 min.

Rising time: 90 min.

Cooking: 45 min.

Level of difficulty: 2

- 1 oz (30 g) fresh
  yeast or 2 (1/4-oz/
  7-g) packages
  active dry yeast
- 1 tsp sugar
- 1 cup (250 ml)
  warm water
- 3 1/3 cups (500 g)
  all-purpose (plain)
  flour
- 1 tsp salt
- 1 large egg
- 1 tbsp finely
  chopped fresh
  sage
- 1 tbsp finely
  chopped fresh
  rosemary
- 1 tbsp extra-virgin
  olive oil
- 6 tbsp pine nuts

To prepare the yeast, place the yeast and sugar in a small bowl and pour in half the water. Stir until the yeast has dissolved then set aside to rest for 10 minutes. • Mix the flour and salt in a large bowl. • Beat the egg, sage, rosemary, and oil in a small bowl. • Gradually stir the yeast mixture into the flour. Add the egg mixture and stir well. Add enough remaining water to make a fairly soft dough. • Transfer to a lightly floured surface and knead for 10–15 minutes, or until smooth and elastic. • Shape into a ball and place in an oiled bowl. Cover with a cloth and place in a warm place to rise for 90 minutes, or until doubled in bulk. • Preheat the oven to 350°F (180°C/gas 4). • Oil a baking sheet. • Punch the dough down. Place on a lightly floured surface and knead in 4 tablespoons of the pine nuts. • Divide the dough in three and roll each piece into a rope. Braid the three pieces of dough together, pulling the ends round and joining them. • Place on the prepared sheet and sprinkle with the remaining 2 tablespoons of pine nuts. • Bake for about 45 minutes, or until well risen and golden brown.

TOMATO PINWHEELS

Prepare the bread dough, knead for 8–10 minutes, then place in an oiled bowl to rise for 1 hour. • Finely chop the carrot, onion, and celery together. • Sauté the chopped vegetables in the oil in a large frying pan over medium heat for 5 minutes. • Blanch the tomatoes in boiling water for 1 minute. Drain and slip off the skins. • Chop the tomatoes coarsely and add to the pan with the vegetables. Season with salt and pepper. Partially cover and simmer over low heat for 30 minutes, stirring often. The sauce should be quite thick.
• Stir in the basil, capers, and anchovy paste, if using. • Preheat the oven to 350°F (180°C/gas 4).
• Oil a large baking sheet. • Punch down the dough and roll out on a lightly floured surface into a rectangle about ¼ inch (5 mm) thick. • Spread evenly with the tomatoes and sprinkle with the oregano. • Roll the rectangle up from the short side. Cut into slices about 1 inch (2.5 cm) thick.
• Transfer to the prepared baking sheet. Let rise for 30 minutes. • Bake for about 25 minutes, or until golden brown. • Serve warm.

Makes: 15—20 pinwheels

Preparation: 30 min.

Rising time: 90 min.

Cooking: 25 min.

Level of difficulty: 2

- **1 recipe Bread Dough (see page 84)**
- **1 medium carrot**
- **1 small onion**
- **1 stalk celery**
- **1 tbsp extra-virgin olive oil**
- **4 large tomatoes**
- **Salt and freshly ground black pepper**
- **8 fresh basil leaves, torn**
- **1 tbsp salted capers, rinsed**
- **Anchovy paste (optional)**
- **¹/₂ tsp dried oregano**

FILLED OLIVE AND ANCHOVY ROLLS

Bread Dough: To prepare the yeast, place the yeast in a small bowl and pour in half the water. Stir until the yeast has dissolved then set aside to rest for 10 minutes. • Place the flour and salt in a large bowl. Add the yeast mixture, oil, and enough of the remaining water to obtain a soft dough. • Transfer the dough to a lightly floured work surface and knead until smooth and elastic, 8–10 minutes. • Break the dough into 12 pieces of the same size. Roll each piece of dough out on a floured work surface until very thin and about 8 inches (20 cm) in diameter. Set aside to rise for 30 minutes. • Preheat the oven to 350°F (180°C/gas 4). • Oil a 12-inch (30-cm) pie pan. • Leaving a ½-inch (1-cm) border around the edge of each piece of dough, sprinkle the rest with olives and anchovies. Drizzle with half the oil. • Roll the disks of pastry into lengths and fold them into spiral shapes. Place each one in the pan, flattening them slightly to fit. Drizzle the tops with the remaining oil. • Bake until golden brown, 35–40 minutes. • Serve hot or at room temperature.

Makes:	12 rolls
Preparation:	25 min
Rising time:	30 min.
Cooking:	35–40 min.
Level of difficulty:	2

Bread Dough
- ¹/₂ oz (15 g) fresh yeast of 1 (¹/₄-oz/ 7-g) package active dry yeast
- ¹/₂ cup (125 ml) lukewarm water
- 2²/₃ cups (400 g) all-purpose (plain) flour
- ¹/₂ tsp salt
- 2 tbsp extra-virgin olive oil

Filling
- 5 oz (150 g) green olives, pitted and chopped
- 8–10 anchovy fillets, chopped
- ¹/₄ cup (60 ml) extra-virgin olive oil
- Freshly ground black pepper

ITALIAN FLATBREAD

Mix the flour, baking soda, and salt into a large bowl. Add the lard and enough water to make a firm dough. • Knead the dough on a lightly floured work surface until smooth. • Place the dough in an oiled bowl and cover with a cloth. Let rise for 30 minutes. • Roll the dough out into a to ⅛ inch (3 mm) thick. • Cut out disks 6–8 inches (15–20 cm) in diameter. • Cook on a griddle or dry-fry in a very hot cast-iron frying pan, turning once, until lightly browned. • Serve very hot filled with cheese, tomatoes, chopped olives, and fresh basil leaves.

Makes: 6–8 flatbreads

Preparation: 25 min.
 + 30 min. to rest

Cooking: 15 min.

Level of difficulty: 2

- **3^{1}/$_3$ cups (500 g) all-purpose (plain) flour**
- **1 tsp baking soda**
- **^{1}/$_2$ tsp salt**
- **4 tbsp lard, melted**
- **1 cup (250 ml) lukewarm water**

OREGANO BREAD STICKS

Prepare the focaccia dough following the instructions on page 90. Gradually work the lard, 3 tablespoons of the oil, and the oregano into the dough as you knead. Let rise in a warm place for 1 hour. • Cover a baking sheet with waxed paper. • Roll out the dough on the paper to ¼ inch (5 mm) thick. Cut it into ⅔-inch (2-cm) thick strips using a fluted pastry wheel. • Place the strips on the baking sheet leaving 1 inch (2.5 cm) between them. • Brush with the remaining oil. Let rise for 30 minutes. • Preheat the oven to 350°F (180°C/gas 4). • Bake until crisp and golden brown, 15–20 minutes. • Serve hot or at room temperature.

Makes: about 40 bread sticks

Preparation: 35 min.

Rising time: 90 min.

Cooking: 20 min.

Level of difficulty: 1

- **1 recipe Basic Focaccia (see page 90)**
- **2 oz (60 g) lard, melted**
- **¹/₃ cup (90 ml) extra-virgin olive oil**
- **3 tbsp finely chopped oregano**

GARBANZO BEAN FLATBREAD

Makes: 4–6 flatbreads

Preparation: 20 min. +
30 min. to rest

Cooking: 20–25 min.

Level of difficulty: 1

- 1¹/₃ cups (200 g) garbanzo bean (chickpea) flour
- 4 bay leaves
- 2 cups (500 ml) cold water
- ¹/₂ cup (125 ml) extra-virgin olive oil
- Salt and freshly ground black pepper
- 1 bunch arugula (rocket), washed and coarsely chopped
- 6 oz (180 g) cherry tomatoes, cut in halves or quarters
- 2 oz (60 g) Parmesan cheese, in flakes

Place the garbanzo bean flour in a medium bowl with the bay leaves and gradually stir in the water. When it has all been absorbed, stir in the oil. Season with salt and set aside for 30 minutes.

- Preheat the oven to 400°F (200°C/gas 6). • Oil a 9-inch (23-cm) square baking dish. • Remove the bay leaves from the garbanzo bean mixture and spoon it into the baking dish. • Bake for 20–25 minutes, or until pale golden brown. • Cool on a rack for 10 minutes in the pan then turn out onto the rack to cool completely. • Cut into 4–6 squares and top with the arugula, tomatoes, and Parmesan. Season lightly with salt and pepper and drizzle with the remaining oil.

BASIC FOCACCIA

To prepare the yeast, place the yeast and sugar in a small bowl and pour in half the water. Stir until the yeast has dissolved then set aside to rest for 10 minutes. • Put the flour and fine salt in a large bowl and pour in the yeast mixture, half the oil, and the remaining water. Stir until well mixed. Transfer to a lightly floured work surface and knead for about 10 minutes. • Place the dough in an oiled bowl, cover the bowl with a cloth, and set aside to rise until doubled in bulk, about 90 minutes. • When the rising time has elapsed, transfer the dough to a lightly floured work surface and knead for 2–3 minutes. • Preheat the oven to 425°F (210°C/gas 7). • Place the dough on an oiled baking sheet and, using your hands, spread it into a 12-inch (30-cm) disk. Dimple the surface with your fingertips, drizzle with the remaining oil, and sprinkle with the coarse salt. • Bake until golden brown, about 20 minutes.

Makes: one (12-inch/ 30-cm) focaccia

Preparation: 20 min.

Rising time: 90 min.

Cooking: 20 min.

Level of difficulty: 1

- $^1/_2$ oz (15 g) fresh yeast or 1 ($^1/_4$-oz/ 7-g) package active dry yeast
- 1 tsp sugar
- 1 cup (250 ml) lukewarm water
- $3^1/_3$ cups (500 g) all-purpose (plain) flour
- 1 tsp fine salt
- $^1/_3$ cup (90 ml) extra-virgin olive oil
- 1 tsp coarse sea salt

SAGE FOCACCIA

Prepare the focaccia dough as described on page 90 and set aside to rise. • Incorporate the sage into the dough as you knead after the rising time has elapsed. • Preheat the oven to 425°F (210°C/gas 7). • Place the dough on an oiled baking sheet and, using your hands, spread it into a 12-inch (30-cm) disk. Dimple the surface with your fingertips, drizzle with the remaining oil, and sprinkle with the coarse salt. • Bake until golden brown, about 20 minutes.

Makes: one (12-inch/ 30-cm) focaccia

Preparation: 20 min.

Rising time: 90 min.

Cooking: 20 min.

Level of difficulty: 1

- **1 recipe Basic Focaccia dough (see page 90)**
- **2 tbsp coarsely chopped fresh sage leaves**

FOCACCINE WITH HERBS

Makes: 6 small
  focaccias

Preparation: 30 min.

Rising time: 90 min.

Cooking: 15 min.

Level of difficulty: 1

- 1 recipe Basic
  Focaccia dough
  (see page 90)
- 4 tbsp finely
  chopped fresh
  parsley
- 2 tbsp finely
  chopped basil
- 1 tbsp finely
  chopped marjoram
  or thyme
- 1 tsp finely
  chopped rosemary
- 1–2 tsp coarse sea
  salt
- 3–4 tbsp extra-
  virgin olive oil

Prepare the focaccia dough as described on page 90 and set aside to rise. • Oil a large baking sheet. • Place the risen dough on a lightly floured work surface. Knead briefly and shape into a ball. Break into 6 equal portions. Shape into balls and place, well spaced, on the prepared baking sheet. Spread a little with your hands. • Sprinkle each little focaccia with herbs and salt. Drizzle with the oil and let rise for 30 minutes. • Preheat the oven to 400°F (200°C/gas 6). • Bake for about 15 minutes, or until pale golden brown. • Serve hot or at room temperature.

FOCACCIA WITH GREEN OLIVES

Prepare the focaccia dough as described on page 90 and set aside to rise. • Incorporate the olives into the dough as you knead after the rising time has elapsed. • Preheat the oven to 425°F (210°C/gas 7). • Place the dough on an oiled baking sheet and, using your hands, spread it into a 12-inch (30-cm) disk. Dimple the surface with your fingertips, drizzle with the remaining oil, and sprinkle with the coarse salt. • Bake until golden brown, about 20 minutes.

Makes: one (12-inch/ 30-cm) focaccia

Preparation: 20 min.

Rising time: 90 min.

Cooking: 20 min.

Level of difficulty: 2

- **1 recipe Basic Focaccia dough (see page 90)**
- **1 cup (125 g) green olives, pitted and chopped**

FOCACCIA WITH SUMMER VEGETABLES

P repare the focaccia dough as described on page 90 and set aside to rise. • Oil a 12 x 10-inch (30 x 25-cm) rectangular pan. • Place the risen dough in the pan and use your fingertips to spread it evenly over the bottom. • Let rise for 30 minutes. • Preheat the oven to 400°F (200°C/gas 4). • Slice the tomatoes and sprinkle with salt. Let drain in a colander for 10 minutes to remove any excess water. Pat dry with paper towels.
• Sauté the garlic and zucchini in 2 tablespoons of oil in a large frying pan for 5 minutes. Season with salt. • Top the dough with the zucchini, garlic, bell peppers, and tomatoes. Season with salt and pepper. Drizzle with the remaining oil. • Bake for 15 minutes. • Sprinkle with the olives, capers, basil, and parmesan. • Bake for 10 minutes more, or until golden brown. • Serve hot.

Makes: one (12 x 10-inch/30 x 25-cm) focaccia

Preparation: 35 min.

Rising time: 90 min.

Cooking: 35 min.

Level of difficulty: 2

- **1 recipe Basic Focaccia dough (see page 90)**
- **2 large ripe tomatoes**
- **Salt and freshly ground black pepper**
- **1 clove garlic, lightly crushed**
- **2 large zucchini (courgettes), sliced**
- **$^1/_3$ cup (90 ml) extra-virgin olive oil**
- **1 large red bell pepper (capsicum), seeded and sliced**
- **1 large yellow bell pepper (capsicum), seeded and sliced**
- **$^1/_2$ cup (50 g) black olives, pitted**
- **1 tbsp salt-cured capers, rinsed and drained**
- **Leaves from 2 sprigs basil, torn**
- **4 oz (125 g) Parmesan cheese,**

POTATO FOCACCIA WITH ROSEMARY

Cook the potatoes in a large pot of salted boiling water for 25 minutes, or until tender. Drain and mash in a large bowl. • Mix the yeast with the water in a small bowl. • Put the flour and salt in a large bowl with the extra-virgin olive oil. Mix well. • Add the yeast mixture and stir until well mixed. Add the potatoes and stir until smooth. Cover and let rise for 1 hour. • Turn the dough out onto a lightly floured work surface and knead for 2 minutes. Divide into 8 portions and flatten each one slightly with your hand. • Heat the peanut oil in a large frying pan over medium heat. Fry the potato bread for 2–3 minutes. Turn it using a spatula and cook for 2–3 minutes, until golden brown all over. • Drain on paper towels. Sprinkle with salt and rosemary. Serve hot.

Makes: 8 focaccias
Preparation: 10 min.
Rising time: 1 hr.
Cooking: 35 min.
Level of difficulty: 2

- 12 oz (350 g) floury (baking) potatoes, peeled
- 1 oz (30 g) fresh yeast or 2 (^{1}/4-oz/ 7-g) package active dry yeast
- ^{1}/3 cup (90 ml) lukewarm water
- 1^1/3 cups (200 g) all-purpose (plain) flour
- ^{1}/2 tsp salt
- 2 tbsp extra-virgin olive oil
- ^{1}/2 cup (125 ml) peanut oil, for frying
- 2 tbsp finely chopped rosemary

CHEESE FOCACCIA

Makes: one (8 x 12-inch/20 x 30-cm) focaccia

Preparation: 30 min.

Rising time: 2 hr.

Cooking: 20–25 min.

Level of difficulty: 2

- **1 recipe Basic Focaccia dough (see page 90)**
- **$^1/_4$ cup (60 ml) extra-virgin olive oil**
- **1 cup (250 g) ricotta cheese, drained**
- **2 large eggs, lightly beaten**
- **2 tbsp finely chopped parsley**
- **2 oz (60 g) salami, cut into small cubes**
- **2 oz (60 g) fresh mozzarella cheese, cut into small cubes**
- **4 tbsp freshly grated Parmesan cheese**
- **Salt and freshly ground black pepper**

Prepare the focaccia dough as described on page 90. Gradually work 2 tablespoons of the oil into the dough as you knead. Let rise in a warm place until doubled in volume, about 2 hours.
- Preheat the oven to 400°F (200°C/gas 6).
- Oil an 8 x 12-inch (20 x 30-cm) baking dish.
- Turn the dough out onto a lightly floured work surface and knead for 5 minutes. • Press the dough into the prepared pan using your fingers.
- Mix together the ricotta, eggs, parsley, salami, mozzarella, Parmesan, salt, and pepper in a medium bowl. • Spread this mixture over the focaccia. Drizzle with the remaining oil. • Bake until golden brown, 20–25 minutes. • Serve hot.

FOCACCIA WITH BELL PEPPER AND EGGPLANT

Makes: one (12-inch/ 30-cm) focaccia

Preparation: 15 min.

Rising time: 90 min.

Cooking: 30 min.

Level of difficulty: 1

- 1 recipe Basic Focaccia dough (see page 90)
- 1 large eggplant (aubergine), thinly sliced
- 1 large red bell pepper (capsicum), thinly sliced
- 1 large yellow bell pepper (capsicum), thinly sliced
- 1 tbsp salt-cured capers, rinsed
- 1 cup (100 g) black olives, pitted and quartered
- 4 anchovy fillets, chopped
- 2 cloves garlic, finely chopped
- 1 fresh red chile pepper, seeded and sliced
- $^1/_4$ cup (60 ml) extra-virgin olive oil
- Salt and freshly ground black pepper
- Leaves from 1 sprig basil, torn

Prepare the focaccia dough as described on page 90 and set aside to rise. • Oil a 12-inch (30-cm) pizza pan. • Place the risen dough in the pan and use your fingertips to spread it evenly over the bottom. • Arrange a layer of the eggplant and bell peppers on top of the dough. Sprinkle with the capers, olives, anchovies, garlic, and chile pepper. Drizzle with the oil and season with salt and pepper. • Let rise for 30 minutes. • Preheat the oven to 400°F (200°C/gas 6). • Bake for about 30 minutes, or until golden brown. • Sprinkle with the basil and serve hot.

RUSTIC FOCACCIA

Prepare the focaccia dough as described on page 90 and set aside to rise. • Oil a 12-inch (30-cm) pizza pan. • Place the risen dough in the pan and use your fingertips to spread it evenly over the bottom. • Boil the eggs for 8–10 minutes. • Drain, shell, and slice them. • Spread the ricotta over the dough with the back of a spoon. Arrange the eggs, sausage meat, and olives over the ricotta. Sprinkle with oregano, salt, and red pepper flakes. Drizzle with the oil and let rise for 30 more minutes. • Preheat the oven to 425°F (220°C/gas 7). • Bake for about 20 minutes, or until golden brown. • Serve hot.

Makes: one (12-inch/ 30-cm) focaccia

Preparation: 30 min.

Rising time: 90 min.

Cooking: 30 min.

Level of difficulty: 1

- **1 recipe Basic Focaccia dough (see page 90)**
- **3 large eggs**
- **1 cup (250 g) ricotta cheese, drained**
- **8 oz (250 g) Italian sausage meat, chopped**
- **10 green olives, pitted and chopped**
- **1 tsp dried oregano**
- **Salt**
- **$^1/_4$ tsp red pepper flakes**
- **2 tbsp extra-virgin olive oil**

FRISEDDE WITH TOMATOES

Frisedde: Dissolve the yeast in ⅓ cup (90 ml) of the water. Add ⅔ cup (100 g) of flour and mix to make a smooth dough. Transfer to a lightly floured bowl, cover, and let rise for 1 hour, or until doubled in bulk. • Put the remaining flour onto a lightly floured surface. Make a well in the center and add a pinch of salt. Add the risen dough and enough of the water to make a smooth dough. Knead for 10–15 minutes, until the dough is smooth and elastic. Transfer to an oiled bowl, cover, and let rise for 2 hours. • Turn the risen dough out onto a lightly floured work surface and knead for 5 minutes. • Divide the dough into pieces the size of golf balls. Roll each one into a sausage about 1 inch (2.5 cm) wide and 6 inches (15 cm) long. Join the ends to make rings. • Arrange half the frisedde on a large oiled baking sheet. Place the remaining frisedde on top, making a series of double rings. Cover with a cloth and let rise for 1 hour. • Preheat the oven to 350°F (180°C/gas 4). • Bake the frisedde for 20 minutes. • Remove from the oven and cut in half horizontally using a sharp knife. • Arrange on the baking sheet and return to the oven. Bake for 10–15 minutes, or until lightly browned. Let cool on a wire rack. • Topping: Rub the cut side of each frisedde with garlic. Dip in a bowl of cold water to soften slightly. Place 2–3 slices of tomato on each frisedde. • Sprinkle with oregano and season with salt and pepper. Drizzle with the oil and serve.

Makes: about 12 frisedde	
Preparation: 1 hr.	
Rising time: 4 hr.	
Cooking: 30–35 min.	
Level of difficulty: 3	

Frisedde
- 1 oz (30 g) fresh yeast or 2 (¹/₄-oz/ 7-g) packages active dry yeas
- 1 cup (250 ml) lukewarm water
- 2 cups (300 g) all-purpose (plain) flour
- Salt

Topping
- 1 clove garlic
- 4 ripe tomatoes, sliced
- 1 tbsp freshly chopped oregano
- Salt and freshly ground black pepper
- ¹/₃ cup (90 ml) extra-virgin olive oil

PIZZA &
CALZONES

PIZZA MARGHERITA WITH CAPERS AND OLIVES

Prepare the pizza dough and set aside to rise.
• Preheat the oven to 425°F (220°C/gas 7).
• Oil a 12-inch (30-cm) pizza pan. • When the rising time has elapsed, knead the dough for 1 minute, then use your fingertips to press it into the pan.
• Spread with the tomatoes and season with salt and pepper. Sprinkle with the mozzarella, olives, and capers. Drizzle with the oil. • Bake for 20–25 minutes, or until the dough is lightly browned and the cheese is melted and bubbling. • Serve hot.

Makes: one (12-inch/ 30-cm pizza)

Preparation: 20 min.

Rising time: 90 min.

Cooking: 20–25 min.

Level of difficulty: 1

- 1 recipe
  Pizza Dough
  (see page 954)
- 1 (14-oz/400 g)
  can tomatoes,
  partially drained,
  mashed
  with a fork
- Salt and freshly
  ground black
  pepper
- 5 oz (150 g)
  mozzarella cheese,
  thinly sliced
- $^1/_2$ cup (50 g)
  black olives
- 2 tbsp salt-cured
  capers, rinsed
- 1 tbsp extra-virgin
  olive oil

ROMAN-STYLE PIZZA

Prepare the pizza dough and set aside to rise.
• Preheat the oven to 425°F (220°C/gas 7).
• Oil a 12-inch (30-cm) pizza pan. • When the rising time has elapsed, knead the dough for 1 minute, then use your fingertips to press it into the pan.
• Spread the tomatoes evenly over the dough and top with the mozzarella, pecorino, and anchovies. Season with salt and pepper and drizzle with 1 tablespoon of oil. • Bake for 20–25 minutes.
• When cooked, sprinkle with the basil leaves, drizzle with the remaining oil, and serve hot.

Makes: one (12-inch/
  30-cm pizza)

Preparation: 30 min.

Rising time: 90 min.

Cooking: 20–25 min.

Level of difficulty: 1

- 1 recipe
  Pizza Dough
  (see page 954)
- 12 oz (350 g)
  canned tomatoes,
  drained and
  chopped
- 5 oz (150 g)
  mozzarella cheese,
  thinly sliced
- 4 tbsp pecorino
  romano cheese,
  freshly grated
- 4–6 anchovy fillets,
  crumbled
- Salt and freshly
  ground black
  pepper
- 2 tbsp extra-virgin
  olive oil
- 6 leaves fresh basil,
  torn

TOMATO AND ONION PIZZA

Makes: one (12-inch/
30-cm pizza)

Preparation: 20 min.

Rising time: 90 min.

Cooking: 20–25 min.

Level of difficulty: 1

- 1 recipe
  Pizza Dough
  (see page 954)
- $^1/_3$ cup (90 ml)
  extra-virgin olive
  oil
- 2 large white
  onions, finely
  sliced
- 1 lb (500 g) fresh
  or canned
  tomatoes, peeled
  and chopped
- 4 leaves basil, torn
- Salt and freshly
  ground black
  pepper
- 8 anchovy fillets
  (optional)
- 2 tbsp black olives

Prepare the pizza dough, incorporating 2 tablespoons of the oil into the dough as you knead, and set aside to rise. • Preheat the oven to 425°F (220°C/gas 7). • Oil a 12-inch (30-cm) pizza pan. • When the rising time has elapsed, knead the dough for 1 minute, then use your fingertips to press it into the pan. Leave a raised border around the outer edge. • Place the remaining oil in a pan over low heat and sauté the onions for 3–4 minutes. Add the tomatoes and basil and season with salt and pepper. Simmer for 10 minutes. Add the anchovies, if using, remove from the heat and stir well. • Spread the sauce over the dough and sprinkle with the olives. • Bake for 20–25 minutes, or until the dough is cooked and golden. • Serve hot.

TOMATO PIZZA WITH ARUGOLA

Prepare the pizza dough and set aside to rise.
• Preheat the oven to 425°F (220°C/gas 7).
• Oil a 12-inch (30-cm) pizza pan. • Blanch the
tomatoes in boiling water for 2 minutes. Drain and
slip off the skins. • Chop the tomatoes, discarding
as many seeds as possible. • Put the chopped
tomatoes into a bowl and season with salt. • When
the rising time has elapsed, knead the dough for 1
minute, then use your fingertips to press it into the
pan. • Top with the seasoned tomatoes, cherry
tomatoes, and buffalo mozzarella. Season with salt
and drizzle with the oil. • Bake for 20–25 minutes,
or until the base is golden and the top is lightly
browned. • Sprinkle with the arugola. • Serve hot,
with the chile-flavored oil, if liked.

Makes: one (12-inch/
30-cm pizza)

Preparation: 15 min.

Rising time: 90 min.

Cooking: 30 min.

Level of difficulty: 1

- 1 recipe
  Pizza Dough
  (see page 954)
- 2 large ripe
  tomatoes
- Salt
- 12 cherry
  tomatoes, halved
- 8 oz (250 g) fresh
  buffalo mozzarella,
  drained and sliced
- 1/4 cup (60 ml)
  extra virgin olive
  oil
- 3 oz (90 g) arugola
  (rocket) leaves
- Olive oil flavored
  with chile pepper,
  to serve (optional)

PIZZA WITH LEEKS AND PANCETTA

Prepare the pizza dough and set aside to rise.
• Preheat the oven to 425°F (220°C/gas 7).
• Oil a 12-inch (30-cm) pizza pan. • Melt the butter
in a frying pan and add the leeks and pancetta.
Sauté over medium-low heat for 10 minutes.
Season with salt and pepper and set aside to cool.
• When the rising time has elapsed, knead the
dough for 1 minute, then use your fingertips to
press it into the pan. • Beat the egg with the cream
in a bowl. Add the leek and pancetta mixture and
the two cheeses. Mix well. • Spread the mixture
evenly over the dough. • Bake until golden brown,
20–25 minutes. • Serve hot.

Makes: one (12-inch/
   30-cm pizza)

Preparation: 25 min.

Rising time: 90 min.

Cooking: 15–20 min.

Level of difficulty: 1

- 1 recipe
  **Pizza Dough
  (see page 954)**
- 2 tbsp butter
- 14 oz (450 g)
  leeks, sliced
- 3 oz (90 g)
  pancetta, diced
- Salt and freshly
  ground black
  pepper
- 1 large egg
- $1^1/_2$ tbsp fresh
  cream
- 4 tbsp Parmesan
  cheese, freshly
  grated
- 2 oz (60 g) Gruyère
  cheese, very thinly
  sliced

PIZZA WITH HAM AND MUSHROOMS

P repare the pizza dough and set aside to rise.
• Preheat the oven to 425°F (220°C/gas 7).
• Oil a 12-inch (30-cm) pizza pan. • Place the
tomatoes in a medium bowl and season with salt
and pepper. Add 2 tablespoons of oil and mix well.
• Heat the remaining oil in a large frying pan over
medium heat. Add the mushrooms and garlic and
sauté until the mushrooms are tender and most of
the cooking juices have evaporated, 6–8 minutes.
• Remove from the heat. Remove and discard the
garlic. • When the rising time has elapsed, knead
the dough for 1 minute, then use your fingertips to
press it into the pan. • Spread with the tomato
mixture. Top with the ham, mushrooms,
mozzarella, and Gorgonzola. • Bake until the base
is crisp and golden brown, 20–25 minutes.
• Sprinkle with the oregano and serve hot.

Makes: one (12-inch/
  30-cm pizza)

Preparation: 30 min.

Rising time: 90 min.

Cooking: 20–25 min.

Level of difficulty: 1

• 1 recipe
  Pizza Dough
  (see page 954)
• 1 (14-oz/400-g)
  can tomatoes,
  drained and
  chopped
• Salt and freshly
  ground black
  pepper
• 1/4 cup (60 ml)
  extra-virgin olive
  oil
• 10 oz (300 g)
  champignon
  mushrooms, sliced
• 1 clove garlic,
  lightly crushed but
  whole
• 4 oz (125 g) ham,
  chopped
• 5 oz (150 g) fresh
  mozzarella cheese,
  drained and cut
  into small cubes
• 4 oz (125 g)
  Gorgonzola, cut
  into small cubes
• 1 tsp dried oregano

PIZZA WITH BROCCOLI AND PANCETTA

Prepare the pizza dough and set aside to rise.
• Preheat the oven to 425°F (220°C/gas 7).
• Oil a 12-inch (30-cm) pizza pan. • Cook the broccoli in a pot of salted boiling water until just tender, 5 minutes. Drain well. • Heat 2 tablespoons of oil in a frying pan over medium heat. Add the garlic and sauté for 1 minute. • Add the broccoli and sauté for 1 minute. • When the rising time has elapsed, knead the dough for 1 minute, then use your fingertips to press it into the pan. • Top the pizza with the broccoli and its cooking juices, the pancetta, and mozzarella. • Drizzle with the remaining oil and season with salt and pepper.
• Bake until the base is cooked and the topping is lightly browned, 20–25 minutes. • Serve hot.

Makes: one (12-inch/ 30-cm pizza)	
Preparation: 25 min.	
Rising time: 90 min.	
Cooking: 30–35 min.	
Level of difficulty: 1	

- 1 recipe
  **Pizza Dough
  (see page 954)**
- 2 small heads
  **broccoli, cut into
  florets**
- $^1/_3$ cup (90 ml)
  **extra-virgin olive
  oil**
- 1 clove garlic,
  finely chopped
- 4 oz (125 g)
  pancetta, chopped
- 8 oz (250 g) fresh
  **mozzarella, cut
  into** $^1/_2$ inch (1 cm)
  cubes
- Salt and freshly
  **ground black
  pepper**

PIZZA WITH CHERRY TOMATOES AND ZUCCHINI

Makes: one (12-inch/ 30-cm pizza)

Preparation: 25 min.

Rising time: 90 min.

Cooking: 30 min.

Level of difficulty: 1

- 1 recipe **Pizza Dough (see page 954)**
- **1/4 cup (60 ml) extra-virgin olive oil**
- **2 cloves garlic, finely chopped**
- **2 medium zucchini (courgettes), thinly sliced**
- **Salt and freshly ground black pepper**
- **1 tbsp finely chopped fresh parsley**
- **10 oz (300 g) cherry tomatoes, halved**
- **5 oz (150 g) fresh mozzarella, cut in small cubes**

Prepare the pizza dough and set aside to rise.
- Preheat the oven to 425°F (220°C/gas 7).
- Oil a 12-inch (30-cm) pizza pan. • Heat 2 tablespoons of the oil in a frying pan over medium heat. • Add the garlic and zucchini and sauté until the zucchini are tender, 3–4 minutes. • Season with salt and pepper and sprinkle with parsley.
- When the rising time has elapsed, knead the dough for 1 minute, then use your fingertips to press it into the pan. • Top the pizza with the tomatoes, zucchini and cooking juices, and the mozzarella. • Drizzle with the remaining oil and season with salt and pepper. • Bake until the base is cooked and the topping is lightly browned, 20–25 minutes. • Serve hot.

EGGPLANT PIZZA

Prepare the pizza dough and set aside to rise.
• Preheat the oven to 425°F (220°C/gas 7).
• Oil a 12-inch (30-cm) pizza pan. • Brush the
eggplant lightly with the oil. • Grill for 3–4 minutes
in a hot grill pan, turning only once. Sprinkle with
salt, garlic, and parsley. • When the rising time has
elapsed, knead the dough for 1 minute, then use
your fingertips to press it into the pan. • Spread
the tomatoes evenly over the pizza and sprinkle
with the mozzarella. • Drizzle with 1 tablespoon of
oil. • Bake for 10–15 minutes. • Take the pizza out
of the oven and cover with the slices of eggplant.
Return to the oven for 5 minutes more. • When
cooked, sprinkle with the basil, drizzle with the
remaining oil, and serve hot.

Makes: one (12-inch/
30-cm pizza)

Preparation: 30 min.

Rising time: 90 min.

Cooking: 20–25 min.

Level of difficulty: 2

- 1 recipe
  Pizza Dough
  (see page 954)
- 10 oz (300 g)
  eggplant
  (aubergine), cut in
  1/2-inch (1-cm)
  thick slices
- 3 tbsp extra-virgin
  olive oil
- Salt
- 2 cloves garlic,
  finely chopped
- 1 tbsp parsley,
  finely chopped
- 12 oz (350 g)
  tomatoes, canned,
  drained and
  chopped
- 5 oz (150 g)
  mozzarella cheese,
  diced
- 6 leaves fresh basil,
  torn

ITALIAN RIVIERA PIZZA

Makes: one (12-inch/
30-cm pizza)

Preparation: 30 min.

Rising time: 2 hr.

Cooking: 45 min.

Level of difficulty: 1

- 1 recipe
  Pizza Dough
  (see page 954)
- $^1/_3$ cup (90 ml)
  extra-virgin olive
  oil
- $^1/_4$ cup (60 ml)
  milk
- 2 large white
  onions, sliced
- Salt and freshly
  ground black
  pepper
- $^1/_8$ tsp cinnamon
- 1 tsp sugar
- 14 oz (400 g)
  tomatoes, peeled
  and sliced
- 8 anchovy fillets,
  chopped
- $^1/_2$ cup (50 g)
  black olives
- 1 clove garlic,
  finely sliced
- 2 tbsp freshly
  grated Parmesan
  cheese
- 1 tsp dried oregano

Prepare the pizza dough and set aside to rise.
• Oil a 12-inch (30-cm) pizza pan. • When the
rising time has elapsed, knead the dough for 1
minute, then use your fingertips to press it into the
pan. • Heat half the oil and milk in a large frying
pan over medium heat. Add the onions and simmer
for about 15 minutes, or until the onions are very
soft and the liquid has evaporated. • Season with
salt and pepper. Add the cinnamon and sugar.
• Arrange the onions on top of the dough. Top with
the tomatoes. Sprinkle with the anchovies, olives,
garlic, Parmesan, and oregano. Drizzle with the
remaining oil and let rise for 30 more minutes.
• Preheat the oven to 425°F (220°C/gas 7).
• Bake for until golden brown, 20–25 minutes.
• Serve hot.

SEAFOOD PIZZA

Prepare the pizza dough and set aside to rise.
• Soak the mussels and clams in cold water for
1 hour. • Preheat the oven to 425°F (220°C/gas
7). • Oil a 12-inch (30-cm) pizza pan. • Heat 1
tablespoon of oil in a large saucepan over medium
heat. • Add the garlic and sauté for 1 minute. •
Add the mussels and clams. • Pour in half the wine
and season with salt and pepper. • Cook for 7–8
minutes, or until the shells open. • Remove the
mussels and clams from their shells, leaving a few
in their shells to garnish the pizza. Discard any
shellfish that did not open. • Cook the shrimps in a
large pot of salted boiling water with the remaining
wine for 1–2 minutes. Drain and shell the shrimps.
• Heat a grill pan to very hot. Drop the squid rings
onto it and cook until just tender, 3–5 minutes.
• Put the shelled mussels, clams, shrimps, and
squid into a large bowl. • Add 1 tablespoon of the
oil and season with salt and pepper. Mix well. •
When the rising time has elapsed, knead the dough
for 1 minute, then use your fingertips to press it
into the pan. • Top with the tomatoes and
mozzarella. Season with salt and drizzle with the
remaining oil. • Bake for 15 minutes, until the top
is lightly browned. • Remove from the oven and top
with the prepared seafood. Decorate with the
mussels and clams in their shells. • Sprinkle with
parsley and bake for 10 minutes, until the base is
cooked through. • Serve hot.

*Makes: one (12-inch/
30-cm pizza)*

Preparation: 40 min.

Rising time: 90 min.

Cooking: 45 min.

Level of difficulty: 3

- **1 recipe
  Pizza Dough
  (see page 954)**
- **1 lb (500 g)
  mussels, in shell**
- **1 lb (500 g) clams,
  in shell**
- **1/3 cup (90 ml)
  extra virgin olive oil**
- **1 clove garlic,
  lightly crushed but
  whole**
- **1/3 cup (90 ml) dry
  white wine**
- **Salt and freshly
  ground black pepper**
- **10 oz (300 g) fresh
  shrimp (prawns)**
- **2 medium squid,
  cleaned and cut
  in rings**
- **10 oz (300 g)
  peeled plum
  tomatoes, pressed
  through a fine
  mesh strainer**
- **5 oz (150 g) fresh
  mozzarella, cut
  into 1/2 inch (1 cm)
  cubes**
- **1 tbsp freshly
  chopped parsley**

PIZZA WITH FOUR-CHEESE TOPPING

Prepare the pizza dough and set aside to rise.
• Preheat the oven to 425°F (220°C/gas 7).
• Oil a 9 x 13-inch (23 x 33-cm) baking pan.
• When the rising time has elapsed, knead the dough for 1 minute, then use your fingertips to press it into the pan. • Spread the surface with the cheeses and drizzle with the oil. • Bake until golden brown and the cheeses are bubbling, 15–20 minutes. • Serve hot.

Makes: one 9 x 13-inch (23 x 33-cm) pizza

Preparation: 30 min.

Rising time: 90 min.

Cooking: 15–20 min.

Level of difficulty: 1

- **1 recipe Pizza Dough (see page 954)**
- **4 oz (125 g) mozzarella cheese, diced**
- **$1/4$ cup (30 g) freshly grated Parmesan cheese**
- **4 oz (125 g) Gorgonzola cheese, diced**
- **2 oz/60 g) Emmental or Swiss cheese, thinly sliced**
- **1 tbsp extra-virgin olive oil**

Makes:	4 calzones
Preparation:	35 min.
Rising time:	90 min.
Cooking:	20–25 min.
Level of difficulty:	1

- **2 recipes Pizza Dough (see page 954)**
- **8 oz (250 g) fresh ricotta cheese, drained**
- **8 oz (250 g) mozzarella cheese, diced**
- **8 oz (250 g) ham, thinly sliced**
- **$^1/_4$ cup (60 ml) extra-virgin olive oil**
- **$^1/_2$ cup (125 ml) chopped canned tomatoes**
- **Salt**

HAM AND EGG CALZONES

Prepare the pizza dough and set aside to rise.
• Preheat the oven to 425°F (220°C/gas 7).
• Oil a baking sheet. • When the rising time has elapsed, knead the dough briefly on a lightly floured work surface, then divide into 4 equal portions. • Roll or stretch the dough into disks about 9 inches (23-cm) in diameter. • Spread half of each disk with the ricotta, then sprinkle with the mozzarella and ham, leaving a 1-inch (2.5-cm) border around the edge. Add 1 raw egg to each calzone. Fold the other half of the dough over the top, pressing down on the edges to seal. • Brush the calzones with 1 tablespoon of oil and arrange them on the prepared baking sheet. • Season the tomatoes with salt and 2 tablespoons of oil. Spread over the calzones. • Bake until puffed and golden brown, 20–25 minutes. • Serve hot.

SWISS CHARD CALZONES

Prepare the pizza dough and set aside to rise.
• Preheat the oven to 425°F (220°C/gas 7).
• Oil a large baking sheet. • Place the Swiss chard
in a heavy-bottomed saucepan with 2–3
tablespoons of oil, the garlic, chilies, and salt to
taste. Cook over medium-low heat, initially with the
lid on, for 10 minutes, stirring from time to time.
The Swiss chard should be tender but not watery.
Add the olives and cook for 2–4 minutes more. Set
aside to cool. • When the rising time has elapsed,
knead the dough briefly on a lightly floured work
surface, then divide into 4 equal portions. • Roll
or stretch the dough into disks about 9 inches
(23-cm) in diameter. • Spread the filling on one
half of each disk, leaving a 1-inch (2.5-cm) border
around the edge. Fold the other half of the dough
over the top, pressing down firmly on the edges to
seal. • Brush the calzones with the remaining oil.
Place on the prepared baking sheet. • Bake until
puffed and golden brown, 20–25 minutes.
• Serve hot.

Makes: 4 calzones

Preparation: 40 min.

Rising time: 90 min.

Cooking: 20–25 min.

Level of difficulty: 2

- 2 recipes
  Pizza Dough
  (see page 954)
- 1¹/₂ lb (750 g)
  fresh Swiss chard
  (silverbeet),
  chopped
- ¹/₄ cup (60 ml)
  extra-virgin olive
  oil
- 2 cloves garlic,
  sliced
- 1 tsp crushed
  chilies
- Salt
- 4 oz (125 g) black
  olives, pitted

APULIAN-STYLE CALZONES

Prepare the pizza dough and set aside to rise.
• Preheat the oven to 425°F (220°C/gas 7).
• Oil a large baking sheet. • Heat 2–3 tablespoons of the oil in a frying pan and sauté the onions until softened, 5 minutes. • Add the tomatoes, olives, anchovies, capers, basil, and salt. Simmer over medium heat for 3–4 minutes. Remove from heat.
• When the mixture is cool, add the pecorino.
• When the rising time has elapsed, knead the dough briefly on a lightly floured work surface, then divide into 4 equal portions. • Roll or stretch the dough into disks about 9 inches (23-cm) in diameter. • Spread the filling on one half of each disk, leaving a 1-inch (2.5-cm) border around the edge. Fold the other half of the dough over the top, pressing down firmly on the edges to seal. • Brush the calzones with the remaining oil. Place on the prepared baking sheet. • Bake until puffed and golden brown, 20–25 minutes. • Serve hot.

Makes: 4 calzones

Preparation: 35 min.

Rising time: 90 min.

Cooking: 20–25 min.

Level of difficulty: 2

- **2 recipes Pizza Dough (see page 954)**
- **1¹/₄ lb (600 g) onions, sliced**
- **¹/₄ cup (60 ml) extra-virgin olive oil**
- **8 oz (250 g) canned tomatoes, drained and chopped**
- **4 oz (125 g) black olives, pitted**
- **8 anchovy fillets, chopped**
- **2 tbsp salt-cured capers, rinsed**
- **8 leaves fresh basil, torn**
- **Salt**
- **4 oz (125 g) pecorino cheese, cut in tiny cubes**

EGGPLANT CALZONES

Makes: 4 calzones

Preparation: 30 min.

Rising time: 90 min.

Cooking: 20–25 min.

Level of difficulty: 2

- 2 recipes
  **Pizza Dough
  (see page 954)**
- 1 lb (500 g)
  **eggplant
  (aubergine), peeled
  and diced**
- $^1/_3$ cup (90 ml)
  **extra-virgin olive
  oil**
- 3 tbsp finely
  **chopped fresh
  marjoram**
- 1 clove garlic,
  finely chopped
- **Salt**
- 12 oz (350 g)
  **tomatoes, canned,
  drained and
  chopped**
- 2 tsp finely
  **chopped fresh
  parsley**
- 6 leaves fresh basil,
  torn
- 5 oz (150 g)
  **pecorino cheese,
  diced**

Prepare the pizza dough and set aside to rise.
• Preheat the oven to 425°F (220°C/gas 7).
• Oil a large baking sheet. • Fry the eggplant in the oil in a large frying pan over high heat. After 8–10 minutes, add the marjoram, garlic, salt, and, if necessary, a little more oil. Cook for 2–3 minutes more, until the eggplant is tender. • Add the tomatoes, parsley, basil, and pecorino. Stir for 1 minute then remove from the heat. • When the rising time has elapsed, knead the dough briefly on a lightly floured work surface, then divide into 4 equal portions. • Roll or stretch the dough into disks about 9 inches (23-cm) in diameter. • Spread the filling on one half of each disk, leaving a 1-inch (2.5-cm) border around the edge. Fold the other half of the dough over the top, pressing down firmly on the edges to seal. • Brush the calzones with the remaining oil. Place on the prepared baking sheet. • Bake until puffed and golden brown, 20–25 minutes. • Serve hot.

SAVORY PIES

RICOTTA AND ZUCCHINI PIE

Preheat the oven to 400°F (200°C/gas 6).
• Oil a 12-inch (30-cm) pie pan. • Heat the butter in a medium saucepan over medium heat and stir in the flour. When smooth remove from the heat and add all the milk at once, stirring constantly. • Return to the heat and stir constantly until thickened, 7–10 minutes. • Remove from the heat and season with salt, pepper, and nutmeg.
• Bring a medium saucepan of water to a boil and blanche the zucchini until almost tender, 3–5 minutes. Drain well and set aside on a clean cloth. • Heat the oil in a large frying pan and sauté the potatoes and mushrooms until almost tender, about 10 minutes. Season with salt and pepper.
• Roll the pastry out on a lightly floured work surface in a disk large enough to line the base and sides of the prepared pie pan. • Stir half the cream sauce into the ricotta and spread over the base of the pie. Use a teaspoon to hollow out the slices of zucchini. Add the zucchini flesh to the potato and mushroom mixture. Stir in the remaining cream sauce. • Arrange the slices of zucchini in the ricotta filling. Fill each slice with some of the filling. • Bake until the pastry is golden brown and the filling is set, 35–40 minutes. • Serve hot.

Serves: 6–8
Preparation: 30 min.
Cooking: 35–40 min.
Level of difficulty: 2

- $1/3$ cup (90 g) butter
- $2/3$ cup (100 g) all-purpose (plain) flour
- Salt and freshly ground white pepper
- Freshly grated nutmeg
- 3 cups (750 ml) milk
- 14 oz (400 g) frozen puff pastry, thawed
- 2 medium zucchini (courgettes), thickly sliced
- 2 tbsp extra-virgin olive oil
- 8 oz (250 g) white mushrooms, diced
- 2 medium potatoes, peeled and cut in small cubes
- 14 oz (400 g) fresh ricotta, drained

ZUCCHINI AND HAM PIE

Sauté the garlic in the oil in a large frying pan over medium heat until pale gold. • Discard the garlic. Add the zucchini and crumble in the stock cube. Cook over low heat for 1 minute. • Pour in the milk and simmer over medium heat for 5 minutes, or until the zucchini are tender and the milk has been absorbed. • Add the potato and cream and set aside. • Preheat the oven to 350°F (180°C/gas 4). • Butter a 9-inch (23-cm) springform pan or pie plate. • Roll the pastry out on a lightly floured work surface to ⅛ inch (3 mm) thick. Line the prepared pan with the pastry. • Arrange the ham in the pastry case and top with the zucchini mixture. Add the Asiago or Fontina. • Cut out decorative shapes from the remaining pastry and arrange on top of the pie. • Bake for about 35 minutes, or until the pastry is golden brown and the filling has set. • Serve warm.

Serves: 6

Preparation: 30 min.

Cooking: 50 min.

Level of difficulty: 1

- 1 clove garlic, lightly crushed but whole
- 2 tbsp extra-virgin olive oil
- 2 zucchini (courgettes), coarsely grated
- ½ vegetable bouillon cube
- ¼ cup (60 ml) milk
- 1 boiled potato, cubed
- 3 tbsp heavy (double) cream
- 8 oz (250 g) frozen puff pastry, thawed
- 4 large thin slices of ham
- 2 oz (60 g) Asiago or Fontina cheese, cut in small cubes

ZUCCHINI FLOWER QUICHE

Serves: 4–6

Preparation: 20 min.
+ 1 hr. to chill

Cooking: 30 min.

Level of difficulty: 1

Pastry
- 2 cups (300 g) all-purpose (plain) flour
- $^{1}/_{2}$ cup (125 g) cold butter, chopped
- $^{1}/_{4}$ tsp salt
- 2 large egg yolks, lightly beaten
- $^{1}/_{4}$ cup (60 ml) chilled water

Filling
- 25 zucchini (courgette) flowers, stamen and green part removed, and halved
- 2 tbsp extra-virgin olive oil
- 5 large eggs
- 1 cup (250 ml) heavy (double) cream
- Salt and freshly ground black pepper
- $1^{1}/_{4}$ cups (150 g) freshly grated Parmesan cheese

Pastry: Process the flour, butter, and salt in a food processor until the mixture is the same consistency as bread crumbs. • Stir in the egg yolks and enough water to make a firm dough. • Knead on a lightly floured work surface until smooth. • Wrap in plastic wrap (cling film) and chill in the refrigerator for 1 hour. • Preheat the oven to 350°F (180°C/gas 4). • Butter a 10-inch (25-cm) springform pan or pie plate. • Filling: Sauté the zucchini flowers in the oil in a small frying pan over medium heat for 2 minutes. Drain well on paper towels. • Beat the eggs and cream in a large bowl. Season with salt and pepper. • Roll the dough out on a lightly floured work surface to ¼-inch (5-mm) thick. • Line the prepared pan with the dough. • Sprinkle with the Parmesan and Emmental. • Add the zucchini flowers and pour the egg mixture over the top. • Bake for about 25 minutes, or until the pastry is golden brown and the filling has set. Let cool slightly. • Serve warm.

RICOTTA AND PROSCIUTTO PIE

Pastry: Place the yeast in a small bowl with half the water and stir until dissolved. Set aside to rest until frothy, 10–15 minutes. • Place the flour and salt in a large bowl. Pour in the yeast mixture, milk, oil, and enough of the remaining water to obtain a fairly firm dough. • Transfer the dough to a floured work surface and knead until smooth and elastic, about 15 minutes. • Place the dough in a clean, lightly oiled bowl, cover with a cloth, and set aside to rise until doubled in bulk, about 1 hour. • Preheat the oven to 350°F (180°C/gas 4). • Oil a 12-inch (30-cm) pie pan. • Divide the risen dough in two, with one piece slightly larger than the other. Roll the larger piece of dough into a disk large enough to line the bottom and sides of the pan. Leave some pastry hanging over the edges of the pan. • Filling: Spread the pastry with the ricotta. Cover with the prosciutto, sprinkle with the pecorino and parsley, and top with slices of boiled egg. Season with salt and pepper. • Roll the remaining piece of dough into a circle large enough to cover the top of the pie. Fold the overhanging dough over the top to seal the pie. Prick the top all over with a fork. • Bake until golden brown, 35–40 minutes. • Serve hot.

Serves: 6–8

Preparation: 30 min. + 1 hr. to rise

Cooking: 35–40 min.

Level of difficulty: 2

Pastry
- 1 oz (30 g) fresh yeast or 2 (1/4-oz/ 7-g) packages active dry yeast
- 1/2 cup (125 ml) lukewarm water, + extra, as required
- 3 1/3 cups (500 g) all-purpose (plain) flour
- 3 tbsp extra-virgin olive oil
- 1 tsp salt
- 1/4 cup (60 ml) milk

Filling
- 8 oz (250 g) fresh ricotta cheese, drained
- 4 oz (125 g) prosciutto (Parma ham), thinly sliced
- 2 oz (60 g) freshly grated pecorino cheese
- 1 tbsp finely chopped fresh parsley
- 2 large eggs, hard boiled, sliced
- Salt and freshly ground black pepper

SWISS CHARD PIE

Serves: 6–8

Preparation: 30 min.

Cooking: 35 min.

Level of difficulty: 2

Preheat the oven to 400°F (200°C/gas 6).
• Rinse the Swiss chard under cold running; do not dry. Cook for a few minutes with just the water left clinging to the leaves. Squeeze out as much moisture as possible and chop coarsely. • Sauté the pancetta, parsley, garlic, and scallions in a frying pan with 1 tablespoon of butter for 3–5 minutes. • Add the Swiss chard, Parmesan, salt, and pepper. Stir well and set aside. • Mix the flour and salt in a bowl. Pour in the lard and stir it into the flour, adding a little warm water at intervals, to form a workable dough. • Transfer to a lightly floured work surface and knead the dough until smooth and elastic. • Divide into two parts, one larger than the other, and roll out into two thin disks. Use the larger one to line a 12-inch (30-cm) pie pan greased with the remaining butter. It should overlap the edges a little. • Fill with the vegetable mixture. Cover with the other disk, sealing the edges well. • Bake for 30 minutes and serve hot.

- 2 lb (1 kg) Swiss chard (silver beet)
- 1/4 cup (60 g) chopped pancetta
- 2 tbsp finely chopped parsley
- 1 clove garlic, finely chopped
- 6 scallions (green onions) finely chopped
- 2 tbsp butter
- 3/4 cup (100 g) freshly grated Parmesan cheese
- Salt and freshly ground pepper
- 3 cups (450 g) all-purpose (plain) flour
- 1/4 cup (60 g) melted lard
- Warm water, for the dough

Serves: 4–6

Preparation: 15 min.

Cooking: 45 min.

Level of difficulty: 1

- 12 oz (350 g) potatoes, peeled and thinly sliced
- 2 tbsp extra-virgin olive oil
- 2 leeks, sliced
- 12 oz (350 g) frozen puff pastry, thawed
- 1 bunch watercress
- Small bunch chives, chopped
- 2 large eggs
- $^1/_3$ cup (90 ml) heavy (double) cream
- $^1/_2$ cup (60 g) freshly grated Parmesan cheese
- Salt and freshly ground white pepper

LEEK AND WATERCRESS PIE

Preheat the oven to 350°F (180°C/gas 4).
• Cook the potatoes in a small pan of salted boiling water until just tender, 5 minutes. Drain well.
• Heat the oil in a large frying pan and sauté the leeks until softened, 5 minutes. • Use the pastry to line a 9-inch (23-cm) springform pan. • Place the potatoes and leeks on the pastry and cover with the watercress and chives. • Beat the eggs, cream, and Parmesan until well mixed. Season with salt and pepper and pour over the vegetables in the pan. • Bake until set and golden brown, about 35 minutes. • Serve hot or warm.

PEAR AND GORGONZOLA QUICHE

P repare the quiche dough. • Shape into a ball and wrap in plastic wrap (cling film). Refrigerate for 30 minutes. • Preheat the oven to 400°F (200°C/gas 6). • Butter a 9-inch (23-cm) springform pan or pie plate. • Roll the dough out on a lightly floured work surface to ¼ inch (5 mm) thick. • Line the prepared pan with the dough. • Filling: Beat the Gorgonzola, ricotta, eggs, cream, and tarragon in a large bowl. Season with salt and pepper. • Add the chopped pears and mix well. • Spread the mixture in the crust. • Top with the remaining pears and drizzle with the butter. • Bake for about 20 minutes, or until the pastry is golden brown and the filling has set. • Serve hot or warm.

Serves: 4–6

Preparation: 15 min. + 30 min. to chill

Cooking: 20 min.

Level of difficulty: 2

- **1 quantity Never-Fail Quiche Crust (see page 959)**

Filling
- **2 oz (60 g) Gorgonzola cheese, crumbled**
- **4 tbsp ricotta cheese**
- **2 large eggs**
- **¹⁄₂ cup (125 ml) heavy (double) cream**
- **1 tbsp finely chopped fresh tarragon**
- **Salt and freshly ground black pepper**
- **2 large pears, peeled and cored, 1 chopped and 1 sliced**
- **1 tbsp butter, melted**

ONION QUICHE

Preheat the oven to 350°F (180°C/gas 4). • Roll the pastry out on a lightly floured work surface to ⅛ inch (3 mm) thick. • Line a 10-inch (25-cm) springform pan or pie plate with the pastry. • Sauté the onions in the oil in a large frying pan over medium heat until softened, about 5 minutes. • Beat the eggs, cream, and Emmental in a large bowl. Season with salt and pepper. • Add the onions and mix well. • Pour the onion mixture into the pastry case. • Bake for 15 minutes. • Increase the oven temperature to 400°F (200°C/gas 6). • Bake for about 15 minutes more, or until the pastry is golden brown and the filling has set. • Serve warm or at room temperature.

Serves: 4–6

Preparation: 30 min.

Cooking: 35 min.

Level of difficulty: 1

- **12 oz (350 g) frozen puff pastry, thawed**
- **2 large white onions, thinly sliced**
- **2 tbsp extra-virgin olive oil**
- **5 large eggs**
- **1 cup (250 ml) heavy (double) cream**
- **1³/₄ cups (215 g) freshly grated Emmental or Swiss cheese**
- **Salt and freshly ground black pepper**

PUFF PASTRY WITH CREAMY MUSHROOM FILLING

Serves: 4–6

Preparation: 15 min.

Cooking: 25 min.

Level of difficulty: 3

- **10 oz (300 g) frozen puff pastry, thawed**
- **$^1/_4$ cup (60 g) butter**
- **$1^1/_2$ lb (750 g) button mushrooms, cut into quarters**
- **2 tbsp finely chopped parsley**
- **2 tbsp all-purpose (plain) flour**
- **$^1/_3$ cup (90 ml) vegetable stock**
- **Salt and freshly ground black pepper**
- **2 large egg yolks**
- **$^1/_2$ cup (125 g) Béchamel Sauce (see page 956)**
- **2 tbsp freshly grated Parmesan cheese**

Preheat the oven to 400°F (200°C/gas 6). • Set out a 10-inch (25-cm) quiche pan. • Roll out the puff pastry on a lightly floured surface to $^1/_4$ inch (5 mm) thick. • Line the pan with the pastry. Prick all over with a fork. • Bake for 15 minutes, or until puffed and golden brown. • Carefully cut off the top of the puff and set aside. • Melt the butter in a large frying pan over medium heat. • Add the mushrooms and parsley and sauté for 2 minutes. • Sprinkle with the flour and mix well. Add the stock and season with salt and pepper. • Lower the heat and simmer for 5 minutes, or until the mushrooms are very tender. • Beat together the egg yolks and Béchamel sauce in a small bowl. Add the mixture to the mushrooms and mix well. Cook over very low heat for 2–3 minutes until it begins to thicken. • Spoon the filling into the pastry case. • Sprinkle with the Parmesan and replace the top of the puff. Serve at once.

SPRING VEGETABLE PIE

Preheat the oven to 350°F (180°C/gas 4).
• Oil a 10-inch (25-cm) quiche or pie pan.
• Cook the cauliflower in a large pot of salted boiling water until just tender, about 5 minutes. Drain well. • Heat the oil in a large frying pan over medium heat. Add the leeks, bell pepper, and zucchini. Sauté until the vegetables begin to soften, about 5 minutes. • Add the cauliflower and sugar peas. Season with salt and pepper. Cover and simmer until the vegetables are tender, 5–10 minutes. Remove from the heat. • Beat the ricotta, one of the eggs, the Parmesan, parsley, and thyme in a large bowl. Add the vegetables and mix well. • Roll out two-thirds of the pastry on a lightly floured surface to ¼ inch (5 mm) thick. • Line the pan with the pastry. Cut away any excess pastry around the edges using a sharp knife. • Fill with the vegetable mixture. • Roll out the remaining pastry on a lightly floured surface. Place over the vegetable filling.
• Beat the remaining egg in a cup. Brush the pastry with the beaten egg. • Bake until puffed and golden brown, about 35 minutes. • Serve hot.

Serves: 4–6

Preparation: 25 min.

Cooking: 1 hr.

Level of difficulty: 2

- 1 small cauliflower, cut into florets
- 2 tbsp extra-virgin olive oil
- 2 small leeks, sliced
- 1 large red bell pepper, (capsicum) seeded and chopped
- 2 small zucchini (courgettes), sliced into julienne
- 5 oz (150 g) sugar peas (mangetout), sliced
- Salt and freshly ground black pepper
- 5 oz (150 g) ricotta cheese, drained
- 2 large eggs
- ½ cup (60 g) freshly grated Parmesan cheese
- 1 tbsp finely chopped fresh parsley
- ½ tbsp finely chopped fresh thyme
- 12 oz (350 g) frozen puff pastry, thawed

156

CHEESE CROSTATA

Serves: 4–6

Preparation: 30 min.

Cooking: 20 min.

Level of difficulty: 1

- 1 recipe
  Shortcrust Pastry
  (see page 959)
- ³/₄ cup (180 ml)
  heavy (double)
  cream
- 14 oz (400 g)
  creamy goat
  cheese (caprino),
  at room
  temperature
- 5 oz (150 g)
  mascarpone (or
  cream cheese), at
  room temperature
- 1 tbsp finely
  chopped fresh
  parsley
- 1 tbsp finely
  chopped basil, +
  extra leaves, torn
- 1 small clove
  garlic, very finely
  chopped (optional)
- Salt and freshly
  ground black
  pepper
- 3 oz (90 g) arugula
  (rocket)
- 1–2 tbsp extra-
  virgin olive oil
- 6–8 pickled
  cucumbers
  (gherkins), sliced

Preheat the oven to 350°F (180°C/gas 4).
• Oil a 9-inch (23-cm) fluted pie pan. • Roll out
the pastry on a lightly floured work surface to
about ⅛ inch (3 mm) thick. Line the base and sides
of the prepared pan with the pastry. Cut away the
over-hanging edges. • Cover the pastry with a
piece of waxed paper and fill with dried beans or
pie weights. • Bake for 20 minutes. Remove the
beans or pie weights and waxed paper and bake
until crisp and pale golden brown. • Let cool for
5 minutes in the pan then carefully remove and
place on a wire rack to cool. • Beat the cream with
an electric mixer on high speed until stiff peaks
form. • Place both cheeses in a medium bowl and
carefully fold in the cream, parsley, basil, and
garlic, if using. Season lightly with salt and plenty
of pepper. • Just before serving, place the arugula
in the baked pie crust and drizzle with the oil.
• Place the cheese mixture in a piping bag with
a plain nozzle and pipe small rounds all over the
salad. • Decorate each round of cheese mixture
with a slice of gherkin or a piece of basil leaf.
• Serve at once.

QUICHE WITH CHEESE AND PEAS

Preheat the oven to 350°F (180°C/gas 4). • Oil a 10-inch (25-cm) quiche pan. • Heat the oil in a frying pan over medium heat. Sauté the scallions until softened, about 5 minutes. • Add the peas and sauté for 5 minutes. Season with salt and pepper. • Beat the eggs and milk in a bowl. Season with salt and pepper. • Roll out the pastry on a lightly floured work surface ¼ inch (5 mm) thick. Line the prepared pan with the pastry. Trim off and discard any excess. • Spoon half the pea mixture into the pastry case. Add the Gorgonzola and remaining pea mixture. Cover with the egg mixture. • Bake until set and golden brown, about 35–40 minutes. • Serve hot.

Serves: 4–6

Preparation: 20 min.

Cooking: 45–55 min.

Level of difficulty: 1

- **2 tbsp extra-virgin olive oil**
- **3 scallions (green onions), sliced**
- **2 cups (300 g) frozen peas**
- **Salt and freshly ground black pepper**
- **14 oz (400 g) frozen shortcrust pastry, thawed**
- **2 large eggs**
- **¹/₃ cup (90 ml) milk**
- **8 oz (250 g) Gorgonzola cheese, cut into small cubes**

RICOTTA TART

Serves: 4–6
Preparation: 25 min.
Cooking: 45–50 min.
Level of difficulty: 1

- 2 tbsp extra-virgin olive oil
- 2 leeks, thinly sliced
- 2 carrots, cut in small cubes
- 1 lb (500 g) ricotta cheese, drained
- 3 tbsp finely chopped fresh herbs (parsley, sage, thyme)
- 2 large eggs, lightly beaten + 1 extra, to brush
- 1/2 cup (60 g) freshly grated Parmesan
- Salt and freshly ground black pepper
- 14 oz (400 g) frozen shortcrust pastry, thawed
- 2 tbsp milk

Preheat the oven to 400°F (200°C/gas 6). • Oil a 10-inch (25-cm) springform pan. • Heat the oil in a large frying pan over medium heat. Sauté the leeks in the oil until softened, about 5 minutes. • Add the carrots and sauté for 5 minutes. • Place the ricotta in a large bowl and stir in the 2 eggs, mixed herbs, cheese, and vegetable mixture. Season with salt and pepper and mix well. • Roll out two-thirds of the pastry and press into the bottom and sides of the prepared pan. • Spoon the filling into the pan. • Roll out the remaining pastry and cut into long thin strips. Arrange over the pan in a lattice patter, • Mix the remaining egg with the milk and brush the top of the tart. • Bake until set and golden brown, 35–40 minutes. • Serve hot.

161

SOUPS

CALABRIAN BREAD SOUP

Heat the oil in a heavy saucepan over medium heat. Add the tomatoes, parsley, garlic, celery, bay leaf, and water. Season with salt and pepper. Bring to a boil then simmer over low heat for 30 minutes. • Preheat the oven to 350°F (180°C/gas 4). • Toast the bread in the oven until crisp and golden brown. Make sure you toast in the oven and not in a toaster—the bread needs to dry out and this can only be achieved in the oven. • Filter the stock, discarding the vegetables. Pour into a clean saucepan over medium heat and bring to a boil. • Add the toasted bread and let simmer until it has absorbed plenty of stock, 2–3 minutes. • Remove the bread with a slotted spoon and place in a heated serving bowl. • Carefully break the eggs into the remaining boiling stock and simmer gently until just set, 3–4 minutes. • Place the eggs in the bowl with the bread and ladle the remaining stock over the top. • Sprinkle with the pecorino and serve hot.

Serves: 4

Preparation: 15 min.

Cooking: 40 min.

Level of difficulty: 1

- $1/4$ cup (60 ml) extra-virgin olive oil
- 2 large ripe tomatoes, coarsely chopped
- 3 sprigs parsley
- 2 cloves garlic
- 2 stalks celery, coarsely chopped
- 1 bay leaf
- 6 cups (1.5 liters) cold water
- Salt and freshly ground black pepper
- 4 day-old bread rolls, sliced
- 4 large eggs
- $1/2$ cup (60 g) freshly grated pecorino cheese

POTATO AND BREAD SOUP WITH ARUGULA

Place the potatoes in a saucepan and cover with the water. Season with salt and bring to a boil. • Simmer for 7–8 minutes then add the arugula. Simmer until the potatoes are tender but not mushy, about 5 minutes. Remove from the heat. • Place the slices of bread in a soup tureen and sprinkle with the garlic. • Pour the potato, arugula, and cooking liquid over the top. Drizzle with the oil then stir gently to mix. • Sprinkle with the chile pepper and serve hot.

166

Serves: 4

Preparation: 15 min.

Cooking: 15 min.

Level of difficulty: 1

- 1 lb (500 g) potatoes, peeled and sliced $^1/_4$-inch (5-mm) thick
- 6 cups (1.5 liters) cold water
- Salt
- 1 lb (500 g) arugula (rocket)
- 8 thick slices firm-textured, day-old bread
- 2 cloves garlic, thinly sliced
- $^1/_3$ cup (90 ml) extra-virgin olive oil
- 1 fresh red chile pepper, finely chopped

BAKED TUSCAN VEGETABLE SOUP

S auté the onion in half the oil. • Purée two-thirds of the cannellini beans in a blender. • Add the puréed beans and stock to the onion. • Add all the vegetables and cook until tender, at least 1 hour. • Preheat the oven to 350°F (180°C/gas 4). • Stir the remaining beans into the soup and season with salt and pepper. • Arrange the bread in an oiled terra-cotta baking dish and ladle the vegetable soup over the top. • Drizzle with the remaining oil and bake for 20 minutes. Serve hot.

168

Serves: 6

Preparation: 20 min.

Cooking: 80 min.

Level of difficulty: 1

- 1 red onion, finely chopped
- 1/4 cup (60 ml) extra-virgin olive oil
- 10 oz (300 g) dried cannellini beans, pre-soaked and boiled in salted water with a sage leaf for 1 hour
- 3 cups (750 ml) Beef Stock (see page 946)
- 1/2 small Savoy cabbage, shredded
- 3 small tomatoes, coarsely chopped
- 8 oz (250 g) Swiss Chard (silverbeet), shredded
- 1 zucchini (courgette), coarsely chopped
- 1 carrot, sliced
- 1 celery stalk, coarsely chopped
- 2 potatoes, diced
- 8 oz (250 g) Tuscan kale, shredded
- 1 leek, sliced
- salt and freshly ground black pepper
- 6 slices firm-textured bread

TUSCAN TOMATO AND BREAD SOUP

Serves: 4

Preparation: 10 min.

Cooking: 25 min.

Level of difficulty: 1

- 4 cloves garlic, finely chopped
- $1/4$ cup (60 ml) extra-virgin olive oil, + extra for serving
- 1 (14-oz/400-g) can tomatoes, with juice
- 12 leaves fresh basil, torn, + extra to garnish
- 10 oz (300 g) firm-textured, day-old bread, cut in thick slices and diced
- $1^1/4$ cups (300 ml) boiling water + extra, as required

Heat the oil in a saucepan over medium heat. Add the garlic and sauté until pale gold, 3–4 minutes. • Add the tomatoes, breaking them up with a wooden spoon. Simmer over low heat until the tomatoes reduce, about 10 minutes. • Add the basil and stir in the bread. • Add about half the water and turn up the heat. • Stir often, adding more water as required to obtain a thick porridge-like consistency. • Turn off the heat and let the soup sit for 5 minutes before serving. • Serve with a drizzle of extra-virgin oil and garnished with basil.

VEGETABLE SOUP WITH PESTO

- 8 cups (2 liters) water
- 1/2 cup (100 g) dried cannellini or borlotti beans, soaked overnight and drained
- 10 oz (300 g) winter squash or pumpkin, peeled and cubed
- 14 oz (400 g) potatoes, peeled and cut into cubes
- 4 zucchini (courgettes), cut into cubes
- 4 oz (150 g) green beans, sliced
- 3/4 cup (90 g) fresh or frozen peas
- 1 tomato, coarsely chopped
- 1 eggplant (aubergine), peeled and cubed
- 1 stalk celery, 1 sprig parsley, 2 cloves garlic, finely chopped
- 1 carrot, chopped
- 1 onion, chopped
- Salt
- 2 tbsp extra-virgin olive oil
- 2 rinds of Parmesan cheese
- 4 oz (150 g) dried egg tagliatelle
- 1/2 cup (125 ml) Pesto (see page 945)

Bring the water to a boil with the beans in a large pot over medium heat. Add the winter squash, potatoes, zucchini, green beans, peas, tomato, eggplant, celery, parsley, garlic, carrot, and onion. Season with salt and drizzle with oil. • Simmer over low heat for 1 hour. • Add the Parmesan rinds and continue cooking for 30 minutes, or until the beans are tender. • Use a wooden spoon to crush the beans and potatoes against the sides of the pot to make a dense soup. Add the pasta and simmer until cooked, about 5 minutes. • Ladle the soup into individual bowls and top each serving with pesto.

CABBAGE SOUP WITH GARLIC CROSTINI

C ut each slice of bread in three. • Heat the oil in a large frying pan over medium heat. Add the garlic and bread and fry until golden brown on both sides. Remove from the heat and drain on paper towels. • Discard the tough outer leaves from the cabbage. Chop the rest into wedges and boil in lightly salted water until tender, 5–7 minutes.
• Drain the cabbage and chop finely. • Heat the stock in a saucepan and add the cabbage. Bring to a boil over medium heat and simmer for 5 minutes.
• Ladle the soup into four individual soup bowls. Sprinkle with the pecorino and garnish with the garlic crostini. Serve hot.

Serves: 4–6

Preparation: 20 min.

Cooking: 20 min.

Level of difficulty: 1

- **6 large slices firm-textured bread**
- **$^1/_3$ cup (90 ml) extra-virgin olive oil**
- **2 cloves garlic**
- **1 medium Savoy cabbage**
- **6 cups (1.5 liters) Beef Stock (see page 946)**
- **$^1/_2$ cup (60 g) freshly grated pecorino cheese**
- **Salt and freshly ground black pepper**

WINTER CABBAGE SOUP

Serves: 4

Preparation: 15 min.

Cooking: 1 hr.

Level of difficulty: 1

- **3 cloves garlic, finely chopped**
- **2 tbsp extra-virgin olive oil**
- **1³/₄ lb (800 g) Savoy cabbage, shredded**
- **4 cups (1 liter) vegetable stock (bouillon cube)**
- **Salt and freshly ground black pepper**
- **4–8 slices of day-old firm-textured bread, toasted**
- **8 tbsp freshly grated Parmesan cheese**

Sauté the garlic in the oil in a large saucepan over low heat until pale gold, 3–4 minutes. • Add the cabbage and cook, stirring often, until it has wilted. • Pour in the vegetable stock and simmer for 40 minutes. Season with the salt and pepper. • Preheat the oven to 350°F (180°C/gas 4). • Place a layer of toasted bread in a terra-cotta pot. Sprinkle with the Parmesan and pour in 1½ cups (375 ml) of the soup. Repeat until all the ingredients are in the pot. • Bake for 10 minutes and serve piping hot.

RICE AND CELERY SOUP

Place half the butter and the oil in a saucepan over low heat. Add the celery, parsley, and bay leaf and simmer, stirring often, until tender, 10–15 minutes. • Turn the heat up to medium and add the water. Season with salt and bring to a boil. Simmer for 5 minutes. • Add the rice and simmer until tender, about 15 minutes. • Remove the bay leaf and stir in the remaining butter. • Serve hot sprinkled with Parmesan.

Serves: 4

Preparation: 15 min.

Cooking: 30 min.

Level of difficulty: 1

- 3 tbsp butter
- 2 tbsp extra-virgin olive oil
- 8 oz (250 g) celery stalks, fairly finely chopped
- 2 tbsp finely chopped fresh parsley
- 1 bay leaf
- 5 cups (1.25 liters) water
- Salt
- 1 1/4 cups (250 g) short-grain rice
- Freshly grated Parmesan cheese

TUSCAN CABBAGE AND RICE SOUP

Serves: 4

Preparation: 15 min.

Cooking: 40–50 min.

Level of difficulty: 1

Bring the carrots, celery, and cabbage to a boil in a large saucepan with the stock. Lower the heat and simmer for 25–30 minutes, or until the vegetables are tender. • Add the rice and cook for 15–18 minutes, or until the rice is cooked. Season with the pepper, oil, and Parmesan and serve hot.

- 2 carrots, finely sliced
- 2 stalks celery, sliced
- 1/2 small Savoy cabbage, coarsely chopped
- 4 cups (1 liter) Beef Stock (see page 946)
- 1 cup (200 g) short-grain rice
- Freshly ground black pepper
- 2 tbsp extra-virgin olive oil
- 2 tbsp freshly grated Parmesan cheese

Serves: 4

Preparation: 20 min.

Cooking: 20 min.

Level of difficulty: 1

- 14 oz (400 g) Belgian endive, rinsed and finely shredded
- 4 large eggs, lightly beaten
- 4 tbsp freshly grated Parmesan cheese
- $1/8$ teaspoon freshly grated nutmeg
- 5 cups (1.25 liters) boiling Beef Stock (see page 946)
- 4 slices firm-textured bread, toasted

BELGIAN ENDIVE SOUP

Cook the Belgian endive in a large saucepan of salted boiling water until tender. • Drain, squeezing it dry, and chop finely. • Transfer to a large bowl and mix in the eggs, Parmesan, and nutmeg. • Pour the boiling stock over the egg mixture, and mix well. • Arrange the bread in individual serving bowls and ladle the soup over the top. Serve hot.

TUSCAN ONION SOUP

Melt 2 tablespoons of butter in a heavy saucepan over low heat. Add the onions, cover, and simmer until tender, about 25 minutes. • Season with salt, pepper, and nutmeg. • Stir in 2 tablespoons of the remaining butter and the flour. • Turn the heat up to medium-high and add the wine and cognac. Cook until the alcohol has evaporated, about 5 minutes. • Pour in the stock and bring to a boil. Lower the heat, cover than pan, and simmer for 45 minutes. • Preheat the oven to 425°F (210°C/gas 7). • Ladle the soup into an earthenware dish. Top four slices of bread with slices of Gruyère and float on the soup. Sprinkle with the Parmesan. Bake until the cheese topping is just golden. • Toast the remaining bread in the oven. • Melt the remaining butter in a small saucepan with the parsley. Spread on the remaining toasted bread. Serve the soup hot garnished with the toast.

Serves: 4

Preparation: 30 min.
+ 4–5 hr. to rest

Cooking: 30 min.

Level of difficulty: 2

- $^1/_3$ cup (90 g) butter
- 1 lb (500 g) white onions, thinly sliced
- Salt and freshly ground black pepper
- Freshly grated nutmeg
- $^1/_4$ cup (30 g) all-purpose (plain) flour
- $^1/_2$ cup (125 ml) dry white wine
- $^1/_3$ cup (90 ml) cognac
- 4 cups (1 liter) vegetable stock
- 8 small slices firm-textured bread
- 3 oz (90 g) Gruyère or Swiss cheese, sliced
- 1 cup (125 g) freshly grated Parmesan cheese

MEAT AND VEGETABLE SOUP

Heat the oil in a large saucepan over medium heat. Sauté the scallions until translucent, 2–3 minutes. • Add the beef and sauté for 2–3 minutes. Stir in the pancetta and cook for 5 minutes more. • Add the fava beans, peas, artichokes, and asparagus. Season with salt and pepper. • Simmer for 10–15 minutes, or until the meat is cooked. • Pour in the stock and cook for 20 minutes more. • Serve in individual soup bowls with the cubes of fried bread.

Serves: 4

Preparation: 15 min.

Cooking: 45 min.

Level of difficulty: 2

- $^1/_4$ cup (60 ml) extra-virgin olive oil
- 4 scallions (spring onions), thinly sliced
- 3 oz (90 g) ground (minced) beef
- 2 oz (60 g) pancetta cut in thin strips
- 3 oz (90 g) fresh or frozen fava (broad) beans
- $^3/_4$ cup (90 g) fresh or frozen peas
- 2 artichokes, cleaned and thinly sliced
- 3 oz (90 g) asparagus tips
- Salt and freshly ground black pepper
- 2 cups (500 ml) Beef Stock (see page 946)
- Firm-textured bread, cut into cubes and sautéed in olive oil

FAVA BEAN AND ARTICHOKE SOUP

Trim the stalks and cut the top third off the tops of the artichokes. Remove the tough outer leaves by bending them down and snapping them off. Cut in half and use a sharp knife to remove any fuzzy choke. Slice into thin wedges. Place in a bowl of cold water with the lemon juice. • Hull the fava beans and place in a bowl of cold water. • Place the oil in a saucepan over medium heat and sauté the scallions and celery until tender, about 5 minutes. • Add the water. Drain the beans and artichokes and add to the pan. Season with salt and pepper. Bring to a boil and simmer over low heat until the vegetables are tender, about 45 minutes. • Serve hot.

Serves: 4

Preparation: 45 min.

Cooking: 50 min.

Level of difficulty: 1

- **6 medium artichokes**
- **Freshly squeezed juice of 1 lemon**
- **3 lb (1.5 kg) fresh fava (broad) beans, in the pod**
- **$1/3$ cup (90 ml) extra-virgin olive oil**
- **4 scallions (green onions), sliced**
- **2 stalks celery, sliced**
- **5 cups (1.25 liters) cold water**
- **Salt**

FAVA BEAN AND PASTA SOUP

S auté the onion and garlic in the oil in a medium saucepan until lightly browned. • Add the potatoes and fava beans. Sauté for 2–3 minutes. • Pour in the vegetable stock. Simmer over low heat for 30–40 minutes, or until the beans are almost tender. • Add the pasta and cook until al dente. • Season with the salt and pepper and serve hot.

Serves: 4

Preparation: 35 min.

Cooking: 50–60 min.

Level of difficulty: 1

- 1 onion, finely chopped
- 2 cloves garlic, finely chopped
- $^1/_4$ cup (60 ml) extra-virgin olive oil
- 2 medium potatoes, peeled and cut in small cubes
- 2 cups (300 g) fresh or frozen fava (broad) beans
- 10 oz (300 g) small penne pasta
- 1 tsp tomato concentrate (purée) dissolved in 2 cups (500 ml) vegetable stock
- Salt and freshly ground black pepper

Serves: 4

Preparation: 1 hr.
+ 12 hr. to soak
the beans

Cooking: 3 hr.

Level of difficulty: 1

- 8 oz (200 g) mixed dried beans, including lentils, fava (broad) beans, and garbanzo beans (chickpeas), soaked overnight and drained
- Salt
- 2 cloves garlic, finely chopped
- 1/2 cup (60 g) diced pancetta
- 1/4 cup (60 ml) extra-virgin olive oil
- 1 onion, finely chopped
- 1 stalk celery, finely chopped
- 1/2 small Savoy cabbage, finely shredded
- 1/2 oz (15 g) dried mushrooms, soaked in warm water for 15 minutes
- 8 oz (200 g) dried short pasta, such as ditalini
- Freshly ground black pepper
- 1/4 cup (30 g) freshly grated pecorino cheese

CALABRIAN BEAN AND PASTA SOUP

Rinse the beans under cold running water and place in a large saucepan. Pour in enough water to cover the beans. • Boil gently for about 1 hour, or until the beans are tender. Season with salt. • Drain, reserving the cooking liquid. • Sauté the garlic and pancetta in the oil in a large frying pan over low heat for 5 minutes. • Add the onion, celery, and cabbage and simmer for 3 minutes. • Drain the mushrooms. Finely chop the mushrooms and add to the pan. • Pour in enough of the reserved cooking water to cover the vegetables. Simmer for about 30 minutes, or until all the vegetables are tender. • Add the beans and cook for 10 minutes more. • Add the pasta and cook until al dente, adding more of the cooking water if needed. • Season with salt. • Serve hot, sprinkled with pepper and pecorino.

TUSCAN GARBANZO BEAN SOUP

P ut the beans in a large pot and pour in the water. Add 2 cloves of garlic and 1 sprig of rosemary. Partially cover and simmer for 1 hour, or until the beans are very tender. Season with salt and remove from the heat. • Drain, reserving the water and discarding the garlic and rosemary. • Purée half of the garbanzo beans in a food processor, leaving the remainder whole. • Sauté the remaining 2 cloves of garlic and sprig of rosemary in 3 tablespoons of oil in a large saucepan over low heat until the garlic is pale gold, 2–3 minutes. • Discard the garlic. Stir in the tomato paste and cook over medium heat for 2 minutes. • Add the puréed and whole garbanzo beans and the reserved cooking liquid and bring to a boil. If the soup is very thick, dilute with a little hot stock. • Add the pasta and cook until al dente. Season with salt and pepper. Drizzle with the remaining 3 tablespoons of oil, discard the rosemary, and serve hot.

Serves: 4

Preparation: 20 min. + 12 hr. to soak the beans

Cooking: 75 min.

Level of difficulty 1

- 1²/₃ cups (160 g) dried garbanzo beans (chickpeas), soaked overnight and drained
- 8 cups (2 liters) cold water
- 4 cloves garlic, lightly crushed but whole
- 2 sprigs fresh rosemary
- Salt
- ¹/₃ cup (90 ml) extra-virgin olive oil
- ¹/₄ cup (60 g) tomato concentrate (paste)
- 1 cup (250 ml) boiling Beef Stock (see page 946) (optional)
- 8 oz (250 g) small dried soup pasta
- Freshly ground black pepper

GARBANZO BEAN, POTATO, AND MUSHROOM SOUP

Serves: 4

Preparation: 15 min.

Cooking: 30 min.

Level of difficulty: 1

- $^1/_3$ cup (90 ml) extra-virgin olive oil
- 1 clove garlic, finely chopped
- 1 tbsp finely chopped fresh rosemary
- 1 oz (30 g) dried porcini mushrooms, soaked in warm water for 15 minutes, drained, and chopped
- 1 lb (500 g) button mushrooms, sliced
- 2 small potatoes, peeled and cut into $^1/_2$ inch (1 cm) cubes
- salt and freshly ground black pepper
- 4 cups (1 liter) boiling vegetable stock
- 14 oz (400 g) canned garbanzo beans (chickpeas), drained
- 2 tbsp finely chopped fresh parsley, to garnish
- Fresh chives, to garnish

Heat 2 tablespoons of the oil in a large saucepan over medium heat. Add the garlic and rosemary and sauté for 2 minutes. • Add the dried mushrooms, button mushrooms, and potatoes. Season with salt and pepper and sauté for 10 minutes, or until the mushrooms are tender. If the mixture begins to stick to the pan add a little of the stock. • Add the garbanzo beans and the stock. • Simmer for 15 minutes, until the garbanzo beans begin to break down. • Ladle the soup into serving bowls. • Sprinkle with chopped parsley. • Drizzle each portion with a little of the remaining oil. • Garnish with the parsley and chives. Serve hot.

MUSHROOM SOUP

Place the mushrooms on a large plate and sprinkle with salt. Let rest for 4–5 hours.
• Heat the oil in a saucepan over medium heat. Add the onion and garlic and sauté until pale gold, 3–4 minutes. • Add the tomatoes and then the mushrooms. Simmer for 3–4 minutes then add the water. Season with salt and pepper. • Bring to a boil and simmer for 15 minutes. • Arrange the toasted bread in four individual soup bowls and ladle the soup over the top. Sprinkle with the parsley and pecorino and serve hot.

Serves: 4–6

Preparation: 30 min.
  + 4–5 hr. to rest

Cooking: 30 min.

Level of difficulty: 1

- 1 $^1/_2$ lb (750 g) mixed fresh mushrooms, cleaned and sliced
- $^1/_4$ cup (60 ml) extra-virgin olive oil
- 1 medium white onion, finely chopped
- 3 cloves garlic, crushed
- $^1/_4$ cup (60 ml) canned tomatoes, chopped, with juice
- 6 cups (1.5 liters) water
- Salt and freshly ground black pepper
- 4–6 slices firm-textured bread, toasted
- 2 tbsp finely chopped parsley
- $^1/_4$ cup (30 g) freshly grated pecorino cheese

PEARL BARLEY AND PORK RIB SOUP

Place the pearl barley in a bowl and cover with cold water. Let soak overnight. • Boil the pearl barley in the soaking water until tender, about 30 minutes (depending on the variety). • Drain the pearly barley and return to the saucepan. Cover with the stock and bring to a boil. • Add the pork ribs, pancetta, potatoes, onions, celery, carrots, and leeks and return to a boil. Season with salt and pepper. • Partially cover the pan and simmer over very low heat for 3 hours. • Serve hot.

Serves: 4

Preparation: 30 min. + 12 hr. to soak

Cooking: 3 hr. 30 min.

Level of difficulty: 1

- **12 oz (350 g) pearl barley**
- **8 cups (2 liters) Beef Stock + extra, as required (see page 946)**
- **8 oz (250 g) baby pork ribs**
- **2 oz (60 g) pancetta, cut in small cubes**
- **2 medium potatoes, cut in small cubes**
- **2 medium white onions, finely chopped**
- **2 stalks celery, thinly sliced**
- **2 medium carrots, cut in small cubes**
- **2 medium leeks, thinly sliced**
- **Salt and freshly ground black pepper**

TAGLIATELLE IN STOCK

Serves: 4–6

Preparation: 30 min. + 30 min. to rest the dough

Cooking: 20 min.

Level of difficulty: 2

P asta Dough: Mound the flour and salt on a work surface and make a well in the center. Break the eggs into the well and mix in to make a smooth dough. Knead for 15–20 minutes, until smooth and elastic. Shape the dough into a ball, wrap in plastic wrap (cling film), and let rest for 30 minutes. • Roll out the dough on a lightly floured surface to ⅛ inch (3 mm) thick. Cut into 4 x 1-inch (10 x 2.5-cm) strips. • Fry the lard in a nonstick frying pan over medium heat for 3 minutes, until lightly golden. • Bring the stock to a boil in a large saucepan and add the lard. • Cook the pasta in the boiling stock until al dente, 3–4 minutes. • Serve hot.

Pasta Dough

- 2 cups (300 g) all-purpose (plain) flour
- $1/4$ tsp salt
- 3 large eggs

To Serve

- $3/4$ cup (90 g) diced lard or fatty pancetta
- 6 cups (1.5 liters) meat stock or broth

Serves: 4

Preparation: 45 min.
+ 1 hr. to rest

Cooking: 30 min.

Level of difficulty: 2

- ¹/₄ cup (60 g) butter
- 8 oz (250 g) veal or beef, sliced
- 7 cups (1.75 liters) Chicken Stock (see page 946)
- Salt and freshly ground white pepper
- ²/₃ cup (80 g) freshly grated Parmesan cheese
- 1 small egg
- ¹/₈ tsp freshly grated nutmeg
- ¹/₂ cup (60 g) fine dry bread crumbs (optional)
- ¹/₂ cup (75 g) all-purpose (plain) flour

MEATBALLS IN STOCK

Melt the butter in a large frying pan and braise the veal for about 15 minutes, or until cooked through, adding about ¾ cup (180 ml) of stock to make sure that the meat does not dry out. Season with salt and pepper. Remove from the heat and let cool. • Chop the veal in a food processor until finely ground. Transfer to a large bowl and mix in the egg, nutmeg, and about two-thirds of the Parmesan. Season with salt. If the mixture is too soft, add some bread crumbs. Cover with plastic wrap (cling film) and let rest for 1 hour at room temperature. • Form into balls the size of walnuts and coat lightly in the flour. • Bring the remaining stock to a boil in a large saucepan. Add the meatballs and simmer for about 5 minutes, or until the meatballs are cooked through. • Serve hot sprinkled with the remaining Parmesan.

PASTA AND PEAS IN STOCK

Serves: 4

Preparation: 30 min.

Cooking: 45 min.

Level of difficulty: 1

- 1/4 cup (60 g) lard or butter, cut up
- 1 onion, finely chopped
- 2 cloves garlic, lightly crushed but whole
- 5 leaves fresh basil
- 2 cups (300 g) frozen peas
- 2 oz (50 g) prosciutto (Parma ham), finely shredded
- 1 tbsp tomato paste (concentrate)
- 6 cups (1.5 liters) Beef Stock (see page 946)
- Salt and freshly ground white pepper
- 4 oz (125 g) quadrucci or any small soup pasta (fresh or dried)
- 1/4 cup (30 g) freshly grated pecorino cheese

Chop together the lard, onion, garlic, and basil.
• Sauté the chopped mixture with the peas and prosciutto in a large saucepan over medium heat.
• Mix the tomato paste with 3/4 cup (180 ml) of stock and add to the saucepan. • Cover and simmer over low heat, adding more stock if needed. Season with salt and pepper. • When the peas are tender, add the remaining stock. • Bring to a boil, add the pasta, and cook until al dente.
• Sprinkle with pecorino and serve hot.

CRÊPES IN STOCK

Mix the flour and salt in a large bowl. • Add the eggs, beating until just blended. • Pour in the milk and add the parsley. Use a balloon whisk to beat the mixture until smooth. Let rest in a cool place for 1 hour. • Heat a small amount of the oil in an 8-inch (20-cm) nonstick crêpe pan or frying pan over medium heat. Stir the batter and pour in about 2 tablespoons, tilting the pan so the batter forms a thin, even layer. Cook until the top is set and the bottom is golden, about 1 minute. Turn the crêpe over and cook until lightly browned, about 30 seconds. Repeat, oiling the pan each time, until all the batter is used. Stack the cooked crêpes between sheets of waxed paper. • Sprinkle each crêpe with pecorino and roll it up. Slice each crêpe into 4–5 short lengths. Place the slices of crêpe in individual serving bowls. Carefully ladle the boiling stock over the top. Serve hot.

Serves: 6

Preparation: 40 min.
+ 1 hr. to rest the batter

Cooking: 30 min.

Level of difficulty: 1

- 1 1/3 cups (200 g) all-purpose (plain) flour
- 1/4 tsp salt
- 4 large eggs
- 1 cup (250 ml) milk
- 1 tbsp finely chopped fresh parsley
- 3–4 tbsp extra-virgin olive oil
- 1/2 cup (60 g) freshly grated pecorino cheese
- 8 cups (2 liters) boiling Chicken or Beef Stock (see page 946)

GNOCCHI & POLENTA

TUSCAN POTATO GNOCCHI

Cook the potatoes in salted boiling water for 15–20 minutes, or until tender. • Slip off the skins and mash until smooth. • Place in a large bowl and season with salt. Let cool to lukewarm. • Mix in the flour, egg, Parmesan, and pepper. • Place the mixture on a lightly floured work surface and shape into a ball. • Break off pieces of dough and form into logs about ⅔ inch (1.5 cm) in diameter and cut into 1-inch (2.5-cm) lengths. • Place the gnocchi on a clean kitchen towel, making sure that they don't touch each other, and dust lightly with flour. Let rest for one hour. • Cook the gnocchi in small batches in a large pot of salted boiling water for 3–5 minutes, or until they rise up to the surface. • Use a slotted spoon to transfer to serving plates. • Melt the butter with the sage in a small saucepan over low heat. Pour over the gnocchi and serve hot.

Serves: 4

Preparation: 40 min. + 1 hr. to rest

Cooking: 40 min.

Level of difficulty: 2

- **2 lb (1 kg) baking (floury) potatoes, with peel**
- **1¹/₃ cups (200 g) all-purpose (plain) flour**
- **1 large egg**
- **2 tbsp freshly grated Parmesan cheese**
- **Salt and freshly ground white pepper**
- **¹/₂ cup (125 g) butter**
- **Fresh sage leaves**

POTATO GNOCCHI WITH TOMATO AND PARMESAN

Potato Gnocchi: Cook the potatoes in salted boiling water for 15–20 minutes, or until tender. • Slip off the skins and mash until smooth. • Place in a bowl and let cool for 15 minutes. • Stir in the flour, salt, egg, and Parmesan. Place the mixture on a lightly floured work surface and shape into a ball. • Break off pieces of dough and form into logs about ⅔ inch (1.5 cm) in diameter and cut into 1-inch (2.5-cm) lengths. • Place the gnocchi on a clean kitchen towel, making sure that they don't touch each other, and dust lightly with flour. Let rest for one hour. • Preheat the oven to 400°F (200°C/gas 6). • Sauce: Melt the butter in a medium saucepan over medium heat. Add the tomatoes, garlic, onion, and salt. • Cover and simmer for about 10 minutes, or until the tomatoes have broken down. Uncover and let reduce for 5 minutes. • Remove from the heat and process in a food processor or blender until pureed. • Cook the gnocchi in small batches in a large pot of salted boiling water until they rise to the surface, 3–4 minutes. Use a slotted spoon to transfer them to a baking dish. Cover with half the sauce and sprinkle with half the Parmesan. Make a second layer with the gnocchi, sauce, and Parmesan. • Bake for 12–15 minutes, or until the cheese is bubbling. • Serve hot.

Serves: 4–6

Preparation: 30 min. + 1 hr. to rest

Cooking: 30 min.

Level of difficulty: 2

Potato Gnocchi
- 2 lb (1 kg) baking (floury) potatoes, with peel
- 1⅓ cups (200 g) all-purpose (plain) flour
- ⅛ tsp salt
- 1 large egg, lightly beaten
- 3 tbsp freshly grated Parmesan cheese

Sauce
- 2 tbsp butter
- 1 lb (500 g) firm-ripe tomatoes, peeled and coarsely chopped
- 1 clove garlic, lightly crushed but whole
- ½ red onion, thinly sliced
- salt
- ¾ cup (90 g) freshly grated Parmesan cheese

POTATO GNOCCHI WITH SCAMPI AND LEEK

Serves: 4–6

Preparation: 45 min.
+ time to make
the gnocchi

Cooking: 50 min.

Level of difficulty: 3

- 1 recipe Potato Gnocchi (see page 206) or 1¹/₂ lb (750 g) store-bought potato gnocchi
- 16 scampi
- 1 large red bell pepper (capsicum)
- ¹/₄ cup (60 g) butter
- 4 leeks, finely sliced
- Salt
- ¹/₄ cup (60 ml) vegetable stock
- 1 tbsp finely chopped fresh chives
- ¹/₂ tbsp finely chopped fresh tarragon
- ¹/₂ tbsp finely chopped fresh marjoram

If using homemade potato gnocchi, prepare them following the instructions on page 206. • Preheat a broiler (grill) on a high setting. • Cook four of the scampi in a pot of salted boiling water for 3 minutes. • Drain and set to one side. Broil (grill) the bell pepper until it is charred all over. • Remove from the heat and transfer to a plastic bag. Set aside for 10 minutes. • Peel the bell pepper and remove the seeds. Chop into small pieces. • Shell and devein the remaining scampi. • Heat 2 tablespoons of butter in a frying pan over medium heat. • Add the leeks and sauté for 2 minutes. Season with salt and add the stock. Simmer for 5 minutes, until the leeks are very tender. • Transfer to a food processor and blend until smooth. • Heat the remaining butter in the same pan over medium heat. Add the shelled scampi and sauté for 2 minutes. • Add the leek purée and the bell pepper. • Mix well and remove from the heat. • Cook the gnocchi in small batches in a large pot of salted boiling water until they rise to the surface, 3–4 minutes. • Scoop the cooked gnocchi out with a slotted spoon, drain well, and add to the pan with the sauce. Mix well. • When all the gnocchi are cooked and in the pan, sprinkle with the chives, tarragon, and marjoram. • Top with the boiled scampi and serve.

GNOCCHI IN TOMATO AND CREAMY GORGONZOLA SAUCE

If using homemade potato gnocchi, prepare them following the instructions on page 206. • Heat the oil in a frying pan over low heat. • Add the onion and garlic and sauté for 5 minutes, or until softened. • Add the tomatoes and basil. Simmer for 15 minutes, or until the tomato has broken down and the sauce is slightly reduced. Season with salt and pepper. • Melt the butter in a saucepan over low heat. • Add the sage and sauté for 2 minutes. • Add the Gorgonzola and cream. Mix well until the Gorgonzola has melted and the ingredients are well incorporated, about 3 minutes. • Cook the gnocchi in small batches in a large pot of salted boiling water until they rise to the surface, 3–4 minutes. • Scoop the cooked gnocchi out with a slotted spoon, drain well, and place in a large heated serving bowl. • Spoon the tomato sauce over one half of the bowl and the Gorgonzola sauce over the other half. • Sprinkle with the cheese and serve hot.

Serves: 4–6

Preparation: 10 min. + time to make the gnocchi

Cooking: 30 min.

Level of difficulty: 2

- 1 recipe Potato Gnocchi (see page 206) or 1 1/2 lb (750 g) store-bought potato gnocchi
- 1 tbsp extra virgin olive oil
- 1 small onion, finely chopped
- 1 clove garlic, finely chopped
- 1 lb (500 g) tomatoes, peeled and chopped
- 2 basil leaves, torn
- Salt and freshly ground black pepper
- 2 tbsp butter
- 2 sage leaves
- 5 oz (150 g) Gorgonzola cheese, cut into small cubes
- 1/2 cup (125 ml) heavy (double) cream
- 4 tbsp freshly grated Parmesan cheese

POTATO GNOCCHI WITH RADICCHIO

If using homemade potato gnocchi, prepare them following the instructions on page 206. • Place the radicchio, garlic, walnuts, pine nuts, cheese, salt, and pepper in a blender or food processor and chop finely. Transfer to a bowl and gradually stir in the oil. • Cook the gnocchi in small batches in a large pot of salted boiling water until they rise to the surface, 3–4 minutes. • Scoop the cooked gnocchi out with a slotted spoon, drain well, and place in a large heated serving bowl. • When all the gnocchi are cooked and in the bowl, spoon the radicchio sauce over the gnocchi. Toss gently and serve hot.

Serves: 4–6

Preparation: 15 min.
+ time to make
the gnocchi

Cooking: 15 min.

Level of difficulty: 1

- **1 recipe Potato Gnocchi (see page 206) or 1^1/$_2$ lb (750 g) store-bought potato gnocchi**
- **2 heads red radicchio, coarsely chopped**
- **2 cloves garlic**
- **3 tbsp pine nuts**
- **6 tbsp coarsely chopped walnut pieces**
- **Salt and freshly ground black pepper**
- **^{2}/$_3$ cup (100 g) freshly grated pecorino cheese**
- **^{1}/$_2$ cup (125 ml) extra-virgin olive oil**

Serves: 4–6

*Preparation: 30 min.
+ time to make
the gnocchi*

Cooking: 45 min.

Level of difficulty: 1

- 1 recipe Potato Gnocchi (see page 206) or 1¹/₂ lb (750 g) store-bought potato gnocchi
- 14 oz (450 g) asparagus (tender green tips only), cut in small pieces
- 5 tbsp butter
- 2 tbsp all-purpose (plain) flour
- 1 cup (250 ml) milk
- ²/₃ cup (185 ml) heavy (double) cream
- Salt and freshly ground black pepper
- ¹/₄ tsp freshly ground nutmeg
- ¹/₂ cup (75 g) freshly grated Parmesan cheese

POTATO GNOCCHI WITH ASPARAGUS

If using homemade potato gnocchi, prepare them following the instructions on page 206. • Cook the asparagus pieces in a saucepan of boiling water until tender,3–4 minutes. Drain well. • Sauté the asparagus in half the butter for 3–4 minutes. • Melt the remaining butter in a small saucepan and stir in the flour. • Gradually add the milk. Simmer, stirring constantly, for 5 minutes. • Remove from the heat. Add the cream, salt, pepper, nutmeg, and asparagus. Chop in a food processor. • Cook the gnocchi in small batches in a large pot of salted boiling water until they rise to the surface, 3–4 minutes. • Scoop the cooked gnocchi out with a slotted spoon, drain well, and place in a large heated serving bowl. • Spoon the sauce over the top and toss gently. Serve hot.

SPINACH POTATO GNOCCHI WITH TOMATO SAUCE

Spinach Gnocchi: Cook the potatoes in salted boiling water until tender, 15–20 minutes. • Slip off the skins and mash until smooth. • Transfer to a large bowl and mix in the flour, spinach, Parmesan, egg, and salt. Stir until smooth and well mixed. • Break off pieces of dough and form into logs about ⅔ inch (1.5 cm) in diameter and cut into 1-inch (2.5-cm) lengths. • Place the gnocchi on a clean kitchen towel, making sure that they don't touch each other, and dust lightly with flour. Let rest for one hour.
• Tomato Sauce: Sauté the pancetta in the butter in a medium saucepan over low heat for 5 minutes.
• Add the tomatoes and simmer over low heat for 25–30 minutes. • Pour in the cream and season with salt. • Cook the gnocchi in small batches in a large pot of salted boiling water until they rise to the surface, 3–4 minutes. • Scoop the cooked gnocchi out with a slotted spoon, drain well, and place in a large heated serving bowl. • When all the gnocchi are in the bowl, spoon top with the sauce and serve hot.

Serves: 4

Preparation: 30 min. + 1 hr. to rest the gnocchi

Cooking: 1 hr.

Level of difficulty: 2

Spinach Gnocchi
- 2 lb (1 kg) baking (floury) potatoes, with peel
- 1 cup (150 g) all-purpose (plain) flour
- 4 oz (125 g) spinach leaves, cooked, squeezed dry, and finely chopped
- 3 tbsp freshly grated Parmesan cheese
- 1 large egg, lightly beaten
- ⅛ tsp salt

Tomato Sauce
- ¾ cup (90 g) thinly sliced pancetta or bacon, cut in thin strips
- ¼ cup 60 g) butter
- 3 cups (750 g) canned tomatoes, with juice
- ⅔ cup (150 ml) heavy (double) cream
- salt

SPINACH AND RICOTTA GNOCCHI

Serves: 4–6

Preparation: 45 min. + time to prepare the sauce

Cooking: 25 min.

Level of difficulty: 2

- **1 recipe Tomato Sauce (see page 948)**

Gnocchi
- **1 small onion, sliced in thin rings**
- **$1/4$ cup (60 g) butter**
- **$1^1/2$ lb (750 g) fresh spinach leaves**
- **$3/4$ cup (180 g) fresh Ricotta cheese, drained**
- **3 large eggs**
- **Pinch of nutmeg**
- **$1^1/2$ cups (180 g) freshly grated Parmesan cheese + extra, to serve**
- **Salt and freshly ground black pepper**
- **$2^1/2$ cups (375 g) all-purpose (plain) flour**

Prepare the tomato sauce. • Gnocchi: Sauté the onion and butter in a saucepan over medium heat until pale gold. Remove the onion with a fork, leaving as much butter as possible in the pan. • Cook the spinach in a pot of salted, boiling water for 8–10 minutes, or until tender. Drain and squeeze out excess moisture. Chop finely. • Add the spinach to the pan with the butter and sauté for 10 minutes. Remove from the heat and transfer to a bowl. Let cool. • When the spinach is cool, add the ricotta, eggs, nutmeg, and Parmesan. Season with salt and pepper and mix well. Stir in the flour gradually until the mixture is firm. • Shape into walnut-size balls and place on a lightly floured plate. • Bring a large pot of salted water to a boil and cook the gnocchi in small batches until they rise to the surface, 3–4 minutes. • Remove with a slotted spoon and place in a pan with the preheated tomato sauce. Stir carefully. Sprinkle with the extra Parmesan and serve hot.

BAKED CHEESE GNOCCHI

P reheat the oven to 400°F (200°C/gas 6).
• Butter a baking dish. • Cook the potatoes in salted boiling water for 15–20 minutes, or until tender. • Slip off the skins and mash until smooth. Let cool. • Mix in the butter, flour, Parmesan, and egg. Season with salt and pepper. • Spread the mixture out on an oiled work surface to ½ inch (5 mm) thick and let cool completely. • Mix the Emmental, cream, and egg yolk into the Béchamel sauce. Season with salt and pepper. • Cut the potato mixture into 1-inch (2.5-cm) squares. Arrange the gnocchi in the prepared baking dish, alternating with the Béchamel sauce. Sprinkle with Parmesan. • Bake for 15–20 minutes, or until the cheese is bubbling. • Serve hot.

Serves: 4–6

Preparation: 30 min.
+ 1 hr. to cool

Cooking: 40 min.

Level of difficulty: 2

- 2 lb (1 kg) baking (floury) potatoes, with peel
- ¹/₃ cup (90 g) butter, cut up
- 1¹/₃ cups (200 g) all-purpose (plain) flour
- 3 tbsp freshly grated Parmesan cheese
- 1 large egg
- Salt and freshly ground white pepper
- ¹/₂ cup (60 g) freshly grated Emmental or Swiss cheese
- ¹/₄ cup (60 ml) heavy (double) cream
- 1 large egg yolk
- 1 recipe Béchamel Sauce (see page 956)
- 6 tbsp freshly grated Parmesan cheese

GNOCCHI WITH SAGE BUTTER

Mix the flour and salt in a large bowl. • Make a well in the center and mix in enough water to form a stiff dough. • Knead on a lightly floured work surface until smooth and elastic, 10 minutes. • Scoop up tablespoons of the dough and cook in batches in a large pot of salted, boiling water until the gnocchi rise to the surface, 3–4 minutes. • Use a slotted spoon to transfer the gnocchi to a large heated bowl. • Meanwhile, melt the butter in a small saucepan with the sage. • Drizzle the butter over the gnocchi and sprinkle with the Parmesan. Serve at once.

Serves: 4

Preparation: 15 min.

Cooking: 15 min.

Level of difficulty: 2

- **2 cups (300 g) all-purpose (plain) flour**
- **$^1/_2$ tsp salt**
- **$^1/_2$ cup (125 ml) water**
- **$^1/_3$ cup (90 g) butter**
- **3 leaves sage, torn**
- **$^1/_2$ cup (60 g) freshly grated Parmesan cheese**

GNOCCHI IN STOCK

Serves: 4

Preparation: 25 min.

Cooking: 10 min.

Level of difficulty: 2

- 1/4 cup (60 g) butter
- 4 large eggs, separated
- 2 cups (300 g) finely ground polenta (yellow cornmeal)
- 1/2 tsp salt
- 1/4 tsp freshly grated nutmeg
- 1 quart (1 liter) Beef Stock (see page 946)
- 4 tbsp freshly grated Parmesan cheese

Beat the butter in a large bowl until pale and creamy. • Add 1 egg yolk and beat well. • Continue to beat in the egg yolks, one at a time, until well blended. • Beat the egg whites in a large bowl with a mixer at high speed until stiff peaks form. • Use a large rubber spatula to fold the cornmeal and beaten whites into the batter. Mix well to make a stiff dough. • Season with salt and nutmeg. • Shape the mixture into balls the size of marbles. If the dough is too moist, add a little flour and mix well. • Bring the stock to a boil in a large saucepan. • Add the gnocchi and simmer for 10 minutes. • Ladle the gnocchi and stock into serving bowls. Sprinkle with the Parmesan and serve.

PRUNE GNOCCHI

Serves: 6

Preparation: 20 min.
+ 30 min. to soak

Cooking: 15–20 min.

Level of difficulty: 3

- 8 oz (250 g) prunes
- Sugar
- 2 lb (1 kg) potatoes
- 1²/₃ cups (250 g) all-purpose (plain) flour
- 1 large egg, lightly beaten
- 1 tbsp butter
- ¹/₃ (50 g) fine dry bread crumbs
- ¹/₂ tsp ground cinnamon

Soak the prunes in lukewarm water for 30 minutes. Pit the prunes and fill each cavity with ½ teaspoon of sugar. • Cook the potatoes in salted boiling water for 15–20 minutes, or until tender. • Slip off the skins and mash until smooth. Spread out on a clean work surface and let cool. • Shape the potato mixture into a ball and add the flour, egg, and butter. Use your hands to mix the potato mixture until well blended. • Shape the dough into dumplings about the size of golf balls. Insert a prune into the center of each one. • Cook the gnocchi in batches in a large pan of salted, boiling water until they bob up to the surface, 3–4 minutes. Scoop out with a slotted spoon, drain well, and transfer to a heated serving dish. • Brown the bread crumbs in a little extra butter and sugar. Dust with the cinnamon. Sprinkle this mixture over the gnocchi and serve hot.

CHESTNUT GNOCCHI

If using fresh chestnuts, cook them in salted boiling water with a bay leaf for 35–45 minutes, or until softened. • Drain and transfer to a large bowl. Use a potato masher to mash the chestnuts until smooth. • Mix in the pecorino and eggs. Season with salt and pepper, and add 2–3 tablespoons of flour to make a smooth dough. Test the consistency by breaking off a small ball of dough, dusting it with flour, and cooking it in boiling water. If it falls apart during cooking, add more flour. • Form the dough into balls the size of marbles. Roll in the flour and lay them out on a plate dusted with flour. • Cook the gnocchi in small batches in a large pot of salted boiling water for until they rise to the surface, 3–4 minutes. • Use a slotted spoon to transfer to serving dishes. Drizzle with the melted butter, and sprinkle with the sage and Parmesan. • Serve hot.

Serves: 4
Preparation: 30 min.
Cooking: 70 min.
Level of difficulty: 2

- 1 1/2 lb (750 g) raw peeled chestnuts or drained canned chestnuts
- 1 bay leaf (optional)
- 1/2 cup (60 g) freshly grated pecorino cheese
- 2 large eggs
- 1/2 cup (75 g) semolina flour + more as needed
- Salt and freshly ground white pepper
- 1/3 cup (90 g) butter, melted
- 4 sprigs fresh sage
- 1/4 cup (30 g) freshly grated Parmesan cheese

SQUASH GNOCCHI IN SAUSAGE SAUCE

Gnocchi: Preheat the oven to 400°F (200°C/gas 6). • Bake the pieces of squash on a large baking sheet for 40–45 minutes, or until tender. • Remove from the oven and let cool. Use a tablespoon to remove the flesh from the peel and chop in a food processor. If the squash is still moist, wrap it in a kitchen cloth and wring out the excess moisture. • Transfer the squash to a large bowl and mix in the eggs, amaretti, bread crumbs, and Parmesan. • Season with nutmeg, salt and pepper. • Sausage Sauce: Sauté the onion in the butter in a small saucepan over a medium heat for 5 minutes, until softened. Add the crumbled sausage and garlic and simmer over low heat for 10 minutes. • Discard the garlic and add the tomato paste mixture. • Season with salt and remove from the heat. • Form tablespoons of the gnocchi mixture into balls the size of walnuts, pressing them into an oval shape. • Dip in the flour until well coated. • Cook the gnocchi in small batches in a large pot of salted boiling water until they rise to the surface, 3–4 minutes. • Use a slotted spoon to transfer to serving dishes and serve hot with the sauce.

Serves: 4

Preparation: 45 min.

Cooking: 75 min.

Level of difficulty: 2

Gnocchi
- 2¹/₄ lb (1.25 kg) winter squash or pumpkin, cut into large pieces unpeeled but seeded
- 2 large eggs
- ¹/₄ cup (50 g) amaretti cookies, crumbled
- 4 tbsp fresh bread crumbs
- ¹/₄ cup (30 g) freshly grated Parmesan cheese
- ¹/₄ tsp ground nutmeg
- Salt and freshly ground white pepper

Sausage Sauce
- 1 small onion, finely chopped
- ¹/₄ cup (60 g) butter
- 4 oz (100 g) Italian sausage, crumbled
- 1 clove garlic, lightly crushed but whole
- 1 tbsp tomato paste (concentrate) mixed with 1 tbsp water
- Salt
- ¹/₄ cup (30 g) all-purpose (plain) flour

RICOTTA GNOCCHI WITH MEAT SAUCE

If the ricotta is very soft, drain it in a fine mesh strainer. • Mix the ricotta, flour, eggs and egg yolks, ¾ cup (90 g) of Parmesan, and salt and pepper in a large bowl to make a fairly stiff dough. Break off pieces of dough, shape them into ⅔-inch (1.5 cm) thick logs on a floured board and cut into 1-inch (2.5-cm) sections. • Cook the gnocchi in small batches in a large pot of salted boiling water until they rise to the surface, 3–5 minutes. • Use a slotted spoon to scoop out the gnocchi and transfer to a heated serving dish. Cover with the meat sauce. Sprinkle with the remaining Parmesan and serve hot.

Serves: 6

Preparation: 40 min. + time to make the meat sauce

Cooking: 20 min.

Level of difficulty: 2

Gnocchi

- 2¹/₂ cups (625 g) fresh ricotta cheese
- 2 cups (300 g) all-purpose (plain) flour
- 2 large eggs + 3 large egg yolks
- 1¹/₄ cups (150 g) freshly grated Parmesan cheese
- Salt and freshly ground white pepper

- 1 recipe Meat Sauce (see page 951)

Serves 6

Prep: 1 hr. + time to make the gnocchi

Cooking: 1 hr.

Level of difficulty: 2

- 1 recipe Potato Gnocchi (see page 206) or 1¹/₂ lb (750 g) store-bought potato gnocchi
- 5 tbsp extra-virgin olive oil
- 1 red or white onion, 1 stalk celery, ¹/₂ carrot, all finely chopped
- 1¹/₂ lb (750 g) goose or duck, excess fat removed and cut into large chunks
- 1 cup (250 ml) dry white wine
- 2 cups (500 g) peeled and chopped tomatoes
- 1¹/₄ cups (150 g) freshly grated pecorino cheese

GNOCCHI WITH DUCK SAUCE

If using homemade potato gnocchi, prepare them following the instructions on page 206. • Heat the oil in a saucepan over medium heat. Add the onion, celery, and carrot and sauté until softened, about 5 minutes. • Add the pieces of meat and cook until browned all over. • Pour in the wine and tomatoes. Cover and simmer over low heat for about 45 minutes, or until the meat is tender. Remove the meat, bone it, and remove the skin. Break it up with your fingers. Return the meat to the pan and cook for 1 minute. • Cook the gnocchi in small batches in a large pot of salted boiling water until they rise to the surface, 3–4 minutes. • Use a slotted spoon to scoop out the gnocchi and transfer to a heated serving dish with the sauce. Sprinkle with the pecorino. Serve hot.

SAFFRON GNOCCHI IN MEAT SAUCE

Saffron Gnocchi: Mix the flour and salt in a bowl and make a well in the center. Mix in enough of the saffron water to make a smooth dough. Knead on a lightly floured work surface for 15–20 minutes, until smooth and elastic. Shape the dough into a ball, wrap in plastic wrap (cling film), and let rest for 30 minutes. • Meat Sauce: Heat the oil in a Dutch oven (casserole) over low heat and add the onion and pancetta. Cover and cook for 10 minutes. • Add the pork and sauté over high heat for 7 minutes until browned all over. • Pour in the wine and let it evaporate, 5 minutes. • Stir in the tomatoes and basil and season with salt and pepper. Bring to a boil and simmer over low heat, partially covered, for at least 2 hours, adding stock or hot water if the sauce begins to stick to the pan. • Form the dough into logs ¼ inch (5 mm) in diameter and cut into ½-inch (1-cm) lengths. • Lay them on a dry cloth dusted with semolina. • Cook the gnocchi in small batches in a large pot of salted boiling water until they rise to the surface, 2–3 minutes. • Drain and serve in the sauce, sprinkled with pecorino.

Serves: 6

Preparation: 1 hr. + 30 min. to rest the dough

Cooking: 40 min.

Level of difficulty: 2

Saffron Gnocchi

- 2²/₃ cups (400 g) semolina flour
- ¹/₄ tsp salt
- ¹/₄ tsp saffron strands, crumbled and dissolved in ³/₄ cup (180 ml) lukewarm water + more as needed

Meat Sauce

- ¹/₄ cup (60 ml) extra-virgin olive oil
- 1 red onion, finely chopped
- 3 oz (90 g) pancetta, bacon, or lard, finely chopped
- 12 oz (300 g) lean ground (minced) pork
- ¹/₂ cup (125 ml) dry red wine
- 3 lb (1.5 kg) peeled plum tomatoes, pressed through a fine mesh strainer (passata)
- 4 leaves fresh basil, torn
- Salt and freshly ground black pepper
- 1 cup (125 g) freshly grated aged pecorino cheese

FRIED GNOCCHI

Serves: 4
Preparation: 50 min.
Cooking: 40 min.
Level of difficulty: 2

- 1 large egg and 5 large egg yolks
- 1 tbsp sugar
- 1 cup (150 g) potato flour
- 2 cups (500 ml) milk
- 1 cup (250 g) butter
- Pinch each of nutmeg, cinnamon, and salt
- $^{1}/_{4}$ cup (30 g) all-purpose (plain) flour
- 1 cup (150 g) fine dry bread crumbs
- $^{1}/_{2}$ cup (60 g) freshly grated Parmesan cheese

Beat the egg yolks in a bowl with the sugar until smooth. • Place the potato flour in a heavy-bottomed saucepan. Gradually stir in the milk. Add the egg mixture, 2 tablespoons of the butter, the nutmeg, cinnamon, and salt. Mix well with a wooden spoon. • Place the pan over medium heat and, stirring constantly, bring to a boil. Simmer for 10 minutes, stirring all the time. Remove from the heat. • Turn the gnocchi batter out onto a flat work surface. Using a spatula dipped in cold water, spread it out to about ½-inch (1-cm) thick and leave to cool for 30 minutes. • Cut the batter into cubes or roll into marble-sized balls. • Beat the remaining egg in a bowl with a fork. • Dust the gnocchi with flour, drop them into the beaten egg, then roll them in the bread crumbs. • Heat the remaining butter in a 12-inch (30-cm) frying pan and fry the gnocchi until golden brown. • Place on a heated serving dish, sprinkle with Parmesan, and serve hot.

SEMOLINA GNOCCHI

P reheat the oven to 400°F (200°C/gas 6).
• Butter a baking dish. • Bring the milk to a
boil with ¼ cup (60 g) of the butter and the salt,
pepper, and nutmeg. Sprinkle in the semolina and
beat vigorously with a whisk to prevent lumps from
forming. • Simmer for 20 minutes, stirring
constantly. Remove from the heat, let cool, and
add 2 tablespoons of the Parmesan and the egg
yolks. • Pour the semolina onto a surface greased
with oil. Use your hands and a spatula to smooth it
out to ⅓ inch (7 mm) thick and let cool completely.
• Use a smooth pastry cutter to cut the dough into
2½-inch (6-cm) rounds. • Arrange the leftover
dough scraps in the bottom of the prepared baking
dish. Top with the rounds, leaning them one against
another, roof tile fashion. • Sprinkle with the
remaining butter and Parmesan. • Bake for 12–15
minutes, or until golden brown. • Serve hot.

Serves: 4

Preparation: 40 min.

Cooking: 45 min.

Level of difficulty: 2

- 4 cups (1 liter) milk
- ⅓ cup (90 g)
  butter
- Salt and freshly
  ground white
  pepper
- ⅛ tsp freshly
  grated nutmeg
- 1⅔ cups (250 g)
  semolina flour
- 1 cup (125 g)
  freshly grated
  Parmesan cheese
- 3 large egg yolks,
  beaten with 1 tbsp
  milk

ROMAN GNOCCHI WITH GORGONZOLA

Prepare the semolina gnocchi following the instructions on page 234. • Arrange the gnocchi in an oiled baking dish, overlapping a little, in roof-tile fashion. • Sauce: Melt the butter in a medium saucepan and stir in the flour. • Gradually add the milk and cook over low heat, stirring constantly, for 5 minutes. Season with salt and pepper. • Sprinkle the Gorgonzola over the gnocchi in the baking dish and pour the sauce over the top. Sprinkle with Parmesan. • Bake for 15 minutes, or until nicely browned. Serve hot.

Serves: 4

Preparation: 15 min.
  + time to make the gnocchi

Cooking: 20 min.

Level of difficulty: 2

- **1 recipe semolina gnocchi (see page 234)**

Sauce
- **3 tbsp butter**
- **3 tbsp all-purpose (plain) flour**
- **2 cups (500 ml) hot milk**
- **Salt and freshly ground black pepper**
- **8 oz (250 g) Gorgonzola cheese, cut in small cubes**
- **4 tbsp freshly grated Parmesan cheese**

BASIC POLENTA

Serves: 6–8

Preparation: 5 min.

Cooking: 40–45 min.

Level of difficulty: 2

- **4 quarts (4 liters) cold water**
- **2 tbsp coarse sea salt**
- **3¹/₂ cups (500 g) polenta (yellow cornmeal)**

B ring the water and salt to a boil in a very large saucepan or polenta cauldron. (If preferred, use an electric polenta maker to prepare the polenta.) • Add the polenta gradually, stirring constantly so that no lumps form. Polenta should always be perfectly smooth. • Stir the polenta over medium-low heat by moving a long, wooden spoon in a circular motion. At a certain point the polenta will begin to draw away from the sides of the pot on which a thin crust will form. The polenta should be stirred constantly for the 40–45 minutes it takes to cook. • Pour the cooked polenta onto a serving board or platter. Serve hot with sauce or let cool to make fried or baked polenta crostini.

FRIED MUSHROOM POLENTA

Serves: 6–8

Preparation: 15 min.

Cooking: 1 hr.

Level of difficulty: 2

- 1 recipe
  **Basic Polenta
  (see page 237)**
- 1 lb (500 g) porcini
  (or other wild)
  mushrooms
- 1/3 cup (90 ml)
  extra-virgin olive
  oil
- 1 onion
- 2 tbsp finely
  chopped parsley
- 6 fresh sage
  leaves, finely
  chopped
- 2 cups (500 ml)
  olive oil, for frying

Prepare the polenta. • While the polenta is cooking, clean the mushrooms, rinse under cold running water, and chop coarsely. • Heat the oil in a large frying pan and sauté the onion until soft. • Add the mushrooms, parsley, and sage and simmer over medium-low heat for 10 minutes, stirring frequently. • Add the mushroom mixture to the polenta just before the polenta is cooked. • Dampen a clean work surface and spread the mixture out in a layer about ½-inch (1-cm) thick. Leave to cool. • Cut the polenta in slices about 2 x 4 inches (5 x 8 cm). • Heat the oil in a large frying until very hot and fry the slices of polenta in batches until golden brown on both sides. Drain on paper towels. Serve hot.

POLENTA AND CHEESE FRITTERS

Bring the water and salt to a boil in a very large saucepan or polenta cauldron. If preferred, use an electric polenta maker to prepare the polenta.
• Add the polenta gradually, stirring constantly so that no lumps form. • Stir the polenta over medium-low heat by moving a long, wooden spoon in a circular motion. At a certain point the polenta will begin to draw away from the sides of the pot on which a thin crust will form. The polenta should be stirred constantly for the 40–45 minutes it takes to cook. Turn the polenta out onto a wooden board and let cool. This will take several hours. •
Cut the cold polenta into very small cubes. • Place the Gruyère, Parmesan, flour, 4 egg yolks, milk, salt, pepper, and nutmeg in a large heavy saucepan, mix well, and bring to a boil over medium heat. Simmer the mixture over low heat for 5 minutes, stirring constantly. • Remove from the heat and stir in the polenta and truffles, if using. Mix well then spread on a large board or plate in a layer about 1 inch (2.5-cm) thick and let cool and harden. • Use a cookie cutter or glass to cut out rounds of the polenta mixture. • Beat the remaining whole eggs and whites in a bowl until frothy. •
Dredge each fritter first in the bread crumbs, then dip in the egg, and dredge again in the bread crumbs. • Heat the oil in a deep fryer or frying pan.
• Fry the fritters in small batches until golden brown on both sides. Drain on paper towels.
• Serve hot.

Serves: 6–8

Preparation: 45 min.
+ several hr. to cool

Cooking: 1 hr.

Level of difficulty: 2

• 8 cups (2 liters) water
• 1 tbsp coarse sea salt
• 2¹/₃ cups (350 g) polenta (yellow cornmeal)
• 12 oz (350 g) freshly grated Gruyère or Swiss cheese
• 1 cup (125 g) freshly grated Parmesan cheese
• 2 tbsp all-purpose (plain) flour
• 6 large eggs
• 1 cup (250 ml) milk
• Salt and freshly ground black pepper
• Freshly grated nutmeg
• White truffles, grated (optional)
• 2 cups (300 g) fine dry bread crumbs
• 2 cups (500 ml) olive oil, for frying

POLENTA WITH TUSCAN BLACK CABBAGE

Serves: 4–6

Preparation: 15 min.

Cooking: 75 min.

Level of difficulty: 2

- 6 cups (1.5 liters) cold water
- 2 cups (300 g) polenta (yellow cornmeal)
- Salt
- 1 1/2 lb (750 g) Tuscan black cabbage or kale, chopped
- 1/3 cup (90 ml) extra-virgin olive oil
- 2 cloves garlic, lightly crushed but whole
- 1 fresh red chile pepper, seeded and sliced
- 4 anchovy fillets, chopped
- 2 cups (500 ml) boiling milk
- 1/2 cup (60 g) freshly grated Parmesan cheese

Bring the water to a boil in a large saucepan over medium heat. • Add the polenta gradually, beating well to prevent lumps forming. • Season with salt and mix well. Cook the polenta for about 45 minutes, stirring almost constantly. • While the polenta is cooking, cook the cabbage in a large pot of salted boiling water until tender, 10–15 minutes. • Drain well. • Heat half the oil in a large frying pan over medium heat. Add the garlic and sauté for until pale golden brown, 3–4 minutes. • Remove and discard the garlic. • Add the cabbage and the half the chile pepper. Sauté over high heat for 3–4 minutes. • Add the anchovies and mix well. Remove from the heat. • Add the milk and Parmesan to the cooked polenta and mix well. • Add two-thirds of the cabbage mixture and mix well. • Spoon the polenta into serving bowls. • Top with the remaining cabbage and drizzle with the remaining oil. • Garnish with remaining chile pepper and serve hot.

POLENTA WITH MEAT SAUCE

Meat Sauce: Heat the oil in a medium saucepan over low heat. Add the onions, carrots, and celery. Cook, covered, for 25–30 minutes. Add the garlic and sausage, turn up the heat to high, and add the beef. Brown well. • Stir in the flour. Pour in the wine and cook until it has evaporated. • Add the tomatoes, parsley, nutmeg, rosemary, sage, bay leaf, lemon zest, salt, and pepper. • Cook for at least 4 hours over low heat, adding a little stock or water to keep it moist. • Prepare the polenta. • When cooked, pour onto a warm serving plate. Top with the meat sauce and sprinkle with Parmesan.

Serves: 6

Preparation: 35 min.

Cooking: 4 hr.

Level of difficulty: 2

Meat Sauce
- 2 tbsp extra-virgin olive oil
- 2 red onions, 2 carrots, 2 stalks celery, finely chopped
- 2 cloves garlic, finely chopped
- 8 oz (250 g) sausage
- 8 oz (250 g) ground (minced) beef
- 1 tbsp all-purpose (plain) flour
- $^{1}/_{2}$ cup (125 ml) red wine
- 1 lb (500 g) tomatoes, peeled and chopped
- 1 tbsp finely chopped fresh parsley
- $^{1}/_{4}$ tsp freshly grated nutmeg
- sprig rosemary
- sprig sage
- 1 bay leaf
- 1 small piece lemon zest
- Salt and freshly ground black pepper
- 1 recipe Basic Polenta (see page 237)
- 4 tbsp freshly grated Parmesan cheese

POLENTA GNOCCHI

Serves: 4

Preparation: 10 min.
+ 1 hr. to cool

Cooking: 45 min.

Level of difficulty: 1

- **4 cups (1 liter) milk**
- **2¹/₂ cups (375 g) polenta (yellow cornmeal)**
- **Salt and freshly ground white pepper**
- **Pinch of nutmeg**
- **²/₃ cup (150 g) butter**
- **1 cup (120 g) freshly grated Parmesan cheese**
- **3 large egg yolks, beaten with 1 tbsp milk**
- **¹/₂ cup (75 g) ham, coarsely chopped**

B ring the milk to a boil in a large, heavy sauce-pan. • Pour in the cornmeal while stirring continuously with a long-handled wooden spoon. Season with salt, pepper, and nutmeg. Add one-third of the butter. Stir for about 30 minutes. • Remove from the heat and add 2 tablespoons of the Parmesan, the egg yolks and milk, and ham. • Dampen a clean work surface and pour the polenta onto it. Spread to about ½ inch (1-cm) thick. Let cool for 1 hour. • Preheat the oven to 400°F (200°C/gas 6). • Use a cookie cutter or glass to cut out disks. • Grease a rectangular ovenproof dish with butter and arrange the disks in overlapping layers, roof-tile fashion. • Heat the remaining butter and pour over the top. Sprinkle with the remaining Parmesan. • Bake for about 10 minutes, or until the topping is golden brown. • Serve hot.

POLENTA WITH PORK AND PRUNES

Serves: 6–8

Preparation: 20 min.

Cooking: 35 min.

Level of difficulty: 2

- 8 cups (2 liters) water
- 3 1/2 cups (500 g) instant polenta
- Salt
- 2 lb (1 kg) pork fillet, cut into 1 inch (3 cm) cubes
- 3 tbsp all-purpose (plain) flour
- 16 prunes, pitted
- 5 oz (150 g) sliced pancetta or bacon
- 1/3 cup (90 g) butter
- Leaves from 1 sprig of sage
- Salt and freshly ground black pepper
- 1/2 cup (125 ml) dry Marsala wine + a little more if required
- 1 cup (250 ml) boiling Beef Stock (see page 946), + extra, as required

Bring the water to a boil in a large saucepan over medium heat. • Add 1 teaspoon of salt and the polenta. Cook for 8–10 minutes, stirring constantly, until the mixture is thickened. • Pour the polenta into an oiled dish and let cool. • Dredge the pork in the flour in a bowl, ensuring that it is evenly coated. Shake the meat gently to remove any excess flour. • Wrap each of the prunes in a small piece of pancetta. • Preheat the oven to 400°F (200°C/gas 6). • Melt the butter in a large frying pan over medium heat. • Add the sage, pork, and the prepared prunes. Sauté for 3 minutes, until the meat is sealed all over. • Season with salt and pepper. • Remove and discard the sage. • Add the Marsala and stock. Simmer for 15 minutes, stirring from time to time, until the meat is cooked through and the sauce is thick and glossy. If the mixture is too dry and sticks to the pan add a little more stock and Marsala. • Turn out the polenta onto a cutting board and slice it. • Arrange the slices on an oiled baking sheet and bake for 10 minutes, until lightly browned. • Remove from the oven and arrange in a large serving dish. • Spoon the pork and its sauce into the center of the dish. • Serve hot.

POLENTA PIE
WITH MEAT SAUCE

Bring the water and salt to a boil in a heavy
saucepan and add the polenta. Simmer over
low heat, stirring constantly until done, about
40 minutes. The polenta should be fairly firm.
If preferred, use an electric polenta maker to
prepare the polenta. • Turn the polenta out onto
a wooden board and let cool. This will take several
hours. • Cut the cold polenta into thin slices. • Melt
1 tablespoon of butter in a heavy saucepan. Add
the pork and sauté until lightly browned, 5 minutes.
• Add the sausages and tomatoes. Cover the pan
and simmer over low heat for 1 hour. • Preheat the
oven to 350°F (180°C/gas 4). • Butter a large
rectangular baking dish (similar to what you would
use for lasagne). • Cover the bottom of the dish
with a layer of polenta slices. Spread with a layer
of the sauce. Cover with another layer of polenta
and sauce. Finish with a layer of polenta. Dot with
the remaining butter and sprinkle with the
Parmesan. • Bake until golden brown and cooked
through, about 35 minutes. • Serve hot.

Serves: 6–8

Preparation: 45 min.
+ several hr. to cool

Cooking: 90 min.

Level of difficulty: 1

- 8 cups (2 liters)
  cold water
- 3$\frac{1}{3}$ cups (500 g)
  polenta (yellow
  cornmeal)
- $\frac{1}{3}$ cup (90 g)
  butter
- 14 oz (400 g)
  ground (minced)
  pork
- 12 oz (350 g)
  Italian sausages,
  peeled
- 4 large tomatoes,
  peeled and
  chopped
- Salt and freshly
  ground black
  pepper
- 1 cup (125 g)
  freshly grated
  Parmesan cheese

POLENTA PIE

B ring the water and salt to a boil in a heavy saucepan and add the polenta. Simmer over low heat, stirring constantly until done, about 40 minutes. The polenta should be fairly firm. If preferred, use an electric polenta maker to prepare the polenta. • Place the dried mushrooms in a small bowl and cover with warm water. Let soak. • Blanche the tomatoes in boiling water for 1 minute then slip off the skins. Chop coarsely. • Drain the mushrooms. • Chop the onion and celery finely with the lard. • Place in a heavy saucepan over medium heat and sauté for 2–3 minutes. • Add the sausages, tomatoes, and mushrooms, season with salt and pepper, and simmer over low heat for 30 minutes. • Preheat the oven to 350°F (180°C/gas 4). • Butter a deep 10-inch (25-cm) round baking dish. • Turn the polenta out onto a wooden board and divide into three pieces; one piece should be twice as large as the other two. • Lightly flour a work surface and roll the larger piece of polenta out into round large enough to line the base and sides of the prepared pan. Spread with a layer of the sauce. Sprinkle with Parmesan and dot with a little of the remaining butter. • Roll out the other pieces of polenta and place one in the pan. Cover with another layer of sauce, Parmesan, and butter. Finish with the remaining piece of polenta, dotted with the remaining butter. • Bake until golden brown and cooked through, about 50 minutes. • Serve hot.

Serves: 4–6

Preparation: 45 min.

Cooking: 90 min.

Level of difficulty: 2

- 8 cups (2 liters) cold water
- 3¹/₃ cups (500 g) polenta (yellow cornmeal)
- 1 oz (30 g) dried porcini mushrooms
- 1 lb (500 g) ripe tomatoes
- 1 white onion
- 1 stalk celery
- 3 tbsp lard
- 8 oz (250 g) Italian sausages, peeled
- ¹/₃ cup (90 g) butter
- 1 cup (125 g) freshly grated Parmesan cheese
- Salt and freshly ground black pepper

SICILIAN COUSCOUS

Serves: 6–8

Preparation: 1 hr. + 30 min. to rest

Cooking: 1 hr.

Level of difficulty: 1

Simmer the fish stock with the white onion, garlic, oil, parsley, saffron, cinnamon, lemon, and salt over low heat for 30 minutes. Strain and set aside. • Sauté the red onion, bay leaf, and cinnamon in ¼ cup (60 ml) of the oil in a Dutch oven (casserole) over low heat for 10 minutes. • Add the garlic, tomato paste, lemon zest, and 1 cup (250 ml) of water. Bring to a boil and add the fish. • Pour in 2 cups (500 ml) of the fish stock. Season with salt, cover, and simmer over very low heat for 15 minutes. • Bring the remaining fish stock back to a boil. Place the couscous in a large saucepan and pour the hot fish stock over it. Stir well. Cover and let rest for 10 minutes. • Place the couscous over low heat and add the remaining 2 tablespoons of oil oil to prevent clumping. Stir well, then transfer to a large, deep serving dish. • Spoon the fish mixture over the top. Serve hot.

- 8 cups (2 liters) fish stock
- 1 white onion, cut into quarters
- 2 cloves garlic, lightly crushed but whole
- ⅓ cup (90 ml) extra-virgin olive oil
- 1 tbsp finely chopped fresh parsley
- ½ tsp saffron threads, crumbled
- 1 small stick cinnamon
- ½ lemon, chopped
- Salt
- 1 red onion, finely chopped
- 1 bay leaf
- 1 small stick cinnamon
- 2 cloves garlic, finely chopped
- 2 tbsp tomato paste (concentrate)
- Finely grated zest of ½ lemon
- 1 cups (250 ml) water + more as needed
- 3 lb (1.5 kg) mixed fish fillets, such as mullet, snapper, grouper, or cod
- 2 lb (1 kg) instant couscous

RICE

SPINACH RISOTTO

Cook the baby spinach leaves in a little salted water until just tender, 3–5 minutes. Drain well and chop finely. • Melt ⅓ cup (90 g) of butter in a large saucepan over low heat. Add the chopped spinach and 4 tablespoons of Parmesan. Season with salt, pepper, and nutmeg. Remove from the heat and set aside. • Heat the remaining butter in a large frying pan over medium heat. Add the onion and sauté until softened, 5 minutes. • Turn the heat up to medium-high and add the rice. Stir constantly for 2–3 minutes. • Add the wine and stir until evaporated. • Begin adding the stock, ½ cup (125 ml) at a time, cooking and stirring until each addition has been absorbed and the rice is tender, 15–18 minutes. • Stir in the spinach mixture and the remaining Parmesan, season with salt and pepper, and serve hot.

Serves: 4–6

Preparation: 25 min.

Cooking: 35 min.

Level of difficulty: 1

- **1 lb (500 g) baby spinach leaves**
- **¹/₂ cup (125 g) butter**
- **1 medium white onion, finely chopped**
- **¹/₂ cup (125 ml) dry white wine**
- **2 cups (400 g) Italian risotto rice**
- **5 cups (1.25 liters) Chicken Stock (see page 946)**
- **¹/₂ cup (60 g) freshly grated Parmesan cheese**
- **Salt and freshly ground black pepper**

HERB RISOTTO

259

Serves: 4–6

Preparation: 15 min.

Cooking: 3 h 30 min.

Level of difficulty: 2

- 3 tbsp extra virgin olive oil
- 1 clove garlic, finely chopped
- 1 large onion, finely chopped
- 1 celery stick, finely chopped
- 1 tbsp finely chopped fresh rosemary
- 1 tbsp finely chopped fresh basil
- 1 tbsp finely chopped fresh sage
- 2 cups (400 g) Italian risotto rice
- $1/3$ cup (90 ml) dry white wine
- 6 cups (1.5 liters) boiling vegetable stock
- 2 tbsp butter
- Salt
- Finely chopped fresh rosemary, basil, and sage, to garnish

Heat the oil in a large saucepan over low heat. • Add the garlic, onion, celery, rosemary, basil, and sage. Sauté for 3–4 minutes, until the onion begins to soften. • Add the rice and mix well. Sauté for 2 minutes. • Add the wine and cook until it evaporates. • Begin adding the stock, ½ cup (125 ml) at a time, cooking and stirring until each addition has been absorbed and the rice is tender, 15–18 minutes. • Remove from the heat and add the butter. Season with salt. • Mix well then let the risotto rest for 2 minutes. • Garnish with the herbs and serve hot.

RICE WITH ARTICHOKES

Trim the stalks and cut the top third off the tops of the artichokes. Remove the tough outer leaves by bending them down and snapping them off. Cut in half and use a sharp knife to remove any fuzzy choke. Slice into thin wedges. Place in a bowl of cold water with the lemon juice and let soak for 2 hours. • Preheat the oven to 400°F (200°C/gas 6). • Place the rice in a deep 9-inch (23-cm) baking dish. Sprinkle with the parsley and garlic and arrange the artichokes on top. Season with salt and pepper and pour in the stock. Drizzle with the oil and sprinkle with the pecorino. • Cover the dish and bake until the rice is tender, 45–55 minutes. Check half way through cooking that the rice has not absorbed all the stock. If it has, add a little more boiling stock or water. Don't add too much liquid; the dish should be moist but not slushy. • Serve hot.

Serves: 4

Preparation: 30 min. + 2 hr. to soak

Cooking: 45–55 min.

Level of difficulty: 1

- **6 medium artichokes**
- **Freshly squeezed juice of 1 lemon**
- **2 cups (400 g) short-grain rice**
- **$1/3$ cup (90 ml) extra-virgin olive oil**
- **$1/2$ cup (60 g) freshly grated pecorino cheese**
- **2 tbsp finely chopped parsley**
- **5 cups (1.25 liters) vegetable stock**
- **2 cloves garlic, thinly sliced**
- **Salt and freshly ground black pepper**

RISOTTO WITH BEANS

Soak the beans in cold water overnight.
• Drain the beans and bring to a boil in fresh cold water. Simmer until tender, about 2 hours.
• When the beans are almost tender, heat 2 tablespoons of butter and the oil in a large frying pan over medium heat. Add the onion, pancetta, parsley, basil, and garlic and sauté until softened, about 5 minutes. • Add the tomatoes and simmer, stirring often, for 10 minutes. • Drain the beans and add to the frying pan. • Add the rice and stir well. Pour in the wine and stir until it has been absorbed. • Begin adding the stock, ½ cup (125 ml) at a time, cooking and stirring until each addition has been absorbed and the rice is tender, 15–18 minutes. • Stir in the remaining butter and the Parmesan and serve hot.

Serves: 4–6

Preparation: 45 min. + 12 hr. to soak the beans

Cooking: 2 hr. 30 min.

Level of difficulty: 2

- 1 cup (100 g) dried borlotti or cranberry beans
- ¹/₃ cup (90 g) butter
- 2 tbsp extra-virgin olive oil
- 1 medium white onion, finely chopped
- 2 oz (60 g) pancetta, diced
- 2 tbsp finely chopped fresh parsley
- 1 tbsp finely chopped fresh basil
- 1 clove garlic, finely chopped
- 2 cups (400 g) Italian risotto rice
- 3 large tomatoes, peeled and chopped
- 5 cups (1.25 liters) Beef Stock (see page 946)
- ¹/₂ cup (125 ml) red wine
- ¹/₂ cup (60 g) freshly grated Parmesan cheese
- Salt and freshly ground black pepper

RICE WITH PEAS AND BEANS

Serves: 4–6

Preparation: 45 min.

Cooking: 1 hr.

Level of difficulty: 1

- 1 lb (500 g) fresh borlotti beans (weight before hulling)
- 1 lb (500 g) fresh peas (weight before hulling)
- 2 carrots, cut in small cubes
- 3 potatoes, peeled and cut in small cubes
- 2 cups (400 g) short-grain rice
- 2 leeks, thinly sliced
- 1 medium zucchini (courgette), cut in small cubes
- 1 stalk celery, thinly sliced
- 1 small cauliflower, broken into florets
- $1/2$ cup (125 g) butter
- 4 leaves sage + extra, to garnish
- $1/3$ cup (45 g) freshly grated Parmesan cheese
- Salt and freshly ground black pepper

Hull the beans. Place in a saucepan of lightly salted boiling water and simmer until tender, about 30 minutes. • Hull the peas and place in a bowl of cold water. • When the beans are almost tender, bring a lightly salted large saucepan of water to a boil. Add the carrots, potatoes, and rice and simmer for 5 minutes. Add the remaining vegetables and simmer until the rice and vegetables are tender. • Heat the butter and sage leaves in a large frying pan over medium heat. • Drain the rice and vegetables and the beans and place in a large, heated serving dish. • Drizzle with the butter and sage and sprinkle with the cheese. Season with salt and pepper. • Garnish with a sprig a sage and serve hot.

MUSHROOM AND PUMPKIN RISOTTO

Serves: 6

Preparation: 40 min.

Cooking: 50 min.

Level of difficulty: 2

Bring the stock to a boil in a large saucepan over medium heat. Add the pumpkin, a sprig of rosemary, and the garlic. Simmer until the pumpkin is tender, 10–15 minutes. Remove and discard the garlic and rosemary. • Transfer the pumpkin to a bowl using a slotted spoon. Keep the stock hot. • Heat 3 tablespoons of the oil in a small frying pan with the remaining rosemary and the orange zest. Sauté for 2 minutes and then remove and discard the rosemary. Set aside to cool. • Heat the remaining oil in a large frying pan over medium heat. Add the onion and sauté until transparent, about 3 minutes. • Add the mushrooms and sauté for 1–2 minutes. Season with salt and pepper • Add the rice and sauté for 2 minutes. • Add ½ cup (125 ml) of the stock and cook until it is absorbed. Stir in the pumpkin and season with salt and pepper. Keep adding the stock ½ cup (125 ml) at a time, cooking and stirring until each addition has been absorbed and the rice is tender, 15–18 minutes. • Remove from the heat and stir in the orange zest and oil. Cover and let rest for 1 minute. • Serve hot.

- • 4 cups (1 liter) boiling vegetable stock
- • 14 oz (400 g) fresh pumpkin flesh, cut into small cubes
- • 2 sprigs of rosemary
- • 1 clove garlic, lightly crushed
- • ⅓ cup (90 ml) extra-virgin olive oil
- • Zest of 1 orange, cut into julienne strips
- • 1 large onion, finely chopped
- • 8 oz (250 g) porcini mushrooms, sliced
- • Salt and freshly ground black pepper
- • 2 cups (400 g) Italian risotto rice

Serves: 4

Preparation: 10 min.

Cooking: 40 min.

Level of difficulty: 1

- 1/3 cup (90 ml) extra-virgin olive oil
- 2 large potatoes, peeled and cut into small cubes
- 1 3/4 cups (350 g) Italian risotto rice
- 1/3 cup (90 ml) dry white wine
- 1 large onion, chopped finely
- 8 oz (250 g) cabbage, shredded
- 3 cups (750 ml) boiling vegetable stock
- Salt
- 1 tbsp finely chopped fresh parsley, to garnish

POTATO AND CABBAGE RISOTTO

Heat 3 tablespoons of oil in a small frying pan over medium heat. Add the potatoes and sauté until tender and golden brown, 8–10 minutes. Remove from the heat. • Heat the remaining oil in a large frying pan over medium heat. Add the rice and sauté for 2 minutes. • Pour in the wine and cook until it evaporates, 2–3 minutes. • Add the onion and cabbage and sauté for 3 minutes. • Begin adding the stock ½ cup (125 ml) at a time, cooking and stirring until each addition has been absorbed and the rice is tender, 15–18 minutes. • Add the potatoes. Season with salt and mix well. • Garnish with parsley and serve hot.

RISOTTO WITH FRESHWATER SHRIMP AND PEAS

B ring the water to a boil and add the shrimp. Boil
for 3 minutes then drain, reserving the cooking
water. • Heat 2 tablespoons of butter and 2
tablespoons of the oil in a frying pan over medium
heat. Add the parsley, carrot, celery, and garlic and
sauté until softened, about 7 minutes. • Remove
the shrimp from their shells and place the shrimp
in a small bowl. Cover with some of the cooking
water. • Chop the shrimp shells with a knife.
• Add the shrimp shells to the frying pan. Add half
the wine and cook until evaporated. • Add the
remaining cooking water and simmer for 20
minutes. • Heat 2 tablespoons of butter and the
remaining oil in a medium saucepan over medium
heat. Add the onion and sauté until softened. Add
the mushrooms and sauté for 2–3 minutes. • Add
the tomatoes and peas, season with salt and
pepper, and simmer over medium heat for 5
minutes. • Drain the shrimp and add to the pan with
the tomato sauce. • Filter the mixture with the
shrimp shells into a small bowl. • Melt half the
remaining butter in a large frying pan over medium-
high heat. Add the rice and sauté for 2 minutes.
• Pour in the wine and cook and stir until it
evaporates. • Begin adding the stock, ½ cup
(125 ml) at a time, cooking and stirring until each
addition has been absorbed and the rice is tender,
15–18 minutes. • Stir in the remaining butter. •
Spoon the tomato and mushroom sauce over the
top and finish with the shrimp stock. • Serve hot.

Serves: 4–6

Preparation: 45 min.

Cooking: 1 hr.

Level of difficulty: 3

- 5 cups (1.25 liters) cold water
- 1 lb (500 g) freshwater shrimp
- $^1/_2$ cup (125 g) butter
- $^1/_4$ cup (60 ml) extra-virgin olive oil
- 2 tbsp finely chopped parsley
- 1 carrot, diced
- 1 stalk celery, finely sliced
- 1 clove garlic, finely chopped
- 1 medium white onion, finely chopped
- 8 oz (250 g) white mushrooms, sliced
- 3 medium tomatoes, sliced
- 1 cup (150 g) frozen peas
- 2 cups (400 g) Italian risotto rice
- $^1/_2$ cup (125 ml) dry white wine
- Salt and freshly ground black pepper

RISOTTO WITH PROSECCO

Serves: 4–6

Preparation: 15 min.

Cooking: 25 min.

Level of difficulty: 1

- $^{1}/_{2}$ cup (125 g) butter
- 2 medium white onions, finely chopped
- 2 medium leeks, thinly sliced
- 1 cup (250 ml) prosecco wine
- 2 cups (400 g) Italian risotto rice
- 5 cups (1.25 liters) Chicken Stock (see page 946)
- $^{1}/_{2}$ cup (60 g) freshly grated Parmesan cheese
- Salt and freshly ground black pepper

Heat half the butter in a large frying pan over low heat. Add the onion and leeks and sauté until well softened, 7–8 minutes. • Turn the heat up to medium-high and add the rice. Stir constantly for 2–3 minutes. • Add the prosecco and cook and stir until evaporated. • Begin adding the stock, $^{1}/_{2}$ cup (125 ml) at a time, cooking and stirring until each addition has been absorbed and the rice is tender, 15–18 minutes. • Stir in the remaining butter and Parmesan, season with salt and pepper, and serve hot.

RICE WITH POTATOES

Heat the oil in a large frying pan over medium heat. Add the onion, tomato, and parsley and sauté for 2–3 minutes. • Season with salt and add the water. Bring to a boil then add the potatoes. Cover the pan and simmer over low heat until the potatoes are tender but not mushy, 10–15 minutes. • Cook the rice in a large pan of salted boiling water until just al dente, 12–15 minutes. • Drain the rice and add to the pan with the potatoes. Stir in the pecorino. Garnish with sprigs of parsley and serve hot.

Serves: 4

Preparation: 30 min.

Cooking: 30 min.

Level of difficulty: 1

- $1/4$ cup (60 ml) extra-virgin olive oil
- 1 medium white onion, thinly sliced
- 2 large tomatoes, peeled and diced
- 1 tbsp finely chopped parsley + extra, to garnish
- $1^1/2$ cups (375 ml) water
- 1 lb (500 g) potatoes, peeled and cubed
- $1^1/2$ cups (300 g) short-grain rice
- $1/2$ cup (60 g) freshly grated pecorino cheese
- Salt

RISOTTO WITH LEEKS

Heat half the butter in a large frying pan over medium heat. Add the pancetta, onion, and leeks and sauté until almost tender, 7–8 minutes.
• Add the wine and pour in the rice and stir until the wine is evaporated. • Begin adding the stock, ½ cup (125 ml) at a time, cooking and stirring until each addition has been absorbed and the rice is tender, 15–18 minutes. • When the rice is almost ready, melt 2 tablespoons of the remaining butter in a small saucepan and stir in the flour. Add the stock cube and cream and stir over low heat until just boiling. Add 2 tablespoons of Parmesan and the two egg yolks, stir well, and remove from the heat. • Stir the remaining butter and Parmesan into the risotto and spoon into individual serving bowls.
• Pour a little of the sauce over each dish and serve hot.

Serves: 4–6

Preparation: 30 min.

Cooking: 30 min.

Level of difficulty: 2

- ½ cup (125 g) butter
- 2 oz (60 g) pancetta, finely chopped
- 1 small white onion, finely chopped
- 6 medium leeks, thinly sliced
- ½ cup (125 ml) dry white wine
- 2 cups (400 g) Italian risotto rice
- 5 cups (1.25 liters) Beef Stock (see page 946)
- 2 tbsp all-purpose (plain) flour
- ½ stock cube
- 1½ cups (325 ml) heavy (double) cream
- 2 large egg yolks
- ½ cup (60 g) freshly grated Parmesan cheese
- Salt and freshly ground black pepper

274

BAKED RICE

Serves: 4

Preparation: 15 min.

Cooking: 35 min.

Level of difficulty: 2

- **1¹/₂ tbsp butter**
- **¹/₂ onion, finely sliced**
- **5 oz (150 g) Italian sausage, skin removed and broken into pieces**
- **1 tbsp dried mushrooms, soaked in warm water for 15 minutes, drained, and chopped**
- **4 tbsp frozen peas**
- **2 artichoke hearts, finely sliced**
- **Salt and freshly ground black pepper**
- **¹/₄ cup (60 ml) Beef Stock (see page 946)**
- **1³/₄ cups (350 g) short-grain rice**
- **2 tbsp freshly grated Parmesan cheese**

Preheat the oven to 375°F (190°C/gas 5.)
• Heat the butter in a large Dutch oven over medium heat. Add the onion and sauté until softened, 5 minutes. • Add the sausage, mushrooms, peas, and artichokes and cook for 2 minutes to brown the sausage. Season with salt and pepper. • Add the stock and lower the heat. • Cook the rice in a large pot of salted, boiling water for 5 minutes. • Drain the rice, leaving enough water to give it the consistency of very thick soup. • Add the rice to the Dutch oven and mix well. Stir in the Parmesan. • Bake for 20 minutes, or until the rice is cooked through and has absorbed the cooking liquid. • Serve hot.

RICE WITH EGGPLANTS

Slice the eggplants thinly and place in layers in a colander. Sprinkle each layer with coarse sea salt. Set aside for 1 hour to drain. • Preheat the oven to 350°F (180°C/gas 4). • Bring a medium saucepan of water to a boil and boil the onions whole for 10 minutes. Drain well and slice. • Heat the butter and 2 tablespoons of oil in a large frying pan over medium heat. Add half the onion and the parsley and basil and sauté for 2–3 minutes. • Add the tomatoes and season with salt and pepper. Turn the heat down to low, cover the pan, and simmer for 15 minutes. • Heat the remaining oil in a Dutch oven or ovenproof saucepan over medium-high heat and add the remaining onion and the rice. Sauté for 3–4 minutes, then pour in the stock. Bring to a boil then bake in the oven for 15 minutes. • Remove the pan from the oven and stir in 2 tablespoons of the cheese. • Turn the oven up to 400°F (200°C/gas 6). • While the rice is baking, rinse the eggplant and dry well. Dredge lightly in the flour. • Heat the frying oil in a large frying pan and fry the eggplant in batches until golden brown on both sides, 5–7 minutes per batch. • Oil a large baking dish. Cover the bottom with half the eggplants in an even layer. Cover with a third of the tomato mixture and top with half the rice. Cover with half the remaining tomatoes and top with the remaining rice. Cover with the remaining tomatoes. • Top with the remaining eggplant and sprinkle with the remaining cheese. • Bake in the oven for 10 minutes. • Serve hot.

Serves: 4

Preparation: 45 min. + 1 hr. to drain the eggplants

Cooking: 1 hr.

Level of difficulty: 3

- 3 medium-large eggplants (aubergines)
- 2 tbsp coarse sea salt
- 2 medium white onions, peeled
- 3 tbsp butter
- 1/4 cup (60 ml) extra-virgin olive oil
- 2 tbsp finely chopped fresh parsley
- 1 tbsp finely chopped fresh basil
- 3 medium tomatoes, peeled and chopped
- Salt and freshly ground black pepper
- 1 1/2 cups (300 g) short-grain rice
- 3 cups (750 ml) boiling Beef Stock (see page 946)
- 1/2 cup (60 g) freshly grated caciocavallo (or pecorino) cheese
- 1 cup (150 g) all-purpose (plain) flour
- 2 cups (500 ml) olive oil, to fry

RICE WITH SUNDRIED TOMATO PESTO AND ARUGULA

Put the almonds, sundried tomatoes, capers, pecorino, oil, and lemon juice in the bowl of a food processor and chop until smooth. • Cook the rice in a large pot of salted, boiling water for about 15 minutes, or until tender. • Drain well and let cool under cold running water. Drain again and transfer to a large bowl. • Stir in the sundried tomato pesto and mozzarella. • Arrange the arugula in 4 serving dishes. Top with the rice and sprinkle with the Parmesan. Serve at once.

Serves: 4

Preparation: 10 min.

Cooking: 15 min.

Level of difficulty: 1

- $1/4$ cup (45 g) blanched almonds, toasted
- 8 sundried tomatoes in oil, drained
- 1 tbsp salt-cured capers, rinsed
- 4 tbsp freshly grated pecorino or Parmesan cheese
- $1/3$ cup (90 ml) extra-virgin olive oil
- Freshly squeezed juice of $1/2$ lemon
- $1^1/2$ cups (300 g) short-grain rice
- 8 oz (280 g) mini mozzarella balls
- 4 oz (125 g) arugula (rocket)
- 4 tbsp freshly grated Parmesan cheese

SALTWATER CRAYFISH AND ASPARAGUS RISOTTO

Serves: 4–6

Preparation: 10 min.

Cooking: 35 min.

Level of difficulty: 2

- 1¼ lb (600 g) large asparagus spears
- ¼ cup (60 g) butter
- 2 scallions (spring onions), chopped
- 1 small onion, thinly sliced
- Salt and freshly ground black pepper
- 2 cups (400 g) Italian risotto rice
- 2 cups (500 ml) fish stock
- 3 tbsp extra-virgin olive oil
- 12 oz (350 g) saltwater crayfish, shelled and cut in half
- ½ cup (125 ml) dry white wine

Rinse the asparagus, cut off the tough ends, and chop into pieces about 1 inch (2.5-cm) long.
• Melt half the butter in a frying pan and sauté 1 scallion and the onion until soft. • Add the asparagus and season with salt and pepper. Cook for 2 minutes, add the rice, and cook for 2 more minutes. • Stir in ½ cup (125 ml) of the stock. Cook, stirring often, until the stock is absorbed. Continue adding the stock, ½ cup (125 ml) at a time, stirring often until each addition is absorbed, until the rice is tender, 15–18 minutes. • Sauté the remaining scallion in the oil in a frying pan for 3 minutes, then add the crayfish. Season with salt and pepper and cook for 2 minutes. • Add the wine and allow to evaporate. Turn off the heat, cover the pan, and set aside. • Add the crayfish and remaining butter to the risotto 3 minutes before the rice is cooked. • Serve hot.

RISOTTO WITH SCALLOPS

Serves: 4

Preparation: 15 min.

Cooking: 35 min.

Level of difficulty: 2

- ¹/₃ cup (90 g) butter
- 2 shallots, finely chopped
- ¹/₃ cup (60 g) blanched almonds, toasted and chopped
- 1 large ripe red apple, cored and chopped
- 2 cups (400 g) Italian risotto rice
- ¹/₂ cup (125 ml) dry white wine
- 5 cups (1.25 liters) boiling vegetable stock
- 1 bay leaf
- 12 scallops, shelled
- 2 tbsp all-purpose (plain) flour
- ¹/₄ cup (60 ml) cognac
- 1 tsp curry powder
- Salt

Melt half the butter in a large frying pan over medium heat. • Add 1 shallot, the almonds, and the apple. Sauté for 3 minutes, until the shallot is transparent. • Add the rice and sauté for 2 minutes. • Add the wine and cook until it evaporates. • Stir in ½ cup (125 ml) of the stock. Cook, stirring often, until the stock is absorbed. Continue adding the stock, ½ cup (125 ml) at a time, stirring often until each addition is absorbed, until the rice is tender, 15–18 minutes. • Reserve one ladleful of the stock. • Remove the risotto from the heat. • Melt the remaining butter in a frying pan over medium heat. Add the bay leaf and remaining shallot and sauté for 2 minutes, until the shallot begins to soften. • Toss the scallops in the flour, ensuring that they are evenly coated. Gently shake each one to remove any excess flour. • Add the scallops to the pan and sauté for 2–3 minutes. • Add the cognac and cook until it evaporates, 1 minute. • Add the reserved stock and the curry powder, and mix well. Season with salt. Cook for 2 minutes, until the sauce begins to thicken. • Spoon the risotto into serving bowls. Arrange the scallop mixture on top of the risotto. • Serve hot.

MUSHROOM AND SOLE RISOTTO

Drain the mushrooms, reserving the liquid. Filter the liquid. Chop the mushrooms. • Heat half the oil in a large frying pan over medium heat. Add the onion and sauté until softened, 5 minutes. • Add the rice and sauté for 2 minutes. Add 2 tablespoons of the wine and let evaporate. Add the mushrooms and reserved liquid and cook until the rice has absorbed the liquid. • Stir in ½ cup (125 ml) of the stock. Cook, stirring often, until the stock is absorbed. Continue adding the stock, ½ cup (125 ml) at a time, stirring often until each addition is absorbed, until the rice is tender, 15–18 minutes. • Heat the remaining oil in a large frying pan over medium heat. Add the sole and remaining wine and sauté for 2–3 minutes. Season with salt and remove from the heat. • Add the Parmesan and butter to the risotto and mix well. • Spoon the risotto onto individual serving dishes. Arrange the sole on top. Sprinkle with parsley and serve hot.

- 2 oz (60 g) dried porcini mushrooms, soaked in warm water for 15 minutes
- $^1/_3$ cup (90 ml) extra virgin olive oil
- 1 large onion, finely chopped
- 2 cups (400 g) Italian risotto rice
- $^1/_4$ cup (60 ml) dry white wine
- 2 cups (500 ml) boiling vegetable stock
- 8 small sole fillets
- Salt
- $^1/_4$ cup (30 g) freshly grated Parmesan cheese
- 1 tbsp butter
- 2 tbsp finely chopped fresh parsley

Serves: 4–6

Preparation: 20 min.
+ 1 hr. to soak the
shellfish

Cooking: 50 min.

Level of difficulty: 2

- **14 oz (400 g) mussels, in shell**
- **14 oz (400 g) clams, in shell**
- **$^1/_2$ cup (125 ml) extra virgin olive oil**
- **1 clove garlic, lightly crushed but whole**
- **1 small onion, finely chopped**
- **1 small carrot, finely chopped**
- **1 celery stick, finely chopped**
- **8 oz (250 g) baby squid, cleaned and sliced**
- **$^1/_2$ cup (125 ml) dry white wine**
- **$1^3/_4$ cups (350 g) Italian risotto rice**
- **3 cups (750 ml) boiling fish stock**
- **Salt and freshly ground black pepper**
- **5 oz (150 g) fresh shelled shrimps (prawns)**
- **8 large shrimp (prawns)**
- **1 tbsp finely chopped parsley**

SEAFOOD RISOTTO

S oak the mussels and clams in cold water for
1 hour. • Heat 3 tablespoons of oil with the garlic
in a large saucepan over high heat. Add the shellfish
and cook until they open, 7–10 minutes. Drain,
reserving the cooking juices. Remove most of the
shells. • Heat 3 tablespoons of the oil in a large frying
pan over medium heat. Add the onion, carrot, and
celery. Sauté until transparent. Add the squid and
sauté for 2 minutes. • Pour in the wine. Add the rice
and sauté for 2 minutes. Add the reserved cooking
juices and cook until absorbed. Begin adding the
stock $^1/_2$ cup (125 ml) at a time, cooking and stirring
until each addition has been absorbed and the rice is
tender, 15–18 minutes. Season with salt and pepper.
• Heat the remaining oil in a large frying pan over
high heat. Add the shrimps. Sauté for 2 minutes. Add
the clams and mussels. • Add to the risotto. Sprinkle
with the parsley and serve hot.

RICE

RICE WITH MUSSELS

S oak the mussels in a bowl of cold water for
1 hour. Rinse well, scrubbing off any beards.
• Place in a large pan over medium heat. Cover the
pan and cook, shaking often, until all the mussels
have opened. Discard any mussels that have not
opened. • Remove the mollusks from their shells
and set aside. Leave one or two mussels in their
shells to garnish the dish. • Filter the cooking liquid
and set aside. • Blanch the tomatoes in boiling
water for 1 minute then slip off the skins. Chop
coarsely. • Heat the oil and garlic in a large frying
pan. Add the tomatoes and the reserved cooking
liquid. Season with salt and pepper and simmer
over low heat. • Cook the rice in a saucepan of
salted water for half the time indicated on the
package. • Drain well and add to the pan with the
tomatoes. Simmer until the rice is almost tender.
• Add the mollusks and stir until heated through.
• Sprinkle with the pecorino. Garnish the dish with
the reserved mussels in shells and serve hot.

Serves: 4–6

*Preparation: 30 min.
+ 1 hr. to soak the
mussels*

Cooking: 30 min.

Level of difficulty: 1

- **2 lb (1 kg) mussels,
  in shell**
- **1 lb (500 g) ripe
  tomatoes**
- **3 tbsp extra-virgin
  olive oil**
- **1 clove garlic,
  finely chopped**
- **1 3/4 cups (350 g)
  rice**
- **1/2 cup (60 g)
  freshly grated
  pecorino cheese**
- **Salt and freshly
  ground black
  pepper**

288

BAKED RICE WITH MUSSELS

Soak the mussels in a bowl of cold water for 1 hour. Rinse well, scrubbing off any beards. Shuck the mussels and set the mollusks aside.
• Preheat the oven to 350°F (180°C/gas 4). • Oil a large baking dish. • Spread the onions in a layer over the bottom of the baking dish. Sprinkle with half the parsley, the garlic, and tomatoes. Top with the pecorino. Season with salt and pepper and cover with half the potatoes. • Cover with the rice and top with the mussels. Sprinkle with the remaining parsley, garlic, and tomatoes and top with the remaining potatoes. • Drizzle with the oil and top up with the water. • Bake until the rice and potatoes are tender, about 1 hour. • Serve hot or at room temperature.

Serves: 4–6

Preparation: 30 min. + 1 hr. to soak the mussels

Cooking: 1 hr.

Level of difficulty: 2

- 1 lb (500 g) mussels, in shell
- 2 large white onions, thinly sliced
- 4 tbsp finely chopped fresh parsley
- 4 cloves garlic, finely chopped
- 1 lb (500 g) tomatoes, coarsely chopped
- Salt and freshly ground black pepper
- 1 lb (500 g) potatoes, peeled and thinly sliced
- 1 1/2 cups (300 g) short-grain rice
- 1/2 cup (60 g) freshly grated pecorino cheese
- 1/4 cup (60 ml) extra-virgin olive oil
- 3 cups (750 ml) water

RICE WITH SAUSAGE
AND ROSEMARY

Serves: 4

Preparation: 10 min.
+ 12 min. to rest
the rice

Cooking: 25 min.

Level of difficulty: 1

- 3 cups (750 ml)
  water
- Salt
- 1³/₄ cups (350 g)
  short-grain rice
- 1 bay leaf
- 10 oz (300 g)
  Italian pork
  sausage, skinned
  and broken into
  bite size pieces
- 2 tbsp extra-virgin
  olive oil
- 2 shallots, finely
  chopped
- 8 oz (250 g)
  canned cannellini
  beans, drained
- 1 tbsp finely
  chopped fresh
  rosemary
- Freshly ground
  black pepper
- 2 tbsp butter
- ¹/₄ cup (30 g)
  freshly grated
  Parmesan cheese

B ring the water to a boil with a pinch of salt
in a medium saucepan over medium heat.
Add the rice and bay leaf, cover, and cook for
12 minutes. Remove from the heat. • Let the rice
rest until it has absorbed all the water, 10–12
minutes. • Remove and discard the bay leaf.
• Sauté the sausage in a large nonstick frying pan
over medium heat until well browned and cooked
through, 4–5 minutes. Transfer the sausage to
a plate and keep warm. • Add the oil to the frying
pan. Add the shallots and sauté until softened,
3–4 minutes. • Add the beans and rosemary.
Sauté for 2 minutes, mixing well. Season with
salt and pepper. • Add the sausage and mix well.
• Add the butter and Parmesan to the rice and mix
well. • Spoon the rice onto serving dishes. Top with
the sausage mixture. • Serve hot.

RISOTTO WITH PEAS AND PARMESAN

Bring the stock to a boil in a large saucepan over medium heat. Add half the peas and simmer until tender, 6–7 minutes. • Transfer to a food processor and chop until smooth. Return the mixture to the saucepan and keep warm. • Heat the oil in a large frying pan over medium heat. Add the pancetta and sauté until golden brown, 3–4 minutes. • Add the onion and sauté until transparent, 3–4 minutes. • Add the remaining peas and the rice and sauté for 2 minutes. • Begin adding the stock and pea mixture, ½ cup (125 ml) at a time, cooking and stirring until each addition has been absorbed and the rice is tender, 15–18 minutes. • Season with salt. Remove from the heat. • Stir in the grated Parmesan. Cover and let rest for 2 minutes. • Sprinkle with the flakes of Parmesan and serve hot.

294

Serves: 4

Preparation: 10 min.

Cooking: 40 min.

Level of difficulty: 1

- 3 cups (750 ml) vegetable stock,
- 1 lb (500 g) fresh or frozen peas
- ¼ cup (60 ml) extra-virgin olive oil
- 5 oz (150 g) pancetta or bacon, chopped
- 1 large onion, finely chopped
- 1¾ cups (350 g) Italian risotto rice
- Salt
- ½ cup (60 g) freshly grated Parmesan cheese
- 1 oz (30 g) Parmesan cheese, flaked

Serves: 8

Preparation: 1 hr.

Cooking: 90 min.

Level of difficulty: 3

- 1 small onion, finely chopped
- 3 tbsp extra-virgin olive oil
- 2 tablespoons tomato paste (concentrate)
- 6 cups (1.5 liters) Beef Stock (see recipe, page 946)
- 2 oz (60 g) dried porcini mushrooms, soaked in warm water for 15 minutes, drained, finely chopped
- 1 cup (150 g) frozen peas
- Salt and freshly ground black pepper
- 1 Italian pork sausage
- 12 oz (350 g) ground (minced) beef
- 3 large eggs
- $^{1}/_{2}$ cup (75 g) fine dry bread crumbs
- $^{1}/_{2}$ cup (60 g) freshly grated Parmesan cheese
- $^{1}/_{2}$ cup (75 g) all-purpose (plain) flour
- $2^{1}/_{2}$ cups (450 g) short-grain rice
- 5 oz (150 g) lard
- 8 oz (250 g) mozzarella cheese, sliced
- 8 oz (250 g) chicken livers, cleaned and chopped

NEAPOLITAN RICE PIE

Heat the oil in a heavy saucepan over medium heat. Sauté the onion until soft. Add the tomato paste diluted in 1 cup (250 ml) of stock, together with the mushrooms and peas. Season with salt and pepper. • Cook for 5 minutes, then add the sausage. Simmer for 20 minutes, then slice the sausage and remove the sauce from heat. • Combine the beef in a bowl with salt, pepper, 1 egg, 2 tablespoons of bread crumbs, and 1 tablespoon of Parmesan. Mix well. Shape into small meatballs and roll in the flour. • Heat the frying oil in a frying pan and fry the meatballs in small batches until golden brown. Drain on paper towels. • Heat half the mushroom sauce in a heavy pan. Add the rice. Begin adding the stock, ½ cup (125 ml) at a time, stirring often until each addition is absorbed, until the rice is tender, 15–18 minutes. • Stir in 2 oz (60 g) lard, ¼ cup (30 g) Parmesan, and the remaining eggs. Mix well and set aside. • Add 2 oz (60 g) of lard and the meatballs to the other half of the sauce. Simmer over low heat. • Heat the remaining lard in a small frying pan and sauté the chicken livers, adding a little stock if they dry out. Season with salt. • Preheat the oven to 350°F (180°/gas 4). • Grease a 3-quart (3-liter) mold with butter and sprinkle with bread crumbs. • Place almost all the rice in the mold and use a spoon to press up the sides. Fill the center with layers of meatballs, sauce, chicken livers, mozzarella, sausage, and Parmesan. Cover with the remaining rice. • Bake for 30 minutes. Serve hot.

BAKED RICE PIE

Prepare the meat sauce. • Preheat the oven to 400°F (200°C/gas 6). • Oil a deep 10-inch (25-cm) springform pan. • Cook the rice in a large pan of salted, boiling water until tender, 12–15 minutes. Drain well. • Roll out the pastry on a lightly floured work surface to ⅛-inch (3 mm) thick. Place the pastry in the pan, lining the bottom and sides. Cut off the extra pieces overhanging the edges. • Place a layer of meat sauce in the bottom of the pan. Cover with a layer of cooked rice and sprinkle with cheese. Repeat this layering process until all the ingredients are in the pan, finishing with a layer of cheese. • Re-roll the scraps of dough and cut into thin strips. Use them to create a decorative criss-cross pattern on the top of the pie. • Bake until golden brown, 25–30 minutes. Serve hot.

Serves: 4–6

Preparation: 25 min. + time to make the meat sauce

Cooking: 40–45 min.

Level of difficulty: 2

- **1 recipe Meat Sauce (see page 951)**
- **1¹/₂ cups (300 g) short-grain rice**
- **14 oz (400 g) frozen puff pastry, thawed**
- **1 cup (120 g) freshly grated Parmesan cheese**

BAKED SWISS CHARD AND RICE

Serves: 4–6

Preparation: 40 min.

Cooking: 45 min.

Level of difficulty: 1

Preheat the oven to 400°F (200°C/gas 6).
• Boil the rice in salted water until almost tender, about 12 minutes. Drain well. • Boil the Swiss chard in salted water until just tender, 7–10 minutes. Drain well, squeeze out the excess moisture, and chop finely. • Mix the Swiss chard and rice together in a bowl. • Heat 2 tablespoons of butter with the oil in a heavy saucepan. Add the onions, leeks, pancetta, sage, and bay leaf and sauté until softened, 5–7 minutes. • Discard the bay leaf and sage and chop the remaining mixture in a food processor until smooth. Stir into the rice mixture. • Stir in the eggs, Parmesan, half the Gruyère, the parsley, garlic, and basil. Season with salt and pepper and mix well. • Butter a rectangular baking dish and sprinkle with a quarter of the bread crumbs. • Spoon the mixture into the baking dish, leveling the top with the back of the spoon. Sprinkle with the remaining bread crumbs mixed with the remaining Gruyère. Dot with the remaining butter. • Bake until bubbling and golden brown, about 30 minutes. • Let rest for 10 minutes before serving.

- 1 cup (200 g) short-grain rice
- 1 lb (500 g) Swiss chard (silverbeet), chopped
- 2 medium white onions, thinly sliced
- 1/4 cup (60 g) butter
- 1 tbsp extra-virgin olive oil
- 2 leeks, thinly sliced
- 2 oz (60 g) pancetta, chopped
- 2 leaves fresh sage
- 1 bay leaf
- 3 large eggs, lightly beaten
- 1/2 cup (60 g) freshly grated Parmesan cheese
- 1/2 cup (60 g) freshly grated Gruyère or Swiss cheese
- 3 tbsp finely chopped fresh parsley
- 2 cloves garlic, finely chopped
- 1 tbsp finely chopped fresh basil
- 1 cup (150 g) fine dry bread crumbs
- Salt and freshly ground black pepper

DRIED
PASTA

SPAGHETTI WITH GARLIC, OIL, AND CHILIES

Cook the spaghetti in a large pot of salted boiling water until al dente. • While the pasta is cooking, heat the oil in a large frying pan over medium heat. Sauté the chile and garlic for 2–3 minutes, until the garlic is pale gold. • Remove from the heat and set aside. • Drain the pasta and add to the frying pan. • Sprinkle with the parsley and toss over medium heat for 2 minutes. Serve hot.

304

Serves: 4

Preparation: 5 min.

Cooking: 20 min.

Level of difficulty: 1

- 1 lb (500 g) spaghetti
- $^1/_3$ cup (90 ml) extra-virgin olive oil
- 6 cloves garlic, finely chopped
- 2–3 dried chile peppers, crumbled
- 2 tbsp finely chopped fresh parsley

SPAGHETTI WITH TOMATO SAUCE

Serves: 4–6

Preparation: 10 min.

Cooking: 45 min.

Level of difficulty: 1

- 3 tbsp extra-virgin olive oil
- 1 onion, thinly sliced
- 2 cloves garlic, finely chopped
- 3 lb (1.5 kg) firm-ripe tomatoes, coarsely chopped
- 1 small bunch fresh basil, torn + extra leaves, to garnish
- $^1/_2$ tsp sugar
- Salt
- 1 lb (500 g) spaghetti

Heat the oil in a large frying pan over medium heat. Add the onion and garlic and sauté until softened, about 5 minutes. • Add the tomatoes, basil, oil, sugar, and salt. Partially cover and simmer over low heat until the sauce is reduced, about 40 minutes. • Cook the spaghetti in a large pan of salted, boiling water until al dente. • Place in a large heated serving bowl and toss with the sauce. • Serve hot.

SPAGHETTI WITH ARTICHOKES

Trim the stalks and cut the top third off the tops of the artichokes. Remove the tough outer leaves by bending them down and snapping them off. Cut in half and use a sharp knife to remove any fuzzy choke. Slice into thin wedges. Place in a bowl of cold water with the lemon juice. • Heat the oil and lard in a large frying pan over medium heat. Add the garlic and sauté until pale golden brown, 3–4 minutes. • Drain the artichokes and add to the pan. Sauté for 2–3 minutes then add ¼ cup (60 ml) of water. Season with salt. Simmer the artichokes gently until tender, stirring often and adding more water as required. • Cook the spaghetti in a large pan of salted, boiling water until al dente. • Drain the pasta and add to the pan with the artichokes. • Sprinkle with the parsley and pecorino, toss well, and serve hot.

Serves: 4–6

Preparation: 20 min.

Cooking: 30 min.

Level of difficulty: 1

- **8 artichokes**
- **1 lemon**
- **¹/₄ cup (60 ml) extra-virgin olive oil**
- **¹/₄ cup (60 g) lard**
- **2 cloves garlic, finely chopped**
- **1 cup (250 ml) water, + extra, as required**
- **1 lb (500 g) spaghetti**
- **2 tbsp finely chopped fresh parsley**
- **6 tbsp freshly grated pecorino cheese**
- **Salt**

HOT AND SPICY SPAGHETTI

Place the oil in a large frying pan over medium heat. Add the garlic and chile pepper and sauté until pale golden brown, 2–3 minutes. • Add the anchovies and stir until they dissolve into the oil. • Add the tomatoes, olives, capers, and tomato concentrate and simmer over low heat for 15–20 minutes. • Meanwhile, cook the spaghetti in a large pot of salted, boiling water until al dente. • Drain the spaghetti and add to the pan with the sauce. • Toss over high heat for 1–2 minutes. • Serve hot.

Serves: 4–6
Preparation: 15 min.
Cooking: 30 min.
Level of difficulty: 1

- $1/3$ cup (90 g) extra-virgin olive oil
- 2 cloves garlic, finely chopped
- 1 red chile pepper, sliced
- 6–8 anchovy fillets
- 1 $1/2$ lb (750 g) firm, ripe tomatoes, peeled and chopped
- 3 oz (90 g) black olives, pitted
- 2 tbsp salt-cured capers, rinsed
- 1 tbsp tomato concentrate
- 1 lb (500 g) spaghetti
- Salt

SPAGHETTINI WITH RICOTTA AND PECORINO

Mix the fresh ricotta, butter, ricotta salata, chile pepper, and salt in a large bowl. • Cook the pasta in a large pot of salted boiling water until al dente, 8–10 minutes. • Drain, reserving 2 tablespoons of the cooking water. Transfer the pasta to the ricotta mixture, adding the reserved cooking water. • Sprinkle with the pecorino, toss well, and serve hot.

Serves: 4–6

Preparation: 10 min.

Cooking: 8–10 min.

Level of difficulty: 1

- 1 cup (250 g) fresh ricotta cheese
- $^1/_3$ cup (90 g) butter, cut up
- $^1/_2$ cup (60 g) freshly grated ricotta salata cheese
- 1 dried chile pepper, crumbled
- Salt
- 1 lb (500 g) spaghettini
- $^1/_2$ cup (60 g) freshly grated pecorino cheese

SPAGHETTINI WITH TOMATO FISH SAUCE

Serves: 4–6

Preparation: 20 min.

Cooking: 20 min.

Level of difficulty: 1

- 2 cloves garlic, lightly crushed but whole
- 1/3 cup (90 ml) extra-virgin olive oil
- 2 lb (1 kg) tomatoes, peeled and chopped
- 1 lb (500 g) tiny fresh fish, such as sardines, whitebait or anchovies
- Salt and freshly ground black pepper
- 1 lb (500 g) spaghettini
- 2 tbsp finely chopped fresh parsley

Sauté the garlic in the oil in a large frying pan over medium heat until pale gold, about 3 minutes. • Stir in the tomatoes and cook over high heat until the tomatoes have broken down, 5–10 minutes. • Add the fish and season with salt and pepper. Cook for 5 minutes, shaking the pan. • Discard the garlic and remove from the heat. • Cook the pasta in a large pot of salted boiling water until al dente, about 8 minutes. • Drain and add to the sauce. Toss over high heat for 1–2 minutes. Sprinkle with the parsley and serve hot.

SPAGHETTI WITH TUNA

Sauté the garlic in the oil in a large frying pan over medium heat for 2 minutes, until pale gold. • Add the tuna and sauté briefly. • Pour in the wine and cook until evaporated. • Add the tomatoes. Season with salt and pepper and simmer for 15 minutes, crushing the tomatoes with a wooden spoon against the sides of the pan. • Cook the pasta in a large pot of salted boiling water until al dente. • Drain and transfer to a heated serving bowl. • Top with the hot sauce. • Sprinkle with parsley and serve hot.

Serves: 4–6

Preparation: 10 min.

Cooking: 30 min.

Level of difficulty: 1

- **2 cloves garlic, finely chopped**
- **$^1/_4$ cup (60 m) extra-virgin olive oil**
- **8 oz (250 g) tuna, packed in oil, crumbled**
- **$^1/_3$ cup (90 ml) dry white wine**
- **$1^1/_2$ lb (750 g) cherry tomatoes, halved**
- **Salt and freshly ground white pepper**
- **1 lb (500 g) spaghetti**
- **1 tbsp finely chopped fresh parsley**

314

SPAGHETTI CARBONARA

Serves: 4–6

Preparation: 15 min.

Cooking: 20 min.

Level of difficulty: 2

- 1 onion, finely chopped
- 3 tbsp extra-virgin olive oil
- 1 cup (125 g) diced bacon
- 4 large egg yolks
- $^1/_4$ cup (60 ml) heavy (double) cream (optional)
- Salt and freshly ground black pepper
- 2 tbsp freshly grated Parmesan cheese
- 1 lb (500 g) spaghetti

Sauté the onion in the oil in a small saucepan over medium heat for until lightly browned, about 5 minutes. • Add the pancetta and sauté for about 5 minutes, or until crisp. Remove from the heat and set aside. • Beat the egg yolks and cream in a large bowl. Season with salt and pepper and sprinkle with the Parmesan. • Cook the pasta in a large pot of salted boiling water until al dente. • Drain and add to the pancetta. Return to high heat, add the egg mixture, and toss the pasta briefly so that the eggs cook lightly but are still creamy. • Serve hot.

SPAGHETTI WITH TOMATO SAUCE AND FRIED EGGPLANT

Place the eggplant slices in a colander and sprinkle with the coarse sea salt. Let drain for 1 hour. • Heat the oil in a large deep frying pan until very hot. • Fry the eggplant in small batches for 5–7 minutes, or until golden brown. • Drain on paper towels. • Sauce: Stir together the tomatoes, onion, garlic, basil, oil, sugar, and salt in a medium saucepan. Cover and simmer over medium heat for 15 minutes, or until the tomatoes have broken down. • Uncover and simmer for about 40 minutes, or until the sauce had thickened.
• Transfer to a food mill or food processor and process until smooth. • Cook the spaghetti in a large pot of salted boiling water until al dente.
• Drain and add to the sauce. Place the fried eggplant on a large serving dish and top with the spaghetti. Sprinkle with Parmesan and serve hot.

Serves: 4

*Preparation: 1 hr.
+ 1 hr. to drain
the eggplant*

Cooking: 1 hr. 20 min.

Level of difficulty: 1

Eggplant
- 1 large eggplant (aubergine), weighing about 1 lb (500 g,) thinly sliced
- Coarse sea salt
- 1 cup (250 ml) olive oil, for frying

Sauce
- 2 lb (1 kg) tomatoes, peeled and coarsely chopped
- 1 red onion, thinly sliced
- 2 cloves garlic, finely chopped
- Leaves from 1 small bunch fresh basil, torn
- 2 tbsp extra-virgin olive oil
- $1/8$ tsp sugar
- Salt

- 1 lb (500 g) spaghetti
- 1 cup (125 g) freshly grated Parmesan cheese

BAVETTE WITH MUSHROOMS

Clean the mushrooms very carefully and cut the larger ones into small pieces. • Cook the onion in the oil in a frying pan, covered, over low heat for 20 minutes. Season with salt and add the garlic and chile. • Increase the heat and pour in the wine. • Add the mushrooms and sauté over high heat for a few minutes. • Stir in the tomatoes, basil, and parsley and cook for about 10 minutes, or until the mushrooms are tender. Season with salt. • Cook the pasta in a large pot of salted boiling water until al dente. • Drain and add to the sauce. Toss well and serve hot.

Serves: 4

Preparation: 30 min.

Cooking: 40 min.

Level of difficulty: 1

- 1 lb (500 g) mixed small mushrooms (porcini, finferli, champignons, chiodini)
- 1 onion, finely chopped
- $^1/_4$ cup (60 ml) extra-virgin olive oil
- Salt
- 2 cloves garlic, finely chopped
- 1 dried hot chile pepper, crumbled
- $^1/_4$ cup (60 ml) dry white wine
- 10 cherry tomatoes, coarsely chopped
- Leaves from 1 bunch fresh basil, torn
- 1 tbsp finely chopped fresh parsley
- 12 oz (350 g) bavette or other long pasta

BUCATINI IN SPICY EGGPLANT SAUCE

Serves: 4–6

Preparation: 20 min.

Cooking: 30 min.

Level of difficulty: 2

- $^1/_3$ cup (90 ml) extra-virgin olive oil
- 2 medium eggplants (aubergines), cut into small cubes
- Salt and freshly ground black pepper
- 2 large white onions
- 2 cloves garlic, finely chopped
- 4–6 medium tomatoes, peeled and coarsely chopped
- 1–2 fresh chile peppers, finely chopped
- 2 tbsp salt-cured capers, rinsed
- 1 lb (500 g) bucatini or other long pasta
- 6–8 fresh basil leaves, torn
- 2 oz (60 g) Pecorino romano cheese, in shavings or flakes

Heat ¼ cup (60 ml) of oil in a large frying pan and sauté the eggplants until tender, about 10 minutes. If the pan dries out too much during cooking add a little water. Season with salt and pepper and set aside. • Heat the remaining oil in a large frying pan and sauté the onions and garlic until softened, about 5 minutes. Add the tomatoes, chile peppers, and capers and cook over medium heat for 15–20 minutes. Add water from the pasta pot if the sauce dries out too much during cooking. • Meanwhile, cook the pasta in a large pan of salted, boiling water until al dente. • Drain the pasta, not too thoroughly, and add to the pan with the eggplant and basil. Toss well until the moisture has all been absorbed, then sprinkle with the pecorino. • Serve hot.

ZITE WITH CAULIFLOWER AND TOMATO SAUCE

Heat the oil in a large frying pan. Add the garlic and sauté until pale gold, 2–3 minutes. Add the tomatoes and parsley. Season with salt and pepper and simmer over low heat for about 20 minutes.
• Place a large pot of lightly salted water over high heat and bring to a boil. Add the cauliflower and pasta and return to a boil. • When the pasta is cooked al dente drain well. • Add the pasta and cauliflower to the sauce and toss gently. • Sprinkle with the pecorino and serve hot.

Serves: 4–6

Preparation: 20 min.

Cooking: 30 min.

Level of difficulty: 1

- 3 tbsp extra-virgin olive oil
- 2 cloves garlic, finely chopped
- 1¹/₂ lb (750 g) tomatoes, peeled and chopped
- 1 tbsp finely chopped parsley
- Salt and freshly ground black pepper
- 1 small cauliflower, broken into florets
- 1 lb (500 g) zite
- 6 tbsp freshly grated pecorino cheese

CONCHIGLIE WITH SAFFRON AND GRILLED VEGETABLES

Remove the seeds and core from the bell peppers, rinse well, and cut into strips. • Heat a grill pan and cook the bell peppers, turning often, until tender, about 10 minutes. • Cut the eggplant lengthwise in slices about ½ inch (1 cm) thick. • Cook the slices in the grill pan, browning on both sides. Remove from heat and cut into squares. • Cook the pasta in a large pan of salted, boiling water until al dente. • Drain well and transfer to a large serving bowl. Add the grilled vegetables, saffron, marjoram, oil, salt, and pepper. Toss well and serve.

Serves: 4–6

Preparation: 20 min.

Cooking: 30 min.

Level of difficulty: 2

- 1 large red bell pepper (capsicum)
- $^1/_2$ large yellow bell pepper (capsicum)
- 1 medium eggplant (aubergine)
- 1 lb (500 g) conchiglie pasta
- 1 tsp saffron threads
- 2 tbsp finely chopped marjoram
- $^1/_4$ cup (60 ml) extra-virgin olive oil
- Salt and freshly ground black pepper

PASTA WITH LEEK AND BELL PEPPER CRUMBLE

Serves: 4–6

Preparation: 20 min.

Cooking: 40 min.

Level of difficulty: 1

- 1/3 cup (90 ml) extra-virgin olive oil
- 2 cloves garlic, finely chopped
- 1 lb (500 g) cherry tomatoes, halved
- 8 leaves fresh basil
- Salt and freshly ground black pepper
- 3 leeks, thinly sliced
- 1 yellow bell pepper (capsicum), cut into small pieces
- 1 lb (500 g) rigatoni
- 8 oz (250 g) toasted bread, cut into small cubes

Heat 1/4 cup (60 ml) of the oil in a large frying pan. Add the garlic and sauté until page golden brown, 2–3 minutes. • Add the tomatoes and basil and season with salt and pepper. Simmer for 10 minutes. • Heat the remaining 2 tablespoons of oil in a small frying pan and add the leeks. Sauté for 3 minutes then add the bell peppers and simmer for 5 minutes. • Cook the pasta in salted boiling water until al dente. • Drain well and add to the pan with the tomatoes. Add the leek and bell pepper mixture and the toasted bread and toss over medium heat for 2–3 minutes. • Serve hot.

RIGATONI WITH ROASTED BELL PEPPER SAUCE

B roil (grill) the bell peppers whole until their skins are blackened. Wrap the blackened bell peppers in a brown paper bag and set aside for 10 minutes. Unwrap and remove the skins and seeds. Chop into small strips. • Heat the oil in a large frying pan over medium heat. Add the tomatoes, garlic, and parsley. Season with salt and pepper and simmer over low heat for 20–30 minutes. • Cook the rigatoni in a large pan of salted, boiling water until al dente. Drain the pasta and add to the pan with the sauce. • Add the bell peppers and pecorino and stir gently. • Serve hot.

328

Serves: 4–6

Preparation: 30 min.

Cooking: 45 min.

Level of difficulty: 2

- **2 large red bell peppers (capsicums)**
- **$1/4$ cup (60 ml) extra-virgin olive oil**
- **1 lb (500 g) rigatoni**
- **$1^1/2$ lb (750 g) tomatoes, peeled and sliced**
- **2 cloves garlic, finely chopped**
- **2 tbsp finely chopped fresh parsley**
- **6 tbsp freshly grated pecorino cheese**
- **Salt and freshly ground black pepper**

PENNE WITH TOMATOES AND WILD ASPARAGUS

Heat the oil in a large frying pan. Add the garlic and sauté until pale gold, 2–3 minutes. Add the tomatoes. Season with salt and pepper and simmer over low heat for about 20 minutes.
• Boil the asparagus in a medium pot of lightly salted water until just tender. Drain well, chop in short lengths, and set aside. • Cook the penne in a large pan of salted, boiling water until al dente.
• Drain the pasta and add to the pan with the tomato sauce. Add the asparagus and stir gently.
• Sprinkle with the pecorino and serve hot.

Serves: 4–6

Preparation: 20 min.

Cooking: 30 min.

Level of difficulty: 1

• $1/4$ cup (60 ml) extra-virgin olive oil
• 4 cloves garlic, finely chopped
• 14 oz (400 g) tomatoes
• 1 lb (500 g) penne
• $1^1/2$ lb (750 g) tender asparagus tips
• 6 tbsp freshly grated pecorino cheese
• Salt and freshly ground black pepper

PENNE WITH RAW ARTICHOKES

Serves: 4–6

Preparation: 20 min.

Cooking: 15 min.

Level of difficulty: 1

- **8 small, fresh artichokes**
- **Freshly squeezed juice of 1 lemon**
- **Salt and freshly ground black pepper**
- **$1/4$ cup (60 ml) extra-virgin olive oil**
- **1 lb (500 g) penne**
- **4 oz (125 g) Parmesan cheese, in flakes**

Trim the artichoke stems, discard the tough outer leaves, and trim the tops. Cut in half lengthwise and scrape any fuzzy choke away with a knife. Cut in very thin slices. Soak in a bowl of cold water with the lemon juice for 15 minutes.
- Drain and pat dry with paper towels. Place in a large serving bowl. Season with salt and pepper and drizzle with the oil. • Meanwhile, cook the pasta in a large pan of salted, boiling water until al dente. • Drain well and place in the bowl with the sauce. Toss well, sprinkle with the Parmesan, and serve.

RIGATONI WITH CAULIFLOWER, PINE NUTS, AND RAISINS

C ook the cauliflower in a large pan of salted, boiling water until just tender. • Remove the cauliflower with a slotted spoon, reserving the water. • Place a large saucepan over medium heat with half the oil. Add the onion and sauté until pale gold, about 5 minutes. Season with salt and pepper. • Add the saffron and water and stir well. • Add the cauliflower, cover, and simmer over very low heat. • Heat the remaining oil in a small saucepan. Add the anchovies and stir until dissolved into the oil. • Add the anchovy mixture to the pan with the cauliflower together with the raisins and pine nuts. • Meanwhile, cook the rigatoni in the water used to cook the cauliflower until al dente. • Drain the pasta and add to the pan with the sauce. Stir in the basil and cheese. Toss gently and serve hot.

Serves: 4–6

Preparation: 15 min.

Cooking: 30 min.

Level of difficulty: 1

- 1 small cauliflower, broken into florets
- $1/3$ cup (90 ml) extra-virgin olive oil
- 1 large white onion, finely chopped
- Salt and freshly ground black pepper
- $1/4$ tsp saffron
- 2 tbsp water
- 6 anchovy fillets
- 1 lb (500 g) rigatoni
- 2 oz (60 g) raisins
- 2 oz (60 g) pine nuts
- 1 tbsp finely chopped basil + sprigs, to garnish
- $1/2$ cup (60 g) freshly grated pecorino cheese

RIGATONI WITH PEAS AND PESTO

Rinse the basil and mint under cold running water. Remove any tough stems and place in a food processor or blender with the garlic, salt, and pepper. Chop for 2–3 minutes, then add the cheese and chop finely. Transfer the sauce to a small bowl and gradually beat in enough of the oil to make a thick pesto sauce. • Meanwhile, cook the pasta and peas in a large pan of salted, boiling water until the pasta is cooked al dente and the peas are tender. • Drain the pasta and peas thoroughly and place in a large serving bowl. • Spoon the herb sauce over the top and toss well • Serve hot.

Serves: 4–6

Preparation: 15 min.

Cooking: 10–15 min.

Level of difficulty: 1

- **Bunch of fresh basil**
- **6–8 fresh mint leaves**
- **2 cloves garlic, finely chopped**
- **Salt and freshly ground white pepper**
- **6 tbsp freshly grated ricotta salata cheese**
- **$^1/_2$ cup (125 ml) extra-virgin olive oil**
- **1 lb (500 g) rigatoni**
- **14 oz (400 g) fresh or frozen peas**

RIGATONI WITH ONION SAUCE

Serves: 4–6

Preparation: 10 min.

Cooking: 30 min.

Level of difficulty: 1

- **²/₃ cup (150 g) butter or diced pork lard**
- **2 large white onions, finely chopped**
- **¹/₄ cup (60 ml) dry white wine**
- **1 lb (500 g) rigatoni**
- **Salt and freshly ground black pepper**
- **4–6 tbsp freshly grated pecorino or Parmesan cheese**

Melt the butter in a medium saucepan over low heat. • Add the onion and sweat until softened and pale golden brown, about 20 minutes. • Increase the heat to medium, pour in the wine, and cook until it evaporates, about 5 minutes. • Cook the pasta in a large pan of salted boiling water until al dente. • Drain and add to the pan with the sauce. Season with salt and pepper. Sprinkle with cheese and toss gently. • Serve hot.

337

FUSILLI WITH MUSHROOMS

Serves: 4–6

Preparation: 10 min.

Cooking: 40 min.

Level of difficulty: 1

- **1 lb (500 g) white mushrooms**
- **3 cloves garlic, finely chopped**
- **1/4 cup (60 ml) extra-virgin olive oil**
- **3 tbsp finely chopped parsley**
- **Salt and freshly ground black pepper**
- **1lb (500 g) fusilli**

Rinse the mushrooms under cold running water. Trim the stems and slice the stems and caps coarsely. • In a large frying pan, sauté 2 cloves of the garlic in 2 tablespoons of oil over medium heat until it begins to color, 2–3 minutes. • Add the mushrooms and half the parsley, season with salt and pepper, and simmer for 10–15 minutes, or until the mushrooms are tender. • Meanwhile, cook the fusilli in a large pot of salted, boiling water until al dente. Drain well and add to the pan with the sauce. • Sprinkle with the remaining garlic and parsley and drizzle with the remaining oil. Toss for 1–2 minutes and serve hot.

339

WHOLE-WHEAT FUSILLI WITH ONION AND BASIL

Heat the oil in a large frying pan and sauté the onions and chile for 2–3 minutes. Add the water and simmer over medium-low heat until the water has evaporated. • Add the zucchini and simmer for 10–15 minutes more. Season with salt and pepper. • Meanwhile, cook the pasta in a large pan of salted, boiling water until al dente. • Drain the pasta, not too thoroughly, and add to the pan with the sauce. Toss over high heat for 1–2 minutes, or until the water has evaporated. Add the Parmesan and basil and toss again. • Serve hot.

Serves: 4–6

Preparation: 15 min.

Cooking: 20 min.

Level of difficulty: 1

- 1/4 cup (60 ml) extra-virgin olive oil
- 2 large white onions, thinly sliced in rings
- 1 fresh red chile pepper, finely chopped
- 1/4 cup (60 ml) cold water
- 3 large zucchini (courgettes), cut in small cubes
- Salt and freshly ground black pepper
- 1 lb (500 g) whole-wheat (wholemeal) fusilli
- 6 tbsp freshly grated Parmesan cheese
- 2–3 tbsp fresh basil leaves, torn

FARFALLE WITH RADICCHIO AND GOAT CHEESE

Serves: 4–6

Preparation: 10 min.

Cooking: 20 min.

Level of difficulty: 1

- 1 lb (500 g) farfalle
- 1 onion, thinly sliced
- $^1/_4$ cup (60 ml) extra-virgin olive oil
- 2 heads radicchio, cut in strips
- Salt and freshly ground black pepper
- $^1/_4$ cup (60 ml) light beer
- 4 oz (125 g) soft fresh goat cheese (caprino) (or other soft, fresh cheeses, such as robiola, Philadelphia, or stracchino)
- 2 tbsp milk

Cook the pasta in a large pan of salted, boiling water until it is al dente. • Sauté the onion in 3 tablespoons of the oil in a large frying pan until softened, about 3 minutes. • Add the radicchio and season with salt and pepper. Sauté for a few minutes, then add the beer. When the beer has evaporated, add the goat cheese and stir well, softening the mixture with the milk. • Drain the pasta well and add to the pan with the sauce. Toss for 2–3 minutes over medium heat. Drizzle with the remaining oil and serve hot.

343

PENNE EN PAPILLOTE

Preheat the oven to 400°F (200°C/gas 6).
• Sauté the onion in the oil and 2 tablespoons of butter over medium heat in a large frying pan for about 5 minutes, then add the shrimp and smoked salmon. • Blend the cream and puréed tomatoes in a small bowl and add this to the pan. Season with salt and pepper, and simmer, uncovered, for 5 more minutes. • Meanwhile, cook the penne in a large pan of salted, boiling water until al dente. Drain and transfer to a bowl. • Mix in the prepared sauce, check the seasoning, and sprinkle with chopped parsley. • Butter a sheet of waxed paper or foil about 13 x 23 inches (35 x 60 cm) and place the penne in their sauce in the center. • Dot with the remaining butter, seal the parcel with a second sheet of waxed paper or foil, and bake in a preheated oven at for 15 minutes.
• Serve hot, straight from the parcel (otherwise the pasta will cool), laid on a serving dish.

Serves: 4

Preparation: 20 min.

Cooking: 45 min.

Level of difficulty: 2

- **1 medium yellow onion, very finely chopped**
- **$^1/_4$ cup (60 g) butter**
- **4 oz (125 g) shrimp (prawns), shelled and deveined, chopped**
- **4 oz (125 g) smoked salmon, chopped**
- **$^1/_3$ cup (90 ml) light (single) cream**
- **1 cup (250 ml) puréed tomatoes (passata)**
- **Salt and freshly ground black pepper**
- **1 lb (500 g) penne**
- **3 tbsp finely chopped fresh parsley**

PENNE WITH MEAT SAUCE

Serves: 4–6

Preparation: 15 min.

Cooking: 75 min.

Level of difficulty: 1

- **1 carrot, finely chopped**
- **2 stalks celery, finely chopped**
- **1 medium onion, finely chopped**
- **2 tbsp butter**
- **1 lb (500 g) ground (minced) pork**
- **5 oz (150 g) ground (minced) beef**
- **1 cup (125 g) diced ham**
- **²/₃ cup (150 ml) dry white wine**
- **6 large tomatoes, peeled and coarsely chopped**
- **Salt and freshly ground black pepper**
- **¹/₄ teaspoon freshly ground nutmeg**
- **1 lb (500 g) penne**
- **¹/₂ cup (60 g) freshly grated Parmesan**

Heat the butter in a large frying pan over medium heat. Add the carrot, celery, and onion and sauté until softened, about 5 minutes. • Add the pork and beef and sauté until browned, 5–7 minutes. • Add the ham and cook for 1 minute. • Increase the heat to high, pour in the wine, and let it evaporate, about 5 minutes. • Stir in the tomatoes. Season with salt, pepper, and nutmeg. • Partially cover the pan and simmer over low heat for about 1 hour. • Cook the pasta in a large pot of salted boiling water until al dente. Drain well and add to the sauce. • Add the cheese and toss well. Serve hot.

PASTA SALAD WITH TUNA AND OLIVES

Chop the tomatoes coarsely, season with salt, and place them in a colander. let drain for 1 hour. • Use a fork to crumble the tuna. • Mix the tuna, tomatoes, olives, scallions, celery, carrot, and garlic. Drizzle with almost all the oil and season with salt, pepper, and oregano. Cover with plastic wrap (cling film) and refrigerate for 1 hour. • Cook the pasta in a large pot of salted boiling water until al dente. • Drain and let cool under running cold water. Drain again and dry on a clean kitchen towel. • Transfer to a serving bowl and drizzle with the remaining oil. • Add the tuna mixture and toss well. Garnish with the parsley and basil.

348

Serves: 4–6

Preparation: 30 min. + 1 hr. to drain the tomatoes + 1 hr. to chill the tuna

Cooking: 15 min.

Level of difficulty: 1

- 12 oz (350 g) cherry tomatoes
- Salt and freshly ground white pepper
- 8 oz (250 g) tuna packed in oil, drained
- 12 black olives, pitted and finely chopped
- 12 green olives, pitted and finely chopped
- 2 scallions (spring onions), coarsely chopped
- 1 stalk celery, coarsely chopped
- 1 carrot, coarsely chopped
- 1 clove garlic, finely chopped
- $^1/_3$ cup (90 ml) extra-virgin olive oil
- 2 tsp dried oregano
- 1 lb (500 g) dried short pasta (such as penne, tortiglioni, or conchiglie)
- 1 tbsp finely chopped fresh parsley
- 4–5 leaves fresh basil, torn

PASTA SALAD WITH EGGPLANT AND PINE NUTS

Serves: 4–6

Preparation: 30 min. +
1 hr. to drain the
eggplant

Cooking: 20 min.

Level of difficulty: 1

- 1 large eggplant
  (aubergine), cut into
  $1/2$ -inch (1-cm)
  thick slices
- Coarse sea salt
- 2 cups (500 ml) olive
  oil, for frying
- 2 tbsp salt-cured
  capers, rinsed
- 2 yellow bell peppers
  (capsicums)
- $1/3$ cup (90 ml) extra-
  virgin olive oil
- 1 medium onion,
  finely chopped
- $1/8$ tsp salt
- 2 cloves garlic,
  finely chopped
- 2 tbsp pine nuts
- 1 lb (500 g) short
  pasta (such as
  ridged ditalini)
- 1 cup (100 g) green
  olives, pitted and
  coarsely chopped
- 1 small bunch fresh
  basil, torn
- 2 tbsp finely chopped
  fresh parsley
- 1 tbsp finely chopped
  fresh oregano

Place the eggplant slices in a colander and sprinkle with the coarse sea salt. Let drain for 1 hour. • Chop into cubes. • Heat the oil in a large deep frying pan until very hot. Fry the eggplant in small batches for 5–7 minutes, or until golden brown. • Broil (grill) the bell peppers until the skins are blackened. Wrap them in a paper bag for 5 minutes, then remove the skins and seeds. Cut into small squares. • Heat 3 tablespoons of the extra-virgin olive oil in a small saucepan and sauté the onion with a pinch of salt over high heat until golden. Cover and simmer over low heat for 15 minutes. • Add the garlic and sauté until pale gold. • Toast the pine nuts in a nonstick frying pan over medium heat for 2 minutes, or until golden. • Cook the pasta in a large pot of salted boiling water until al dente. • Drain and let cool under running cold water. Drain again and dry on a clean kitchen towel. • Transfer to a large serving bowl and toss well with the fried eggplant, capers, bell peppers, onions, pine nuts, olives, basil, parsley, and oregano.

PASTA SALAD WITH TUNA

Place the tuna in a bowl. Drizzle with the lemon juice and ¼ cup (60 ml) of the oil. Add the olives. Let marinate for 30 minutes. • Sauté the garlic in ¼ cup (60 ml) of oil in a frying pan over medium heat for 1-2 minutes. Remove from the heat and let cool. Discard the garlic. • Chop the tomatoes, salt them, and place in a colander. Let drain for 15 minutes. • Mix the tomatoes and garlic-infused oil into the tuna. Season with salt and pepper. • Cook the pasta in a large pot of salted boiling water until al dente. • Drain and let cool under running cold water. Drain again and dry on a clean kitchen towel. • Transfer to a serving bowl and drizzle with the remaining oil. Add the tuna sauce and basil. Toss well and serve.

Serves: 4

Preparation: 40 min. + 45 min. to marinate and drain

Cooking: 15 min.

Level of difficulty: 1

- **14 oz (400 g) fresh tuna, in a single slice, skinned, boned, and chopped**
- **Freshly squeezed juice of 1 lemon**
- **¾ cup (180 ml) extra-virgin olive oil**
- **20 black olives, pitted and chopped**
- **2 cloves garlic, lightly crushed but whole**
- **1 lb (500 g) tomatoes, peeled and chopped**
- **Salt and freshly ground white pepper**
- **1 lb (500 g) conchiglie**
- **4–5 leaves fresh basil, torn**

WHOLE-WHEAT PENNE WITH PUMPKIN AND WALNUTS

Heat the oil in a large frying pan over medium heat. • Add the garlic, walnuts, and shallots. Sauté for 4 minutes, until the shallots are tender. • Add the pumpkin and vegetable stock. Cover and cook for 15 minutes, or until the pumpkin begins to break down. • Cook the pasta in a large pot of salted boiling water until not quite al dente. • Drain and add to the pan with the pumpkin. • Mix well and sauté over high heat for 2 minutes. • Add the cheese and mix well. • Transfer to a serving dish. Season with freshly ground black pepper and serve hot.

354

Serves: 4–6
Preparation: 10 min.
Cooking: 25 min.
Level of difficulty: 2

- 1/4 cup (60 ml) extra-virgin olive oil
- 1 clove garlic, finely chopped
- 1 cup (150 g) walnuts, crushed
- 2 shallots, finely chopped
- 1 lb (500 g) pumpkin flesh, cut into 1/2 inch (1 cm) cubes
- 1/3 cup (90 ml) vegetable stock
- 1 lb (500 g) whole-wheat (wholemeal) penne
- 3 oz (90 g) Fontina or other firm creamy cheese, sliced very thinly
- Freshly ground black pepper

BAKED RIGATONI WITH HAM AND MUSHROOMS

Serves: 6

Preparation: 25 min.

Cooking: 35 min.

Level of difficulty: 2

- $^1/_2$ cup (60 g) freshly grated Parmesan cheese
- 1 recipe Béchamel Sauce (see page 956)
- 5 oz (150 g) white mushrooms, thinly sliced
- $^1/_4$ cup (60 g) butter, cut into flakes
- $^3/_4$ cup (90 g) diced ham
- 1 lb (500 g) dried pasta tubes, such as rigatoni
- 5 oz (150 g) prosciutto (Parma ham), cut into thin strips

B ring a large pot of salted water to a boil over high heat. • Preheat the oven to 400°F (200°C/gas 6). • Butter a large baking dish. • Mix half the Parmesan into the Béchamel. • Sauté the mushrooms in 2 tablespoons of the butter in a frying pan over high heat until pale gold, 2–3 minutes. • Add the ham and sauté until crisp, about 5 minutes. • Meanwhile, cook the pasta in the boiling water until just al dente. • Drain and place half in the baking dish. Top with half the mushrooms and ham. Cover with half the Béchamel. Make a second layer with the pasta, mushrooms, ham, and Béchamel. Sprinkle with the remaining Parmesan and dot with the remaining butter. • Bake until the surface is golden brown, 10–15 minutes. • Serve hot.

BAKED ZITE

Place the oil in a large frying pan over medium heat. Add the sausage meat and sauté until lightly browned, 4–5 minutes. Add the wine and sauté until it has evaporated. • Add the tomatoes and basil and season with salt and pepper. Simmer until reduced, about 20 minutes. • Place a quarter of the pecorino in a bowl with the beef, bread crumbs, parsley, garlic, and eggs. Stir until smooth. • Heat the oil in a large frying pan. • Shape the meat and bread crumb mixture into balls about the size of marbles. • Fry the meatballs in the oil until crisp and golden brown. Drain on paper towels. • Cook the pasta in a large pan of salted boiling water until very al dente (it should be slightly undercooked). • Preheat the oven to 400°F (200°C/gas 6). • Spread a layer of filling over the bottom of an ovenproof baking dish. Cover with a layer of pasta and top with meatballs, sliced of mozzarella, pecorino, and sauce. Repeat this layering process until al the ingredients are in the dish. Finish with a layer of sauce and pecorino. • Bake until the cheese is browned and the sauce is bubbling, about 20 minutes. • Serve hot.

Serves: 4–6

Preparation: 20 min.

Cooking: 45 min.

Level of difficulty: 2

- 2 tbsp extra-virgin olive oil
- 8 oz (250 g) Italian pork sausages, peeled and crumbled
- $^1/_4$ cup (60 ml) dry white wine
- 1 (14-oz/400-g) can tomatoes, with juice
- 1 tbsp finely chopped fresh basil
- Salt and freshly ground black pepper
- 6 oz (180 g) freshly grated pecorino cheese
- 8 oz (250 g) ground (minced) beef
- $^1/_2$ cup (75 g) fine dry bread crumbs
- 1 tbsp finely chopped fresh parsley
- 1 clove garlic, finely chopped
- 2 large eggs
- $^1/_4$ cup (60 ml) extra-virgin olive oil
- 1 lb (500 g) zite pasta
- 4 oz (125 g) mozzarella cheese, sliced

BAKED RIGATONI PASTA

Sauté the onion in the oil in a large frying pan over medium heat for 10 minutes. Season with salt. • Pierce the sausages with a fork and blanch in boiling water for 3 minutes. Drain, remove the casings, and crumble the meat. • Add the sausage meat, salami, and beef to the onion. Simmer over medium heat for 30 minutes, adding some stock if the mixture starts to stick to the pan. • Add the eggs and season with salt and pepper. • Cook the pasta for half the time on the package. • Drain and let cool. • Preheat the oven to 350°F (180°C/gas 4). • Butter a baking dish and sprinkle with bread crumbs. • Fill the pasta with the meat sauce. • Arrange the pasta in the baking dish with the tomato sauce and pecorino. • Bake for 40–45 minutes, or until bubbling and golden. • Serve hot.

Serves: 4–6

Preparation: 45 min.

Cooking: 90 min.

Level of difficulty: 2

- **1 large onion, finely chopped**
- **$1/4$ cup (60 ml) extra-virgin olive oil**
- **Salt and freshly ground black pepper**
- **2 sausages, weighing about 8 oz (250 g)**
- **1 cup (150 g) diced salami**
- **1 lb (500 g) ground (minced) beef**
- **1 cup (250 ml) Beef Stock (optional), (see page 946)**
- **3 hard-boiled eggs, crumbled**
- **1 lb (500 g) large rigatoni pasta**
- **1 recipe Tomato Sauce (see page 948)**
- **1 cup (125 g) freshly grated aged pecorino cheese**

BAKED PENNE PIE

Serves: 4–6

Preparation: 20 min.

Cooking: 40 min.

Level of difficulty: 1

- 1 lb (500 g) penne
- 2 tbsp extra-virgin olive oil
- $1/3$ cup (90 g) butter
- 1 tbsp all-purpose (plain) flour
- 3 cups (750 ml) milk
- Salt and freshly ground white pepper
- Freshly grated nutmeg
- 6 oz (180 g) freshly grated pecorino cheese
- 6–8 large thinly sliced caciocavallo cheese

Preheat the oven to 400° F (200°C/gas 6). • Cook the penne in a large pan of salted, boiling water until al dente. • Drain well and place in a large bowl. Stir in the oil and set aside. • Melt ¼ cup (60 g) of butter in a medium saucepan. Stir in the flour. Gradually add the milk, stirring constantly. Bring to a boil and simmer for 5 minutes. Remove from the heat. Season with salt, pepper, nutmeg, and pecorino. • Butter a large ovenproof baking dish. • Place the pasta in the baking dish and pour the sauce over the top. Cover with the slices of caciocavallo. • Bake until the cheese is melted and bubbling, about 25 minutes. • Serve hot.

BAKED PASTA WITH EGGPLANT

Place the eggplant slices in a colander and sprinkle with the coarse sea salt. Let drain for 1 hour. • Preheat the oven to 400°F (200°C/gas 6). • Butter a 10-inch (25-cm) baking dish and sprinkle with ¼ cup (30 g) of the bread crumbs. • Heat the oil in a large deep frying pan until very hot. Fry the eggplant in small batches over medium heat for 5–7 minutes, or until golden brown. • Drain well on paper towels. • Arrange the eggplant in a single layer on the bottom and sides of the prepared pan, letting the edges of the eggplant overhang. • Cook the pasta in a large pot of salted boiling water until al dente. • Drain and transfer to a large bowl. Mix in the meat sauce, oregano, basil, the cheeses, and season with pepper. • Spoon the pasta into the pan, taking care not to displace the eggplant. Fold over the overhanging eggplant and top with the remaining slices of eggplant. • Sprinkle with bread crumbs and dot with butter. • Bake for 25–30 minutes, or until golden brown on top. • Remove from the oven and let rest for 10 minutes. • Serve warm.

Serves: 6

Preparation: 40 min. + 1 hr. to drain the eggplants + time to make meat sauce

Cooking: 1 hr.

Level of difficulty: 2

- **3 eggplants, each weighing about 1 lb (500 g), thinly sliced**
- **Coarse sea salt**
- **³/4 cup (60 g) fine dry bread crumbs**
- **1 cup (250 ml) olive oil, for frying**
- **1 lb (500 g) bucatini**
- **1 recipe Meat Sauce (see page 951)**
- **¹/2 tsp dried oregano**
- **Leaves from 1 small bunch fresh basil, torn**
- **1¹/4 cups (150 g) freshly grated mixed firm cheeses, such as caciocavallo, Parmesan, and pecorino**
- **Freshly ground black pepper**
- **¹/4 cup (60 g) butter, cut into flakes**

SARDINIAN GNOCCHI WITH SAUSAGES AND PECORINO

Serves: 4–6

Preparation: 10 min.

Cooking: 30 min.

Level of difficulty: 1

- **14 oz (400 g) Italian pork sausages, skinned and crumbled**
- **1 large onion, finely chopped**
- **3 cloves garlic, finely chopped**
- **8 basil leaves, torn**
- **2 tbsp extra-virgin olive oil**
- **1 1/2 lb (750 g) tomatoes, peeled and chopped**
- **Salt and freshly ground black pepper**
- **1 lb (500 g) Malloreddus (Sardinian gnocchi) or other small, dried pasta shape**
- **1/2 cup (125 g) freshly grated pecorino cheese**

Sauté the sausages, onion, garlic, and basil in the oil in a large frying pan over medium heat until the onion is soft. • Add the tomatoes and season with salt and pepper. Simmer for 15–20 minutes, or until the sauce has reduced. • Meanwhile, cook the pasta in a large pot of salted, boiling water until al dente. Drain well and place in a heated serving dish. Pour in the sauce and sprinkle with the pecorino. • Toss well and serve hot.

BAKED PASTA WITH GREENS

B reak the eggs, one at a time, into salted, simmering water. Add the vinegar and simmer until the whites are set and the yolks are still slightly soft, about 10 minutes. • Use a slotted spoon to remove the eggs and set aside. • Preheat the oven to 350°F (180°C/gas 4). • Oil a baking dish. • Cook the Swiss chard and spinach in salted boiling water for 5–7 minutes, or until tender. • Remove with a slotted spoon. • Return to a boil and cook the pasta in the same cooking water until al dente. • Drain and transfer the pasta to the baking dish. Top with the Swiss chard and spinach and sprinkle with pecorino. Continue to layer the ingredients, finishing with pecorino. • Top with the eggs and pour the cream over the top. • Bake for 10–15 minutes, or until the egg whites begin to brown at the edges. • Serve warm.

Serves: 6

Preparation: 30 min.

Cooking: 45–60 min.

Level of difficulty: 2

- **6 large eggs**
- **1 tbsp malt vinegar**
- **1 lb (500 g) Malloreddus (Sardinian gnocchi) or other small, dried pasta shape**
- **8 oz (200 g) Swiss chard (silverbeet) leaves, shredded**
- **8 oz (200 g) spinach leaves, shredded**
- **1 cup (125 g) freshly grated pecorino cheese**
- **$^1/_2$ cup (125 ml) light (single) cream**

RIGATONI BAKED IN PASTRY WITH MEAT SAUCE

Serves: 6

Preparation: 30 min.
+ time to make the
pastry and sauces

Cooking: 30 min.

Level of difficulty: 3

- 1 recipe Meat Sauce (see page 951)
- 1 recipe Béchamel Sauce (see page 956)
- 1 recipe Shortcrust Pastry (see page 959)
- 1 lb (500 g) rigatoni pasta
- 2 tbsp butter
- 4 tbsp fine dry bread crumbs
- 1 whole white truffle, in shavings
- 1 cup (120 g) freshly grated Parmesan cheese

Prepare the Meat and Béchamel sauces. • Prepare the pastry. • Preheat the oven to 350°F (180°C/gas 4). • Cook the rigatoni in a large pot of salted, boiling water for half the time indicated on the package. Drain well and mix with half the meat sauce. • Grease a 12-inch (30-cm) ovenproof baking dish with the butter and sprinkle with the bread crumbs. • Roll the dough out to about ¼ inch (3 mm) thick and line the baking dish. • Cover the bottom with a layer of Béchamel, followed by layers of pasta and meat sauce. Sprinkle with the truffle. Repeat until all the ingredients are in the baking dish. The last layer should be of Béchamel. Sprinkle with the Parmesan. • Bake for about 30 minutes. Serve hot.

FRESH
PASTA

TAGLIATELLE WITH WALNUT AND GARLIC SAUCE

Pasta: Place the flour in a mound on a clean work surface. Make a well in the center and add the eggs. Use a fork to gradually incorporate the eggs into the flour. When almost all the flour has been absorbed, use your hands to gather the dough up into a ball. • Knead the dough by pushing down and forward on the ball of pasta with the palm of your hand. Fold the dough in half, give it a quarter-turn, and repeat. After 15–20 minutes, the dough should be smooth and silky with tiny air bubbles visible near the surface. • Wrap in plastic wrap (cling film) and let rest for 30 minutes. • Roll the dough through a pasta machine, reducing the thickness setting by one notch each time, until you reach the thinnest setting. • Put the pasta machine on the setting for tagliatelle and cut each sheet. Fold the tagliatelle into "nests" and set aside until ready to cook. • Walnut Sauce: Place the bread crumbs in a small bowl. Pour in the milk. • Shell the walnuts. Place in a food processor with the garlic and chop briefly. Don't make the sauce too smooth—you should still be able to feel the texture of the walnuts. • Add the bread crumbs and milk (without squeezing the bread crumbs) and season with salt. Set aside to rest for 30 minutes. • Cook the tagliatelle in a large pan of salted, boiling water until al dente. • Drain the tagliatelle and place in a bowl with the butter and walnut sauce. Toss gently and serve hot.

Serves: 4

Preparation: 1 hr.
+ 30 min. to rest

Cooking: 5 min.

Level: 2

Pasta
- 3 cups (450 g) all-purpose (plain) flour
- 4 large very fresh eggs, beaten

Walnut Sauce
- 3 oz (90 g) fresh bread crumbs
- $^{1}/_{2}$ cup (125 ml) milk
- $1^{1}/_{2}$ lb (750 g) walnuts, in shell
- $^{1}/_{4}$ cup (60 g) very fresh butter
- 4 cloves garlic
- Salt

SPINACH TAGLIATELLE WITH BUTTER AND ROSEMARY

Serves: 4

*Preparation: 5 min.
+ time to make the
pasta*

Cooking: 5 min.

Level of difficulty: 2

- $^3/_4$ cup (180 g)
  butter
- **5 sprigs fresh
  rosemary**
- **1 recipe
  Spinach Tagliatelle
  (see page 376)**

C ook the butter and rosemary in a heavy-bottomed pan over very low heat until the butter turns pale gold. • Remove the rosemary. • Cook the pasta in a large pot of salted, boiling water until al dente. Drain well and place in a heated serving dish. • Pour the hot sauce over the top, toss carefully, and serve.

BAKED SPINACH TAGLIATELLE

Pasta: Cook the spinach leaves in a little lightly salted water until tender, 3–5 minutes. • Drain well, squeeze out excess moisture, and chop finely. • Place the flour in a mound on a clean work surface. Make a well in the center and add the eggs and spinach. Use a fork to gradually incorporate the egg mixture into the flour. When almost all the flour has been absorbed use your hands to gather the dough up into a ball. • Knead the dough by pushing down and forward on the ball of pasta with the palm of your hand. Fold the dough in half, give it a quarter-turn, and repeat. After 15–20 minutes, the dough should be smooth and silky with tiny air bubbles visible near the surface. • Wrap in plastic wrap (cling film) and let rest for 30 minutes. • Roll the dough through a pasta machine, reducing the thickness setting by one notch each time, until you reach the thinnest setting. • Put the pasta machine on the setting for tagliatelle and cut each sheet. Fold the tagliatelle into "nests" and set aside until ready to cook. • Prepare the Béchamel Sauce. • Preheat the oven to 350°F (180°C/gas 4). • Cook the pasta in a large pan of salted, boiling water until al dente, 3–4 minutes. • Drain well. • Butter an ovenproof baking dish and spread with a layer of Béchamel. Cover with pasta and top with pieces of butter and Parmesan. Repeat this layering process until all the ingredients are in the dish, finishing with a layer of butter and cheese. • Bake until the top is golden brown, about 20 minutes. Serve hot.

Serves: 4–6

Preparation: 1 hr.

Cooking: 25 min.

Level: 3

Pasta
- 1 lb (500 g) fresh tender spinach leaves
- 3$^1/_3$ cups (500 g) all-purpose (plain) flour
- $^1/_4$ tsp salt
- 3 large eggs
- $^1/_4$ cup (60 g) butter
- 1 cup (120 g) freshly grated Parmesan cheese

- 1 recipe Béchamel Sauce (see page 956)

TAGLIATELLE WITH CREAM AND HAM

Serves: 4

Preparation: 15 min.
+ time to make
the pasta

Cooking: 15 min.

Level of difficulty: 2

- **1 recipe tagliatelle (see page 372) or 14 oz (400 g) store-bought tagliatelle**
- **1/4 cup (60 g) butter**
- **4 oz (125 g) ham, cut into thin strips**
- **3/4 cup (200 ml) heavy (double) cream**
- **Salt and freshly ground white pepper**
- **1/8 tsp freshly grated nutmeg**
- **1/2 cup (60 g) freshly grated Parmesan cheese**

If using homemade pasta, prepare the tagliatelle following the instructions on page 372. • Melt the butter in a large frying pan over medium heat. Add the ham and sauté until crisp, about 5 minutes. • Pour in the cream and simmer until thickened, about 5 minutes. • Season with salt, pepper, and nutmeg. • Cook the pasta in a large pot of salted boiling water until al dente, 3–5 minutes. • Drain and add to the pan with the sauce. Toss gently. • Sprinkle with the Parmesan and serve hot.

WATERCRESS TAGLIOLINI WITH BASIL SAUCE

Cook the watercress in a pan of salted, boiling water for 2–3 minutes. Drain well and finely chop in a food processor. • Place both flours and the salt in a large bowl. Add the watercress and gradually stir in the water a little at a time. You may not need it all. The dough should be reasonably firm. • Transfer the dough to a lightly floured work surface and knead for 7–8 minutes, or until smooth and elastic. • Roll the pasta using a pasta machine or by hand, then cut into tagliolini (thin ribbon pasta). • Place the basil, oil, cream cheese, pine nuts, and garlic in a food processor or blender and chop until smooth and creamy. Add a little hot water from the pasta pan if the sauce is too thick. • Cook the tagliolini in a large saucepan of salted, boiling water for 2–3 minutes. • Drain and place in a heated serving dish. Spoon the sauce over the top and toss gently.

Serves: 4

Preparation: 1 hr.

Cooking: 5 min.

Level of difficulty: 3

- 8 oz (250 g) watercress
- 1¹/₂ cups (250 g) all-purpose (plain) flour
- 1¹/₂ cups (250 g) whole-wheat (wholemeal) flour
- ¹/₂ tsp salt
- ³/₄ cup (180 ml) water
- 2¹/₂ oz (75 g) fresh basil
- ¹/₄ cup (60 ml) extra-virgin olive oil
- 3 oz (90 g) cream cheese
- 3 tbsp pine nuts
- 3 cloves garlic

TAGLIOLINI WITH SCAMPI AND RADICCHIO

Serves: 4
Preparation: 45 min.
Cooking: 15 min.
Level of difficulty: 2

- 14 oz (400 g) store-bought tagliolini
- 1 lb (500 g) scampi (Dublin Bay prawns)
- 3 tbsp butter
- 1 clove garlic, finely chopped
- $^{1}/_{4}$ cup (60 ml) brandy
- 1 medium tomato, peeled and chopped
- Salt and freshly ground white pepper
- $^{3}/_{4}$ cup (180 ml) heavy (double) cream
- 8 oz (250 g) red radicchio, cut in julienne strips

Peel the scampi and chop coarsely. Remove the flesh from the heads and claws as well. • Melt the butter in a large frying pan and sauté the garlic with the scampi meat from the heads and claws. • Pour in the brandy and cook until evaporated. • Add the tomato and cook for 3 minutes. Add the remaining scampi. Season with salt and pepper and simmer over low heat for 1–2 minutes. Add the cream and simmer until reduced. • Cook the pasta in a large pan of salted boiling water until al dente, about 2 minutes. Drain the pasta and add to the pan with the scampi. • Add the radicchio, toss gently, and serve immediately.

TAGLIATELLE WITH BEANS

Soak the beans overnight in cold water. • If using homemade pasta, prepare the tagliatelle following the instructions on page 372. • Lightly salt the water and bring to a boil. Drain the beans and add to the pot. Add the lard, oil, onion, celery, potatoes, tomatoes, garlic, and basil and simmer over very low heat for 2 hours. • Five minutes before the sauce is ready, add the tagliatelle to the pan and cook until al dente, 3–5 minutes. • Serve hot garnished with the extra sprigs of basil.

Serves: 4

Preparation: 15 min. + 12 hr. to soak

Cooking: 2 hr.

Level: 2

- 1¹/₂ cups (150 g) dried cannellini or white kidney beans
- 1 recipe tagliatelle (see page 372) or 14 oz (400 g) store-bought tagliatelle
- Salt
- 3 quarts (3 liters) water
- 2 oz (60 g) lard
- 2 tbsp extra-virgin olive oil
- 1 medium white onion, coarsely chopped
- 1 stalk celery, sliced
- 1 tbsp chopped fresh basil, + extra sprigs, to garnish
- 3 medium potatoes, peeled and diced
- 3 medium tomatoes, peeled and chopped
- 4 cloves, garlic, finely chopped

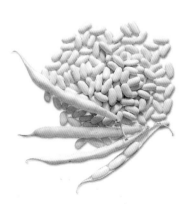

TAGLIATELLE WITH PINE NUT AND WALNUT PESTO

Serves: 4

Preparation: 30 min.
+ time to make
the pasta

Cooking: 15 min.

Level of difficulty: 2

- 1 recipe tagliatelle
  (see page 372) or
  14 oz (400 g)
  store-bought
  tagliatelle
- 1/3 cup (45 g) pine
  nuts
- 1 lb (500 g)
  walnuts, in shells
- 2 cloves garlic
- 1 cup chopped
  parsley
- 1/3 cup (90 ml)
  extra-virgin olive
  oil
- Salt

If using homemade pasta, prepare the tagliatelle following the instructions on page 372. • Preheat the oven to 350°F (180°C/gas 4). • Roast the pine nuts until pale gold, 5–10 minutes. • Shell the walnuts and chop finely in a food processor with the pine nuts, garlic, parsley, and oil. Season with salt. • Cook the pasta in a large pot of salted, boiling water until al dente. • Drain and place in a heated serving dish. Cover with the sauce, toss carefully, and serve.

CHESTNUT TAGLIATELLE

Chestnuts: Bring the milk and salt to a boil in a large saucepan. • Add the chestnuts and simmer for 1 hour, or until tender. • Use a fork or potato masher to mash the chestnuts in a large bowl until smooth, adding a little of the cooking liquid to form a purée. • Pasta Dough: Place both flours and the salt in a mound on a work surface and make a well in the center. Gradually stir in the eggs and enough water to make a smooth dough. Shape the dough into a ball, wrap in plastic wrap (cling film), and let rest for 30 minutes. • Roll out the dough into a sheet that is not too thin. Cut into ¾-inch (2-cm) wide strips. • Sauce: Heat the cream in a medium saucepan over low heat. Mix in the ricotta, nutmeg, and salt. • Cook the pasta in a large pot of salted boiling water until al dente. • Drain and add to the sauce along with the Parmesan and almost all the chestnut purée. • Garnish with the remaining chestnut purée and serve hot.

Serves: 4

Preparation: 90 min. +30 min. to rest the dough

Cooking: 1 hr. 15 min.

Level of difficulty: 3

Chestnuts
- 2 cups (500 ml) milk
- ¹/₄ tsp salt
- 15 dried chestnuts

Pasta Dough
- 8 oz (250 g) chestnut flour
- ³/₄ cup (125 g) all-purpose (plain) flour
- ¹/₄ tsp salt
- 2 large eggs, beaten
- ³/₄ cup (180 ml) lukewarm water, + more as needed

Sauce
- ¹/₄ cup (60 ml) heavy (double) cream
- ³/₄ cup (200 g) ricotta cheese
- ¹/₈ tsp freshly grated nutmeg
- 4 tbsp freshly grated Parmesan cheese
- Salt

TAGLIATELLE WITH LEEKS AND FONTINA CHEESE

If using homemade pasta, prepare the tagliatelle following the instructions on page 372. • Heat the oil in a medium saucepan. Add the leeks and just enough water to cover them. Cook over medium heat until the leeks are tender. • Season with salt and pepper, add the cheese and mustard, if using, and cook until the cheese has almost melted. • Cook the tagliatelle in a large pan of salted, boiling water until al dente. Drain well and place in a heated serving dish. • Pour the leek sauce over the top, toss gently, and serve.

Serves: 4–6

Preparation: 15 min. + time to make the pasta

Cooking: 3–5 min.

Level of difficulty: 2

- **1 recipe tagliatelle (see page 372) or 14 oz (400 g) store-bought tagliatelle**
- **$1/4$ cup (60 ml) extra-virgin olive oil**
- **4 leeks, thinly sliced**
- **Salt and freshly ground black pepper**
- **5 oz (150 g) Fontina cheese, diced**
- **1 tbsp spicy mustard (optional)**

LASAGNE WITH POPPY SEEDS

Serves: 4–6

Preparation: 15 min. + time to make the pasta

Cooking: 3–5 min.

Level of difficulty: 2

- **1 recipe pasta dough (see page 372) or 14 oz (400 g) store-bought lasagne**
- **$^1/_3$ cup (90 g) butter**
- **1 oz (30 g) sugar**
- **$^2/_3$ oz (20 g) poppy seeds**

I f using homemade pasta, prepare the pasta dough following the instructions on page 372. To make lasagne, cut the dough into 3 x 12-inch (8 x 30-cm) sheets. • Cook the lasagne in a large pot of salted water until cooked al dente. • Melt the butter in a small saucepan and add the sugar and poppy seeds. • Drain the pasta and place in a heated serving dish. • Pour the butter sauce over the top and toss gently. • Serve hot.

TAGLIATELLE WITH LAMB SAUCE

If using homemade pasta, prepare the tagliatelle following the instructions on page 372. • Sauté the garlic and rosemary in the oil in a medium saucepan over medium heat for 2 minutes until the garlic is pale gold. • Add the lamb and sauté for 5 minutes, until browned all over. • Increase the heat and pour in the wine. • Stir in the tomatoes and season with salt and pepper. Cover and simmer over low heat for about 1 hour, or until the lamb is very tender. • Cook the pasta in a large pot of salted boiling water until al dente. • Drain and add to the sauce. Toss gently with the sauce and serve hot.

Serves: 4

Preparation: 45 min. + time to make the pasta

Cooking: 75 min.

Level of difficulty: 1

- **1 recipe tagliatelle (see page 372) or 14 oz (400 g) store-bought tagliatelle**
- **3 cloves garlic, finely chopped**
- **1 sprig fresh rosemary**
- **1/3 cup (90 ml) extra-virgin olive oil**
- **1 lb (500 g) fatty or lean lamb, cut into small chunks**
- **1/3 cup (90 ml) dry white wine**
- **1 lb (500 g) tomatoes, peeled, seeded, and coarsely chopped**
- **Salt and freshly ground black pepper**

TAGLIATELLE WITH BEEF SAUCE

If using homemade pasta, prepare the tagliatelle following the instructions on page 372. • Sprinkle the salt, pepper, 1 tablespoon of parsley, and half the garlic on a cutting board. Roll the lard in this mixture. • Lard the meat by cutting holes in the direction of the grain with a long, thin knife and inserting strips of lard. Tie up the meat with kitchen string so it keeps its shape. • Heat the oil and butter in a large saucepan over medium heat. Add the remaining garlic, parsley, onion, and celery and sauté until the garlic is pale gold, 2–3 minutes. • Add the beef and sear all over. Season with salt, pepper, nutmeg, and the crushed cloves. • When the vegetables begin to brown, pour in the wine. Simmer for 30 minutes, adding water if the mixture becomes too thick. • Stir in the tomatoes and enough water or stock to cover the meat. • Simmer over very low heat until the meat is tender, about 2 hours. • Serve the sauce with tagliatelle. Serve the meat as a main course to follow the pasta.

Serves: 4

Preparation: 30 min. + time to make the pasta

Cooking: 3 hr.

Level of difficulty: 2

- 1 recipe tagliatelle (see page 372) or 14 oz (400 g) store-bought tagliatelle
- Salt and freshly ground black pepper
- 2 tbsp finely chopped fresh parsley
- 3 cloves garlic, finely chopped
- $1/3$ cup (90 g) lard or fatty cooked ham, cut into strips
- 2 lb (1 kg) beef rump
- 3 tbsp extra-virgin olive oil
- 2 tbsp butter
- 1 red onion, finely chopped
- 1 stalk celery, finely chopped
- $1/8$ tsp freshly grated nutmeg
- 3 cloves, crushed
- Generous $3/4$ cup (200 ml) dry red wine
- 1 cup (250 g) peeled plum tomatoes, pressed through a fine mesh strainer (passata)
- Water or Beef Stock (see page 946)

MALTAGLIATI WITH SAUSAGES

If using homemade pasta, prepare the pasta dough following the instructions on page 372. To make maltagliati, roll the dough in strips about 2 inches (5 cm) wide and cut into diamond shapes. • Prick the sausages well with a fork and cook for 3 minutes in a pan of boiling water. Drain, peel, and chop coarsely. • Heat the oil in a large frying pan over low heat and sweat the onion with a pinch of salt for 10 minutes. • Add the sausage meat and sauté over high heat for 5 minutes. • Season with the cinnamon, salt, and pepper. Pour in the wine and cook until it has evaporated. • Add the tomatoes and simmer for 20 minutes over low heat. • Cook the pasta until al dente. • Drain and add to the pan with the sauce. Toss gently and sprinkle with the Parmesan. • Serve hot.

Serves: 4

Preparation: 30 min. + time to make the pasta

Cooking: 45 min.

Level of difficulty: 2

- **1 recipe pasta dough (see page 372) or 14 oz (400 g) fresh store-bought maltagliati**
- **12 oz (350 g) fresh Italian sausages**
- **2 tbsp extra-virgin olive oil**
- **1 red onion, finely chopped**
- **Salt and freshly ground black pepper**
- **$1/2$ tsp ground cinnamon**
- **$1/2$ cup (125 ml) dry red wine**
- **1 (14-oz/400-g) can tomatoes, with juice**
- **4 tbsp freshly grated Parmesan cheese**

Serves: 4

Preparation: 30 min. +
time to make
the pasta

Cooking: 90 min.

Level of difficulty: 1

- **1 recipe tagliatelle (see page 372) or 14 oz (400 g) store-bought tagliatelle**
- **1 red onion, 1 small carrot, 1 small stalk celery, finely chopped**
- **$^1/_4$ cup (60 ml) extra-virgin olive oil**
- **8 oz (200 g) lean ground (minced) beef**
- **$^1/_3$ cup (90 ml) dry red wine**
- **4 oz (125 g) chicken livers, trimmed and diced**
- **1$^1/_4$ cups (300 g) peeled tomatoes, pressed through a fine mesh strainer (passata)**
- **$^1/_2$ oz (15 g) dried porcini mushrooms, soaked in warm water for 15 minutes, drained and finely chopped**
- **1 bay leaf**
- **Salt and freshly ground black pepper**
- **1 cup (125 g) freshly grated Parmesan cheese**
- **$^1/_4$ cup (60 g) butter**

ROMAN STYLE TAGLIATELLE

If using homemade pasta, prepare the tagliatelle following the instructions on page 372. • Sauté the onion, carrot, and celery in the oil in a large saucepan over medium heat until softened, about 5 minutes. • Stir in the beef and cook for 3 minutes until browned all over. • Increase the heat and pour in the wine. • Add the chicken livers and simmer over low heat for 15 minutes. • Add the tomatoes, mushrooms, and bay leaf and season with salt and pepper. Simmer over low heat for 1 hour. • Cook the pasta in a large pot of salted boiling water until al dente. • Drain and add to the sauce. Sprinkle with the Parmesan, dot with the butter, letting it melt into the pasta, and serve.

BAKED TAGLIOLINI

Preheat the oven to 400°F (200°C/gas 6).
• Butter a baking dish and sprinkle with the bread crumbs. • Mix the Parmesan and cinnamon in a small bowl. • Arrange one-third of the pasta in the dish, dot with 1 tablespoon of butter, and sprinkle with one-third of the cinnamon-Parmesan mixture. Continue until all the pasta, butter, and Parmesan are used up. • Bake for 15–20 minutes, or until golden brown. • Remove from the oven and pour over the boiling stock. • Return to the oven and bake for 20–25 minutes, or until almost all of the liquid is absorbed, but taking care not to dry the pasta out. • Serve piping hot.

Serves: 4

Preparation: 30 min.

Cooking: 35–40 min.

Level of difficulty: 2

- $^1/_2$ cup (60 g) fine dry bread crumbs
- $^2/_3$ cup (80 g) freshly grated Parmesan cheese
- $^1/_8$ tsp ground cinnamon
- 12 oz (350 g) store-bought fresh tagliolini
- 3 tbsp butter, in flakes
- $1^1/_4$ cups (300 ml) boiling Beef Stock (see page 946)

TAGLIATELLE CAKE

Prepare the tagliatelle following the instructions on pages 372. Shape the tagliatelle into nests and place on a lightly flour cloth until ready to use. • Shortcrust Pastry: Sift the flour into a large bowl and add the butter, confectioners' sugar, egg yolks, lemon zest, and salt. Mix rapidly with your hands and shape into a ball. Wrap in plastic wrap (cling film) and refrigerate for 30 minutes. • Place a large pan of water over high heat with the coarse sea salt. Cover and bring to a boil. • Preheat the oven to 400°F (200°C/gas 6). • Roll the pastry out on a lightly floured work surface. Place in an 8-inch (20-cm) round springform pan and prick well with the tines (prongs) of a fork. • Cover the pastry with aluminum foil and fill with dried beans. • Bake for 15–20 minutes, or until the edges are pale golden brown. Remove from the oven and let cool. Remove the beans and foil. • Filling: Soak the sultanas, pine nuts, and citron peel in a small bowl with the rum or brandy. • In a separate bowl, beat the egg yolks with the sugar until pale and creamy. Beat in the milk or cream. • Cook the tagliatelle in the boiling water for 2 minutes. Drain well and mix with the egg and sugar mixture and dried fruit. Mix well and spoon into the precooked pastry shell. • Bake for 30 minutes, or until the filling mixture is dried out. • Serve warm or at room temperature.

398

Serves: 6–8

Preparation: 1 hr.
  + time to make
  the pasta

Cooking: 1 hr.

Level of difficulty: 2

Pasta
- **¹/₂ recipe tagliatelle (see page 372)**
- **2 tbsp coarse sea salt**

Shortcrust Pastry
- **2 cups (300 g) all-purpose (plain) flour**
- **¹/₂ cup (125 g) cold butter, cut up**
- **³/₄ cup (125 g) confectioners' (icing) sugar**
- **3 large egg yolks**
- **Finely grated zest of ¹/₂ lemon**
- **Pinch of salt**

Filling
- **4 tbsp golden raisins (sultanas)**
- **4 tbsp pine nuts**
- **3 tbsp candied citron peel, cut in small cubes**
- **3 tbsp rum or brandy**
- **3 large egg yolks**
- **6 tbsp sugar**
- **2–3 tbsp milk or cream**
- **Salt**

HOMEMADE SPAGHETTI WITH GARLIC SAUCE

Pasta Dough: Mound the flour and salt onto a work surface and make a well in the center. Mix in half an egg (reserve the remaining portion for another use) and enough water to make a fairly sticky dough. Knead for 15–20 minutes, until smooth. • Roll out the dough out on a lightly floured surface to ¼-inch (1 cm) thick. Cover with a damp cloth and set aside to rest for 30 minutes. • Tear off strips of dough, pulling them until the diameter of the strips is the size of large spaghetti. Wrap into nests and let dry on a floured cloth for about 30 minutes before cooking. • Garlic Sauce: Sauté the garlic in the oil in a large saucepan over low heat for 2 minutes, until pale gold. • Add the tomatoes and chile and season with salt. • Cook over low heat for 40 minutes, or until the garlic has almost dissolved. Season with salt. • Cook the pasta in a large pot of salted boiling water for 4–5 minutes, depending on the diameter. • Drain and add to the sauce. Serve immediately.

Serves: 4–6

Preparation: 1 hr.
+ 30 min. to rest
the dough

Cooking: 1 hr.

Level of difficulty: 3

Pasta Dough

- 3¹/₃ cups (500 g) all-purpose (plain) flour
- ¹/₄ tsp salt
- 1 large egg, lightly beaten
- 1 tbsp water + more if needed

Garlic Sauce

- 8–10 cloves garlic, lightly crushed but whole
- 5 tbsp extra-virgin olive oil
- 2 lb (1 kg) tomatoes, peeled and finely chopped
- ¹/₄ tsp crumbled dried chile pepper
- Salt

PIZZOCCHERI WITH CABBAGE, POTATO, AND CHEESE

Serves: 6

Preparation: 1 hr.

Cooking: 40 min.

Level of difficulty: 2

- 2^1/$_2$ cups (375 g) buckwheat flour
- 1^1/$_2$ cups (225 g) all-purpose (plain) flour
- 3 large eggs
- ^{1}/$_2$ cup (125 ml) milk
- 1 tsp salt
- 8 oz (250 g) potatoes, cut into small cubes
- 6 oz (180 g) Savoy cabbage, shredded
- ^{2}/$_3$ cup (180 g) butter
- 2 cloves garlic, finely chopped
- 4 leaves fresh sage
- Freshly ground black pepper
- 1 cup (120 g) freshly grated Parmesan cheese
- 6 oz (180 g) Fontina cheese, thinly sliced

Preheat the oven to 350°F (180°C/gas 4). • Combine both flours in a large bowl. Add the eggs, milk, and salt and stir to obtain a firm dough. • Place on a lightly floured work surface and knead until smooth, 10 minutes. Set aside for 30 minutes. • Roll the pasta out until about ^{1}/$_8$-inch (3 mm) thick. Roll the sheet of pasta loosely and cut into strips ^{1}/$_2$-inch (5 mm) wide and 3 inches (8 cm) long. • Bring a large saucepan of lightly salted water to a boil and cook the potatoes and cabbage. Put the potatoes in 5 minutes before the cabbage. • When the potatoes are almost cooked, add the pasta. • When the vegetables and pasta are cooked, drain carefully. • Melt the butter with the garlic and sage in a small saucepan. Cook for 2 minutes. • Butter an ovenproof dish. • Place a layer of pasta in the bottom of the dish and cover with a layer of potato and cabbage. Drizzle with a little butter, sprinkle with pepper and Parmesan, and cover with slices of Fontina. Repeat this layering process two or three times until all the ingredients are in the dish. Finish with a layer of Parmesan. • Bake for 25 minutes, or until the cheese is golden brown on top. Serve hot.

POTATO AND BROCCOLI PIZZOCCHERI

Melt the butter in a large frying pan over medium heat. • Add the garlic, rosemary, and sage. Sauté for 2–3 minutes, until the garlic is pale golden brown. • Remove and discard the garlic and the herbs. • Cook the potatoes in a large pot of salted boiling water for 5 minutes. • Add the pizzoccheri and cook for 8 minutes. • Add the broccoli and cook until the pasta is al dente and the potatoes and the broccoli are tender. • Drain well. • Add the pasta and the vegetables to the frying pan with the herb butter and sauté over high heat for 1 minute. • Transfer to a serving dish. • Sprinkle with Parmesan and serve.

404

Serves: 4

Preparation: 15 min. + time to make the pasta

Cooking: 20 min.

Level of difficulty: 2

- $^1/_3$ cup (90 g) butter
- 2 cloves garlic, lightly crushed but whole
- 1 sprig of rosemary
- 1 sprig of sage
- 3 large floury (baking) potatoes, peeled and cut into 1 inch (3 cm) cubes
- 1 recipe pizzoccheri (see page 403) or 14 oz (400 g) store-bought pizzoccheri
- 2 small heads broccoli, cut into florets
- $^3/_4$ cup (90 g) freshly grated Parmesan cheese

ORECCHIETTE WITH BROCCOLI

Serves: 4

Preparation: 15 min.

Cooking: 40 min.

Level of difficulty: 1

- 1 lb (500 g) broccoli
- 2 cloves of garlic, finely chopped
- $^1/_4$ cup (60 ml) extra-virgin olive oil
- 1 hot red chile, thinly sliced
- Salt to taste
- 1 lb (500 g) fresh orecchiette
- 1$^3/_4$ cups (200 g) freshly grated pecorino cheese

Trim the stem of the broccoli and dice into small cubes. Divide the broccoli heads into small florets. Boil the stem and florets in a large pot of salted water for about 8 minutes, or until tender. • Drain the broccoli well, reserving the water to cook the pasta. • In a large frying pan, sauté the garlic in the oil until pale golden brown. • Add the broccoli and chile, season with salt, and cook over low heat for 5 more minutes. • Remove from heat. • Meanwhile, bring the water used to cook the broccoli back to a boil, add the pasta, and cook until al dente (about 20 minutes). • Drain well, and add to the broccoli in the pan. • Toss over high heat for 1–2 minutes. Remove from heat, sprinkle with the pecorino, and serve.

ORECCHIETTE WITH POTATOES AND PECORINO

Bring a large pan of salted water to a boil. Add the potatoes and simmer for 10 minutes.
• Add the orecchiette and simmer until al dente.
• Drain the pasta and potatoes and place in a large serving bowl. Chop the potatoes into bite-size pieces. • Add the hot tomato sauce, parsley, and pecorino and toss gently. • Serve hot.

Serves: 4–6

Preparation: 15 min.

Cooking: 20 min.

Level of difficulty: 1

• 1 lb (500 g) fresh orecchiette
• 4 medium potatoes, peeled and cut in half
• 1 recipe Tomato Sauce (see page 948)
• 1 tbsp finely chopped fresh parsley
• $^1/_2$ cup (60 g) freshly grated pecorino cheese

LEMON ORECCHIETTE

Serves: 4

Preparation: 10 min.

Cooking: 20 min.

Level of difficulty: 2

Heat the oil in a large frying pan over medium heat. • Add the garlic and sauté for 1 minute. Add the fennel and sauté until tender, 5–7 minutes. • Drizzle with the lemon juice and season with salt. • Transfer the fennel to a plate using a slotted spoon. • Add the bread crumbs to the frying pan and sauté over medium heat for 3–4 minutes, until golden brown and crispy. • Return the fennel to the pan. Add the lemon zest and the pepper flakes. Mix well and then remove from the heat. • Cook the pasta in a large pot of salted boiling water until al dente. • Drain and add to the sauce. • Sauté over high heat for 1 minute. • Sprinkle with the pecorino and serve.

- $^1/_4$ cup (60 ml) extra-virgin olive oil
- 2 cloves garlic, finely chopped
- 2 bulbs fennel, sliced
- Freshly squeezed juice of $^1/_2$ lemon
- Salt
- 1 cup (60 g) fresh bread crumbs
- Finely grated zest of $^1/_2$ lemon
- Pinch of red pepper flakes
- 14 oz (400 g) fresh orecchiette
- $^1/_2$ cup (60 g) freshly grated pecorino or Parmesan cheese

Preparation: 30 min.
+ 2 hr. to soak the
tofu

Cooking: 2 hr

Level of difficulty: 3

- 2 tbsp extra-virgin olive oil
- 1 carrot, finely chopped
- 1 stalk celery, finely chopped
- 1 onion, finely chopped
- 1 clove garlic, finely chopped
- 2 tbsp finely chopped fresh parsley
- $^1/_2$ cup (125 ml) dry red wine
- 2 cups (500 g) chopped tomatoes
- 1 lb (500 g) dehydrated tofu, soaked for 2 hours, drained
- 1 lb (500 g) lasagne
- 2 tbsp butter
- 1 cup (125 g) freshly grated Parmesan cheese
- 1 recipe Béchamel Sauce (see page 956)

VEGETARIAN LASAGNE

Heat the oil in a large frying pan and sauté the carrot, celery, onion, garlic, and parsley for 7–8 minutes. • Add the wine and cook until evaporated. • Add the tomatoes and tofu, season with salt and pepper, and simmer over low heat for 90 minutes. • Preheat the oven to 400°F (200°C/gas 6). • Blanch the pasta and lay the sheets out on a damp cloth. • Prepare the Béchamel. • Smear the bottom of a large baking dish with butter. Line with a single layer of cooked lasagne sheets. Cover with thin layers of Béchamel and tomato sauce. Sprinkle with grated Parmesan, followed by another layer of lasagne. Repeat until there are at least 6 layers. Finish with a layer of Béchamel and Parmesan. Top with the butter.
- Bake until golden brown, 15–20 minutes.
- Serve hot.

LASAGNA WITH MEATBALLS

If using homemade pasta, prepare the pasta dough following the instructions on page 372. To make lasagne, cut the dough into 3 x 12-inch (8 x 30-cm) sheets. • Blanch the pasta and lay the sheets out on a damp cloth. • Prepare the meat sauce. • Preheat the oven to 400°F (200°C/gas 6). • Oil a baking dish. • Meatballs: Mix the beef, eggs, and pecorino in a large bowl. Season with salt and pepper and form into balls the size of hazelnuts. • Add the meatballs to the meat sauce and cook for 10 minutes. • Lay the first layer of lasagna in the prepared baking dish along the bottom and against the sides of the dish, extending far enough so that you can lay it back over the top layer. Cover with some of the meat sauce, the mozzarella, hard-boiled eggs, and pecorino. Continue to layer the ingredients for a total of five layers. Fold the extra pasta over the top. Dot with the butter and sprinkle with any remaining Pecorino. • Bake for 35–40 minutes, or until golden brown. • Let rest at room temperature for 20 minutes before serving.

Serves: 6

Preparation: 1 hr. + time to make the pasta

Cooking: 2 hr.

Level of difficulty: 2

- **1 recipe pasta dough (see page 372) or 14 oz (400 g) store-bought lasagne**
- **1 recipe Meat Sauce (see page 951)**

Meatballs
- **12 oz (300 g) ground (minced) beef**
- **2 large eggs**
- **2 tbsp freshly grated pecorino cheese**
- **Salt and freshly ground black pepper**
- **8 oz (250 g) mozzarella cheese, sliced**
- **3 hard-boiled eggs, finely chopped**
- **$^3/_4$ cup (90 g) freshly grated pecorino cheese**
- **2 tbsp butter, cut into flakes**

SOUTHERN LASAGNA WITH MEATBALLS

If using homemade pasta, prepare the pasta dough following the instructions on page 372. To make lasagne, cut the dough into 3 x 12-inch (8 x 30-cm) sheets. • Blanch the pasta and lay the pieces out on a damp cloth. • Meatballs: Mix the beef, egg, parsley, and salt and pepper in a large bowl until well blended. Form into small balls the size of hazelnuts. • Heat the frying oil in a large frying pan until very hot. Fry the meatballs in small batches for 5–7 minutes, or until golden brown. • Drain and pat dry on paper towels. • Preheat the oven to 400°F (200°C/gas 6). • Grease a baking dish with oil and sprinkle with bread crumbs. • Lay the first layer of pasta in the baking dish and top with the eggs, one-fifth of the sauce, and one-fifth of the meatballs. Continue until you have a total of five layers. Sprinkle with the cheeses. • Bake for 40–45 minutes, or until the top is golden brown. • Serve hot.

Serves: 6

Preparation: 2 hr.

Cooking: 60–80 min.

Level of difficulty: 2

- 1 recipe pasta dough (see page 372) or 14 oz (400 g) store-bought lasagne

Meatballs

- 12 oz (300 g) ground (minced) beef
- 1 egg
- 1 tbsp finely chopped fresh parsley
- Salt and freshly ground black pepper
- $1^1/_4$ cups (300 ml) olive oil, for frying
- 3 hard-boiled eggs, finely chopped
- 2 cups (500 ml) store-bought unseasoned tomato sauce
- 10 oz (300 g) Caciocavallo or ricotta salata cheese, thinly sliced
- 7 oz (200 g) mozzarella cheese, thinly sliced
- $^3/_4$ cup (90 g) freshly grated pecorino cheese

Serves: 6

Preparation: 1 hr.
+ time to make
the pasta

Cooking: 3 hr.

Level of difficulty: 2

- 1 recipe pasta
  dough (see page
  372) or
  14 oz (400 g)
  store-bought
  lasagne

Meat Sauce
- 5 oz (150 g)
  prosciutto (Parma
  ham), chopped
- 1 onion, chopped
- 1 stalk celery,
  chopped
- 1 carrot, finely
  chopped
- 8 oz (250 g) ground
  (minced) beef
- $1/3$ cup (90 ml) dry
  white wine
- $2/3$ cup (150 g)
  chopped tomatoes
- $1/2$ cup (125 ml)
  Beef Stock (see
  page 946) + more
  as needed
- Salt and freshly
  ground black
  pepper
- 1 recipe
  Béchamel Sauce
  (see page 956)
- $3/4$ cup (90 g)
  freshly grated
  Parmesan cheese

LASAGNA, FERRARA STYLE

If using homemade pasta, prepare the pasta dough following the instructions on page 372. To make lasagne, cut the dough into 3 x 12-inch (8 x 30-cm) sheets. • Blanch the pasta and lay the pieces out on a damp cloth. • Meat Sauce: Sauté the prosciutto, onion, celery, and carrot in the butter in a large frying pan over medium heat for 2 minutes until browned. • Add the beef and cook for 2–3 minutes until browned all over. • Pour in the wine and let it evaporate. • Stir in the tomatoes and ½ cup (125 ml) of stock. Season with salt, cover, and simmer over low heat for about 2 hours, adding more stock if needed. Season with salt and pepper. • Preheat the oven to 400°F (200°C/gas 6). • Butter a baking dish. • Place alternate layers of pasta, meat sauce, Béchamel, and Parmesan in the prepared dish. • Bake for 20–25 minutes, or until bubbling. • Serve hot.

FILLED PASTA

TORTELLINI WITH TRUFFLES

Prepare the pasta dough. Wrap in plastic wrap (cling film) and let rest. • Filling: Heat the butter in a large frying pan and sauté the pork and chicken over medium heat for about 5 minutes. Remove from the pan and chop finely in a food processor. • Sauté the prosciutto and mortadella in the same pan for 2–3 minutes. • Combine the pork, chicken, prosciutto, and mortadella in a bowl. Add the eggs, ½ cup (60 g) of Parmesan, nutmeg, salt, and pepper. Mix well and set aside. • Prepare the tortellini: Use a pasta machine to roll the pasta dough out into thin sheets. Cut the sheets in strips about 2 inches (5 cm) wide, then cut into squares. • Place teaspoons of the filling mixture at the center of each. • Moisten the edges of the pasta with a little water and fold over into a triangular shape. Fold the top of the triangle over and twist around your index finger. Pinch the edges together and seal them. • Lay the tortellini out on clean cloths for 2 hours before cooking. • Cook the tortellini in a large pot of salted, boiling water until the sealed edges of the pasta are al dente. • To make the sauce, melt the remaining butter in a saucepan over low heat. Stir in the cream and cook for 2–3 minutes. • When the tortellini are cooked, drain well and place in the pan with the cream. Add the remaining Parmesan, the truffle, salt, and pepper, and toss gently over medium-low heat for 2–3 minutes. Serve hot.

Serves: 4

Preparation: 25 min. + 3 hr. to make the pasta

Cooking: 10 min.

Level of difficulty: 3

- **1 recipe pasta dough (see page 372)**

Filling
- **2 tbsp butter**
- **2 oz (60 g) boneless lean pork, coarsely chopped**
- **2 oz (60 g) chicken breast, coarsely chopped**
- **2 oz (60 g) prosciutto (Parma ham), finely chopped**
- **4 oz (125 g) mortadella, finely chopped**
- **2 large eggs**
- **³/₄ cup (90 g) freshly grated Parmesan cheese**
- **¹/₄ tsp nutmeg**
- **Salt and freshly ground black pepper**

Sauce
- **¹/₃ cup (90 g) butter**
- **¹/₂ cup (125 ml) heavy (double) cream**
- **1 small truffle, white or black, in shavings**

TORTELLINI WITH WOODCUTTERS' SAUCE

Prepare the pasta dough. Wrap in plastic wrap (cling film) and let rest. • Prepare the tortellini filling and set aside. • Cook the peas in boiling water. Drain and set aside. • Put the mushrooms, garlic, and parsley in a large frying pan with the oil and cook for 5 minutes, or until the mushroom liquid has evaporated. Add the tomatoes and simmer for about 20 minutes. Add the peas and season with salt and pepper. Cook for 3–4 more minutes. • While the sauce is cooking, prepare the tortellini as explained on page 420. • Cook in a large pot of salted, boiling water until the sealed edges of the pasta are al dente. Drain well and place in the pan with the sauce. Toss gently and serve hot.

Serves: 4–6

Preparation: 25 min. + 3 hr. to make the pasta

Cooking: 35 min.

Level of difficulty: 3

- 1 recipe pasta dough (see page 372)
- 1 recipe filling (see page 420)
- 2 cups (300 g) frozen peas
- 14 oz (400 g) coarsely chopped mushrooms
- 2 cloves garlic, finely chopped
- 3 tbsp finely chopped fresh parsley
- 1/4 cup (60 ml) extra-virgin olive oil
- 2 (14-oz/400-g) cans tomatoes, chopped
- Salt and freshly ground black pepper

TORTELLI WITH SWISS CHARD

Prepare the pasta dough. Wrap in plastic wrap (cling film) and let rest. • Filling: Boil the Swiss chard in a large pan of salted, boiling water until tender, about 10 minutes. Drain well, squeezing out excess moisture, and chop finely. • Melt the butter in a large frying pan and add the Swiss chard. Season with salt and nutmeg and sauté for 10 minutes. • Remove from the heat and let cool a little. • Add the ricotta and Parmesan, mixing well. • Use a pasta machine to roll the pasta dough out into thin sheets. Lay the pasta sheets out on a clean work surface. • Shape the filling into balls the size of marbles and place at regular intervals on half the sheets of pasta. Cover with the remaining sheets of pasta, pressing down gently between the mounds of filling with your fingertips. Cut out the tortelli using a fluted pasta cutter. • Bring a large pan of salted water to a boil. • Cook the tortelli in batches until al dente, 3–4 minutes per batch. • Remove with a slotted spoon and place in a heated serving dish. • Serve hot with the butter and freshly grated Parmesan cheese.

Serves: 4–6

Preparation: 45 min. + 30 min. to rest the pasta

Cooking: 15 min.

Level of difficulty: 3

- 1 recipe pasta dough (see page 372)

Filling
- 1 1/2 lb (750 g) tender Swiss chard (silver beet) leaves, tough stalks removed
- 1/3 cup (90 g) butter
- Salt
- Pinch of nutmeg
- 8 oz (250 g) fresh ricotta cheese, drained
- 1 cup (120 g) freshly grated Parmesan cheese

To Serve
- 1/2 cup (125 g) butter, melted
- 1 cup (120 g) freshly grated Parmesan cheese

POTATO TORTELLI WITH MEAT SAUCE

Prepare the meat sauce. • Prepare the pasta dough. Wrap in plastic wrap (cling film) and let rest. • Cook the potatoes in a pot of salted, boiling water for 25 minutes, or until tender. Drain, slip off their skins, and mash. Place in a large bowl with the egg, half the Parmesan, the butter, nutmeg, salt, and pepper. Mix well and set aside. • Use a pasta machine to roll the pasta dough out into thin sheets. Lay out on a clean work surface. • Place heaped teaspoons of the filling at regular intervals on half the sheets of pasta. Cover with the remaining sheets of pasta, pressing down gently between the mounds of filling with your fingertips. Cut out the tortelli using a fluted pasta cutter.
• Cook the tortelli in a large pot of salted, boiling water until the sealed edges of the pasta are al dente. Drain and transfer to a serving dish. • Serve with the meat sauce and remaining Parmesan.

Serves: 4

Preparation: 30 min. + time to make the pasta and sauce

Cooking: 35 min.

Level of difficulty: 3

- 1 recipe Meat Sauce (see page 951)
- 1 recipe pasta dough (see page 372)

Filling
- 2 lb (1 kg) potatoes
- 1 large egg
- 1 cup (120 g) freshly grated Parmesan cheese
- 2 tbsp butter
- Pinch of nutmeg
- Salt and freshly ground black pepper

AMARETTI AND SPICE TORTELLI

Serves: 6

Preparation: 1 hr.
+ time to make
the pasta

Cooking: 20 min.

Level of difficulty: 3

- **1 recipe pasta dough (see page 372)**

Filling
- **3 tbsp fresh bread crumbs**
- **2 tbsp butter**
- **1¹/₄ cups (150 g) crushed amaretti cookies**
- **1¹/₄ cups (150 g) freshly grated Parmesan cheese**
- **¹/₄ cup (50 g) golden raisins (sultanas)**
- **¹/₂ cup (50 g) finely chopped candied lemon peel**
- **1 large egg**
- **1 tsp allspice (cloves, nutmeg, cinnamon in equal quantities)**
- **Salt and freshly ground white pepper**
- **1–2 tbsp vegetable stock (optional)**

To Serve
- **²/₃ cup (150 g), melted**
- **¹/₂ cup (60 g) freshly grated Parmesan cheese**

Prepare the meat sauce. • Prepare the pasta dough. Wrap in plastic wrap (cling film) and let rest. • Filling: Toast the bread crumbs in 2 tbsp of the butter in a medium pan over medium heat for 5 minutes until crispy. • Transfer to a large bowl with the amaretti cookies, 1¹/₄ cups (150 g) of the Parmesan, raisins, candied lemon peel, egg, and spices. Season with salt and pepper. If the mixture is dry and crumbly, add the stock. • Use a pasta machine to roll the pasta dough out into thin sheets. Use a fluted pastry wheel to cut into 2-inch (5-cm) squares. • Drop a teaspoon of filling into the center of each one. Fold into triangles and seal well. • Cook the pasta in a large pot of salted boiling water for 3–5 minutes until al dente. • Remove with a slotted spoon and transfer to a serving dish. Drizzle with the melted butter and sprinkle with the Parmesan.

POTATO AND RICOTTA TORTELLI

Prepare the pasta dough. Wrap in plastic wrap (cling film) and let rest. • Boil the potatoes in a large pan of lightly salted water until tender. Drain well and slip off the skins. Mash until smooth. • Sauté the pancetta, onion, and garlic in a large frying pan over medium heat until pale golden brown, about 5 minutes. • Season generously with pepper and add to the potatoes. • Stir in the ricotta and Parmesan and season with salt, pepper, and nutmeg. Set aside to cool completely. • Use a pasta machine to roll the pasta dough out into thin sheets. Lay out on a clean work surface. • Shape the filling into balls the size of large marbles and place at regular intervals on half the sheets of pasta. flatten them slightly. Cover with the remaining sheets of pasta, pressing down gently between the mounds of filling with your fingertips. Cut out the tortelli using a fluted pasta cutter. • Bring a large pan of salted water to a boil. • Cook the tortelli in batches until al dente, 3–4 minutes per batch. • Remove with a slotted spoon. • Serve hot with melted butter and plenty of freshly grated Parmesan cheese.

Serves: 6–8

Preparation: 1 hr. + time to make the pasta

Cooking: 15 min.

Level: 3

- 1 **recipe pasta dough (see page 372)**

Filling
- 2 lb (1 kg) potatoes
- 3 oz (90 g) pancetta, finely chopped
- 1 medium white onion, finely chopped
- 2 cloves garlic, finely chopped
- 5 oz (150 g) ricotta cheese, drained
- $^1/_2$ cup (60 g) freshly grated Parmesan cheese
- Freshly grated nutmeg
- Salt and freshly ground black pepper

- Melted butter and freshly grated Parmesan cheese to serve

POTATO RAVIOLI WITH ZUCCHINI SAUCE

Serves: 4–6

Preparation: 40 min.

Cooking: 50 min.

Level of difficulty: 3

- 1 lb (500 g) floury (baking) potatoes
- 1¹/₃ cups (200 g) all-purpose (plain) flour
- 2 large egg yolks, lightly beaten
- Salt
- 4 oz (125 g) soft goat cheese
- 1 tbsp freshly grated Parmesan
- 1 large egg white, lightly beaten
- ¹/₄ cup (60 ml) extra-virgin olive oil
- 1 shallot, finely chopped
- 3 large zucchini (courgettes), sliced
- ³/₄ cup (180 ml) boiling vegetable stock
- Leaves from 2 sprigs of basil

Cook the potatoes in a large pot of salted boiling water until tender, 20–25 minutes. Drain well and transfer to a large bowl. • Purée the potatoes using a potato ricer and let cool. Add the flour and the egg yolks. Season with salt and mix well to make a smooth dough. • Turn the dough out onto the lightly floured surface and knead until smooth and elastic, 5 minutes. • Roll out the dough on a lightly floured surface to ¼-inch (5 mm) thick. • Cut into 2 inch (5 cm) disks using a cookie cutter. • Beat the goat cheese with the Parmesan in a small bowl to make a smooth paste. • Put hazelnut-sized balls of this mixture on half the disks. • Brush the edges of the disks with the beaten egg white. • Cover with the remaining disks and press gently around the edges of each ravioli to seal. • Arrange the ravioli on a lightly floured plate. • Heat the oil in a large frying pan over medium heat. • Add the shallot and sauté until tender, 3–4 minutes. • Add the zucchini and stock. • Mix well, cover, and simmer until the zucchini are very tender, about 10 minutes. • Transfer the zucchini to a blender, reserving 2 tablespoons. • Add the basil and blend to make a smooth purée. • Cook the ravioli in small batches in a large pot of salted boiling water for 3–5 minutes. • Transfer to a serving dish using a slotted spoon. • Serve hot with the zucchini sauce and reserved zucchini.

TORTELLONI WITH BEEF, SPINACH, AND ROSEMARY

Prepare the pasta dough. Wrap in plastic wrap (cling film) and let rest. • Filling: Heat ¼ cup (60 g) of butter with the rosemary in a medium saucepan and sauté for 2–3 minutes. Add the beef and wine, and simmer over low heat for 2 hours. When the beef is very tender, chop finely in a food processor. • Cook the spinach in a pot of salted water for 8–10 minutes, or until tender. Squeeze out excess moisture and chop finely. • Combine the beef and spinach in a bowl and add the eggs, Parmesan, and nutmeg. Season with salt and pepper. Mix well and set aside for 1 hour. • Use a pasta machine to roll the pasta dough out into thin sheets. Prepare the tortelli as explained on page 428. • Cook the tortelli in a large pot of salted, boiling water until al dente. Drain and place in a heated serving dish. • Put the Fontina, remaining butter, and nutmeg in a small saucepan over very low heat until the cheese has melted.
• Pour over the tortelli and serve hot.

Serves: 4

Preparation: 25 min. + time to make the pasta

Cooking: 2 hr. 15 min.

Level of difficulty: 3

- 1 recipe pasta dough (see page 372)

Filling
- ³/₄ cup (180 g) butter
- 1 tbsp finely chopped fresh rosemary
- 12 oz (350 g) lean beef
- 2 tbsp dry white wine
- 8 oz (250 g) spinach
- 1 large egg and 1 large egg yolk
- ¹/₄ cup (30 g) freshly grated Parmesan cheese
- Pinch of nutmeg
- Salt and freshly ground black pepper

- 8 oz (250 g) Fontina cheese, diced
- ¹/₂ tsp nutmeg

TORTELLONI WITH PUMPKIN

Prepare the pasta dough. Wrap in plastic wrap (cling film) and let rest. • Preheat the oven to 400°F (200°C/gas 6). • Without peeling the pumpkin, scrape away the seeds and fibers and cut it in slices about 1½ inches (4 cm) thick. • Bake in the oven until tender. • Remove the flesh from the skin. Mash and place in a mixing bowl while still hot. • Stir in three-quarters of the Parmesan, the egg, nutmeg, bread crumbs, and salt. • Cover the bowl with plastic wrap (cling film) and leave to stand for 2 hours. • Use a pasta machine to roll the pasta dough out into thin sheets. Prepare the tortelloni as explained on page 420. • Cook the tortelloni in a large pot of salted, boiling water until the sealed edges of the pasta are al dente. • Drain well. Drizzle with the butter and sprinkle with the remaining Parmesan. Serve hot.

Serves: 4

Preparation: 1 hr.
+ time to make
the pasta

Cooking: 30 min.

Level of difficulty: 3

- **1 recipe pasta dough (see page 372)**

Filling
- **2½ lb (1.25 kg) fresh pumpkin**
- **1¾ cups (200 g) freshly grated Parmesan cheese**
- **1 large egg**
- **Pinch of nutmeg**
- **¾ cup (120 g) fine dry bread crumbs**
- **Salt**
- **¾ cup (180 g) butter, melted**

Serves: 6–8

Preparation: 2 hr. +
12 hr. to marinate

Cooking: 5–6 hr.

Level: 3

- **1 recipe pasta dough (see page 372)**

Filling
- **2 tbsp butter**
- **3 tbsp cooking juices from roast meat**
- **3 oz (90 g) Savoy cabbage, finely chopped**
- **1 small leek, white part only, finely chopped**
- **2 oz (60 g) Italian sausage meat**
- **6 oz (180 g) each of lean roast beef and pork, chopped**
- **1 large egg**
- **2 tbsp freshly grated Parmesan cheese**
- **Dash of nutmeg**
- **Dalt and freshly ground white pepper**

Sauce
- **$^1/_2$ cup (125 g) butter, melted**
- **6 fresh sage leaves**
- **Freshly grated Parmesan cheese**

AGNOLOTTI WITH BUTTER AND SAGE

Prepare the pasta dough. Wrap in plastic wrap (cling film) and let rest. • Filling: Melt the butter in a saucepan and add the meat juices, cabbage, leek, and sausage meat. Simmer for 5–6 minutes, stirring frequently and moistening, if necessary, with a little water. Let cool a little. • Place the filling in a bowl with the chopped roast meats, egg, Parmesan, nutmeg, salt, and pepper. Transfer to a food processor and chop finely. • Use a pasta machine to roll the pasta dough out into thin sheets. Prepare the agnolotti following the instructions for tortelli as explained on page 428. • Spread out in a single layer on a lightly-floured clean cloth and leave to dry in a cool place for at least 2 hours. • Cook the agnolotti in a large pot of salted, boiling water until the pasta round the sealed edges is al dente. • Drain thoroughly and transfer to a heated serving dish. • Heat the butter and sage until golden brown and drizzle over the ravioli. Sprinkle with Parmesan and serve hot.

437

AGNOLOTTI WITH MEAT SAUCE

Prepare the meat sauce. • Prepare the pasta dough. Wrap in plastic wrap (cling film) and let rest. • Prepare the filling. • Use a pasta machine to roll the pasta dough out into thin sheets. Prepare the agnolotti following the instructions for tortelli as explained on page 428. • Spread out in a single layer on a lightly-floured clean cloth and leave to dry in a cool place for at least 2 hours. • Cook the agnolotti in a large pot of salted, boiling water until the pasta round the sealed edges is al dente. Drain well and place on a heated serving dish. • Cover with the meat sauce. Sprinkle with the Parmesan and, if using, shavings of white truffle. Serve hot.

Serves: 4

Preparation: 30 min. + time to make the pasta and meat sauce

Cooking: 15 min.

Level of difficulty: 3

• 1 recipe pasta dough (see page 372)

• 1 recipe filling (see page 436)
• 1 recipe Meat Sauce (see page 952)
• $1/4$ cup freshly grated Parmesan cheese
• 1 white truffle, in shavings (optional)

MARENGO AGNOLOTTI

Place the onion, carrot, and celery in a medium stainless steel or enamel saucepan. Add the beef and pork. Cover with the garlic, rosemary, bay leaf, sage, cinnamon, cloves, nutmeg, salt, and peppercorns. Pour in the wine. Marinate in the refrigerator for 12 hours. • Remove the meat from the marinade and set aside. Discard the sage, rosemary, and garlic. Set the cinnamon stick, cloves, bay leaf, and peppercorns aside. Reserve the wine. • Chop the remaining vegetables in a food processor. • Return the chopped vegetables to the saucepan used to marinate them. Add the oil, lard, and butter and simmer over low heat until softened, 7–8 minutes. • Add the beef and pork. Sauté on medium heat until the meat is browned, about 10 minutes. • Pour in the reserved wine and simmer until it has evaporated. Add the cinnamon stick, cloves, bay leaf, and peppercorns. • Pour in the water, partially cover the pan, and simmer on low for 2 hours. • Bring a large pan of salted water to a boil. Add the cabbage leaves and simmer until tender, about 15 minutes. • Drain well, squeezing out excess moisture. • Remove the sauce from the heat and let cool for a few minutes. Take out the beef and pork and chop in a food processor with the cabbage and sausage meat. • Return to very low heat and simmer until ready to serve. • Stir the egg, Parmesan, and bread crumbs into the filling mixture. Season with salt. • Prepare the agnolotti following the instructions on page 438. • Cook the agnolotti in batches until al dente, 3–4 minutes per batch. • Serve hot with the sauce.

Serves: 4

Preparation 2 hr.
+ 12 hr. to marinate

Cooking 3 hr.

Level: 3

- 1 white onion, 1 carrot, 1 stalk celery, finely chopped
- 5 oz (150 g) beef, in bite-size pieces
- 2 oz (60 g) pork in bite-size pieces
- 2 cloves garlic
- 1 sprig rosemary
- 1 bay leaf
- 3 sage leaves
- 1 stick cinnamon
- 2 cloves
- Freshly grated nutmeg
- Salt
- 4 black pepper corns
- $^1/_2$ cup (125 ml) dry red wine
- $^1/_4$ cup (60 ml) extra-virgin olive oil
- 3 tbsp lard
- 1 tbsp butter
- 4 oz (125 g) Italian sausage meat
- 2 cups (500 ml) boiling water
- 4 oz (125 g) cabbage
- 1 egg
- $^1/_2$ cup (60 g) freshly grated Parmesan cheese
- 2 tbsp fine dry bread crumbs
- 1 recipe pasta dough (see page 372)

CHESTNUT TORTELLI

Pasta Dough: Mound both flours with the salt on a work surface and make a well in the center. Add the eggs and enough water to make a smooth dough. Knead for 15–20 minutes, until smooth and elastic. Shape the dough into a ball, wrap in plastic wrap (cling film), and let rest for 30 minutes. • Filling: Blanch in boiling water for 10 minutes. • Drain and peel. Transfer to a large saucepan and add enough water to cover. Season with salt and add the bay leaf. • Simmer for 35–45 minutes, or until tender. Drain. • Mash the chestnuts and add the ricotta, eggs, and ¾ cup (90 g) Parmesan. Season with salt and pepper. • Roll out the pasta dough on a lightly floured work surface until paper-thin. Cut into 2-inch (5-cm) rounds and drop a small amount of filling in the center. Fold over to seal in a semi-circular shape. • Cook in a large pot of salted boiling water for 3–5 minutes. • Drain well. Drizzle with the butter and sprinkle with the remaining Parmesan.

Serves: 6–8

Preparation: 2 hr.

Cooking: 45 min.

Level of difficulty: 3

Pasta Dough
- 2¹/₃ cups (350 g) all-purpose (plain) flour
- 1 cup (150 g) chestnut flour
- ¹/₄ tsp salt
- 3 large eggs, beaten
- 2–3 tbsp warm water

Filling
- 1¹/₂ lb (750 g) chestnuts, cut in half
- Salt
- 1 bay leaf
- ³/₄ cup (200 g) ricotta cheese
- 2 large eggs
- 1¹/₂ cups (180 g) freshly grated Parmesan cheese
- ¹/₂ cup (125 g) butter, melted
- Salt and freshly ground black pepper

SWEET FRIED RAVIOLI

Serves: 4

*Preparation: 40 min.
+ 30 min. to rest
the dough*

Cooking: 30 min.

Level of difficulty: 3

Pasta Dough
- 1¹/₃ cups (200 g) all-purpose (plain) flour
- ¹/₄ tsp salt
- 2 large eggs, beaten

Ricotta Filling
- 1³/₄ cups (480 g) ricotta cheese, well-drained
- 1 large egg + 1 egg yolk, beaten
- 1 tbsp sugar
- ¹/₄ tsp ground cinnamon

To Serve
- 1 cup (250 ml) peanut oil, for frying
- ¹/₂ cup (75 g) confectioners' (icing) sugar, to dust

Pasta Dough: Mound the flour and salt on a work surface and make a well in the center. Add the eggs and mix in to form a firm dough. Knead for 15–20 minutes, until smooth and elastic. • Press the dough into a disk, wrap in plastic wrap (cling film), and let rest for 30 minutes. • Ricotta Filling: Mix the ricotta, egg and egg yolk, sugar, and cinnamon in a large bowl. • Roll out the dough on a lightly floured work surface until very thin. Cut into 8-inch (20-cm) long strips and arrange pellets of filling near one edge about ¾ inch (2 cm) apart. Fold each strip of dough lengthwise to cover the filling. Seal, then cut into squares with a fluted pasta wheel. • Heat the oil in a large frying pan until very hot. Fry the ravioli in small batches until golden brown. • Drain and pat dry on paper towels. • Dust with confectioners' sugar and serve hot.

RAVIOLI WITH ZUCCHINI IN BUTTER AND ROSEMARY SAUCE

Serves: 4

Preparation: 30 min.
+ time to make
the pasta

Cooking: 10 min.

Level of difficulty: 3

- 1 recipe pasta dough (see page 372)

Filling
- 2 medium zucchini (courgettes)
- 1 cup crushed amaretti cookies
- $^2/_3$ cup (150 g) fresh ricotta cheese
- 1 cup (120 g) freshly grated Parmesan cheese
- $^1/_4$ tsp nutmeg
- Salt
- 1 clove garlic, finely chopped
- $^1/_2$ cup (125 g) butter
- 2 tbsp finely chopped fresh rosemary

Prepare the pasta dough. Wrap in plastic wrap (cling film) and let rest. • Cook the zucchini in a pot of salted, boiling water until tender. Drain, place in a bowl, and mash with a fork. Add the amaretti, ricotta, two-thirds of the Parmesan, and nutmeg. Season with salt. Mix well to form a thick cream. If the filling is too liquid, add dry bread crumbs; if it is too thick, add a little milk. • Prepare the ravioli as shown on page 428. • Cook the ravioli in a large pot of salted, boiling water until the sealed edges of the pasta are al dente. Drain well and place in a heated serving dish. • Place the garlic in a small saucepan with the butter and rosemary and cook for 3–4 minutes over medium heat, stirring frequently. • Pour the sauce over the ravioli, sprinkle with the remaining Parmesan, and serve hot.

FISH RAVIOLI

P ut the garlic and oil in a small bowl and let stand for at least 2 hours. Discard the garlic.
• Prepare the pasta dough. Wrap in plastic wrap (cling film) and let rest. • Filling: Melt the butter in a saucepan over low heat. Add the fish and cook for 1 minute. • Increase the heat to high and pour in the vermouth and cook until evaporated. • Stir in the flour and cook briefly. • Add the cream and fish stock and season with salt and pepper. Simmer for 5 minutes. • Remove from the heat and let cool. • Process with the eggs, 2 tablespoons of the garlic oil, and parsley in a food processor. • Transfer to a pastry bag and set aside. • Roll out the dough on a lightly floured surface until paper-thin. Cut into 4-inch (10-cm) wide strips and arrange small heaps of filling near one edge, about 3 inches (7 cm) apart. Fold each strip of dough lengthwise to cover the filling. • Use a fluted pasta wheel to cut out ravioli. • Lay them on a floured surface to dry.
• Tomato Sauce: Heat the remaining garlic oil in a large frying pan. Add the tomatoes and thyme.
• Cook the pasta in a large pot of salted boiling water for 3–4 minutes. • Drain, reserving 2 tablespoons of the cooking water. Add the pasta and cooking water to the sauce and serve hot.

Serves: 6

Preparation: 2 hr.
+ 30 min. to rest

Cooking: 30 min.

Level of difficulty: 3

• 2 cloves garlic, lightly crushed but whole
• $1/4$ cup (60 ml) extra-virgin olive oil

• 1 recipe pasta dough (see page 372)

Filling
• $1/3$ cup (90 g) butter
• $1^3/4$ lb (800 g) white fish fillets, coarsely chopped (such as sole or sea bass)
• $1/4$ cup (60 ml) dry vermouth
• $1/2$ cup (75 g) all-purpose (plain) flour
• $2/3$ cup (150 ml) heavy (double) cream
• $2/3$ cup (150 ml) fish stock
• Salt and freshly ground white pepper
• 2 large eggs
• 2 tbsp finely chopped parsley

Tomato Sauce
• 2 cups (500 g) chopped tomatoes
• 1 tbsp finely chopped fresh thyme
• Salt

FISH RAVIOLI WITH VEGETABLE SAUCE

Prepare the pasta dough. Wrap in plastic wrap (cling film) and let rest. • Melt the butter in a frying pan. Add the fish and cook over medium heat for 5 minutes, or until tender. Chop the fish very finely. • Cook the Swiss chard in a pot of salted water for 8–10 minutes, or until tender. Squeeze out excess moisture and chop finely. • Combine the fish and chard in a bowl with the Ricotta, eggs, half the Parmesan, and nutmeg. Season with salt and mix well. • Prepare the ravioli as shown on page 428. • Put the mushrooms in a small bowl of warm water and soak for 15 minutes. • Drain well and chop finely. • Put the celery, onion, parsley, and butter in the pan used to cook the fish. Add the tomatoes and water, and simmer over low heat for 20 minutes. Season with salt and add the pine nuts. • Cook the ravioli in a large pot of salted boiling for 3-4 minutes. Drain and place in a heated serving dish. • Pour the sauce over the top, sprinkle with the remaining Parmesan, and serve.

Serves: 4

Preparation: 30 min. + time to make the pasta

Cooking: 40 min.

Level of difficulty: 3

- **1 recipe pasta dough (see page 372)**

Filling
- **$^1/_4$ cup (60 g) butter**
- **14 oz (400 g) bass fillets**
- **12 oz (350 g) fresh Swiss chard**
- **2 oz (60 g) fresh ricotta cheese**
- **2 large eggs**
- **1 cup (120 g) freshly grated Parmesan cheese**
- **$^1/_4$ tsp nutmeg**
- **Salt**

Sauce
- **2 tbsp dried mushrooms**
- **1 stalk celery, 1 onion, 1 tbsp parsley, all finely chopped**
- **$^1/_2$ cup (125 g) butter**
- **4 ripe tomatoes, peeled and chopped**
- **1 cup (250 ml) water**
- **$^1/_4$ cup (30 g) pine nuts, toasted and finely chopped**

Serves: 6

*Preparation: 1 hr.
+ 30 min. to rest the
dough*

Cooking: 30 min.

Level of difficulty: 3

- **1 recipe pasta dough
(see page 372)**

Filling

- **1 $2/3$ cups (400 g)
ricotta cheese**
- **2 large eggs**
- **5 tbsp sugar**
- **1 tbsp finely chopped
fresh parsley**
- **Finely grated zest
of $1/2$ lemon**
- **$1/8$ tsp freshly grated
nutmeg**
- **$1/8$ tsp cinnamon**
- **Salt and freshly
ground white pepper**

Tomato Sauce

- **3 tbsp extra-virgin
olive oil**
- **1 clove garlic, lightly
crushed but whole**
- **2 lb (1 kg) tomatoes,
peeled and chopped**
- **Salt and freshly
ground white pepper**
- **1 tbsp finely chopped
fresh parsley**
- **4 leaves basil, torn**
- **3 tbsp butter**
- **1 cup (125 g) freshly
grated Parmesan
cheese**

RICOTTA RAVIOLI WITH TOMATO SAUCE

Prepare the pasta dough. Wrap in plastic wrap (cling film) and let rest. • Filling: Mix the ricotta, eggs, sugar, parsley, lemon zest, nutmeg, cinnamon, salt, and pepper. • Use a pasta machine to roll the pasta dough out into thin sheets. Cut into 3-inch (8-cm) strips. • Place 1 tablespoon of the filling on each strip at regular intervals. Top with another strip of dough and use a fluted pasta wheel to cut into ravioli. • Tomato Sauce: Heat the oil in a large frying pan over medium heat. Add the garlic and sauté until pale gold, 3–4 minutes. Add the tomatoes and season with salt and pepper.
• Simmer for 20 minutes. • Discard the garlic and add the parsley, basil, and butter. • Cook the pasta in a large pot of salted boiling water until al dente, 2–3 minutes. • Drain well and transfer to a serving dish. Cover with the sauce and Parmesan and serve hot.

RAVIOLI WITH BEET FILLING

Prepare the pasta dough. Wrap in plastic wrap (cling film) and let rest. • Filling: Chop the beets and sauté in half the butter and a pinch of salt over high heat. • Remove from heat, stir in the ricotta, adding some bread crumbs if the mixture is too moist. • Prepare the ravioli as shown on page 428. • Cook the ravioli in a large pot of salted, boiling water until the sealed edges of the pasta are al dente. • Drain well. Place in a serving dish, dot with the remaining butter, and sprinkle with the poppy seeds. • Sprinkle with the Parmesan and serve hot.

Serves: 4

Preparation: 1 hr. + time to make the pasta

Cooking: 20 min.

Level of difficulty: 3

- **1 recipe pasta dough (see page 372)**

Filling
- **2 lb (1 kg) boiled beets (beet root)**
- **1 1/2 cups (375 g) butter**
- **Salt**
- **4 oz (125 g) fresh ricotta cheese**
- **1/2 cup (75 g) fine dry bread crumbs (optional))**
- **4 tsp poppy seeds**
- **1/2 cup (60 g) freshly grated Parmesan cheese**

CANNELLONI WITH RICOTTA

Preheat the oven to 400°F (200°C/gas 6).
• Cook the spinach in a pot of salted water until tender (about 5–6 minutes). Drain, squeeze out excess moisture and chop finely. • Put half the butter in a frying pan with the spinach. Season with salt and pepper. Cook briefly over high heat until the spinach has absorbed the flavor of the butter. • Transfer to a bowl and mix well with the ricotta, half the Parmesan, and the eggs. Season with salt and pepper. • Prepare the Béchamel. • Cook the cannelloni in a large pot of salted, boiling water until half-cooked (about 5 minutes). Drain in a colander and pass under cold running water. Dry with paper towels and stuff with the ricotta and spinach. • Line the bottom of a baking dish with a layer of Béchamel and place the cannelloni in a single layer on it. Cover with the remaining Béchamel sauce. Sprinkle with the remaining Parmesan and dot with butter. • Bake for about 20 minutes, or until a golden crust has formed on top. Serve hot.

Serves: 4

Preparation: 40 min.

Cooking: 20 min.

Level of difficulty: 2

- 1 lb (500 g) spinach
- $1/4$ cup (60 g) butter
- 1 cup (250 g) fresh ricotta cheese
- 1 cup (125 g) freshly grated Parmesan cheese
- 2 large eggs
- Salt and freshly ground black pepper
- 1 recipe Béchamel Sauce (see page 956)
- 12 store-bought fresh or dried cannelloni

SPINACH ROLL

Serves: 4–6

Preparation: 1 hr.

Cooking: 40 min.

Level of difficulty: 3

- ½ recipe pasta dough (see page 372)
- 2 cups (500 g) cooked, drained spinach
- ½ cup (125 g) butter, melted
- 1¼ cups (300 g) ricotta cheese
- 1 cup (125 g) freshly grated Parmesan cheese
- Salt and freshly ground white pepper
- 1 small bunch sage

Prepare the pasta dough. Wrap in plastic wrap (cling film) and let rest. • Finely chop the spinach and sauté in 7 tablespoons of butter in a large frying pan over medium heat for 2 minutes. • Remove from the heat and let cool completely. • Drain the ricotta in a fine mesh strainer and mix it in with ¾ cup (90 g) of Parmesan. Season with salt and pepper. • Roll out the pasta dough into a rectangle measuring about 8 x 15 inches (20 x 38 cm). • Use a large rubber spatula to spread the mixture over the pasta rectangle, leaving a small border at the edges. • Roll up and wrap the dough in a clean kitchen cloth. Tie each end with kitchen string and tie the roll in the center. • Bring a long saucepan (a fish poacher is ideal) filled with salted water to the boil. Lower the pasta roll into it and simmer over low heat for 30 minutes. • Remove from the water and remove from the cloth. • Slice the pasta roll ½-inch (1-cm) thick and arrange on serving plates. • Melt the remaining tablespoon of butter with the sage in a small saucepan. Discard the sage. Pour over the slices and sprinkle with remaining Parmesan.

SEAFOOD

GROUPER WITH PESTO

Prepare the pesto. • Rinse the grouper steaks under cold running water and dry with paper towels. • Heat a broiler (grill) to very hot and broil (grill) the grouper on both sides until cooked. Place in a warm oven. • Peel the tomatoes and chop finely. Crush the anchovies with the back of a fork. • Heat the oil in a small saucepan and add the tomatoes and anchovies. Simmer over medium heat for 10 minutes. • Add the pesto to the pan and heat, without letting it boil. • Pour the sauce over the grouper steaks and serve at once.

Serves: 4

Preparation: 10 min.

Cooking: 15 min.

Level of difficulty: 1

- 1 recipe Pesto (see page 945)
- 4 large grouper steaks, about 8 oz (250 g) each
- 2 large tomatoes
- 4 anchovy fillets
- 2 tbsp extra-virgin olive oil
- Salt and freshly ground black pepper

SEA BASS BAKED WITH WINE

Serves: 4

Preparation: 10 min.

Cooking: 25–30 min.

Level of difficulty: 1

- **2 lb (1 kg) sea bass, cleaned**
- **1 bottle (750 ml) dry white wine**
- **2 tbsp butter**
- **Salt**
- **2 lb (1 kg) potatoes, peeled, to serve**
- **Sprig of fresh parsley, to garnish**

Preheat the oven to 375°F (190°/gas 5). • Place the fish in a fish poacher. Pour in the wine and add the butter and salt. • Bake in the oven until the fish is tender, 25–30 minutes. • Cook the potatoes in a large pan of salted water until tender. Drain well. • Place the fish on a heated serving dish with the potatoes around it. Garnish with the parsley and serve hot.

GRILLED FISH FILLETS WITH FRESH HERBS

Place the fillets in a deep-sided dish and pour in the oil and lemon juice. Sprinkle with the parsley, thyme, sage, bay leaves, garlic, salt, and pepper. Marinate for 1 hour. • Broil (grill) the fillets on both sides until cooked, basting frequently with the marinade. • Arrange the toast on a heated serving platter and cover with the fillets. Spoon a little of the marinade over the top and serve hot.

464

Serves: 4

*Preparation: 10 min.
+ 1 hr. to marinate*

Cooking: 10 min.

Level of difficulty: 1

- 2 lb (1 kg) gilthead sea bream, (or grouper, pollack, sea bass) fillets
- $^1/_2$ cup (125 ml) extra-virgin olive oil
- Freshly squeezed juice of 1 large lemon
- 1 tbsp each finely chopped parsley, thyme, sage
- 2 bay leaves
- 4 cloves garlic, finely chopped
- Salt and freshly ground white pepper
- 4 slices firm-textured bread, toasted

BREAM WITH ROAST VEGETABLES

Preheat the oven to 400°F (200°C/gas 6).
• Put the onions, zucchini, rosemary, thyme, and garlic in an oiled baking dish. Season with salt and pepper and add the oil. • Bake until the vegetables are tender and golden brown, about 20 minutes. • Melt half the butter in a large frying pan over low heat. • Add the caper berries and sauté for 3 minutes. • Add the lemon juice and chives and sauté for 3 minutes. • Put the flour on a plate and dredge the fish in it, ensuring that it is evenly coated. Shake off any excess. • Melt the remaining butter in a large frying pan over medium heat. • Add the fish and cook for 2 minutes. Turn and cook for 2 minutes. • Transfer to the frying pan with the caper berries and simmer over medium heat for 1–2 minutes, until the fish is cooked through.
• Season with salt and pepper. • Serve hot with the roast vegetables.

Serves: 4
Preparation: 15 min.
Cooking: 15 min.
Level of difficulty: 2

• 2 large onions, sliced into wedges
• 2 large zucchini (courgettes), cut into batons
• 1 tbsp finely chopped fresh rosemary
• 1 tbsp finely chopped fresh thyme
• 1 clove garlic, sliced
• Salt and freshly ground black pepper
• $^1/_4$ cup (60 ml) extra-virgin olive oil
• $^1/_4$ cup (60 g) butter
• 2 oz (60 g) caper berries
• Freshly squeezed juice of 1 lemon
• 2 tbsp finely chopped fresh chives
• 2 tbsp all-purpose (plain) flour
• 4 large fillets bream (or porgy, grouper, gilthead, pollack)

TURBOT WITH MUSHROOMS

Serves: 4–6

Preparation: 20 min.

Cooking: 35 min.

Level of difficulty: 1

- 2 tbsp extra-virgin olive oil
- $1/3$ cup (90 g) butter
- 1 turbot or brill, weighing about 4 lb (2 kg), cleaned
- $1/2$ cup (75 g) all-purpose (plain) flour
- Salt and freshly ground white pepper
- 1 cup (250 ml) dry white wine
- 12 oz (350 g) mushrooms, sliced

Preheat the oven to 400°F (200°C/gas 6).
• Place the oil and 2 tablespoons of butter in an oval ovenproof dish. • Coat the fish lightly all over with flour and place in the dish. Season with salt and pepper. Dot the fish with 2 tablespoons of butter. • Bake for 8–10 minutes. • Remove from the oven. Sprinkle the wine over the fish and return to the oven for 15 minutes more. • Sauté the mushrooms over medium heat in the remaining butter for 15 minutes. Season with salt and pepper and remove from the heat. • Remove the fish from the oven and transfer to a heated serving plate. Add the cooking liquid to the mushrooms and reduce over medium heat for 5 minutes. • Spoon the mushrooms and liquid over the fish and serve.

STUFFED SALMON FILETS

Preheat the oven to 300°F (150°C/gas 2). • Chop the smooth hound finely with the spinach and shallots. Season with salt and pepper and place in a small bowl. • Remove any bones from the salmon fillets. Place in an oiled baking dish. Use a sharp knife to make incisions in the flesh and fill with the spinach mixture. Sprinkle the rest of the mixture on top. • Season with salt and pepper and sprinkle with the butter and parsley. • Bake in the oven until tender, about 20 minutes. • Serve hot.

Serves: 4

Preparation: 20 min.

Cooking: 20 min.

Level of difficulty: 1

- **5 oz (150 g) smooth hound**
- **4 oz (125 g) fresh tender spinach leaves, well rinsed**
- **3 shallots**
- **Salt and freshly ground black pepper**
- **1¹/₂ lb (750 g) salmon fillets, with skin**
- **1 tbsp extra-virgin olive oil**
- **2 tbsp butter, cut up**
- **1 tbsp finely chopped parsley**

FRESH TUNA WITH TOMATOES AND OREGANO

Preheat the oven to 350°F (180°C/gas 4).
• Put the tomatoes in a medium bowl with the garlic, capers, oregano, a pinch of salt, and a generous grinding of pepper. • Rinse the tuna and dry with paper towels. • Pour half the oil into an ovenproof dish and arrange the tuna slices in a single layer. • Cover with the tomato mixture and drizzle with the remaining oil. Bake for 30 minutes. Serve hot.

Serves: 4

Preparation: 10 min.

Cooking: 30 min.

Level of difficulty: 1

- **1 lb (500 g) fresh or canned tomatoes, peeled and chopped**
- **2 cloves garlic, finely chopped**
- **1 tbsp salt-cured capers, rinsed**
- **2 tbsp finely chopped fresh oregano**
- **Salt and freshly ground black pepper**
- **6 slices fresh tuna, about 4 oz (125 g) each**
- **$^1/_2$ cup (125 ml) extra-virgin olive oil**

SWORDFISH WITH CHERRY TOMATOES AND CAPERS

Serves: 4
Preparation: 20 min.
Cooking: 20–25 min.
Level of difficulty: 1

- 4 anchovy fillets
- 2 tbsp salt-cured capers, rinsed
- 4 cloves garlic
- Small bunch of parsley
- 2 lb (1 kg) slice of swordfish, cleaned
- 12 oz (350 g) cherry tomatoes, cut in half
- Salt and freshly ground black pepper
- $1/3$ cup (90 ml) extra-virgin olive oil

Preheat the oven to 400°F (200°C/gas 6).
• Finely chop the anchovy fillets and capers with 2 cloves of garlic and the parsley. • Tie the swordfish with kitchen string. • Place the swordfish in a large baking dish. Use a sharp knife to make deep incisions into the flesh. Fill each incision with some of the chopped anchovy mixture. • Arrange the tomatoes around the swordfish. Place the remaining cloves of garlic (whole, unpeeled) in the pan with the tomatoes. Season well with salt and pepper and drizzle with the oil. • Bake in the oven until tender, 20–25 minutes. • Serve hot with the tomatoes spooned over the top.

SWORDFISH STEAKS WITH ARUGULA AND BASIL SAUCE

Rinse and dry the swordfish steaks without removing the skins. Place on a plate and sprinkle with salt and pepper. Drizzle with the oil, coating both sides, and set aside. • Heat a grill pan (or broiler or barbecue). Cook the swordfish steaks for 10–15 minutes, turning twice. • Put the garlic, parsley, basil, arugula, and remaining oil in a small bowl, add a pinch of salt, a grinding of pepper, and the lemon juice, and whisk with a fork until thoroughly emulsified. • When the steaks are done, place on a heated serving platter. Spoon the sauce over the top and serve.

Serves: 4

Preparation: 10 min.

Cooking: 15 min.

Level of difficulty: 1

- 4 steaks swordfish, cut ¹/₂ inch (1-cm) thick, about 8 oz (250 g) each
- Salt and freshly ground black pepper
- ¹/₂ cup (125 ml) extra-virgin olive oil
- 2 cloves garlic, finely chopped
- 1 tbsp finely chopped parsley
- 12 basil leaves, torn
- 1 bunch arugula (rocket), coarsely chopped
- Freshly squeezed juice of 1 lemon

BAKED COD WITH ONIONS AND CABBAGE

P reheat the oven to 350°F (180°C/gas 4). •
Heat half the butter in a large frying pan over
medium heat. • Add the onions and sauté until
softened, about 5 minutes. • Add the water and
cook until it evaporates. • Cook the cabbage in a
large pot of salted boiling water until tender, 8–10
minutes. • Drain well. Put half the cabbage and half
the onions into an oiled baking dish. • Add the wine
and juniper berries. • Season with salt and pepper.
• Arrange the cod on the bed of cabbage and
onions. • Cover with the remaining cabbage and
onions. • Drizzle with the remaining butter and
bake for 20 minutes, or until the fish is cooked
through. • Serve hot.

Serves: 4

Preparation: 10 min.

Cooking: 30 min.

Level of difficulty: 1

- $^1/_4$ cup (60 g) butter, melted
- 4 red onions, each one cut into 8 wedges
- $^1/_3$ cup (90 ml) water
- 1 head of cabbage, chopped
- 1 cup (250 ml) dry white wine
- 1 tbsp juniper berries
- Salt and freshly ground black pepper
- $1^3/_4$ lb (800 g) cod fillets, skinned and boned

BAKED SALT COD WITH TOMATOES AND PINE NUTS

Serves: 6

Preparation: 10 min.
+ overnight to soak
the fish

Cooking: 45 min.

Level of difficulty: 2

- $^1/_2$ cup (125 ml) extra-virgin olive oil
- 2 cloves garlic, finely sliced
- $1^1/_2$ lb (750 g) peeled plum tomatoes, seeded and chopped
- $1^3/_4$ lb (800 g) salt cod, soaked overnight in cold water, skinned, boned, and cut into pieces
- Salt and freshly ground black pepper
- 2 tbsp golden raisins (sultanas)
- 1 tbsp pine nuts
- 1 tbsp chopped parsley

Preheat the oven to 350°F (180°C/gas 4).
• Heat 3 tablespoons of oil in a medium frying pan over medium heat. • Add the garlic and sauté for 2 minutes. • Add the tomatoes. Simmer for 15 minutes, or until the tomatoes have broken down and the sauce has reduced. • Heat the remaining oil in a large frying pan. Fry the salt cod for 2–3 minutes on each side until lightly browned all over. • Remove the salt cod with a slotted spoon and transfer to an ovenproof dish. Cover with the sauce. Season with salt and pepper. • Sprinkle with the raisins, pine nuts, and parsley. • Bake for 20 minutes. • Serve hot.

477

Serves: 6–8

Preparation: 50 min. +
   1 hr. to soak

Cooking: 75 min.

Level of difficulty: 2

- 14 oz (400 g)
  mussels, in shell
- 14 oz (400 g) clams,
  in shell
- 1 onion, stalk celery,
  1 carrot, cut in half
- 1 bunch parsley
- 5 basil leaves
- 1 bay leaf
- Salt
- 8 oz (250 g) hake
- 8 oz (250 g) red
  mullet
- 8 oz (250 g) monkfish
- 6 cloves garlic, 5
  chopped + 1 whole
- $^1/_2$ cup finely
  chopped parsley
- 1 red chile, chopped
- 8 oz (250 g) octopus,
  chopped
- 8 oz (250 g) squid,
  chopped
- 1 cup (250 ml) wine
- 8 oz (250 g) fish
  fillets, chopped
- 14 oz (400 g)
  tomatoes, chopped
- $^1/_3$ cup (90 ml) extra-
  virgin olive oil
- 4 cups (1 liter) fish
  stock
- 4 shrimp (prawns)
- 8 oz (250 g) dogfish
- 6–8 slices bread

TUSCAN FISH SOUP

S oak the mussels and clams in cold water for
1 hour. • Place in a frying pan over high heat
and cook until they are all open. Discard any that
have not opened. Set aside. • Half fill a medium
pan with water, and add the onion, celery, carrot,
parsley, basil, bay leaf, and 1 teaspoon of salt.
Place over medium heat, cover, and bring to a
boil. • Add the hake, red mullet, and monkfish and
bring to a boil again. Lower the heat, partially
cover the pan and cook for 20 minutes. Turn off
the heat. • Strain the stock into a tureen, discard
the monkfish head, onion, celery, carrot, parsley,
basil, and bay leaf. • Push the fish through a food
mill and set aside. • Heat the oil into a large frying
pan and sauté the chopped garlic and parsley
over medium heat for 5 minutes. Add the chile,
squid, and octopus. • Cook for 10 minutes, or
until reduced. • Pour in the wine and cook for 4
minutes. Lower the heat, add the diced tomatoes,
stir, and check the seasoning. • Cover and
simmer for 20 minutes then add the creamed fish
mixture, stock, the shrimp, the dogfish, mussels,
and clams. Cook for 10 minutes. • Toast the
bread and rub the slices with garlic. • Place a
piece of toast in each of 4 individual soup bowls
and ladle the soup over the top. Serve hot.

BAKED COD WITH CARROTS

Serves: 4
Preparation: 15 min.
Cooking: 15 min.
Level of difficulty: 1

- **6 large carrots, sliced**
- **$^1/_2$ cup (125 ml) extra-virgin olive oil**
- **2 large slices day-old bread, crumbled**
- **2 tbsp finely chopped parsley**
- **1 clove garlic, finely chopped**
- **1 teaspoon wholegrain mustard**
- **Salt and freshly ground black pepper**
- **2 lb (1 kg) cod fillets**

Preheat the oven to 400°F (200°C/gas 6).
• Blanch the carrots in a large pot of boiling water for 3 minutes. Drain and arrange in an oiled baking dish. Drizzle with 2 tablespoons of the oil.
• Place the bread, parsley, garlic, and mustard in the bowl of a food processor. Blend until finely chopped. • Add ¼ cup (60 ml) of the remaining oil and mix well. Season with salt and pepper. • Brush the cod with oil and dip it in the bread mixture, ensuring that each piece is evenly coated. • Arrange the coated cod on the bed of carrots. Drizzle with the remaining oil and bake until the fish is cooked through and the coating is lightly browned, 10–15 minutes. • Garnish with parsley and serve hot.

GILTHEAD SEA BREAM WITH SPINACH

P lace the fish in a large saucepan. • Cover with the onion, garlic, parsley, nutmeg, salt, and pepper. Pour in the wine and half the oil. Turn the fish in the marinade a few times. Marinate for 2 hours. • Place the golden raisins in a small bowl and cover with warm water. Soak for 15 minutes. • Cook the spinach in a little salted water until tender, about 5 minutes. Drain and chop finely. • Place the pan with the fish and marinade over medium heat. Bring to a boil and simmer until tender, about 20 minutes. Turn once, half way through the cooking time. • Drain the liquid from the fish. Cover with half the butter and place in a warm oven. • Strain the cooking liquid. Return to the pan with the anchovies and simmer until the anchovies have dissolved. Add the spinach and drained golden raisins. Serve hot with the fish.

Serves: 4

Preparation: 10 min.

Cooking: 15 min.

Level of difficulty: 1

- 2 gilthead sea bream, 1^1/$_2$ lb (750 g) each, cleaned
- 1 onion, chopped
- 2 cloves garlic, sliced
- 2 tbsp finely chopped parsley
- ^{1}/$_4$ tsp freshly grated nutmeg
- Salt and freshly ground black pepper
- ^{1}/$_2$ cup (125 ml) dry white wine
- ^{1}/$_2$ cup (125 ml) extra-virgin olive oil
- 4 tbsp golden raisins (sultanas)
- 1^1/$_2$ lb (750 g) spinach
- ^{1}/$_4$ cup (60 g) butter
- 2 tbsp pine nuts
- 4 salt-cured anchovy fillets

482

SOLE FILLETS WITH ORANGES

Rinse the sole fillets in cold running water and dry with paper towels. • Peel the oranges with a very sharp knife, removing all the white part under the peel. Slice in very thin rounds, discarding any seeds. • Heat half the butter in a frying pan large enough to hold the sole in a single layer. • Season the sole with salt and pepper and dust with the flour. Add to the pan with the butter and cook until nicely browned on both sides. • Heat the remaining butter in a small, heavy-bottomed saucepan until golden brown. • Place the cooked sole on a large heated serving platter and cover with the slices of orange. • Sprinkle with the parsley and pour the hot butter over the top. Serve hot.

Serves: 4

Preparation: 10 min.

Cooking: 10 min.

Level of difficulty: 1

- 1 1/2 lb (750 g) sole fillets
- 2 large oranges
- 1/3 cup (90 g) butter
- Salt and freshly ground black pepper
- 2 tbsp all-purpose (plain) flour
- 1/4 cup finely chopped parsley

SOLE AND SCALLOPS IN PHYLLO PASTRY

Serves: 4
Preparation: 45 min.
Cooking: 15–20 min.
Level of difficulty: 2

- $1/2$ cup (125 ml) extra-virgin olive oil
- 2 cloves garlic, finely chopped
- 1 tbsp finely chopped fresh marjoram
- 12 oz (350 g) tender asparagus spears, cut in short lengths
- 1 medium zucchini (courgette), cut in small dice
- 3 tbsp dry white wine
- 2 tbsp butter
- 8 sole fillets
- 8 scallops, in shell
- 4 tbsp pine nuts
- 1 large bunch fresh basil
- 4 sheets phyllo pastry

Heat 2 tablespoons of the oil in a large frying pan over medium heat. Add the garlic and marjoram and sauté until the garlic is pale gold.
• Add the asparagus and zucchini and drizzle with the wine. Season with salt and pepper and simmer until the vegetables are tender. Remove the vegetables from the pan and set aside. • Melt the butter in the same pan and sauté the scallops and sole filets until cooked, about 5 minutes. • Chop the basil, pine nuts, and remaining oil in a food processor until smooth. Season with salt and pepper. • Preheat the oven to 400°F (200°C/gas 6). • Fold each piece of phyllo pastry in half. Place two sole fillets and 2 scallops and some of the vegetable mixture in the center of each piece. Fold the phyllo pastry around the filling, sealing well.
• Brush with the egg white. Bake until pale golden brown, about 10 minutes. • Serve hot.

BAKED SOLE AND PROSCIUTTO WRAPS

Preheat the oven to 400°F (200°C/gas 6.) • Lay out the slices of prosciutto on a work surface. Put a sole fillet on each slice and brush with butter. Season with salt and pepper. • Wrap the prosciutto around the sole fillets and secure each one with a cocktail stick. • Insert a sprig of rosemary into each parcel. • Arrange on an oiled baking sheet and bake for 10–15 minutes, until the fish is cooked through. • Heat the oil in a small frying pan over medium heat. • Add the shallot, bay leaves, garlic, and parsley. Sauté for 3 minutes, until the shallot is transparent. • Mix the wine and the cornstarch together in a small cup. Add to the frying pan and mix well. Cook for 2–3 minutes, until the sauce has thickened. • Place the fish in a serving dish. • Drizzle with the sauce and serve.

Serves: 4

Preparation: 10 min.

Cooking: 20 min.

Level of difficulty: 2

- 8 slices of prosciutto (Parma ham)
- 8 small sole fillets
- 2 tbsp butter, melted
- Salt and freshly ground black pepper
- 8 small sprigs fresh rosemary
- $1/4$ cup (60 ml) extra-virgin olive oil
- 1 shallot, finely chopped
- 2 bay leaves
- 2 cloves garlic, finely chopped
- 2 tbsp freshly chopped parsley
- $1/3$ cup (90 ml) dry white wine
- $1/2$ tbsp cornstarch (cornflour)

STUFFED CALAMARI

Serves: 4
Preparation: 15 min.
Cooking: 75 min.
Level of difficulty: 2

- **3 large floury (baking) potatoes, peeled**
- **16 shelled shrimps (prawns), chopped**
- **Salt and freshly ground black pepper**
- **1/4 cup (60 ml) extra-virgin olive oil**
- **1 tbsp finely chopped fresh dill**
- **1 tbsp finely chopped chives**
- **8 medium squid, cleaned**
- **1 large onion, chopped**
- **1 bay leaf**
- **2 heads of radicchio, shredded**

Cook the potatoes in a large pot of salted boiling water for 25 minutes, until tender. • Drain and mash until smooth. • Add the chopped shrimps and season with salt and pepper. • Add 2 tablespoons of the oil, the dill, and chives. • Chop the squid tentacles. • Spoon the shrimp mixture into the squid bodies and secure each one with a cocktail stick. • Heat the remaining oil in a large frying pan over medium heat. • Add the onion and bay leaf and sauté until the onion is transparent, 3 minutes. • Add the chopped squid tentacles and the stuffed squid. • Cover and simmer over low heat until the squid is tender, 45 minutes. • Transfer the squid to a serving dish. • Add the radicchio to the pan and sauté for 2–3 minutes. Season with salt and pepper. • Discard the bay leaf. • Spoon this mixture on to the serving dish with the squid. • Garnish with dill and serve hot.

STUFFED BAKED SQUID

Heat 2 tablespoons of the oil in a medium frying pan over medium heat. Add the garlic and sauté until pale golden brown, 3–4 minutes. • Add the tomatoes and season with salt and pepper, Simmer for 10 minutes. • Preheat the oven to 350°F (280°C/gas 4). • Remove the tomato mixture from the heat and stir in the egg, parsley, and bread crumbs. • Remove the tentacles from the bodies of the squid. Chop the tentacles coarsely. • Rinse the bodies of the squid and shake dry. Season with salt and pepper. • Fill each squid with some of the stuffing. • Pour 2 tablespoons of the remaining oil into an ovenproof baking dish and cover the bottom with the sliced potatoes. Position the squid on top and the chopped tentacles round about. Sprinkle with the extra parsley and bread crumbs and drizzle with the remaining oil. • Bake in the oven until the squid and potatoes are tender, 50–60 minutes. • Serve hot.

Serves: 4

Preparation: 30 min.

Cooking: 75 min.

Level of difficulty: 2

- **4 large squid, cleaned**
- **$^1/_3$ cup (90 ml) extra-virgin olive oil**
- **2 cloves garlic, finely chopped**
- **2 firm, ripe tomatoes, peeled and chopped**
- **$1^1/_2$ lb (750 g) potatoes, peeled and sliced**
- **1 large egg**
- **1 tbsp finely chopped parsley + extra, to sprinkle**
- **1 cup (150 g) fine dry bread crumbs + extra, to finish**
- **Salt and freshly ground black pepper**

MINI SEAFOOD KEBABS

Serves: 2–4

Preparation: 35 min.
+ 30 min. to
marinate

Cooking: 10 min.

Level of difficulty: 2

- **8 small squid, cleaned**
- **1 swordfish steak, weighing about 5 oz (150 g)**
- **8 scampi or giant shrimp (prawns)**
- **2 cloves garlic, finely sliced**
- **$1/4$ cup (60 ml) dry white wine**
- **$1/4$ cup (60 ml) extra-virgin olive oil**
- **Salt and freshly ground black pepper**
- **4 oz (125 g) salad greens**
- **1 tbsp finely chopped fresh parsley**

Remove the tentacles from the squid and set aside. • Skin the swordfish and remove the bone. Cut into 8 bite-size pieces. • Rinse the scampi carefully. • Thread the seafood onto the skewers alternating swordfish, scampi, and squid on each skewer. • Arrange the kebabs in a dish and sprinkle with the garlic. • Drizzle with the wine and 1 tablespoon of the oil. Season with salt and pepper. • Let the kebabs marinade for 30 minutes in the refrigerator. • Preheat the broiler (grill) to high. Drizzle the kebabs with the remaining oil and broil (grill) for 5 minutes. • Turn them over and broil for another 5 minutes. Arrange the salad on serving dishes. • Transfer the kebabs to the serving dishes and sprinkle with the parsley. Serve hot.

BAKED SCALLOPS

Preheat the oven to 400°F (200°C/gas 6).
• Melt the butter in a medium saucepan over medium heat. Add the mushrooms and sauté for 3–4 minutes. • Stir in the flour and fish stock and simmer over low heat for 10 minutes, stirring constantly. • Remove from the heat and stir in the egg yolk, cream, and parsley. Season with salt and pepper. • Shuck the scallops and place three in each shell. • Spoon the sauce over the top. Sprinkle each shell with bread crumbs. • Bake in the oven until the scallops are tender and browned, 3–5 minutes. Serve hot.

Serves: 4

Preparation: 30 min.

Cooking: 15 min.

Level of difficulty: 1

- **2 tbsp butter**
- **2 oz (60 g) champignons, finely chopped**
- **18 scallops, in shell**
- **1 cup (250 ml) fish stock**
- **$1/4$ cup (60 ml) heavy (double) cream**
- **$1/4$ cup (30 g) all-purpose (plain) flour**
- **1 large egg yolk**
- **1 tbsp finely chopped parsley**
- **Salt and freshly ground black pepper**
- **$1/3$ cup (50 g) fine dry bread crumbs**

CLAMS WITH TOMATO AND GARLIC

Serves: 4

Preparation: 10 min. + 1 hr. to soak the clams

Cooking: 25–30 min.

Level of difficulty: 1

- **2 lb (1 kg) clams, in shell**
- **$1/3$ cup (90 ml) extra-virgin olive oil**
- **4 cloves garlic, finely chopped**
- **2 tbsp finely chopped fresh parsley**
- **1 lb (500 g) tomatoes, peeled and chopped**
- **Salt and freshly ground black pepper**

Place the clams in a large bowl of lightly salted cold water and let soak for 1 hour. • Heat the oil in a large frying pan and add the garlic and parsley. Sauté until the garlic is pale golden brown. • Add the tomato, season with salt and pepper, and simmer for 10 minutes. • Add the clams and simmer until all the clams have opened. Discard any clams that do not open. • Serve hot.

MUSSELS WITH LEMON AND PARSLEY

Place the mussels in a large bowl of lightly salted cold water and soak for 1 hour. • Rinse thoroughly and scrub off any beards. • Place the mussels in a large frying pan, cover, and place over medium heat until the mussels have opened. Shake the pan from time to time during cooking. Discard any mussels that haven't opened. • Place the mussels in a large serving dish. Sprinkle with the parsley and season with salt and pepper. Drizzle with the lemon juice and olive oil. Serve hot.

498

Serves: 4

Preparation: 10 min.
+ 1 hr. to soak the
mussels

Cooking: 25–30 min.

Level of difficulty: 1

- 3 lb (1.5 kg) mussels, in shell
- 2 tbsp finely chopped parsley
- Salt and freshly ground black pepper
- 1 lemon
- 1/4 cup (60 ml) extra-virgin olive oil

BAKED MUSSELS WITH TOMATO AND ONION

Place the mussels in a large bowl of lightly salted cold water and let soak for 1 hour. • Preheat the oven to 300°F (150°C/gas 2). • Rinse thoroughly and scrub off any beards. Place in a large frying pan over medium heat until they open. Discard the empty half of each shell and place the full half on a plate. Discard any mussels that do not open. • Filter the water the mussels have produced during cooking into a small bowl and set aside.
• Oil a large baking dish and cover the bottom with the potatoes in a single layer. Cover with a layer of onions. Season lightly with salt and pepper and cover with a layer of mussels. Top with a layer of zucchini and pieces of tomato and sprinkle with cheese. Repeat this layering process until all the ingredients are in the pan. • Pour in the reserved cooking liquid and drizzle with the oil. • Bake in the oven for 90 minutes. • Serve hot or at room temperature.

Serves: 4–6

Preparation: 30 min. + 1 hr. to soak the mussels

Cooking: 1 hr. 45 min.

Level of difficulty: 1

- 3 lb (1 .5 kg) mussels, in shell
- 2 medium potatoes, peeled and sliced
- 2 medium white onions, thinly sliced
- Salt and freshly ground black pepper
- 2 lb (1 kg) firm, ripe tomatoes, peeled and chopped
- 2 medium zucchini (courgettes), sliced
- $1/4$ cup (60 ml) extra-virgin olive oil
- $1/2$ cup (60 g) freshly grated pecorino cheese

BAKED MUSSELS

Preheat the oven to 400°F (200°C/gas 6).
• Shuck the mussels using a sharp knife.
Discard one half of each shell and place the
mussels, mollusk side up, in a large baking pan.
Pour in about 1 inch (2.5 cm) of lightly salted
water. • Mix the bread crumbs, parsley, salt,
pepper and ¼ cup (60 ml) of the oil in a small
bowl. Place a little of this mixture in each mollusk.
• Bake in the oven for 10 minutes. • Season the
beaten eggs with salt and pepper and drizzle over
the mussels. • Bake until the egg has set, 10–15
minutes. • Serve hot.

502

Serves: 4

Preparation: 30 min.

Cooking: 25–30 min.

Level of difficulty: 2

- 3 lb (1.5 kg)
  mussels, in shell
- 1 cup (150 g) fine
  dry bread crumbs
- 2 tbsp finely
  chopped parsley
- Salt and freshly
  ground black
  pepper
- $^1/_3$ cup (90 ml)
  extra-virgin olive
  oil
- 2 large eggs,
  lightly beaten

POULTRY

CHICKEN WITH TOMATOES AND PROSCIUTTO

H eat the oil in a large frying pan over medium heat and add the prosciutto and garlic. Sauté until the garlic is pale golden brown, 3–4 minutes. • Add the chicken pieces and sauté over medium-high heat until golden brown, 8–10 minutes. Season with salt and pepper. • Pour in the wine and simmer until the wine has evaporated. • Add the tomatoes and simmer until the chicken is tender and the tomatoes have reduced, about 25 minutes. • Serve hot.

Serves: 4

Preparation: 15 min.

Cooking: 45 min.

Level of difficulty: 1

- $1/4$ cup (60 ml) extra-virgin olive oil
- 2 oz (60 g) prosciutto (Parma ham), chopped
- 2 cloves garlic, finely chopped
- Salt and freshly ground black pepper
- $1/2$ cup (125 ml) dry white wine
- 1 chicken, about 3 lb (1.5 kg), cut into 8 pieces
- 14 oz (400 g) firm, ripe tomatoes, peeled and chopped

CHICKEN WITH MUSHROOMS

Dice the mushroom caps and stems into fairly large cubes. • Melt half the butter in a large frying pan over medium heat. Add 1 tablespoon of oil and sauté the garlic for 2–3 minutes. • Add the mushrooms and thyme. Sprinkle with salt and pepper and simmer for a few minutes. Sprinkle with the parsley, remove from heat, and set aside. • Place the remaining butter and oil in another large frying pan over medium heat. Add the chicken and brown well. Season with salt and pepper. • Pour in the wine and cook over high heat until it evaporates. • Add the onion and cook until softened. • Pour in the milk and reduce the heat. Add salt and pepper to taste, cover the pan, and simmer for 25 minutes, stirring frequently. • Remove the lid; if the sauce is too liquid, raise the heat until it reduces a little. • Add the mushrooms, stir well, and cook over medium-low heat for 10 minutes. • Serve hot.

Serves: 4–6

Preparation: 30 min.

Cooking: 1 hr.

Level of difficulty: 2

- 1 chicken, about 3 lb (1.5 kg), cut into 8 pieces
- 1 lb (500 g) white mushrooms
- 2 tbsp butter
- $^1/_4$ cup (60 ml) extra-virgin olive oil
- 2 cloves garlic, finely chopped
- 2 sprigs fresh thyme
- Salt and freshly ground black pepper
- 2 tbsp finely chopped parsley
- $^1/_2$ cup (125 ml) dry white wine
- 1 white onion, coarsely chopped
- $^3/_4$ cup (180 ml) milk

CHICKEN WITH BELL PEPPERS

510

Heat the oil in a large frying pan over medium heat and add garlic. Sauté until the garlic is pale golden brown, 3–4 minutes. • Add the chicken pieces and sauté over medium-high heat until golden brown. Season with salt and pepper. • Pour in the wine and simmer until it has evaporated. • Add the tomatoes and bell peppers and simmer until the chicken and bell peppers are tender and the tomatoes have reduced, about 35 minutes. • Serve hot.

Serves: 4

Preparation: 15 min.

Cooking: 55 min.

Level of difficulty: 1

- $1/4$ cup (60 ml) extra-virgin olive oil
- 2 cloves garlic, finely chopped
- Salt and freshly ground black pepper
- $1/2$ cup (125 ml) dry white wine
- 1 chicken, about 3 lb (1.5 kg), cut into 8 pieces
- 14 oz (400 g) firm, ripe tomatoes, peeled and chopped
- 3 medium green bell peppers (capsicums), cleaned and chopped into squares

SPICY CHICKEN WITH ONION

Serves: 4
Preparation: 15 min.
Cooking: 45 min.
Level of difficulty: 1

- $1/4$ cup (60 ml) extra-virgin olive oil
- 1 onion, coarsely chopped
- Salt and freshly ground black pepper
- $1/2$ cup (125 ml) dry white wine
- 1 chicken, about 3 lb (1.5 kg), cut into 8 pieces
- 14 oz (400 g) tomatoes, peeled and chopped
- 2 tbsp finely chopped fresh parsley
- 2 tbsp finely chopped fresh basil, + extra sprigs, to garnish
- 1–2 tsp hot paprika
- 3 medium potatoes, peeled and cut into thin wedges

Heat the oil in a large frying pan over medium heat and add the onion. Sauté until the onion is softened, about 5 minutes. • Add the chicken pieces and sauté over medium-high heat until golden brown. Season with salt and pepper. • Pour in the wine and simmer until the wine has evaporated. • Add the tomatoes, parsley, basil, and paprika. Cover the pan and simmer until the chicken and potatoes are tender, about 30 minutes. Add a little water during cooking if the pan dries out during cooking. • Serve hot.

BAKED CHICKEN WITH APPLES

Preheat the oven to 400°F (200°C/gas 6).
• Sprinkle the inside of the chicken with salt.
• Place the apples in a bowl and add the prunes, bread crumbs, eggs, oregano, and pepper. Mix well and use the mixture to stuff the chicken.
• Wrap the chicken in the bacon. • Roast in the oven for 15 minutes. • Turn the heat down to 375°F (190°C/gas 5) and roast until tender, about 45 minutes. • Place the chicken in a serving dish and bring to the table still wrapped in the bacon. Unwrap, slice, and include some of the bacon with each serving.

Serves: 6

Preparation: 10 min.

Cooking: 1 hr.

Level of difficulty: 2

- **1 chicken, about 4 lb (2 kg), cleaned**
- **Salt and freshly ground black pepper**
- **4 tart apples, such as Granny Smith, Cortland, or Empire, peeled, cored, and coarsely chopped**
- **6 prunes, soaked in warm water for 5 minutes, then pitted and chopped**
- **2 cups (120 g) fresh, soft bread crumbs**
- **2 large eggs, lightly beaten**
- **1 tsp dried oregano**
- **8–12 large slices bacon**

MARENGO CHICKEN

Serves: 4–6
Preparation: 15 min.
Cooking: 1 hr.
Level of difficulty: 1

- 1 chicken, about 3 lb (1.5 kg) cut into 6–8 pieces
- 2 tbsp butter
- 2 tbsp extra-virgin olive oil
- Salt and freshly ground black pepper
- Dash of nutmeg
- $^1/_2$ cup (125 ml) dry white wine
- 1 tbsp all-purpose (plain) flour
- 1 cup (250 ml) Beef Stock (see page 946)
- Freshly squeezed juice of $^1/_2$ lemon

Place the chicken in a heavy-bottomed pan with the butter and oil and sauté until lightly browned. Season with salt, pepper, and nutmeg.

- Discard most of the liquid that may have formed in the pan. Add the wine and stir in the flour.
- Simmer over medium-low heat until the chicken is tender, about 50 minutes. Add the stock as required during cooking to keep the chicken moist.
- Arrange the chicken on a serving dish and drizzle with the lemon juice. • Serve hot.

PISTOIA POT ROAST CHICKEN

Put the strips of pancetta and rosemary into the cavity of the chicken. Season with salt and pepper. • Heat a large Dutch oven or casserole over medium heat. Sauté the prosciutto and garlic until lightly browned, about 5 minutes. • Add the stock and vinegar and bring to a boil. Transfer the chicken to the Dutch oven, cover, and simmer for 1 hour. Remove the lid and add the potatoes and a little more stock to stop the chicken sticking to the casserole. Cook until the potatoes are tender, 35–40 minutes. • Serve hot.

Serves: 6

Preparation: 15 min.

Cooking: 1 hr. 45 min.

Level of difficulty: 2

- **3 oz (90 g) pancetta, sliced thinly**
- **2 sprigs of rosemary**
- **3 lb (1.5 kg) chicken**
- **Salt and freshly ground black pepper**
- **2 oz (60 g) fatty prosciutto (Parma ham), chopped**
- **2 cloves garlic, finely chopped**
- **1/3 cup (90 ml) stock + more as required**
- **1 tbsp white wine vinegar**
- **1 1/2 lb (750 g) potatoes, cut into chunks**

BOILED CHICKEN WITH ANCHOVY SAUCE

Serves: 4

Preparation: 20 min.

Cooking: 90 min.

Level of difficulty: 2

- 1 carrot, cut in 4
- 1 leek, cut in 4
- 1 stalk celery, chopped
- Zest of 1 lemon
- 1 chicken, about 3 lb (1.5 kg) cut in 4
- 3 sprigs rosemary
- 1 sprig thyme
- 1 sprig parsley
- 1 bay leaf
- $^1/_4$ cup (60 ml) extra-virgin olive oil
- 2 cloves garlic, lightly crushed but whole
- 4 anchovy fillets
- 1 tbsp salt-cured caper, rinsed
- Sprigs of parsley, to garnish
- 1 lemon, cut into wedges, to garnish

Bring 2 quarts (2 liters) of water to a boil in a large saucepan over medium heat. Add the carrot, leek, celery, lemon zest, and chicken. • Tie a sprig of rosemary, the thyme, a sprig of parsley, and the bay leaf together with a piece of thread and add to the saucepan. • Cover and simmer for 90 minutes. • Heat the oil in a small frying pan over medium heat. Add the garlic and remaining rosemary and sauté until the garlic turns pale gold, 3–4 minutes. • Discard the garlic and rosemary. Add the anchovies and simmer, mashing with a fork until they dissolve in the oil. • Add the capers and simmer for 5 minutes. Remove from the heat. • Drain the chicken, reserving the stock for another recipe. Remove the skin from the chicken and discard. Transfer the chicken to a serving dish and drizzle with the sauce. Garnish with the remaining parsley and wedges of lemon. • Serve hot.

BRAISED CHICKEN AND VEGETABLES

Sauté the onion and garlic in the oil in a large frying pan until softened, about 5 minutes. • Add the chicken and brown well. • Pour in the wine and cook until it evaporates. Add the potatoes, carrots, celery, and parsley and season with salt and pepper. • Pour in enough stock to moisten the dish. Cover and cook over medium heat for 25–30 minutes, stirring frequently. Add more stock as required during cooking. • When the chicken is cooked and the vegetables tender, remove from heat and serve hot.

Serves: 4

Preparation: 10 min.

Cooking: 45 min.

Level of difficulty: 1

- **1 chicken, about 4 lb (2 kg), cut into 8 pieces**
- **2 medium onions, finely chopped**
- **2 cloves garlic, finely chopped**
- **$1/4$ cup (60 ml) extra-virgin olive oil**
- **$1/4$ cup (60 ml) dry white wine**
- **14 oz (400 g) potatoes, peeled and coarsely chopped**
- **4 large carrots, peeled and coarsely chopped**
- **4 stalks celery, cut in short lengths**
- **2 tbsp finely chopped fresh parsley**
- **Salt and freshly ground black pepper**
- **$2/3$ cup (150 ml) Chicken Stock (see page 946)**

HUNTER'S CHICKEN WITH EGGPLANT

Place the eggplants in a large colander and sprinkle with the sea salt. Set aside to drain for 1 hour. • Heat 2 tablespoons of the oil in a large frying pan over medium heat and add the pancetta and garlic. Sauté until the garlic is pale golden brown, 3–4 minutes. • Add the chicken pieces and sauté over medium-high heat until golden brown. Season with salt and pepper. • Pour in the wine and simmer until it has evaporated. • Add the tomatoes. Cover and simmer until the chicken is almost tender, about 35 minutes. • Dry the eggplants with a clean cloth. • Heat the remaining oil in a large frying pan and fry the eggplant until tender and browned. Chop coarsely. • Stir the eggplant into the chicken about 5 minutes before serving. • Serve hot.

Serves: 4–6

Preparation: 30 min.
+ 1 hr. to drain the eggplants

Cooking: 1 hr.

Level of difficulty: 1

- 3 large eggplants (aubergines), cut in strips (with peel)
- 2 tbsp coarse sea salt
- $^1/_2$ cup (125 ml) extra-virgin olive oil
- 3 oz (90 g) pancetta, chopped
- 2 cloves garlic, finely chopped
- Salt and freshly ground black pepper
- $^1/_2$ cup (125 ml) dry white wine
- 1 chicken, about 3 lb (1.5 kg), cut into 8 pieces
- 14 oz (400 g) tomatoes, peeled and chopped

CHICKEN STEW WITH VINEGAR AND ROSEMARY

Lightly flour the chicken pieces. • Heat ¼ cup (60 g) butter with the rosemary in a large frying pan. When the butter turns deep gold, remove the rosemary and add the chicken and pancetta. Sauté until the chicken is lightly browned. Remove the chicken and pancetta (leaving as much of the butter as possible in the pan) and set aside in a warm oven. Sprinkle with salt and pepper. • Pour the vinegar into the pan and mix well. Add the anchovies and stir until they dissolve. Stir in the garlic and remaining butter and cook until the mixture thickens. • Add the chicken and pancetta and cook for 10–15 minutes more. • Serve hot.

Serves: 4–6

Preparation: 10 min.

Cooking: 30 min.

Level of difficulty: 1

- 1 cup (150 g) all-purpose (plain) flour
- 4 skinless, boneless chicken breast halves, about 2 lb (1 kg) total weight, cut into bite-sized pieces
- ¹/₄ cup (60 g) butter + 1 tbsp
- 2 twigs fresh rosemary
- ¹/₄ cup (30 g) diced lean pancetta
- Salt and freshly ground black pepper
- ¹/₂ cup (125 ml) white wine vinegar
- 6 anchovy fillets
- 4 cloves garlic, finely chopped

STUFFED CHICKEN LEGS WITH POTATOES

Serves: 4

Preparation: 30 min.

Cooking: 1 hr.

Level: 2

- **4 large chicken legs**
- **1 lb (500 g) Italian pork sausages, peeled and crumbled**
- **Black truffles, cut in tiny cubes (optional)**
- **5 tbsp butter**
- **3–4 sprigs rosemary**
- **1¹/₂ lb (750 g) potatoes, peeled**
- **¹/₂ cup (60 g) freshly grated Parmesan cheese**
- **3 tbsp milk**
- **Salt and freshly ground black pepper**

Preheat the oven to 350°F (180°C/gas 4). • Use a sharp knife to open the chicken legs up and remove the bone. Leave the bottom bone in to be used as a handle (If preferred, ask your butcher to do this for you). • Place the sausage meat and truffles, if using, in a bowl and mix well. • Stuff the chicken legs with this mixture. Tie with kitchen string. • Place the stuffed chicken legs in a baking dish with the 3 tablespoons of butter and the rosemary. Season with salt and pepper and bake until tender, about 40 minutes. • Meanwhile boil the potatoes in a pan of salted water until tender. • Drain and mash well, adding the remaining butter, cheese, and milk. • Serve the chicken on a heated platter with the mashed potatoes.

TUSCAN FRIED CHICKEN

P ut the chicken into a large bowl and sprinkle with the parsley. • Add the lemon juice and olive oil. Season with salt and pepper. Cover and let marinate for 2 hours. • Beat the eggs in a bowl. • Heat the sunflower oil in a large frying pan over medium-high heat. • Drain the chicken. • Dredge in the flour, ensuring that it is evenly coated. Shake to remove any excess flour. • Dip each piece of chicken in the beaten egg. • Fry in the oil until the meat is cooked through and golden brown, about 15 minutes. • Drain on paper towels and serve hot.

Serves: 4

Preparation: 15 min.
+ 2 hr. to marinate

Cooking: 15 min.

Level of difficulty: 2

- 3 lb (1.5 kg) chicken thighs
- 3 tbsp finely chopped fresh parsley
- Freshly squeezed juice of 1 lemon
- 3 tbsp extra virgin olive oil
- Salt and freshly ground black pepper
- 2 large eggs
- 2 cups (500 ml) sunflower oil, for frying
- 2 tbsp all-purpose (plain) flour

CHICKEN GALANTINE

Serves: 6–8

Preparation: 40 min. + 12 hr. to chill

Cooking: 90 min.

Level of difficulty: 3

C ombine the beef, pork, turkey, veal, and mortadella in a large bowl. Mix well and add the pistachios, egg, and truffle, if using. Sprinkle with salt and pepper and mix thoroughly. • Stuff the boned chicken with the mixture and sew up the neck and stomach cavities with a trussing needle and string. • Use your hands to give it a round shape. Wrap in a piece of cheesecloth (muslin) and tie with kitchen string. • Place a large saucepan of salted water over medium heat. Add the onion, carrot, celery, parsley, peppercorns, and stock cube. • When the water is boiling, carefully add the stuffed chicken and simmer over low heat for 90 minutes. • Remove from the heat and drain the stock. • Remove the cheesecloth and place the chicken between two trays, with a weight on top. • When cool, transfer to the refrigerator, with the weight still on top, and leave for at least 12 hours. • In the meantime, prepare the gelatin, following the directions on the packet. Be sure to add the lemon juice while the gelatin is still liquid. • Serve the galantine thinly sliced on a serving dish, topped with the diced gelatin.

- 1 lb (500 g) lean ground (minced) beef
- 6 oz (180 g) lean ground (minced) pork
- 6 oz (180 g) ground (minced) turkey breast
- 6 oz (180 g) ground (minced) suckling veal
- 4 oz (125 g) ground (minced) mortadella
- 1/2 cup (60 g) shelled pistachios
- 1 large egg
- 1 oz (30 g) black truffle, finely sliced (optional)
- Salt and freshly ground black pepper
- 1 chicken, boned, weighing about 4 lb (2 kg)
- 1 onion, cut in half
- 1 carrot, cut in 3
- 1 stalk celery, cut in 3
- 2 sprigs parsley
- 7–8 peppercorns
- 1 chicken stock cube
- 2 gelatin cubes
- Juice of 1/2 lemon

CHICKEN MEAT LOAF

Serves: 4

Preparation: 15 min.

Cooking: 45 min.

Level of difficulty: 1

- **1¹/₂ lb (750 g) ground (minced) chicken breast,**
- **4 oz (125 g) fresh bread crumbs**
- **¹/₂ cup (100 g) canned corn (sweet corn), drained**
- **1 cup (150 g) frozen peas**
- **1 large egg**
- **Salt and freshly ground black pepper**
- **¹/₄ cup (60 ml) extra-virgin olive oil**

Preheat the oven to 350°F (180°C/gas 4).
• Place the chicken breast, bread crumbs, corn, peas, egg, salt, and pepper in a bowl and mix well. • Shape the chicken mixture into a meat loaf shape and wrap in damp waxed paper. Tie with kitchen string. • Place in a baking dish and drizzle with the oil. • Bake until tender and cooked through, about 45 minutes. • Unwrap and discard the waxed paper. Cut in slices and serve hot.

CHICKEN BREASTS WITH BRANDY SAUCE

Place half the butter in a large frying pan and add the chicken breasts and garlic. Sprinkle with salt and simmer for 5 minutes, turning the chicken breasts frequently. • Remove the garlic and pour in a little of the wine. Turn the chicken breasts in the wine. Add wine as required and simmer until the chicken breasts are tender. • Meanwhile, place the remaining butter in a small frying pan and sauté the onion over medium heat until softened. Pour in the brandy, followed by the cream and chile pepper. Cook for 4–5 minutes, stirring all the time. • Arrange the chicken breasts in a heated serving dish and pour the sauce over the top. Serve hot.

Serves: 4

Preparation: 10 min.

Cooking: 30 min.

Level of difficulty: 1

- $^1/_4$ cup (60 g) butter
- 4 boneless, skinless chicken breasts, about $1^1/_2$ lb (750 g) total weight
- 2 cloves garlic, cut in half
- Salt
- 1 cup (250 ml) dry white wine
- 2 onions, finely chopped
- $^1/_2$ cup (125 ml) brandy
- $^1/_2$ cup (125 ml) heavy (double) cream
- $^1/_2$ small dried red chile pepper, crumbled

CHICKEN BREAST STUFFED WITH FENNEL AND CHEESE

Make an incision almost all the way through the meat lengthwise down the side of each chicken breast to make a pocket for the stuffing. • Preheat the oven to 350°F (180°C/gas 4). • Heat 2 tablespoons of oil in a large frying pan over medium heat. Add the fennel, season with salt, and sauté until the fennel is tender, about 10 minutes. If the fennel sticks to the pan add the stock. • Stir in the pecorino and cream cheese. Remove from the heat. • Spoon the filling into the cavity in the chicken breasts. Wrap the breasts in pieces of pancetta and tie with kitchen string. • Heat the remaining oil in a Dutch oven over medium heat. • Add the chicken and garlic. Sauté until lightly browned all over. • Add the wine and let evaporate. • Place in the oven and bake until the chicken is tender, about 30 minutes. • Slice the chicken. Drizzle with the cooking juices and serve.

Serves: 4
Preparation: 20 min.
Cooking: 45 min.
Level of difficulty: 2

- **4 boneless, skinless chicken breasts, about 1 1/2 lb (750 g) total weight**
- 1/4 cup (60 ml) extra-virgin olive oil
- 1 large fennel bulb, chopped
- Salt
- 3 tbsp vegetable stock, if required
- 1/4 cup (30 g) freshly grated pecorino
- 5 oz (150 g) cream cheese
- 4 large slices pancetta
- 1 clove garlic, lightly crushed but whole
- 1/2 cup (125 ml) dry white wine

536

AROMATIC ROAST CHICKEN

Serves: 4

Preparation: 20 min.

Cooking: 90 min.

Level of difficulty: 1

- **1 chicken about 3 lb (1.5 kg) in weight**
- **2 oz (60 g) lard or rigatino, sliced into thin strips**
- **4 cloves of garlic, lightly crushed but whole**
- **4 tbsp chopped wild fennel**
- **Salt and freshly ground black pepper**
- **1 lb (500 g) new potatoes**
- **Leaves from 1 sprig of rosemary**
- **4 sage leaves, torn**
- **1/2 cup (125 ml) extra virgin olive oil**

Preheat the oven to 350°F (180°C/gas 4). • Arrange the strips of lard inside the cavity of the chicken. Add the garlic and fennel. Season with salt and pepper. Seal the cavity and secure with a skewer. • Transfer the chicken to a large roasting pan and arrange the potatoes around it. Season with salt and pepper. Sprinkle with the rosemary and sage. • Drizzle with oil and roast for about until the chicken is browned and the juices run clear when tested with a skewer, about 90 minutes. • Serve hot.

MARINATED BROILED TURKEY BREASTS

C ut the turkey breasts into 6 or 12 pieces.
Place the turkey in a bowl. • Mix the oil,
vinegar, cloves, garlic, marjoram, salt, and pepper
together and pour over the turkey. Marinate in the
refrigerator for at least 3 hours. • Cook the
breasts under a broiler (grill) or over the hot
embers of a barbecue. Baste with the marinade as
they cook to stop them from drying out. Serve hot.

538

Serves: 6

Preparation: 10 min.
+ 3 hr. to marinate

Cooking: 15 min.

Level of difficulty: 1

- **2 lb (1 kg) boneless, skinless turkey breasts**
- **$^2/_3$ cup (150 ml) extra-virgin olive oil**
- **$^1/_4$ cup (60 ml) white wine vinegar**
- **4 cloves, crushed**
- **2 cloves garlic, finely chopped**
- **2 tbsp finely chopped fresh marjoram**
- **Salt and freshly ground black pepper**

TURKEY WITH PROSCIUTTO

Preheat the oven to 375°F (190°C/gas 5).
• Sprinkle the turkey with the prosciutto,
cloves, rosemary, sage, salt, and pepper, and rub
all over. Wrap in ovenproof parchment paper and
drizzle with the water. • Bake until very tender,
almost 3 hours. • Unwrap the turkey and cut in
strips. • Heat the butter in a frying pan and add the
turkey. Pour in the cream, season with salt and
pepper, and simmer over medium heat for 10
minutes, or until most of the cream is absorbed.
Serve hot.

Serves: 6

Preparation: 25 min.

Cooking: 3 hr.

Level of difficulty: 2

- **1 young, tender turkey, about 4 lb (2 kg), boneless**
- **4 oz (125 g) thinly sliced prosciutto (Parma ham), with fat, chopped**
- **4 cloves, crushed**
- **1 tbsp finely chopped rosemary**
- **1 tbsp finely chopped sage**
- **Salt and freshly ground black pepper**
- **$^1/_4$ cup (60 ml) water**
- **2 tbsp butter**
- **1 cup (250 ml) heavy (double) cream**

DUCK STUFFED WITH RICE AND PARMESAN

Serves: 6
Preparation: 45 min.
Cooking: 3 hr.
Level of difficulty: 2

- 2 large red bell peppers (capsicums), broiled (see recipe, page 85)
- 1 duck, about 4 lb (2 kg), boneless
- Salt and freshly ground black pepper
- Pinch of nutmeg
- 1 cup (200 g) short-grain rice
- 2/3 cup (150 g) butter
- 8 oz (250 g) chicken livers, finely chopped
- 1 onion
- 1 stalk celery
- 4 cloves
- 12 whole black peppercorns
- 1/2 cup (125 ml) dry white wine
- 2 tbsp all-purpose (plain) flour
- Freshly squeezed juice of 1 lemon
- 1/2 cup (125 ml) heavy (double) cream
- 1 cup (120 g) freshly grated Parmesan cheese

Place the bell peppers until a hot broiler (grill) and cook until the skins are completely blackened. Place in a brown paper bag and set aside for 10 minutes. Remove from the bag and peel off the skin. Discard the seeds. Cut into small squares. • Rub the insides of the duck with salt, pepper, and nutmeg. • Cook the rice in a large pot of salted, boiling water until tender. Drain and place in a bowl. • Place half the butter in a small frying pan and cook the chicken livers for 5 minutes. Stir the chicken livers into the rice then add the bell peppers. Mix well and use this mixture to stuff the duck. Sew up the duck using a trussing needle and kitchen thread. • Place all but 1 tablespoon of the remaining butter in a cast-iron pot or Dutch oven that will hold the duck snugly. Add the onion, celery, cloves, peppercorns, and salt and sauté until softened. • Put the duck in the pot and cook over medium heat, turning often until evenly browned. Pour in the wine and continue cooking until the duck is tender, about 2 hours. • Preheat the oven to 375°F (190°C/gas 5). • Remove the duck from the pot and set aside in a warm oven. • Stir the remaining butter and flour into the cooking juices. Add the lemon juice then the cream. Simmer for 2–3 minutes. Pour the sauce over the duck, sprinkle with the Parmesan, and place in the oven for 10 minutes to brown.
• Serve hot.

ROAST TURKEY WITH POMEGRANATE

Preheat the oven to 350°F (180°C/gas 4).
• Sprinkle the cavity of the turkey with a little salt and place half the butter inside. Tie up the turkey so that the legs and wings sit snugly against its sides. • Place the turkey in a fairly deep roasting pan or ovenproof dish. Smear with the remaining butter, drizzle with ½ cup (125 ml) of oil, and sprinkle with the sage. • Roast for 3 hours. Baste with its own juices at intervals as it cooks.
• Place the seeds of 2 of the pomegranates in a blender and process to obtain a smooth juice.
• After the turkey has been in the oven for 90 minutes, drizzle with half the pomegranate juice.
• Rinse and trim the liver. Chop coarsely and fry in 1 tablespoon of the oil over high heat. Add the remaining pomegranate juice, season with salt and pepper, and remove from the heat. • When the turkey is done, cut it into 10–12 pieces. Place in an ovenproof dish and pour the liver and pomegranate sauce over the top. Sprinkle with the seeds of the remaining pomegranate and roast again for 10 minutes before serving.

Serves: 6

Preparation: 20 min.

Cooking: 3 hr.

Level of difficulty: 2

- **1 young, tender turkey, about 4 lb (2 kg), with liver**
- **Salt and freshly ground black pepper**
- **¼ cup (60 g) butter**
- **⅔ cup (150 ml) extra-virgin olive oil**
- **4 fresh sage leaves, finely chopped**
- **3 whole ripe pomegranates**

POT ROASTED CHICKEN WITH PANCETTA AND POTATOES

Place the pancetta and rosemary in the cavity of the chicken. Season with salt and pepper. • Heat the oil a large Dutch oven over medium heat. Sauté garlic until lightly browned, 3–4 minutes. • Add the stock and vinegar, and bring to a boil. • Wrap the chickens in slices of prosciutto and place in the Dutch oven. Cover and simmer over low heat for 1 hour. • Remove the lid from the Dutch oven and add the potatoes and a little more stock to stop the chicken from sticking to the casserole. Simmer until the potatoes are tender, 35–40 minutes. • Serve hot.

Serves: 4–6

Preparation: 25 min.

Cooking: 1 hr. 45 min.

Level: 1

- 3 oz (90 g) pancetta, chopped
- 2 sprigs of rosemary
- $^1/_2$ cup (125 ml) dry white wine
- 2 chickens, about 4 lb (2 kg) total weight
- Salt and freshly ground black pepper
- 2 tbsp extra-virgin olive oil
- 2 oz (60 g) fatty prosciutto (Parma ham), thinly sliced
- 2 cloves garlic, finely chopped
- $^1/_3$ cup (90 ml) chicken stock + more as required
- 1 tbsp white wine vinegar
- 1 lb (500 g) small new potatoes, peeled

DUCK WITH CELERY BALLS

Serves: 4
Preparation: 40 min.
Cooking: 1 hr.
Level of difficulty: 2

- 1 clove garlic,
  1 onion,
- 1 stalk celery,
  1 carrot, all finely
  chopped
- 1 lb (500 g)
  tomatoes, peeled
  and chopped
- 1 duck, about 3 lb
  (1.5 kg), cut into
  8 pieces
- 1/2 cup (125 ml)
  robust dry red wine
- 2 cups (500 ml)
  Beef Stock
  (see page 946)
- 1/3 cup (90 ml)
  extra-virgin olive
  oil
- Salt and freshly
  ground black
  pepper
- 2 large stalks
  celery
- 3/4 cup (100 g) all-
  purpose (plain)
  flour
- 1 large egg, beaten
- 1 cup (250 ml)
  olive oil, for frying

Sauté the chopped vegetables with the oil in a heavy-bottomed pan over medium heat. • After about 5 minutes, add the duck. Season with salt and pepper and simmer until the duck is brown. • Pour in the wine and cook until it evaporates. • Stir in the tomatoes, partially cover the pan, and simmer until the duck is tender, about 90 minutes. Stir frequently, gradually adding the stock as the sauce reduces. • In the meantime, wash the celery stalks and cut into large pieces. Boil in a little salted water for 25–30 minutes. Drain well, squeeze out excess moisture and chop (not too finely). • Shape the celery into small balls, dip in the flour, then the egg. • Fry the celery balls in the oil in a heavy-bottomed pan over medium heat. Drain and set aside on paper towels. • Add the celery balls to the duck during the last 15 minutes of cooking. Take care when stirring or the balls may come apart. • Serve hot.

ROAST SQUAB PIGEON WITH SAUSAGE STUFFING

Preheat the oven to 375°F (190°C/gas 5).
• Clean the pigeons, discarding all internal organs except the livers. Wash the pigeons under cold running water and dry with paper towels. • Finely chop the pigeon livers with the chicken livers and sausages. Place the mixture in a bowl. Season with salt and pepper and mix well. • Fill each pigeon with the stuffing and close them up with toothpicks. • Fix 2 leaves of sage to each pigeon with a toothpick. • Sprinkle the birds with salt and pepper and transfer to a roasting pan. Drizzle with the oil and roast until cooked through, about 45 minutes. • Serve hot.

Serves: 4

Preparation: 25 min.

Cooking: 45 min.

Level of difficulty: 1

- **2 squab pigeons, with their livers**
- **2 chicken livers**
- **2 Italian pork sausages**
- **Salt and freshly ground black pepper**
- **8 leaves sage**
- **$1/4$ cup (60 ml) extra-virgin olive oil**

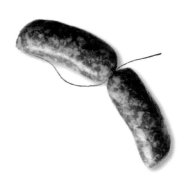

VEAL &
BEEF

VEAL ROLL WITH POTATOES

Preheat the oven to 375°F (190°C/gas 5). • Lay the veal slice out flat on a work surface. Use a sharp knife to trim the sides to make a fairly even rectangle. Pound lightly, taking care not to break the meat. • Sprinkle with the truffle, pistachios, pancetta, garlic, and trimmings of veal. Season with salt and pepper. • Roll the veal up tightly, with the grain of the meat parallel to the length of the roll. Tie with kitchen string. Tuck the rosemary under the string against the roll. • Place the roll in a roasting pan with the butter and oil and place in the oven. Turn often during roasting, basting with the wine and cooking juices. • After the meat has been cooking for about 75 minutes, add the potatoes, basting well in the cooking juice. Continue cooking until the potatoes are golden brown and the meat is very tender, about 45 minutes. • Serve hot.

Serves: 4

Preparation: 25 min.

Cooking: 2 hr.

Level of difficulty: 2

- 1 lb (500 g) slice of veal, preferably topside
- 1 black truffle, thinly sliced
- 2 tbsp pistachios
- 2 tbsp chopped pancetta
- 1 clove garlic, finely chopped
- Salt and freshly ground black pepper
- 2 sprigs rosemary
- $^1/_4$ cup (60 g) butter
- $^1/_4$ cup (60 g) extra-virgin olive oil
- $^1/_4$ cup (60 ml) dry white wine
- 1 lb (500 g) potatoes, peeled and cut in bite-size pieces

PAN ROASTED WHOLE VEAL SHANKS

Heat the butter and oil in a heavy-bottomed pan (large enough to contain both shanks) over medium heat. • Add the shanks and brown well all over, 8–10 minutes. • Add the garlic and leeks and simmer until softened, about 5 minutes. • Season with salt and pepper and pour in the wine. Cover the pan and simmer over low heat until the meat is almost tender, 1 hour 30 minutes–2 hours. • Add the potatoes and simmer until the meat is very tender and the potatoes are cooked. Serve hot.

Serves: 4

Preparation: 15 min.

Cooking: about 2 hr.

Level of difficulty: 1

- 3 tbsp butter
- 3 tbsp extra-virgin olive oil
- 2 whole veal shanks
- 2 cloves garlic, finely chopped
- 2 leeks, sliced
- 6 medium potatoes, peeled and cut in bite-sized pieces
- 1 cup (250 ml) dry white wine
- Salt and freshly ground black pepper

BEEF PARCELS WITH COGNAC

Serves: 6

*Preparation: 25 min.
+ 2 hr. to marinate
the meat + 1 hr. to
rest the dough*

Cooking: 75 min.

Level of difficulty: 3

- 1 tbsp freshly chopped rosemary
- 2 sage leaves, chopped
- 2 cloves garlic, lightly crushed but whole
- $1/4$ cup (60 ml) cognac
- $1^3/4$ lb (800 g) silverside beef
- Salt and freshly ground black pepper
- 2 tbsp butter
- $1/3$ cup (90 ml) dry white wine + extra, as required
- 1 recipe Bread Dough (see page 84)
- 1 tbsp all-purpose (plain) flour
- 1 large egg yolk, lightly beaten

Put the rosemary, sage, garlic, and cognac in a large bowl. Mix well and add the meat. Marinate for 2 hours at room temperature, turning often. • Preheat the oven to 375°F (190°C/gas 5). • Drain the meat, reserving the marinade. • Season with salt and pepper. • Melt 1 tablespoon of butter in a large casserole over medium heat. • Add the meat and sauté for 10 minutes, turning so that it is sealed all over. • Add the reserved marinade and let evaporate for 5 minutes. • Remove and discard the garlic. • Add a little of the wine then transfer to the oven. Roast for 35 minutes, adding a little more wine and turning the meat from time to time. • Remove from the oven and let cool. • Knead the bread dough on a lightly floured work surface for 5 minutes. Roll out to $1/4$-inch (5 mm) thick. • Cut the dough into 6 squares. Remove the meat from the casserole and cut into 6 portions. • Place a piece of meat on each square of dough. Wrap around the meat, sealing the edges well. • Place on an oiled baking sheet and let rise for 1 hour. • Return the casserole to the heat and add the remaining wine, remaining butter, and the flour. Mix well to prevent lumps forming. • Simmer the sauce for 2–3 minutes, or until thick. • Brush the bread dough with the beaten egg yolk. • Bake the meat parcels for 20 minutes, until golden brown. • Drizzle each parcel with a little sauce. • Serve hot.

PAN ROASTED BEEF WITH BEANS AND GRAPES

S oak the beans in cold water overnight. • Drain the beans, then simmer in lightly salted water until tender, about 90 minutes. • Heat the oil in a heavy-bottomed pan (with a tight-fitting lid) over medium heat. Add the beef and brown well all over, 8–10 minutes. Season with salt and pepper. • Add the shallots and sauté until golden brown, about 5 minutes. • Add ½ cup (125 ml) of stock, cover the pan, and simmer over low heat until the meat is almost tender, about 2 hours. Add more stock as required during cooking, making sure that the meat doesn't stick to the pan. • Drain the beans and add to the pan with the grapes. Simmer over low heat until the beef is tender and the beans and grapes are heated through. • Serve hot.

Serves: 4–6

Preparation: 15 min. + 12 hr. to soak the beans

Cooking: 3 hr. 30 min.

Level of difficulty: 1

- 1 cup (150 g) dried borlotti or cranberry beans
- $^1/_4$ cup (60 ml) extra-virgin olive oil
- 2 lb (1 kg) boneless beef roast
- Salt and freshly ground black pepper
- 6 shallots, sliced
- 2 cups (500 ml) boiling Beef Stock (see page 946)
- 1 bunch white grapes, preferably seedless

VEAL COOKED WITH SAGE AND ORANGE

Remove the zest from the orange using a sharp knife and cut into julienne strips. Peel the white pith off the orange with a sharp knife and cut the fruit into segments. • Fold each slice of prosciutto in 3 and lay on a piece of veal. Add a sage leaf to each one and secure with a cocktail stick. Sprinkle with the flour. • Heat the oil in a large frying pan over medium heat. Add the veal, prosciutto side down. Sauté for 2–3 minutes. Add the orange juice and simmer until the meat is cooked through and the sauce is slightly reduced, about 5 minutes. Add the orange zest and season with salt and pepper. • Garnish with the orange segments and serve hot.

Serves: 4

Preparation: 15 min.

Cooking: 10 min.

Level of difficulty: 1

- **1 large ripe orange**
- **12 slices prosciutto (Parma ham)**
- **12 veal escalopes**
- **12 sage leaves**
- **1 tbsp all-purpose (plain) flour**
- **3 tbsp extra virgin olive oil**
- **Freshly squeezed juice of 2 oranges**
- **Salt and freshly ground black pepper**

VEAL BRAISED WITH BABY ONIONS AND RAISINS

Serves: 4–6

Preparation: 15 min.

Cooking: 75 min.

Level of difficulty: 2

- 1/4 cup (60 ml) extra virgin olive oil
- 14 oz (400 g) baby onions
- 1 large carrot, peeled and chopped
- 2 celery sticks, chopped
- 1 cinnamon stick
- pinch of dried chili pepper flakes
- 1 3/4 lb (800 g) veal, cut into bite size chunks
- Salt and freshly ground black pepper
- 1/3 cup (60 g) raisins, soaked in warm water for 15 minutes and drained
- 1 cup (250 ml) dry white wine
- Boiled potatoes, to serve

Heat half the oil in a large casserole over medium heat. Add onions, carrots, celery, cinnamon stick, and chile pepper. • Sauté until the vegetables begin to soften, 3–4 minutes. • Heat the remaining oil in a large frying pan over medium heat. • Add the meat and sauté until well browned, about 5 minutes. Season with salt and pepper. • Add the meat to the casserole with the vegetables. Add the raisins and wine. • Cover and simmer over low heat until the meat is tender, about 1 hour. • Remove the lid and let the sauce reduce for 3–4 minutes. • Remove and discard the cinnamon. • Serve hot with boiled potatoes.

563

STUFFED VEAL ROLL

Serves: 4

Preparation: 15 min.

Cooking: 1 hr.

Level of difficulty: 1

- 1 lb (500 g) boned breast of veal
- 4 oz (125 g) fatty prosciutto (Parma ham), sliced
- 2 tbsp finely chopped fresh rosemary leaves
- 4 fresh sage leaves, finely chopped
- 2 cloves garlic, finely chopped
- Salt and freshly ground white pepper
- $1/4$ cup (60 g) butter
- $3/4$ cup (180 ml) dry white wine
- $1/2$ cup (125 ml) Beef Stock (see page 946)

Lay the veal out between 2 sheets of waxed paper and beat carefully until about ½-inch (1-cm) thick. • Spread the prosciutto over the veal and sprinkle with the rosemary, sage, garlic, salt, and pepper. • Roll up the veal and tie with kitchen string. Do not salt the outside. • Heat the butter in a large Dutch oven or casserole over high heat. Add the meat and brown for 6–7 minutes. • Add one-third of the wine, reduce the heat to low, and cover. • Turn the meat at frequent intervals, adding more wine as the liquid evaporates. Add a little stock, if necessary, when you have used up all the wine. • After 45 minutes, the veal roll will be cooked. Turn off the heat and let rest in the casserole for 6–8 minutes. • Remove the string and carve into slices about ½ inch (1 cm) thick.
• Serve hot or at room temperature.

ROAST VEAL WITH LEMON SAUCE

Tie the veal with kitchen string. Heat 2 tablespoons of the butter in a heavy-bottomed saucepan. Season the meat with salt and brown well in the butter. • Stir in the flour and stock. Cover the pan and simmer over low heat until tender, about 90 minutes. • About 5 minutes before the veal is cooked, heat the remaining butter in a small saucepan. Add the parsley and lemon juice and simmer over low heat. • Slice the veal on a heated serving platter and spoon the sauce over the top. Serve hot.

Serves: 4–6

Preparation: 15 min.

Cooking: 1 hr. 45 min.

Level of difficulty: 1

- 1$^1/_2$ lb (750 g) veal, preferably rump
- 3 tbsp butter
- Salt
- 1 tbsp all-purpose (plain) flour
- 1 cup (250 ml) Beef Stock (see page 946)
- 2 tbsp finely chopped fresh parsley
- Freshly squeezed juice of 2 lemons

ITALIAN VEAL STEW

Serves: 4–6

Preparation: 20 min.

Cooking: 90 min.

Level of difficulty: 1

- **2 lb (1 kg) boned veal shoulder or shank, cut into bite-sized cubes**
- **¹/₄ cup (60 g) butter**
- **¹/₄ cup (60 g) extra-virgin olive oil**
- **4–6 fresh sage leaves**
- **2–3 sprigs rosemary**
- **1 cup (250 ml) boiling Beef Stock (see page 946)**
- **1 tbsp tomato concentrate**
- **Salt**
- **1 lb (500 g) potatoes, peeled and cut in bite-sized pieces**
- **1 cup (250 ml) vegetable oil, for frying**

Heat the butter and oil in a heavy-bottomed pan (with a tight-fitting lid) over medium heat. Add the veal, sage, and rosemary. Season with salt and sauté until nicely browned, 6–8 minutes. • Dissolve the tomato concentrate in the stock and add to the pan. Cover the pan and simmer over low heat until the meat is almost tender, about 1 hour. • While the meat is cooking, fry the potatoes in the oil until just tender, 15–20 minutes. • Add the potatoes to the veal after it has been cooking for about 1 hour. Cover and simmer until the meat is tender enough to cut with a fork, about 30 minutes. • Serve hot.

BEEF POT ROAST WITH POLENTA

Use a sharp knife to make deep incisions in the meat and fill with pieces of garlic. Season the meat with salt and pepper. • Finely chop the onion, celery, carrot, and lard together. • Heat the butter in a heavy-bottomed pot (with a tight-fitting lid) over medium heat and sauté the onion and lard mixture until softened, about 5 minutes. • Add the beef roast to the pot and sauté until lightly browned. Dissolve the tomato concentrate in 1 cup (250 ml) of beef stock and gradually add this mixture to the pot as you brown the meat. • Cover the pot and simmer over very low heat until the meat is very tender, 5–6 hours. Turn the meat often during cooking, adding the remaining stock gradually.
• About an hour before the meat is done, bring the water and salt to a boil in a large saucepan. Add the polenta gradually, stirring constantly so that no lumps form. Stir the polenta over low heat until it begins to draw away from the edges of the pan, 40–50 minutes. If preferred use a polenta pan or pre-cooked polenta (which will be ready in about 10 minutes. • Place the polenta on a large serving plate. • Remove the pot roast from the pot and slice thinly. Place on the polenta and spoon the cooking juices over the top. • Serve hot.

Serves: 6–8

Preparation: 15 min.

Cooking: 5–6 hr.

Level of difficulty: 1

- 3 lb (1.5kg) boneless beef roast
- 2 cloves garlic, sliced
- Salt and freshly ground black pepper
- 1 large white onion
- 2 stalks celery
- 1 large carrot
- 2 oz (60 g) lard
- $^1/_3$ cup (90 g) butter
- About 4 cups (1 liter) boiling Beef Stock (see page 946)
- 1 tbsp tomato concentrate
- 3 quarts (3 liters) cold water
- 2 tbsp coarse sea salt
- 3 cups (450 g) polenta (yellow cornmeal)

BEEF COOKED IN WINE

Heat the butter and oil in a large saucepan over medium heat. Add the bay leaf and sage and sauté for 1–2 minutes. • Increase the heat to medium and add the beef. Season with salt and pepper and cook for 2 minutes. • Turn the beef over and cook for 2 minutes. • Add the wine and let it evaporate. • As soon as it has almost all evaporated transfer the beef to a serving dish. Discard the sage and bay leaf. • Drizzle the remaining cooking juices over the meat and serve.

Serves: 4–6

Preparation: 5 min.

Cooking: 10 min.

Level of difficulty: 2

- $^1/_4$ cup (60 g) butter
- $^1/_3$ cup (90 ml) extra-virgin olive oil
- 1 bay leaf
- 2 leaves fresh sage, torn
- 2 lb (1 kg) thinly sliced beef fillet
- Salt and freshly ground black pepper
- $^1/_2$ cup (125 ml) sweet white wine

BEEF AND APPLE STEW

Serves: 4–6

Preparation: 10 min.

Cooking: 85 min.

Level of difficulty: 2

- 2 lb (1 kg) lean beef, cut into bite-size chunks
- 2 tbsp all-purpose (plain) flour
- 1/3 cup (90 ml) extra-virgin olive oil
- 1 large onion, chopped
- 5 cloves garlic, unpeeled
- 2 bay leaves
- 1 sprig rosemary
- Salt and freshly ground black pepper
- 2 cups (500 ml) vegetable stock
- 1 1/2 lb (750 g) potatoes, peeled, cut into bite size chunks
- 2 tbsp white wine vinegar
- 2 tbsp butter
- 2 large ripe apples, cored and cut into small cubes
- Boiled white rice, to serve

Dust the beef with flour. • Heat 2 tablespoons of oil in a frying pan over medium heat. • Sauté the beef until browned all over. Set aside. • Heat 2 tablespoons of oil in a large frying pan over medium heat. Add the onion, garlic, bay leaves, and rosemary. Sauté for 3 minutes. • Add the meat and season with salt and pepper. • Add the stock, cover, and simmer over low heat until the meat is tender, 1 hour. • Parboil the potatoes with the vinegar in a large pot of salted boiling water for 5 minutes. Drain well. • Heat the remaining oil with the butter in a large frying pan over medium heat. • Add the potatoes and sauté until well browned. Season with salt and pepper. • Add the apples and cook for 3–4 minutes,. • Add the potato mixture to the stew and mix well. • Discard the garlic, rosemary, and bay leaves. • Serve hot with rice.

BREADED VEAL WITH ARUGULA AND TOMATOES

Put the flour on a plate. Put the bread crumbs on another plate. Beat the eggs in a bowl. • Place the veal between 2 sheets of waxed paper and flatten lightly with a meat pounder. • Dredge the veal in the flour, coating evenly. Shake to remove any excess flour. • Dip the veal in the beaten egg and then in the bread crumbs, coating evenly. • Heat ¼ cup (60 ml) of the oil in a large frying pan over high heat. • Fry in the oil for 2–3 minutes, then turn and sauté the other side until crisp golden brown and all over. • Drain on paper towels while you cook the remaining meat. • Heat the remaining oil in a small frying pan over medium heat. • Add the tomatoes and arugula and sauté for 3 minutes. • Season with salt and remove from the heat. Arrange the veal on a serving dish and drizzle with the balsamic vinegar. • Serve hot with the tomatoes and arugula.

Serves: 4–6

Preparation: 15 min.

Cooking: 15 min.

Level of difficulty: 2

- ¹/₃ cup (50 g) all-purpose (plain) flour
- ¹/₂ cup (75 g) fine dry bread crumbs
- 2 large eggs
- 1¹/₂ lb (750 g) veal cutlets
- ¹/₃ cup (90 ml) extra virgin olive oil
- 12 cherry tomatoes, halved
- 6 oz (180 g) arugula (rocket)
- Salt
- 2 tbsp balsamic vinegar

BOLOGNESE CUTLETS

Pound the veal lightly with a meat pounder.
• Beat the egg in a shallow dish with the salt.
• Dip the cutlets into the egg and then coat with
the bread crumbs, pressing so they stick. • Fry the
cutlets in the butter until golden brown on both
sides. • Arrange the veal in a single layer in a very
wide skillet or flameproof casserole. Place a slice
of prosciutto on each and cover with the Parmesan
shavings. • Mix the tomatoes with the meat stock
and pour into the pan. Cover and simmer for
about 15 minutes, until the cheese has melted.
• Serve hot.

Serves: 4

Preparation: 20 min.

Cooking: 25 min.

Level of difficulty: 1

- **4–8 veal cutlets,
  about 1 lb (500 g)
  in total**
- **1 large egg**
- **Pinch of salt**
- **1 cup (150 g) fine
  dry bread crumbs**
- **$^1/_2$ cup (125 g)
  butter**
- **6 thin slices
  prosciutto
  (Parma ham)**
- **1 cup (120 g)
  Parmesan cheese,
  in small shavings**
- **1 cup (250 g)
  sieved tomatoes
  (passata)**
- **$^1/_2$ cup (125 ml)
  Beef Stock
  (see page 946)**

VEAL CUTLETS WITH FONTINA CHEESE

Serves: 4

Preparation: 10 min.

Cooking: 15 min.

Level of difficulty: 1

- **4 veal cutlets with bone, about 6 oz (180 g) each**
- **4 oz (125 g) Fontina cheese, thinly sliced**
- **Wafer-thin slices of fresh white truffle (optional)**
- **Salt and freshly ground black pepper**
- **1 tbsp all-purpose (plain) flour**
- **1 large egg, lightly beaten**
- **$^1/_2$ cup (75 g) fine dry bread crumbs**
- **$^1/_3$ cup (90 g) butter**

Use a very sharp, pointed knife to cut horizontally into the cutlets toward the bone to form a pocket. • Place a quarter of the Fontina inside each pocket, together with a few slivers of truffle, if using. • Beat the sides of the pockets lightly to make the cut edges stick together, enclosing the contents. • Sprinkle the cutlets with a little salt and pepper and dust with flour. Dip in the egg and coat with bread crumbs. • Heat about two-thirds of the butter over high heat in a large frying pan. Add the cutlets and fry until golden brown on both sides. Add the remaining butter as you turn them. • Serve hot.

579

VEAL CUTLETS WITH PARMESAN CHEESE

Pound the veal lightly with a meat pounder.
• Lightly beat the egg and a pinch of salt in a small bowl. Dip the cutlets in the mixture. • Heat the butter in a frying pan over medium-high heat and fry the cutlets until light golden brown on both sides. • Top with a layer of the Parmesan shavings. Add the stock, cover, and cook over low heat until the cheese has melted. • Serve hot.

Serves: 4

Preparation: 15 min.

Cooking: 25 min.

Level of difficulty: 1

- 4 veal cutlets, about 6 oz (180 g) each
- 1 large egg
- Salt
- $^1/_3$ cup (90 g) butter
- 1 cup (120 g) Parmesan cheese, in small shavings
- $^1/_2$ cup (125 ml) Beef Stock (see page 946)

RUMP STEAK COOKED WITH VEGETABLES AND WHITE WINE

Serves: 4

Preparation: 10 min.

Cooking: 20 min.

Level of difficulty: 2

- 8 oz (250 g) frozen mixed vegetables
- 1/3 cup (50 g) all-purpose (plain) flour
- 1 1/2 lb (600 g) rump steak, flattened with a meat pounder, excess fat removed
- 1 tbsp extra-virgin olive oil
- 3 tbsp butter
- 1/2 onion, finely chopped
- 1/4 cup (50 g) canned corn kernels (sweet corn), drained
- 2 tbsp freshly chopped marjoram
- 1/2 cup (125 ml) dry white wine
- Salt and freshly ground black pepper
- 1 tbsp tomato paste (concentrate)
- 3 tbsp hot water

Cook the mixed vegetables in a large pot of salted boiling water until tender, about 5 minutes. Drain well. • Put the flour on a plate and dredge the steak, coating evenly. Shake gently to remove any excess flour. • Heat the oil and butter in a large frying pan over medium heat. • Add the onion and sauté until softened, about 5 minutes. • Add the steak and sauté for 2 minutes. Turn the meat and add the vegetables, corn kernels, and marjoram. Sauté for 2 minutes. • Add the wine and season with salt and pepper. • Turn the meat and lower the heat. • Cook for 6–8 minutes, until the wine has evaporated and the meat is cooked through but still a little pink in the center. • Mix the tomato paste and water in a cup. • Transfer the meat to a serving dish. • Add the diluted tomato paste to the frying pan and mix well. Cook for 1 minute and then spoon the vegetables and the sauce over the meat. • Garnish with marjoram and serve.

BAKED FILLET STEAK WITH ARTICHOKES

Preheat the oven to 450°F (225°C/gas 8).
• Clean the artichokes, removing the tough outer leaves and tops. Cut in half and scrap out any fuzzy choke. Slice thinly and place In a bowl of water with the lemon juice. • Brush the meat with a little of the oil and place on an oiled baking sheet. Season with salt and pepper and sprinkle with thyme. • Bake until the meat well cooked on the outside but still pink in the center, 15–20 minutes.
• Slice on a cutting board and arrange in a serving dish. • Drain the artichokes and pat dry with paper towels. Add to the serving dish with the meat.
• Drizzle with the remaining oil and the balsamic vinegar. Season with salt. • Serve hot.

Serves: 4

Preparation: 15 min.

Cooking: 15–20 min.

Level of difficulty: 2

- **2 artichokes**
- **Freshly squeezed juice of $^{1}/_{2}$ lemon**
- **2 lb (1 kg) beef fillet**
- **$^{1}/_{3}$ cup (90 ml) extra virgin olive oil**
- **Salt and freshly ground black pepper**
- **1 tbsp finely chopped fresh thyme**
- **1 tsp balsamic vinegar**

584

FLORENTINE STEAK

Serves: 2

Preparation: 5 min.

Cooking: 5–10 min.

Level of difficulty: 1

- 1¹/₂ lb (800 g) T-bone steak, at least 1¹/₂ inches (4 cm) thick
- Salt and freshly ground black pepper

Season the steak well with pepper. • Place on a grill about 4 inches (10 cm) above the glowing embers of a wood fire or barbecue. • Sprinkle the seared surface with a little salt, and cook for 4–5 minutes. Turn and cook the other side, sprinkling again with salt and a little more pepper. • When cooked, the steak should be well-browned and sealed on the outside, rare and juicy inside. • Serve hot.

585

PAN FRIED STEAK WITH GREEN SAUCE

S auce: Shell the egg and place in the bowl of a food processor. Add the anchovies, pickled cucumbers, garlic, parsley, and oil. • Mix the vinegar and wine in a small bowl. Dip the bread in this mixture and then squeeze to remove excess liquid. • Add the moist bread to the food processor bowl. Add the capers and blend to make a smooth sauce. Meat: Beat the mustard, Worcestershire sauce, and oil in a small bowl. • Brush each piece of meat with some of this mixture. • Put the herbs on a plate. Press the meat into the herbs, ensuring that each piece is evenly coated. • Cook the meat in a large grill pan or nonstick frying pan over medium-high heat. Season with salt and pepper, and sauté for until cooked to yor liking, 5–10 minutes. • Transfer to a cutting board and slice into strips. • Arrange the salad and the cucumbers on serving dishes. Add some of the steak to each dish. • Drizzle with the prepared sauce and serve.

Sauce

- 1 hard-boiled egg
- 4 anchovy fillets
- 4 pickled cucumbers (gherkins), sliced
- 1 clove garlic, finely chopped
- 4 tbsp finely chopped fresh parsley
- $^1/_3$ cup (90 ml) extra virgin olive oil + extra, as required
- 1 tbsp white wine vinegar
- 3 tbsp dry white wine
- 1 slice white bread, crusts removed
- 1 tbsp salt-cured capers rinsed

Steak

- 2 tbsp French mustard
- $^1/_2$ tsp Worcestershire sauce
- 2 tbsp extra virgin olive oil
- 1 lb (500 g) rump steak
- 3 tbsp dried herbs of Provence
- Salt and freshly ground black pepper
- 6 oz (180 g) mixed salad greens
- 4 small pickled cucumbers (gherkins), sliced

MIXED MEAT AND VEGETABLE SKEWERS

P reheat the oven to 400°F (200°C/gas 6).
• Remove any fat from the meat. • Chop the
meat, vegetables, and bread into large cubes or
squares. Slice the sausages thickly. • Thread the
cubes onto wooden skewers, alternating pieces of
meat, sausage, vegetables, bread, and sage
leaves. • Arrange the skewers in a roasting dish
and season with salt and pepper. Drizzle with the
oil. • Bake in for 30 minutes, turning occasionally
and adding beef stock to moisten, if required.
• When the meat is well browned, remove
from the oven and serve hot.

Serves: 6

Preparation: 1 hr.

Cooking: 30 min.

Level of difficulty: 2

- 12 oz (350 g) pork
- 12 oz (350 g) boned veal shoulder or shank
- 1 lb (500 g) chicken breast
- 1 yellow and 1 red bell pepper (capsicum)
- 12 oz (350 g) baby onions
- 20 cherry tomatoes
- 5 slices crusty bread
- 3 fresh Italian pork sausages
- 20 leaves fresh sage
- Salt and freshly ground black pepper
- $^1/_4$ cup (60 ml) extra-virgin olive oil
- $^1/_2$ cup (125 ml) Beef Stock (see page 946)

BEEF SKEWERS IN HERB SAUCE

Place 1¼ cups (300 ml) of the wine in a bowl with the vinegar, onions, and marjoram. Add the meat and marinate in the refrigerator for 4 hours. • Remove the meat from the marinade and drain well. • Heat the butter in a frying pan and pour in the marinade. Season with salt and pepper. • Bring to a boil, then add the remaining wine and the parsley. Simmer for 5 minutes until the sauce reduces a little. • Preheat a broiler (grill) or barbecue. • Thread the meat and vegetables onto skewers and broil or grill until cooked through. Turn frequently, basting with olive oil as required. Serve hot.

Serves: 4

Preparation: 15 min.
  + 4 hr. to marinate

Cooking: 30 min.

Level of difficulty: 1

- 1¾ cups (450 ml) dry white wine
- ¾ cup (180 ml) white wine vinegar
- 6 large white onions, finely chopped
- 1 tbsp finely chopped fresh marjoram
- 1¼ lb (600 g) veal shank or shoulder, cut into bite-sized pieces
- ½ cup (125 g) butter
- Salt and freshly ground white pepper
- 2 tbsp finely chopped parsley
- 1 red bell pepper (capsicum), cut into 1-inch (2.5-cm) pieces
- 15 baby onions
- Olive oil for basting

PARMESAN VEAL ROLLS

Serves: 4

Preparation: 20 min.

Cooking: 15 min.

Level of difficulty: 1

- 1/2 cup (125 g) butter
- 2 tbsp finely chopped fresh parsley
- 2 cloves garlic, finely chopped
- 1 cup (150 g) fine dry bread crumbs
- 1 1/4 cups (150 g) freshly grated Parmesan cheese
- 2 large eggs
- Salt and freshly ground black pepper
- 12 veal escalopes
- 1 small onion, finely chopped
- 2 tbsp tomato paste diluted in 1/2 cup (125 ml) water

Melt half the butter and mix well with the parsley, garlic, bread crumbs, Parmesan, eggs, salt, and pepper in a bowl. • Spread this mixture on the slices of veal. Roll each slice up and secure with toothpicks. • Sauté the onion in the remaining butter in a large frying pan. • Add the diluted tomato paste and season with salt and pepper. • Place the veal rolls in the pan in a single layer. Cover and cook over low heat for about 15 minutes, turning them frequently. • Serve hot.

ARTICHOKE ROLLS

Remove any small pieces of fat from the veal and pound lightly with a meat pounder. • Beat the eggs in a small bowl with the parsley, garlic, and salt. • Heat 2 tablespoons of oil in a small frying pan, pour in the egg mixture and cook until firm on both sides. Set aside to cool. • To clean the artichokes, remove the tough outer leaves and trim the stalk and tips. Only the tender inner heart should remain. Wash well in cold water and lemon juice. Cut each artichoke into 6 wedges. • Heat 2 tablespoons of oil in a frying pan over medium heat and cook the artichokes for 10 minutes. Season with salt and pepper and set aside. • Lay the slices of veal flat and place a piece of mortadella on each. • Cut the cooked egg into 12 pieces. Place a piece of egg and a wedge of artichoke on the mortadella. • Roll the veal up and secure with a toothpick. • Dredge in the flour. Heat the remaining oil in a frying pan and brown the rolls well all over. Season with salt and pepper. • Pour in the wine and cook for 20 minutes, adding stock if the pan becomes too dry. • Serve hot.

594

Serves: 4–6

Preparation: 25 min.

Cooking: 30 min.

Level of difficulty: 2

- **12 veal escalopes**
- **4 large eggs**
- **2 tbsp finely chopped fresh parsley**
- **2 cloves garlic, finely chopped**
- **Salt and freshly ground black pepper**
- **$^1/_2$ cup (125 ml) extra-virgin olive oil**
- **2 medium artichokes**
- **Freshly squeezed juice of $^1/_2$ lemon**
- **4 oz (125 g) mortadella slices, cut in half (12 pieces)**
- **$^1/_4$ cup (30 g) all-purpose (plain) flour**
- **$^1/_2$ cup (125 ml) dry white wine**
- **$^1/_2$ cup (125 ml) Beef Stock (see page 946)**

PUGLIA-STYLE BEEF PARCELS

Lightly pound the escalopes using a meat pounder. • Mix the Parmesan, parsley and 1 tablespoon of oil in a small bowl. Spread each slice of meat with this mixture. • Place a clove of garlic in the center of each slice of meat. • Fold in the edges and then roll up each escalope. Secure each parcel with a cocktail stick. • Put the flour on a plate and roll the parcels in it, coating evenly. Shake to remove any excess. • Heat the remaining oil in a large frying pan over medium heat. Add the parcels and sauté for 3–4 minutes, turning so that they are sealed all over. • Season with salt and pepper. Add the tomatoes and stock and simmer until the sauce is reduced and the meat is cooked through, about 40 minutes. • Transfer the parcels to a serving dish. Discard the cocktail sticks. Spoon the sauce over the top and serve hot.

Serves: 6

Preparation: 15 min.

Cooking: 45 min.

Level of difficulty: 1

- **12 veal escalopes**
- **1¹/₂ cups (185 g) freshly grated Parmesan cheese**
- **¹/₂ cup (60 g) finely chopped fresh parsley**
- **¹/₄ cup (60 ml) extra virgin olive oil**
- **12 cloves garlic, crushed but whole**
- **2 tbsp all-purpose (plain) flour**
- **Salt and freshly ground black pepper**
- **1 (14-oz/400-g) can tomatoes, with juice**
- **¹/₂ cup (125 ml) vegetable stock**

TUSCAN BEEF STEW

Serves: 4–6

Preparation: 20 min.

Cooking: 2 hr.

Level of difficulty: 1

- 2 lb (1 kg) shank or shoulder (shin) or shoulder of veal, or beef chuck
- $^1/_2$ cup (75 g) all-purpose (plain) flour
- 2 cloves garlic, finely chopped
- 1 tbsp finely chopped fresh sage
- 1 tbsp finely chopped fresh rosemary
- 5 tablespoons extra-virgin-olive oil
- 1 (14-oz/400-g) can tomatoes, with juice
- Salt and freshly ground black pepper
- 1 cup (250 ml) dry red wine
- 1 cup (250 ml) Beef Stock (see page 946)

Trim the meat and cut into 1-inch (2.5-cm) cubes. Lightly coat all over with flour, shaking off the excess. • Sauté the garlic, sage, and rosemary in the oil in a heavy-bottomed saucepan for 3–4 minutes. • Add the meat and brown the pieces all over for 5–6 minutes. • Add the tomatoes and salt and pepper and cook for another 5 minutes. • Pour in the wine, cover and simmer for 1 hour (longer for beef) until tender, adding more stock to moisten if necessary. • Serve hot.

597

MEAT LOAF

Place the beef, lard, Parmesan, cinnamon, salt, pepper, and ¼ cup (30 g) of bread crumbs in a medium bowl and mix well. Gradually stir in the milk, lemon juice, and eggs. The mixture should be quite stiff; add more bread crumbs if required.

• Shape the mixture into a meat loaf and roll in the remaining bread crumbs. • Preheat the oven to 390°F (190°C/gas 5). • Heat the oil in a large frying pan over medium-high heat. Carefully add the meat loaf and brown all over, about 10 minutes.

• Set aside on paper towels. • Melt the butter in a Dutch oven over medium heat. Add the onion and sauté until softened, about 5 minutes. • Add the meat loaf to the Dutch oven and bake in the oven until golden brown, about 30 minutes. • Serve hot or at room temperature.

Serves: 4

Preparation: 20 min.

Cooking: 45 min.

Level of difficulty: 1

- **1 lb (500 g) ground (minced) beef**
- **¹/₃ cup (90 g) butter**
- **¹/₄ cup (60 g) lard, chopped**
- **¹/₄ cup (30 g) freshly grated Parmesan cheese**
- **¹/₃ tsp ground cinnamon**
- **1 cup (150 g) fine dry bread crumbs + extra, as required**
- **¹/₄ cup (60 ml) milk**
- **Freshly squeezed juice of 1 lemon**
- **2 large eggs**
- **¹/₄ cup (60 ml) extra-virgin olive oil**
- **1 medium white onion**
- **Salt and freshly ground black pepper**

MEAT LOAF IN A PUFF PASTRY CRUST

Preheat the oven to 400°F (200°C/gas 6). • Put the bread crumbs in a large bowl and drizzle with the milk. Mix well. Add the pork, beef, mortadella, pistachios, prunes, chives, and paprika. Add 1 of the eggs, season with salt, and mix well using your hands. • Transfer the mixture to an oiled baking sheet lined with waxed paper. Shape it into a large meat loaf using your hands.
• Sprinkle the surface with a little salt and pepper. Bake for 8 minutes and then remove from the oven and gently turn the meat loaf using 2 spatulas.
• Bake for 8 more minutes, until the surface is browned all over. • Remove from the oven and let cool. • Roll out the pastry on a lightly floured sheet of waxed paper until ¼-inch (5-mm) thick. • Prick the surface of the pastry with a fork. • Place the cooled meat loaf in the center of the pastry.
• Wrap the pastry around the meat loaf pinching the edges together to seal. • Transfer to an oiled baking sheet and brush with the remaining egg.
• Bake until the pastry is golden brown all over and the meat is cooked through, about 35 minutes.
• Serve hot or at room temperature.

Serves: 4

Preparation: 25 min.

Cooking: 55 min.

Level of difficulty: 2

- 1¼ cups (150 g) fresh bread crumbs
- 3 tbsp milk
- 5 oz (150 g) ground (minced) pork
- 5 oz (150 g) ground (minced) beef
- ²/₃ cup (80 g) chopped mortadella
- ¼ cup (30 g) blanched pistachios, chopped
- 3 oz (90 g) prunes, pitted and coarsely chopped
- 1 tbsp fleshly chopped chives
- ¼ tsp paprika
- Salt
- 2 large eggs, lightly beaten
- Freshly ground black pepper
- 8 oz (250 g) puff pastry

MEAT LOAF
WITH MUSHROOMS

Serves: 6

Preparation: 20 min.

Cooking: 1 hr.

Level of difficulty: 1

- 6 oz (180 g) white bread, crusts removed
- 2 cups (500 ml) milk
- 1¼ lb (600 g) lean ground (minced) veal
- 2 large eggs
- ¼ cup (30 g) freshly grated pecorino cheese
- 2 oz (60 g) prosciutto (Parma ham), finely chopped
- Salt and freshly ground black pepper
- 2 tbsp fine dry bread crumbs
- 2 tbsp all-purpose (plain) flour
- ¼ cup (60 ml) extra-virgin oil
- ½ cup (125 ml) dry white wine
- 4 large tomatoes, peeled and chopped
- 8 oz (250 g) white mushrooms, coarsely chopped
- 1 clove garlic, finely chopped
- 2 tbsp finely chopped fresh parsley

Preheat the oven to 350°F (180°C/gas 4). • Soak the bread in the milk for 5 minutes. Squeeze well and place in a medium bowl bowl. Add the veal, eggs, pecorino, prosciutto, salt, and pepper. • Shape the mixture into a meat loaf and roll carefully first in the bread crumbs and then in the flour. • Heat the oil in a large, heavy pan over medium heat and brown the loaf on all sides. • Pour in the wine and cook for 5 minutes. • Add the tomatoes, mushrooms, garlic, and parsley. Stir well and transfer to an ovenproof dish or roasting pan. Bake until golden brown and cooked through, about 45 minutes. Serve hot or at room temperature.

BEEF CROQUETTES WITH APPLE

Rinse the apples and grate into a medium bowl. • Add the beef, eggs, Parmesan, garlic, salt, and pepper and mix well. • Form the mixture into oblong croquettes and dredge in the flour. • Heat the butter in a large frying pan and fry the croquettes until golden brown. • Dissolve the sugar in the wine and drizzle spoonfuls over the croquettes. • Serve hot when the wine has all been absorbed.

Serves: 4

Preparation: 10 min.

Cooking: 15 min.

Level of difficulty: 1

- 2 medium apples (Granny Smith are ideal)
- 1^1/$_4$ lb (600 g) finely ground (minced) lean beef
- 2 large eggs, beaten
- ^{1}/$_2$ cup (60 g) freshly grated Parmesan cheese
- 2 cloves garlic, finely chopped
- Salt and freshly ground black pepper
- 1 cup (150 g) all-purpose (plain) flour
- ^{1}/$_2$ cup (125 g) butter
- 2 tbsp sugar
- ^{1}/$_4$ cup (60 ml) dry white wine

VEAL CROQUETTES WITH LEMON

Mix the veal, eggs, Parmesan, lemon juice, salt, and pepper until smooth. • Heat the oil in a large frying pan until very hot. Fry tablespoons of the mixture until golden brown all over. • Drain on paper towels. Drizzle with the remaining lemon juice and serve hot.

Serves: 4

Preparation: 10 min.

Cooking: 20 min.

Level of difficulty: 1

- 1 lb (500 g) finely ground (minced) lean veal
- 4 large eggs
- $^1/_2$ cup (60 g) freshly grated Parmesan cheese
- Freshly squeezed juice of 1 lemon
- Salt and freshly ground white pepper
- 2 cups (500 ml) oil, for frying

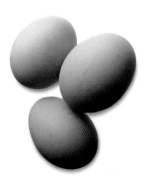

GROUND BEEF

Serves: 4

Preparation: 10 min.

Cooking: 50 min.

Level of difficulty: 1

S auté the garlic and rosemary in the oil and butter over medium heat for 2 minutes. • Add the beef, breaking it up with a fork. Cook for 5–7 minutes, stirring frequently, until all the meat changes color and its liquid has evaporated. Season with salt and pepper. • Add the bay leaf and half the wine and simmer gently over low heat for 40 minutes. Stir now and then during cooking and gradually add the remaining wine. • Remove the bay leaf and serve hot.

- **2 large cloves garlic, finely chopped**
- **1 tbsp finely chopped fresh rosemary leaves**
- **$1/4$ cup (60 ml) extra-virgin olive oil**
- **3 tbsp butter**
- **$1^1/4$ lb (600 g) lean ground (minced) beef**
- **Salt and freshly ground black pepper**
- **1 bay leaf**
- **$1^1/4$ cups (300 ml) dry, full-bodied red wine**

Serves: 4

Preparation: 15 min.

Cooking: 40 min.

Level of difficulty: 1

- 2 large floury (baking) potatoes, peeled
- 1³/₄ cups (100 g) fresh bread crumbs
- 3 tbsp milk
- 1¹/₂ lb (750 g) lean ground (minced) beef
- 1 large egg, lightly beaten
- 2 tbsp freshly grated Parmesan cheese
- 1 tbsp finely chopped fresh marjoram
- 1 tbsp finely chopped fresh parsley
- Salt and freshly ground black pepper
- 2 tbsp all-purpose (plain) flour
- 3 tbsp butter
- 2 shallots, finely chopped
- 2 cups (300 g) peas

MEATBALLS COOKED WITH PEAS

Cook the potatoes in a large pot of salted boiling water for 25 minutes, until tender. • Drain and mash until smooth. • Drizzle the bread crumbs with the milk in a large bowl. • Add the meat, potatoes, egg, Parmesan, marjoram, and parsley. Season with salt and pepper and mix well. • Shape the mixture into balls the size of walnuts using your hands. • Put the flour on a plate and roll the balls in it, coating evenly. • Heat the butter in a large frying pan over medium heat. Add the shallots and sauté until tender, 4–5 minutes. • Add the meatballs and sauté until well browned, 3–5 minutes. • Add the peas and sauté over medium heat until the meatballs are cooked and the peas are tender. • Serve hot.

MIXED BOILED MEATS

Serves: 10
Preparation: 10 min.
Cooking: 4 hr.
Level of difficulty: 2

- 2 medium onions, peeled, stuck with 4–6 cloves
- 3 stalks celery, trimmed and washed
- 3 medium carrots, peeled
- 20 black peppercorns
- 3 tbsp coarse salt
- 6 quarts (6 liters) boiling water
- 4 lb (2 kg) boneless beef cuts from brisket, bottom round, or rump roast
- 2 lb (1 kg) boneless veal cuts from breast or shoulder
- 1 large chicken
- 1¼ lb (600 g) calf's tongue
- 1 cotechino sausage, about 1½ lb (750 g)

Place 1 onion, 2 stalks celery, 2 carrots, 15 peppercorns, and 2 tablespoons of salt in the boiling water. • Add the beef and when the water has returned to a boil, reduce the heat a little and cover. Simmer for 1 hour, then add the veal and chicken. • Cook for 2 more hours, topping up with boiling water if necessary. Test the meats with a thin skewer: if they are not tender, simmer for 30 more minutes or longer. • Meanwhile, in a separate pot, cook the calf's tongue with the remaining onion, celery, carrot, peppercorns, and salt. This will take about 2 hours. Time it so that it is ready at the same time as the other meats. • Cook the cotechino sausage according to the instructions on the package. • All the meats should be ready at the same time, but they will not spoil if kept in their cooking liquid until everything is done. • Slice the cotechino sausage, but leave the other meats whole. Arrange on heated serving platters. Serve hot or at room temperature.

VEAL SHANKS (OSSOBUCHI) WITH SAFFRON RICE

Melt ¼ cup (60 g) of the butter in a large frying pan over medium heat. Add the onion and garlic and sauté until pale golden brown, about 5 minutes. • Add the veal shanks and season with salt and pepper. Dissolve the tomato concentrate in 1 cup (250 ml) of boiling water and add to the pan. Add enough of the remaining boiling water to cover the veal shanks. Cover the pan and simmer over low heat until the water has completely evaporated. • Add the Marsala and simmer until it has half evaporated. • Meanwhile, cook the rice in a large pan of lightly salted water until almost tender. • Remove from the heat and drain. • Heat the remaining butter in a small saucepan and add ¼ cup (60 ml) of water. Add the saffron and stir over medium heat until dissolved. Pour into the rice. • Add the Parmesan to the rice and stir well. • Place the rice on a large serving dish and place the veal shanks and their cooking liquid on top. • Serve hot.

Serves: 4

Preparation: 30 min.

Cooking: 2 h

Level of difficulty: 1

- ¹/₃ cup (90 g) butter
- 1 medium onion, finely chopped
- 2 cloves garlic, finely chopped
- 4 marrow bone steaks (ossobuchi)
- Salt and freshly ground black pepper
- 1 tbsp tomato concentrate
- 3 cups (750 ml) boiling water
- ¹/₂ cup (125 ml) dry Marsala wine
- 1¹/₂ cups (300 g) short-grain rice
- ¹/₄ tsp saffron
- ¹/₂ cup (60 g) freshly grated Parmesan cheese

BRAISED SWEET AND SOUR VEAL SHANKS (OSSOBUCHI)

Serves: 6

Preparation: 10 min.

Cooking: 90 min.

Level of difficulty: 2

- 1 lb (500 g) baby onions, peeled
- $^1/_3$ cup (50 g) all-purpose (plain) flour
- 6 marrow bone steaks (ossobuchi)
- $^1/_4$ cup (60 ml) extra virgin olive oil
- 2 cloves garlic, lightly crushed but whole
- 2 bay leaves
- $^3/_4$ cup (200 ml) dry white wine
- $^1/_3$ cup (75 g) sultanas, soaked in warm water for 10 minutes and drained
- 1 cup (250 ml) boiling Beef Stock (see page 946) + a little more if required
- Salt and freshly ground black pepper
- 2 tbsp finely chopped fresh parsley

Cook the onions in a large pot of salted boiling water until they begin to soften, about 5 minutes. Drain well. • Put the flour on a plate and dredge the meat, coating evenly. Gently shake each of the steaks to remove any excess flour. • Heat the oil in a large casserole. Add the meat and sauté for 2 minutes. Add the garlic and the bay leaves. Turn the meat and sauté for 2–3 minutes, until sealed all over. • Add the wine and let it evaporate, 2 minutes. • Add the sultanas, onions, and stock and season with salt and pepper. Cover and cook over low heat for until the meat is very tender, about 90 minutes. Add a little more stock if the meat begins to stick to the casserole during the cooking time. • Remove and discard the garlic and the bay leaves. • Transfer the meat to a serving dish and drizzle with the cooking juices. Garnish with the parsley and serve.

TRIPE WITH TOMATO SAUCE

Rinse the tripe thoroughly in cold running water. Use kitchen scissors or a sharp knife to cut into thin strips. • Place the tripe in a heavy-bottomed pan over medium heat and sauté for 15 minutes. Remove from the heat and let cool on a plate for 15 minutes. • Melt the butter in the same pan and sauté the celery, onion, and garlic until softened, about 5 minutes. • Add the tripe, tomatoes, bouillon cube, and bay leaf. Season with salt and pepper. Cover the pan and simmer over low heat until the tripe is tender, about 2 hours 30 minutes. • Stir the parsley, basil, and Parmesan into the tripe about 5 minutes before serving.
• Serve hot.

Serves: 4

Preparation: 15 min.

Cooking: 3 hr.

Level of difficulty: 1

- 2 lb (1 kg) calf's honeycomb tripe
- 3 tbsp butter
- 2 stalks celery, finely sliced
- 2 medium onions, finely chopped
- 2 cloves garlic, finely chopped
- 2 (14-oz/400-g) cans tomatoes, with juice
- 1 bouillon cube
- 1 bay leaf
- Salt and freshly ground black pepper
- 4 tbsp finely chopped fresh parsley
- 2 tbsp finely chopped basil
- $1/4$ cup (30 g) freshly grated Parmesan cheese

CARPACCIO

Arrange the slices of beef on a platter, cover with a sheet of plastic wrap (cling film), and place in the refrigerator for 15 minutes while you prepare the dressing. • Mix the egg yolks in a bowl with the mustard powder, lemon juice, and a dash of salt. Beat with a balloon whisk or electric beater as you add the oil in a tiny trickle until the sauce has thickened and you have used most, if not all, the oil. • Add the Worcestershire sauce and vinegar. • Take the beef out of the refrigerator and spoon some of the sauce over it, letting it trickle off a fork in a grid pattern. • Serve at once, handing round the remainder of the sauce separately.

Serves: 6

Preparation: 20 min.

Level of difficulty: 1

- 1³/₄ lb (800 g) prime beef fillet or tenderloin, sliced wafer-thin
- 4 egg yolks
- 2 tsp mustard powder
- Freshly squeezed juice of ¹/₂ lemon
- Salt
- 2 cups (500 ml) extra-virgin olive oil
- 3 drops Worcestershire sauce
- 1 tbsp white wine vinegar

VENETIAN-STYLE LIVER

Serves: 6

Preparation: 15 min.

Cooking: 20 min.

Level of difficulty: 1

- 1¹/₂ lb (750 g) white onions, thinly sliced
- ¹/₄ cup (60 g) butter
- 2 tbsp extra-virgin olive oil
- 1¹/₂ lb (750 g) calf's liver, cut into thin strips
- Salt and freshly ground black pepper
- 2 tbsp finely chopped parsley

Place the onions, butter, and oil in a large frying pan over low heat. Let sweat gently for 15 minutes, then add the liver. • Cook over high heat, stirring and turning constantly for 5 minutes at most (or the liver will become tough). Sprinkle with salt just before removing from the heat.
• Season with pepper, sprinkle with the parsley, and serve hot.

LIVER WITH MARSALA

Serves: 4

Preparation: 10 min.

Cooking: 5–10 min.

Level of difficulty: 1

- 1 lb (500 g) calf's liver, thinly sliced
- Salt and freshly ground black pepper
- $^1/_2$ cup (75 g) all-purpose (plain) flour
- $^1/_3$ cup (90 g) butter
- $^1/_3$ cup (90 ml) dry Marsala wine
- Mashed potatoes, to serve (optional)

Season the liver with salt and pepper and dredge in the flour. • Place the butter in a large frying pan over medium-high heat. Add the liver and cook on one side until tender, 2–3 minutes. Turn and add the Marsala. Cook until tender, 2–3 minutes. • Place in a heated serving dish. • Serve hot with the mashed potatoes, if liked.

LIVER WITH BUTTER AND SAGE

S eason the liver with salt and pepper and dredge in the flour. • Place the butter and sage leaves in a large frying pan over medium-high heat. Add the liver and cook on one side until tender, 2–3 minutes. Turn and cook the other side. • Place in a heated serving dish. Pour the butter and sage mixture over the top. • Serve hot with the potatoes, if liked.

Serves: 4

Preparation: 10 min.

Cooking: 5–10 min.

Level of difficulty: 1

- **1 lb (500 g) calf's liver, thinly sliced**
- **Salt and freshly ground black pepper**
- **$^{1}/_{2}$ cup (75 g) all-purpose (plain) flour**
- **$^{1}/_{2}$ cup (125 g) butter**
- **8–10 fresh sage leaves**
- **Oven-baked potatoes, to serve (optional)**

CALF'S LIVER, MILANESE STYLE

Season the liver with salt and pepper and dredge in the flour. • Dip in the egg and then dredge in the bread crumbs. • Heat the butter and oil in a large frying pan over medium heat. Add the liver and fry until golden brown on both sides. • Put the salad greens, if using, on a large platter and place the liver on top. Slice the lemon into wedges and arrange around the liver. • Serve hot.

Serves: 4

Preparation: 15 min.

Cooking: 10 min.

Level of difficulty: 1

- 1 lb (500 g) calf's liver, thinly sliced
- Salt and freshly ground black pepper
- $1/2$ cup (75 g) all-purpose (plain) flour
- 1 large egg, lightly beaten
- 1 cup (150 g) fine dry bread crumbs
- $1/3$ cup (90 g) butter
- 1 tbsp extra-virgin olive oil
- Salad greens, to serve (optional)
- 1 lemon

BRAISED KIDNEYS

Serves: 4

Preparation: 15 min.
+ 4 hr. to rest

Cooking: 45 min.

Level of difficulty: 1

- 1 lb (500 g) calf's kidneys
- 2 tbsp butter
- 1/3 cup (90 ml) extra-virgin olive oil
- 1 medium white onion, finely chopped
- 2 cloves garlic, finely chopped
- 2 tbsp finely chopped fresh parsley
- 1 lb (500 g) tomatoes, peeled and chopped
- Salt and freshly ground black pepper

Remove the fatty parts from the kidneys. Bring a pot of water to a boil and blanch the kidneys twice for 1 minute each. Drain well and sprinkle with a little salt. Set aside for 4 hours. • Rinse the kidneys and dry well. Use a sharp knife or kitchen scissors to cut into thin strips. • Heat the butter and 2 tablespoons of oil in a medium saucepan. Add the onion, garlic, and parsley and sauté until softened, about 5 minutes. • Add the tomatoes and season with salt and pepper. Cover and simmer over low heat for 30 minutes. • Meanwhile, heat the remaining oil in a frying pan over medium-high heat and sauté the kidneys for 2–3 minutes, or until lightly browned. • Add the kidneys to the pan with the sauce and simmer for 10 more minutes. • Serve hot.

PORK

NEAPOLITAN PORK ROLLS

Place the raisins in a cup and cover with warm water. Let soak for 15 minutes. • Gently pound the slices of pork to flatten. Use a sharp knife to trim the edges. • Drain the raisins and dry well. • Place the raisins on a chopping board with the prosciutto, capers, and pine nuts and chop finely with a sharp knife. • Place in a small bowl. Stir in the bread crumbs and season with salt and pepper. • Sprinkle the filling over the pieces of meat, leaving a border around the edges. Roll the meat up and secure with toothpicks. • Heat the oil in a large frying pan over medium heat. Add the pork rolls and sauté in the oil until nicely browned, 8–10 minutes. • Pour in the tomato sauce and add chile pepper to taste. Season with salt and pepper. Cover the pan and simmer over low heat for 2 hours. • Remove the toothpicks and serve the pork rolls hot with the tomato sauce spoon over the top.

Serves: 4

Preparation: 20 min.
+ 15 min. to soak
the raisins

Cooking: 2 hr. 15 min.

Level of difficulty: 2

- 4 tbsp raisins
- 8 thin slices pork loin (escalopes)
- 4 oz (125 g) prosciutto (Parma ham)
- 3 tbsp salt-cured capers, rinsed
- 2 tbsp pine nuts
- 4 tbsp fine dry bread crumbs
- Salt and freshly ground black pepper
- $^1/_4$ cup (60 ml) extra-virgin olive oil
- 2 cups (500 ml) tomato passata
- Chile pepper

PORK CHOPS WITH WINE AND HERBS

Preheat the oven to 375°F (190°C/gas 5). •
Lightly pound the pork chops to flatten a little.
• Place the sage, rosemary, marjoram, and garlic
on a chopping board and chop finely together with
a sharp knife. • Season the pork chops with salt
and pepper and sprinkle with the herb and garlic
mixture. • Place the oil in a large Dutch oven or
casserole dish. Add the pork chops and wine, and
pour in enough water to cover the chops. Bake in
the oven until tender and the sauce has reduced,
about 1 hour. • Serve hot.

Serves: 4

Preparation: 20 min.

Cooking: 1 hr.

Level of difficulty: 1

- **4 large pork chops**
- **8 leaves fresh sage**
- **Sprig of fresh rosemary**
- **Sprig of fresh marjoram**
- **2 cloves garlic**
- **2 tbsp extra-virgin olive oil**
- **Salt and freshly ground black pepper**
- **$^1/_2$ cup (125 ml) dry white wine**

PORK LOIN ROAST WITH ORANGE AND PANCETTA

Preheat the oven to 425°F (220°C/gas 7).
• Remove the outer, orange-colored zest from the oranges using a sharp knife and cut into julienne strips. Blanch the zest for 2 minutes in boiling water. Drain and set aside. • Squeeze the juice from the oranges and set aside. • Chop one-third of the pancetta. Arrange the remaining slices of pancetta on a work surface to make a single sheet. Sprinkle the chopped pancetta on top. Add the rosemary and garlic. Season with salt and pepper. • Lay the pork on top and wrap the pancetta around it, securing with kitchen string.
• Place in a roasting pan and drizzle with the oil. Bake until lightly browned, about 10 minutes.
• Remove from the oven and add the vermouth.
• Return to the oven for 5 minutes. • Lower the temperature to 350°F (180°C/gas 4). • Add the stock to the meat and roast for 30 minutes. • Add the orange juice. Roast, turning the meat from time to time, until cooked through, about 30 minutes.
• Transfer the meat to a sheet of aluminum foil. Wrap in the foil and let rest for 10 minutes.
• Transfer the cooking juices to a saucepan over low heat. Add the butter and let it melt. Add the wine and let it evaporate for 2 minutes. Add the sugar and reduce the sauce over medium heat for 2–3 minutes. Add the orange zest and segments of orange and mix well. Remove from the heat.
• Unwrap the meat and slice it. Spoon the orange sauce over it. Serve hot.

Serves: 4

Preparation: 25 min.
+ 10 min. to rest
the meat

Cooking: 80 min.

Level of difficulty: 3

- 4 oranges
- 6 oz (180 g) sliced pancetta or bacon
- 1 tbsp finely chopped fresh rosemary
- 1 clove garlic, finely chopped
- Salt and freshly ground black pepper
- 2 lb (1 kg) pork loin
- 3 tbsp extra-virgin olive oil
- $^1/_3$ cup (90 ml) vermouth
- $^1/_3$ cup (90 ml) Beef Stock (see page 946)
- 1 tbsp butter
- $^1/_3$ cup (90 ml) dry white wine
- 2 tbsp sugar

PORK CHOPS ROAST WITH POTATOES

Preheat the oven to 475°F (250°C/gas 9).
• Parboil the potatoes in a large pot of salted boiling water with the vinegar for 5 minutes. Drain well and drain on paper towels. Transfer to a roasting pan. • Add the bay leaves, juniper, and onion. Season with salt and pepper. Drizzle with half the oil and bake for 15 minutes. • Remove from the oven and add the pork chops. Season with a little more salt and pepper and drizzle with the remaining oil. • Bake until the meat is cooked through and browned, 15–20 minutes. • Serve hot.

Serves: 4

Preparation: 10 min.

Cooking: 40 min.

Level of difficulty: 1

- 1³/₄ lb (800 g) floury (baking) potatoes, peeled and cut into small cubes
- 2 tbsp white wine vinegar
- 3 bay leaves
- ¹/₂ tsp juniper berries
- 1 large onion, cut into segments
- Salt and freshly ground black pepper
- ¹/₂ cup (125 ml) extra virgin olive oil
- 4 large pork chops

STUFFED ROAST PORK WITH MARSALA

Serves: 4–6

Preparation: 15 min.

Cooking: 85 min.

Level of difficulty: 2

- **3 lb (1.5 kg) lean pork loin, in 1 large flat piece**
- **Salt and freshly ground black pepper**
- **5 large eggs**
- **$1/4$ cup (60 ml) milk**
- **$1/4$ cup (40 g) freshly grated Parmesan**
- **$1/3$ cup (30 g) chopped almonds**
- **$1/2$ cup (80 g) salt-cured capers, rinsed**
- **2 tbsp finely chopped fresh basil**
- **$1/4$ cup (60 ml) extra-virgin olive oil**
- **$1/2$ cup (125 ml) vegetable stock**
- **$1/3$ cup (80 ml) dry Marsala wine**

Preheat the oven to 350°F (180°C/gas 4).
• Flatten the pork lightly using a meat pounder. Season with salt and pepper. • Beat the eggs in a bowl with the milk. Add the Parmesan, almonds, capers, and basil. • Heat half the oil in a large frying pan over medium heat. • Pour in the egg mixture and cook until the egg is almost set, 5 minutes.
• Turnout onto the meat. Roll up the meat and secure it with kitchen string. • Heat the remaining oil in a large frying pan over high heat. • Transfer the meat to the pan and sauté for 2–3 minutes, turning so it is sealed all over. • Transfer to a roasting pan and roast until cooked through, about 70 minutes.
• Place the meat in a serving dish. • Skim off any excess fat that has collected in the pan. Add the stock and Marsala and let reduce over medium heat for 5 minutes. • Slice the meat and drizzle with the sauce.

PORK

PORK SCALOPPINE WITH MARSALA WINE

Heat the lard and oil in a large frying pan over medium heat. Add the garlic and sauté until pale golden brown. Remove and discard the garlic.
• Add the pork and season with salt and pepper. Cook until tender on one side, 2–3 minutes, then turn and cook the other side. • Set the scaloppine aside on a heated serving dish in a warm oven.
• Add the Marsala, butter, and cornstarch to the pan and simmer over low heat until thickened.
• Pour the sauce over the pork and serve hot.

Serves: 4

Preparation: 15 min.

Cooking: 15 min.

Level of difficulty: 1

- 1 tbsp lard, chopped
- 2 tbsp extra-virgin olive oil
- 2 cloves garlic, crushed but whole
- 8 thin slices pork loin (escalopes)
- Salt and freshly ground black pepper
- $^1/_2$ cup (125 ml) dry Marsala wine
- 1 tbsp butter
- 1 tsp cornstarch (cornflour) flour

638

PORK LOIN AND SAUSAGES

Serves: 4–6

Preparation: 25 min.

Cooking: 1 hr.

Level of difficulty: 1

Polenta
- **3 quarts (3 liters) cold water**
- **2 tbsp coarse sea salt**
- **3 cups (450 g) polenta (yellow cornmeal)**

Meat
- **3 tbsp butter**
- **3 medium white onions, sliced**
- **Salt and freshly ground black pepper**
- **1 lb (500 g) boned pork loin, sliced thinly**
- **$^1/_2$ cup (75 g) all-purpose (plain) flour**
- **1 lb (500 g) Italian pork sausages**
- **1 cup (250 g) tomato passata**

Polenta: Bring the water and salt to a boil in a large saucepan. Add the polenta gradually, stirring constantly so that no lumps form. Stir the polenta over low heat until it begins to draw away from the edges of the pan, 40–50 minutes. If preferred, use a polenta pan or pre-cooked polenta (which will be ready in about 10 minutes). • Meat: Melt the butter in a large frying pan over medium heat. Add the onions, season with salt and pepper, and sauté until pale golden brown, 5–6 minutes. • Add the sausages and sauté until lightly browned, about 5 minutes. Pour in the tomato passata and simmer for 5 minutes. • Add the slices of pork and simmer until cooked, about 10 minutes. • Place the polenta on a heated serving dish and spoon the meat and cooking liquid over the top. • Serve hot.

PORK WITH PRUNES AND WILD MUSHROOMS

Sauté the shallots in 1 tablespoon of butter in a small frying pan over medium heat until softened. • Add the peppercorns and 1 sprig of sage. Pour in ⅔ cup (150 ml) of wine. Bring to a boil. • Put the pork in a large bowl and pour the hot wine mixture over the meat. Let marinate for 2 hours. • Drain the pork and pat dry with paper towels. • Sauté the pork and remaining sage in 1 tablespoon of butter in a large frying pan over medium heat for 4 minutes. • Transfer the pork to a large saucepan. Pour the remaining wine over the pork and add the prunes. Bring to a boil and simmer over low heat for 6–8 minutes, or until the meat is cooked through and the prunes have softened. • Season with salt. Transfer the meat to a serving dish and keep warm. • Cook the sauce over medium heat for 2–3 minutes, or until slightly thickened. • Spoon the prune sauce over the pork and keep warm. • Heat the remaining butter in a large frying pan over medium heat. Add the mushrooms and sauté until tender. • Top the pork with the mushrooms and serve hot.

Serves: 4–6

Preparation: 20 min.
+ 2 hr. to marinate

Cooking: 30 min.

Level of difficulty: 2

- 2 shallots, finely chopped
- ¼ cup (60 g) butter
- ½ tsp crushed black peppercorns
- 3 sprigs sage
- 2 cups (500 ml) full-bodied red wine
- 8 slices pork fillet, weighing about 1 lb (500 g)
- 8 prunes, pitted and coarsely chopped
- Salt
- 14 oz (400 g) mixed wild mushrooms

PORK BRAISED IN RED WINE

Heat half the oil in a large casserole over medium heat. • Add 3 carrots, the celery, chopped onion, and meat. Sauté until the meat is well browned, 5–7 minutes. • Add the cinnamon and paprika. Season with salt and add the wine.
• Cover and simmer over low heat until tender, 50 minutes. If it begins to stick to the casserole add a little stock. • Cook the baby onions in the remaining stock in a small saucepan over medium heat until tender, about 7 minutes. Drain well.
• Melt the butter with the remaining oil in a large frying pan over medium heat. Add the pumpkin, lovage, and remaining carrots. Season with salt and pepper. Add the mushrooms and baby onions. Sauté the vegetables over very low heat until tender and well browned, about 30 minutes.
• Transfer the meat to a serving dish. Add the vegetables, drizzle with the sauce, and serve.

Serves: 4

Preparation: 20 min.

Cooking: 1 hr. 40 min.

Level of difficulty: 2

- $^1/_4$ cup (60 ml) extra virgin olive oil
- 4 large carrots, cut into small cubes
- 1 celery stick, chopped
- 1 medium onion, chopped
- $1^3/_4$ lb (800 g) lean pork, diced
- $^1/_2$ tsp ground cinnamon
- $^1/_2$ tsp hot paprika
- Salt
- $1^2/_3$ cups (400 ml) red wine
- 1 cup (250 ml) vegetable stock
- 14 oz (400 g) baby onions
- 2 tbsp butter
- 8 oz (250 g) pumpkin flesh, cut in cubes
- 5 oz (150 g) lovage, chopped
- Freshly ground pepper
- 8 oz (250 g) button mushrooms, quartered

AREZZO MEAT STEW

- 5 tbsp extra-virgin olive oil
- 2 cloves garlic, finely chopped
- 1 medium onion, 1 small carrot, 1 small stalk celery, all finely chopped
- 1/2 tbsp finely chopped fresh parsley
- 1 tbsp finely chopped fresh basil
- 2 crumbled dried chile peppers
- 3 lb (1.3 kg) assorted meats (pork, poultry, game veal, rabbit, guinea fowl) cut in small pieces
- 1/2 cup (125 ml) full-bodied, dry red wine
- 3 tbsp tomato concentrate
- Salt and freshly ground black pepper
- 4 cups (1 liter) hot Beef Stock (see page 496)
- 6 slices firm-textured bread, 2 days old
- 1 clove garlic, whole

Pour the oil into a heavy-bottomed saucepan and sauté the garlic, onion, carrot, celery, parsley, basil, and chile peppers. • After 5 minutes, add the beef, poultry, and game and cook over slightly higher heat for 8 minutes. • Pour in the wine and cook, uncovered, for about 7 minutes to reduce the liquid. • Add the tomato purée, season with salt and pepper, and stir well. • Pour in the stock. Lower the heat, cover and simmer for about 1 hour, stirring occasionally. There should be plenty of liquid when the dish is cooked; it should be halfway between a hearty soup and a casserole. • Cut each piece of bread in half and toast. Rub the toast with the remaining garlic, place in heated soup bowls, and ladle the stew over the top. • Let stand for 2–3 minutes before serving so that the bread can absorb some of the liquid.

645

MEATBALL KEBABS

P ut the bread in the bowl of a food processor. Drizzle with the milk and blend for a few seconds. • Add the garlic, eggs, beef, pork, Parmesan, and parsley. Season with salt and mix well. • Shape the mixture into balls the size of walnuts. Roll the balls in bread crumbs. • Heat the oil in a large frying pan over medium-high heat. • Sauté the meatballs for 2–3 minutes, or until browned all over. • Add the wine and sage. Cover the pan and cook for 7–10 minutes, or until cooked through. • Transfer the meatballs to a plate and keep warm. • Preheat a broiler (grill) on a medium-high setting. • Blanch the carrots in salted, boiling water for 2 minutes. • Drain well. • Roll half the meatballs in the slices of carrot and thread onto metal skewers. • Roll the remaining meatballs in the lard and thread them onto metal skewers. • Grill the kebabs for 2–3 minutes, or until the lard begins to melt and color. Turn often while grilling. • Serve hot.

Serves: 4

Preparation: 10 min.

Cooking: 20 min.

Level of difficulty: 2

- 1 bread roll, crusts removed
- 2 tbsp milk
- 2 cloves garlic, finely chopped
- 2 large eggs, lightly beaten
- 8 oz (250 g) ground (minced) beef
- 8 oz (250 g) ground (minced) pork
- 2/3 cup (100 g) freshly grated Parmesan cheese
- 1 tbsp finely chopped fresh parsley
- Salt
- 1/2 cup (60 g) fine dry bread crumbs
- 3 tbsp extra-virgin olive oil
- 2 tbsp dry white wine
- 1 sprig sage
- 2 large carrots, peeled and thinly sliced lengthwise
- 4 oz (125 g) sliced lard (or streaky bacon)

ZAMPONE SAUSAGE WITH POTATOES

C ook the zampone in a pot of boiling water according to the instructions on the package.
• About 30 minutes before the sausage is cooked, boil the potatoes in a large pot of salted water for 25 minutes, or until tender. Mash the potatoes and stir in the milk and butter. Season with nutmeg, salt, and pepper. • Slice the cooked sausage and serve on a heated serving dish with the potatoes.

Serves: 6

Preparation: 15 min.

Cooking: 3 hr.

Level of difficulty: 1

- **1 zampone sausage, about 2 lb (1 kg)**
- **1^1/$_2$ lb (750 g) potatoes, peeled**
- **^{1}/$_2$ cup (125 ml) whole milk**
- **1 tbsp butter**
- **Salt and freshly ground black pepper**
- **Pinch of nutmeg**

COTECHINO SAUSAGE WRAPPED IN BEEF

Use a meat pounder to flatten the slice of beef.
• Skin the cotechino sausage. Wrap it up in the slice of beef, enveloping it completely. Tie the resulting roll securely but not too tightly with kitchen string. • Sauté the onion, celery, and carrot in the butter for a few minutes. • Add the meat and sausage roll, and brown well all over. • Pour in the wine and cook until it has evaporated. • Add the mushrooms and the water they were soaked in.
• Simmer gently for 90 minutes. • Untie the string and slice. Serve hot with the cooking juices.

Serves: 4

Preparation: 25 min.

Cooking: 90 min.

Level of difficulty: 2

- 1 large, thin slice of beef, cut from the rump, about 8 oz (250 g)
- 1 large cotechino sausage
- 1 small onion, 1 stalk celery, 1 small carrot, all coarsely chopped
- 2 tbsp butter
- $^1/_2$ cup (125 ml) dry red wine
- 2 oz (60 g) dried porcini mushrooms, soaked in warm water, drained, and chopped
- 2 cups (500 ml) water

SAUSAGES WITH FLOWERING TURNIP TOPS

Serves: 4

Preparation: 5 min.

Cooking: 25 min.

Level of difficulty: 1

- 2 cloves garlic, finely chopped
- 1 fresh red chile pepper, thinly sliced
- 2 tbsp extra-virgin olive oil
- 8 large Italian pork sausages
- 1¼ lb (600 g) flowering turnip tops (or broccoli, if preferred)
- Salt and freshly ground black pepper

Sauté the garlic and chile pepper in the oil in a large frying pan over medium heat until pale gold. • Add the sausages and brown all over, pricking well with a fork to let some of the fat run out. • Add the flowering turnip tops to the pan. Season with salt and pepper. Cook for 20 minutes, or until the greens are tender, but not overcooked. Add a little water during cooking if the pan dries out too much. • Serve hot.

ITALIAN SAUSAGE STEW

Bring a medium pan of water to a boil and add the sausages. Pierce the sausages here and there with a shark knife and boil for 2–3 minutes. Drain well. • Place in a saucepan just large enough for the sausages to stay in a single layer over medium heat. Pour in the wine and enough water to just cover the sausages. Simmer until the cooking liquid has almost all evaporated. • Add the tomatoes, potatoes, onion, celery, carrot, bay leaf and cloves. Season with salt and pepper. Simmer over low heat until the vegetables are tender, about 30 minutes. • Remove the bay leaf and cloves and serve hot.

Serves: 4

Preparation: 20 min.

Cooking: 1 hr.

Level of difficulty: 1

- **4–8 Italian pork sausages**
- **¹/₂ cup (125 ml) dry white wine**
- **2 cups (500 ml) tomato passata**
- **4 large potatoes, peeled and cut into bite-sized pieces**
- **1 medium white onion, chopped**
- **2 stalks celery, sliced**
- **2 carrots, sliced**
- **1 bay leaf**
- **2 cloves**
- **Salt and freshly ground black pepper**

SAUSAGES WITH WHITE WINE SAUCE

Serves: 4–6

Preparation: 25 min.

Cooking: 1 hr.

Level of difficulty: 1

- 8 Italian pork sausages
- 1/3 cup (90 g) butter
- 1 cup (250 ml) Beef Stock (see page 946)
- 1 cup (250 ml) dry white wine
- 2 tbsp all-purpose (plain) flour
- 1 large egg
- 2 tbsp freshly squeezed lemon juice

Bring a medium pan of water to a boil and add the sausages. Pierce the sausages here and there with a shark knife and boil for 2–3 minutes. Drain well. • Melt ¼ cup (60 g) of butter in a large frying pan over medium heat. Add the sausages and sauté until nicely browned, about 10 minutes. • Melt the remaining butter in a small saucepan and stir in the flour. Gradually add the stock, stirring constantly so that no lumps form. Bring to a boil. • Place the pan with the sauce in a larger pan of barely simmering water and keep warm. • Remove all the fat that has formed in the bottom of the pan with the sausages. Pour in the wine and simmer until about half the sauce has reduced. • Place the sausages in a heated serving dish and keep warm. • Pour the beef stock sauce into the pan with the wine. Add the egg yolk and lemon juice and season with salt and pepper. Stir constantly over low heat until almost boiling; do not let the sauce boil. • Pour the sauce over the sausages and serve hot.

SALAMI IN RED WINE

$\mathbf{C}$ut the salami into slices of medium thickness. • Heat a little water in a large frying pan and add the salami. When it begins to sizzle, add the vinegar and then the wine. When the wine has evaporated, add the garbanzo beans. • Heat the tomatoes in another pan then add to the pan with the salame. • Season with salt and pepper and cook for 15 minutes. • Serve hot.

Serves: 6

Preparation: 10 min.

Cooking: 25 min.

Level of difficulty: 1

- 1 1/4 lb (600 g) fresh salame milanese
- 1/2 cup (125 ml) red wine vinegar
- 2/3 cup (200 ml) red wine
- 1 (14-oz/400-g) can garbanzo beans (chickpeas), drained
- 8 oz (250 g) canned tomatoes, finely chopped
- Salt and freshly ground black pepper

SOPPRESSATA AND BEAN SALAD

Serves: 6

Preparation: 10 min.

Cooking: 15 min.

Level of difficulty: 1

- 3 cloves garlic,
  1 sprig rosemary,
  2 sage leaves,
  all finely chopped
- 5 tbsp extra-virgin
  olive oil
- 1 lb (500 g)
  cannellini or white
  kidney beans,
  cooked
- 1 head of Belgian
  endive, diced
- 12 oz (350 g)
  soppressata
- 3 tbsp vinegar
- 4 tbsp finely
  chopped fresh
  parsley

In a frying pan, sauté the garlic, rosemary, and sage in the oil. When the garlic is pale gold, add the beans, and cook for 1 minute. Add the endive, cover the pan, and simmer over low heat for 10 minutes. • Add the soppressata and cook until the fat begins to melt. • Remove from heat and sprinkle with the vinegar and parsley. • Serve hot.

HAM COOKED IN SPUMANTE

Crush ½ tablespoon of the juniper berries.
• Place the ham in a large casserole. Add the crushed juniper berries, lemon zest, and wine. Push the cloves into the onion and add to the casserole. Add the carrot, celery, garlic, and a bay leaf. • Cover with spumante and bring to a boil. Simmer until the ham is cooked through, about 30 minutes. Remove from the heat. • Filter a generous ¾ of a cup (200 ml) of the cooking liquid through a fine mesh strainer and let cool. • Preheat the oven to 425°F (220°C/gas 7). • Line a baking pan with waxed paper and brush with a little butter. • Arrange a layer of bay leaves on the paper. • Add the ham and brush with butter. • Chop the rosemary and 1 tablespoon of the juniper berries in a food processor until very fine. Place in a small bowl and add 2 tablespoons of the melted butter. Season with pepper and mix well. Rub over the ham. • Bake for 10 minutes. • Beat 2 tablespoons of the remaining butter, the brandy, a little more pepper, and sugar in a small bowl. Remove the ham from the oven and brush with this mixture, coating well. • Bake until glazed and well browned, about 15 minutes. Place in a serving dish. Place the remaining butter in a saucepan over medium heat. • Add the flour and mix well. Remove from the heat and gradually add the reserved cooking liquid, beating to prevent lumps forming. • Return to the heat and cook until thickened. • Add the remaining juniper berries and mix well. Drizzle with the sauce and serve hot.

Serves: 6–8

Preparation: 20 min. + 2 hr. to soak the ham

Cooking: 1 hr.

Level of difficulty: 2

- 2 tbsp juniper berries
- 3 lb (1.5 kg) boned ham, in 1 piece
- Finely grated zest of ½ a lemon
- 1 bottle (750 ml) dry Spumante (sparkling wine)
- 2 cloves
- 1 onion, peeled and quartered
- 1 carrot, peeled
- 1 celery stick
- 1 clove garlic
- 12 bay leaves
- ½ cup (125 g) butter, melted
- Leaves from 1 sprig of rosemary
- Freshly ground black pepper
- 1 tbsp brandy
- 2 tbsp brown sugar
- 1 tbsp all-purpose (plain) flour

WILD BOAR IN RED WINE AND TOMATO SAUCE

Place the wild boar in a large bowl with the onion, carrot, celery, garlic, cloves, bay leaves, salt, and pepper. Cover with the wine and place in the refrigerator to marinate for 24 hours. • Prepare the tomato sauce. • Drain the marinade from the wild boar. Reserve the liquid, discard the cloves and bay leaves, and coarsely chop the vegetables. • Heat the oil in a large, heavy-bottomed pan over medium heat and sauté the vegetables for 5–7 minutes. • Add the meat and sauté until brown. • Stir in the tomato sauce, then add the liquid from the marinade. Partially cover the pan and cook over medium-low heat for 2 hours, stirring from time to time. • Serve hot.

Serves: 6

Preparation: 30 min.

Cooking: 2 hr. 30 min. + 24 hr. to marinate

Level of difficulty: 2

- 3 lb (1.5 kg) wild boar, cut in pieces
- 1 onion, sliced
- 1 carrot, thickly sliced
- 1 stalk celery, thickly sliced
- 1 clove garlic, cut in half
- 2 cloves
- 2 bay leaves
- Salt and freshly ground black pepper
- 1 cup (250 ml) robust red wine
- $1/2$ quantity Tomato Sauce (see page 948)
- $1/4$ cup extra-virgin olive oil

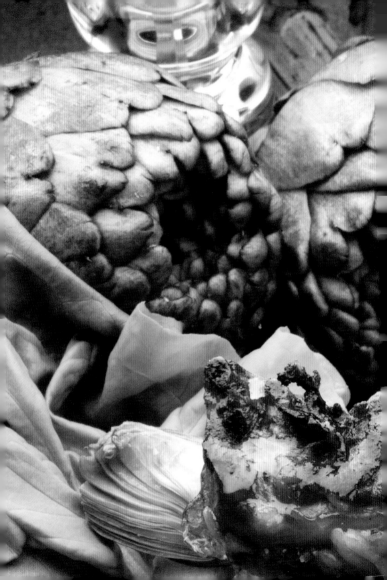

LAMB

LAMB STEW WITH PEAS

Heat the oil in a heavy-bottomed saucepan over medium heat. Add the onion and pancetta and sauté until the onion is softened and the pancetta lightly browned, about 5 minutes. • Add the lamb and sauté until lightly browned, 7–10 minutes.
• Season with salt and pepper and add the peas. Pour in the stock, cover the pan, and simmer over low heat until the lamb is tender, about 1 hour.
• Beat the eggs and cheese in a small bowl.
• Uncover the lamb and simmer until almost all the liquid has reduced. • Turn the heat up to medium and add the egg mixture. Stir constantly until the egg is cooked. • Serve hot.

Serves: 4–6
Preparation: 15 min.
Cooking: 75 min.
Level of difficulty: 1

• 2 tbsp extra-virgin olive oil
• 1 large white onion, finely chopped
• $^3/_4$ cup (90 g) diced pancetta
• $1^1/_2$ lb (750 g) lamb shoulder or leg, boned and cut in bite-size pieces
• Salt and freshly ground white pepper
• 2 cups (500 ml) hot Beef Stock (see page 946)
• $1^1/_2$ lb (750 g) fresh or frozen peas
• 2 large eggs
• 4 tbsp freshly grated pecorino cheese

664

SICILIAN LAMB STEW

Heat the oil and lard in a heavy-bottomed saucepan over medium heat. Add the onion, garlic, and parsley and sauté until the onion is softened, about 5 minutes. • Add the lamb and sauté until lightly browned, 7–10 minutes. • Pour in the wine and simmer until the wine has evaporated. • Add the stock and season with salt and pepper. Cover the pan and simmer over low heat for 30 minutes. • Add the potatoes. Cover and simmer until the potatoes and lamb are tender, about 30 minutes. • Add the cheese, cover the pan, and simmer for 10 more minutes. • Serve hot.

Serves: 4–6

Preparation: 30 min.

Cooking: 75 min.

Level of difficulty: 1

- 2 tbsp extra-virgin olive oil
- 2 tbsp lard
- 1 small white onion
- 4 cloves garlic, finely chopped
- 2 tbsp finely chopped fresh parsley
- $1^1/2$ lb (750 g) lamb shoulder or leg, boned and cut in bite-size pieces
- $1/2$ cup (125 ml) dry red wine
- Salt and freshly ground black pepper
- 1 cup (250 ml) Beef Stock (see page 946)
- 4 medium potatoes, peeled and cut into bite-size pieces
- 2 oz (60 g) pecorino cheese, cut in small dice

LAMB WITH PEAS AND EGGS CAMPANIA STYLE

Serves: 4

Preparation: 20

Cooking: 75 min.

Level of difficulty: 1

- **2 tbsp extra-virgin olive oil**
- **1 medium white onion, thinly sliced**
- **2 oz (60 g) pancetta, cut in thin strips**
- **2 lb (1 kg) lamb shoulder or leg, with bone, cut in large pieces**
- **Salt and freshly ground black pepper**
- **1 lb (500 g) fresh or frozen peas**
- **1/2 cup (125 ml) Beef Stock (see page 946)**
- **2 large eggs**
- **2 tbsp freshly grated pecorino cheese**

Heat the oil in a heavy-bottomed saucepan over medium heat. Add the onion and pancetta and sauté until the onion is softened and the pancetta lightly browned, about 5 minutes. • Add the lamb and sauté over high heat until lightly browned, 7–10 minutes. • Season with salt and pepper and add the peas. Pour in the stock, cover the pan, and simmer over low heat until the lamb is tender, about 1 hour. • Beat the eggs and cheese in a small bowl. • Remove the pieces of lamb from the pan and keep warm in a warming oven. • Turn the heat up to medium and add the egg mixture to the peas. Stir constantly until the egg is creamy. • Place the pea mixture on a heated serving plate. Top with the lamb and serve hot.

SWEET AND SOUR LAMB

Heat the oil in a heavy-bottomed saucepan over medium heat. Add the onion and sauté until softened, about 5 minutes. • Add the lamb and sauté over high heat until lightly browned, 7–10 minutes. • Season with salt and pepper and add the tomatoes. Cover the pan and simmer over low heat until the lamb is tender, about 1 hour. • Turn the heat up to medium and add the vinegar and sugar. Stir until the sugar has dissolved and the sauce has thickened. • Serve hot.

Serves: 4

Preparation: 15 min.

Cooking: 75 min.

Level of difficulty: 1

- 2 tbsp extra-virgin olive oil
- 1 large white onion, thinly sliced
- 1 1/2 lb (750 g) lamb shoulder or leg, boned and cut in bite-size pieces
- 1/2 cup (125 ml) tomato passato (sieved tomatoes)
- Salt and freshly ground black pepper
- 1/2 cup (125 ml) white wine vinegar
- 3 tbsp sugar

LAMB STEW WITH BELL PEPPERS

Heat the oil in a heavy-bottomed saucepan over high heat. Add the garlic, bay leaves, and lamb and sauté until lightly browned, 7–10 minutes.
• Turn the heat down to medium-low and pour in the wine. Simmer until the wine has evaporated.
• Add the tomatoes, bell peppers, and chile pepper. Season with salt. Cover the pan and simmer over low heat until the lamb is tender, about 1 hour. • Serve hot.

Serves: 4

Preparation: 30 min.

Cooking: 75 min.

Level of difficulty: 1

• $1/4$ cup (60 ml) extra-virgin olive oil
• 2 cloves garlic, finely chopped
• 2 bay leaves
• 2 lb (1 kg) lamb shoulder or leg, with bone, cut in small pieces
• $1/2$ cup (125 ml) dry white wine
• Salt
• 1 lb (500 g) firm ripe tomatoes, chopped
• 3 large bell peppers (capsicums), seeded and cut in thin strips
• 1 fresh red chile pepper

LAMB FRICASSEE

Heat the butter and the oil in a large casserole over medium heat. Add the onion and sauté until softened, about 5 minutes. • Add the lamb and brown all over, 7–10 minutes. • Pour in the wine and simmer until it evaporates. • Add the stock and tomatoes. Lower the heat, cover, and simmer until the lamb is tender, about 1 hour. • Add the potatoes and artichokes, if using. Cover and simmer until the vegetables are tender, about 30 more minutes. • Beat the eggs, salt, pepper, pine nuts, lemon juice, and parsley in a bowl. • Add the egg mixture to the casserole and stir until the sauce thickens slightly. • Serve hot.

- 3 tbsp butter
- 2 tbsp extra-virgin olive oil
- 1 large onion, finely chopped
- 2^1/$_2$ lb (1.25 kg) lamb shoulder, boned and cut into bite-size pieces
- ^{1}/$_2$ cup (125 ml) dry white wine
- 1^1/$_2$ cups (375 ml) boiling Beef Stock (see page 946)
- 3 peeled plum tomatoes, seeded and chopped
- 4 large potatoes, peeled and cut into bite size pieces (optional)
- 3 artichoke hearts, cut into bite-size segments (optional)
- 2 large eggs
- Salt and freshly ground black pepper
- 2 tbsp pine nuts
- Freshly squeezed juice of 1 lemon
- 1 tbsp finely chopped fresh parsley

Serves: 4

Preparation: 15 min.

Cooking: 75 min.

Level of difficulty: 2

- 2 tbsp extra-virgin olive oil
- 2 tbsp butter
- 1¹/2 lb (750 g) lamb, cut into cubes
- 1 large onion, finely chopped
- 4 tbsp finely chopped fresh parsley
- Salt and freshly ground black pepper
- 8 oz (250 g) small new potatoes
- 2 artichoke hearts, cut into segments
- ¹/2 cups (375 ml) boiling Beef Stock (see page 946)
- 1²/3 cups (300 g) peas
- 2 large egg yolks
- Juice of ¹/2 lemon

LIGURIAN LAMB STEW

Heat the oil and the butter in a large casserole over a moderate heat. Add the lamb and brown all over. • Add the onion and the parsley. Season with salt and pepper. • Add the potatoes and artichokes and mix well. Cook for 5 minutes until the onion is softened. • Add the stock and cook for 1 hour until the meat is tender. Add a little more stock during the cooking time if necessary. • Add the peas and cook for 5 minutes. • Beat together the egg yolks with the lemon juice. • Add the egg mixture to the stew and mix gently. • Remove the stew from the heat and serve immediately.

HOT AND SPICY LAMB AND TOMATO STEW

Heat the oil in a large, heavy-bottomed pan and sauté the onion, carrot, celery, garlic, parsley, pepper flakes, and pancetta over medium-high heat. • When the pancetta and onion are light golden brown, add the lamb and cook with the vegetable mixture, stirring continuously for 7–8 minutes. • Season with salt and pepper and add the wine. Cook until the wine has evaporated. • Add the tomatoes, then lower the heat to medium and partially cover. Cook for about 1 hour, adding a little hot water if the sauce reduces too much. • Serve hot.

Serves: 4–6

Preparation: 15 min.

Cooking: 75 min.

Level of difficulty: 1

- 1/4 cup (60 ml) extra-virgin olive oil
- 1 onion, 1 carrot, 1 stalk celery, coarsely chopped
- 2 cloves garlic, finely chopped
- 2 tbsp finely chopped parsley
- 1 tsp crushed red pepper flakes
- 1 cup (150 g) diced pancetta
- 2 lb (1 kg) lamb, shoulder or leg, cut in bite-sized pieces
- Salt and freshly ground black pepper
- 2/3 cup (150 ml) dry white wine
- 1 lb (500 g) firm ripe tomatoes, peeled and chopped

LAMB AND POTATO CASSEROLE

Serves: 4–6

Preparation: 10 min.

Cooking: 90 min.

Level of difficulty: 1

- **1 large white onion, finely chopped**
- **2 lb (1 kg) boned lamb shoulder or leg, cut in bite-size pieces**
- **1 lb (500 g) firm ripe tomatoes, peeled and chopped**
- **1 lb (500 g) potatoes, peeled and cut in bite-size pieces**
- **2 tsp finely chopped fresh oregano**
- **Salt and freshly ground black pepper**
- **$^{1}/_{4}$ cup (60 ml) extra-virgin olive oil**

Preheat the oven to 325°F (160°C/gas 2).
• Place the onion, lamb, tomatoes, potatoes, oregano, salt, pepper, and oil in a Dutch oven or casserole dish. Cook in the oven until the lamb and potatoes are tender, about 90 minutes. • Stir from time to time during cooking. • Serve hot.

679

BABY LAMB WITH OLIVES

S eason the flour with salt. Dredge the slices of lamb in the flour, shaking off any excess.
• Heat the oil in a large frying pan over high heat. Add the lamb and cook on both sides until tender, about 10 minutes. • Add the olives, oregano, and chile pepper. Pour in the lemon juice and simmer for 2–3 minutes. • Serve hot.

Serves: 4–6

Preparation: 10 min.

Cooking: 15 min.

Level of difficulty: 1

- $1/2$ cup (75 g) all-purpose (plain) flour
- Salt
- $1^1/2$ lb (750 g) boned very young lamb shoulder or leg, sliced
- $1/4$ cup (60 ml) extra-virgin olive oil
- 4 oz (125 g) pitted black olives, coarsely chopped
- 1 tbsp finely chopped fresh oregano
- 1 fresh red chile pepper, finely chopped
- $1/4$ cup (60 ml) freshly squeezed lemon juice

LAMB STEW PUGLIA-STYLE

Place the lamb, onion, celery, tomatoes, chile pepper, garlic, bay leaves, and thyme. Season with salt and pepper and pour in enough cold water to just cover the meat. • Place over medium-high heat and bring to a gentle boil. Simmer until the lamb is very tender, about 1 hour. Add more water during cooking as required. • Serve hot.

Serves: 4

Preparation: 15 min.

Cooking: 1 hr.

Level of difficulty: 1

- **2 lb (1 kg) boned shoulder or leg of lamb, cut in bite-sized pieces**
- **1 medium white onion, coarsely chopped**
- **2 stalks celery, coarsely chopped**
- **2 large ripe tomatoes, peeled and chopped**
- **1 fresh red chile pepper**
- **2 cloves garlic**
- **2 bay leaves**
- **Sprig of fresh thyme**
- **Salt and freshly ground black pepper**

LAMB WITH SUNDRIED TOMATOES AND ZUCCHINI

Heat the oil in a large, heavy-bottomed pan and sauté the lamb over medium heat until browned all over. Season with salt. • Add the garlic and sauté for 2–3 minutes more. • Stir in the tomatoes and oregano and cook for 10 more minutes. • Meanwhile, cook the zucchini in a pot of salted, boiling water for about 7 minutes. They should be cooked but still quite firm. • Drain the zucchini and add to the lamb, together with 2–3 tablespoons of their cooking water. Stir well until the liquid has been absorbed. • Serve hot.

Serves: 4

Preparation: 10 min.

Cooking: 35 min.

Level of difficulty: 1

- $^1/4$ cup (60 ml) extra-virgin olive oil
- 2 lb (1 kg) lamb shoulder, boned and cut into bite-size cubes
- Salt
- 2 cloves garlic, finely chopped
- 4 oz (125 g) sundried tomatoes, finely chopped
- 1 tsp dried oregano
- 4 large zucchini (courgettes), sliced

GRILLED LAMB CHOPS

Serves: 4

Preparation: 5 min.

Cooking: 15 min.

Level of difficulty: 1

- **2 lb (1 kg) lamb chops**
- **2 tbsp extra-virgin olive oil**
- **Salt and freshly ground black pepper**

Place the chops on a large plate and drizzle with the oil. Sprinkle with salt and a generous grinding of pepper. • Arrange the chops in a grill pan and place over high heat. Turn frequently until well-cooked. If you don't have a grill pan, arrange the chops on a broiler (grill) rack and place under the broiler (grill). Turn frequently until they are done. • Serve very hot.

CALABRIAN LAMB CHOPS

Heat half the oil in a heavy-bottomed saucepan over medium heat and add the onion, tomatoes, olives, parsley, and bell peppers.
• Simmer until the vegetables and tender, about 15 minutes. Season with salt and pepper. Stir often during the cooking time. • In the meantime, heat the remaining oil in a large frying pan and fry the lamb chops on both sides until tender and cooked through, 5–10 minutes. • Serve the meat and vegetables together on a heated serving dish.

Serves: 6

Preparation: 30 min.

Cooking: 15 min.

Level of difficulty: 1

- $1/3$ cup (90 ml) extra-virgin olive oil
- 1 medium white onion, finely chopped
- 1 lb (500 g) tomatoes, peeled and chopped
- 3 oz (90 g) pitted green olives
- 2 tbsp finely chopped parsley
- 2 large red bell peppers (capsicum) seeded and sliced
- Salt and freshly ground black pepper
- $1^{1}/_{2}$ lb (750 g) lamb chops

ROAST LAMB WITH POTATOES AND ARTICHOKES

Preheat the oven to 350°F (180°C/gas 4).
• Season the lamb generously with salt and pepper. Make incisions in the meat and insert pieces of garlic. • Place the lamb in the roasting pan and drizzle with the oil. Roast until tender, about 60–90 minutes. • Add the potatoes about 45 minutes before the lamb is cooked, basting well with the cooking juices. • Clean the artichokes by cutting off the top third of the leaves and by snapping off the tough outer leaves. Trim the stalk and cut in half. remove any fuzzy choke with a sharp knife then cut into quarters. • Boil the artichokes in lightly salted water for 5 minutes. Drain well, squeezing out excess moisture. • Add the artichokes to the roasting pan about 20 minutes before the lamb is cooked, basting well with the cooking juices. • Serve the lamb hot accompanied by the potatoes and artichokes and green salad, if liked.

Serves: 4

Preparation: 20 min.

Cooking: 60–90 min.

Level of difficulty: 1

- 3 lb (1.5 kg) loin of lamb
- $^1/_3$ cup (90 ml) extra-virgin olive oil
- Salt and freshly ground black pepper
- 2–3 cloves garlic, cut in half
- Fresh sage leaves
- 1 lb (500 g) roasting potatoes, peeled and cut into chunks
- 4 artichokes
- Salad greens, to serve (optional)

BABY LAMB WITH HERBS AND POTATOES

Serves: 4

Preparation: 15 min.

Cooking: 1 hr.

Level of difficulty: 1

- 3 lb (1.5 kg) baby lamb (shoulder, loin, or leg), cut into large pieces
- 4 large potatoes, peeled and cut in small wedges
- 1 tbsp finely chopped fresh thyme
- 1 tbsp finely chopped fresh
- 1 tbsp finely chopped fresh rosemary
- Salt and freshly ground black pepper
- $^1/_3$ cup (90 ml) extra-virgin olive oil
- $1^1/_2$ lb (750 g) roasting potatoes, peeled and cut into wedges

Preheat the oven to 350°F (180°F/gas 4).
• Mix the finely chopped herbs in a small bowl with plenty of salt and pepper. Season the lamb generously with this mixture. • Place the lamb and potatoes in a roasting pan and drizzle with the oil. Roast until tender, about 1 hour.

ROAST LAMB AND POTATOES

Place the lamb, potatoes, tomatoes, and onion in an ovenproof casserole. • Drizzle with the oil and season with a little salt and plenty of pepper. Sprinkle with the rosemary and oregano. • Cover and cook in a preheated oven at 400°F (200°C/gas 6) for about 1 hour, or until the meat is very tender. Baste at frequent intervals with a little hot water. • Serve hot

Serves: 4

Preparation: 15 min.

Cooking: 1 hr.

Level of difficulty: 2

- 2 lb (1 kg) lamb, cut into bite-sized pieces
- 1 1/2 lb (750 g) yellow, waxy potatoes, thickly sliced or in wedges
- 4 large tomatoes, quartered or cut into 6 pieces
- 1 medium onion, sliced
- 1/4 cup (60 ml) extra-virgin olive oil
- Salt and freshly ground black pepper
- Leaves from a small sprig of fresh rosemary
- 1 tsp dried oregano

ASPARAGUS LAMB ROLL

Serves: 4

Preparation: 45 min.

Cooking: 1 hr.

Level of difficulty: 3

- 1 lb (500 g) slice boned lamb
- 1 recipe Bread Dough (see page 84)
- 8 oz (250 g) tender asparagus stalks
- 1 large egg
- 2 oz (60 g) fresh bread crumbs
- Salt and freshly ground black pepper
- 4 scallions (green onions), thinly sliced
- 3 tbsp butter
- 1 tbsp all-purpose (plain) flour
- $^1/_2$ cup (125 ml) milk

Preheat the oven to 375°F (190°C/gas 5).
• Lay the meat out on a clean work surface and use a sharp knife to trim into an evenly shaped rectangle. Sprinkle the trimmings over the meat.
• Trim the tough lower parts from the asparagus and boil in salted water until tender, 7–10 minutes.
• Drain well and chop in a food processor. • Beat the egg lightly in a small bowl. Season with salt and pepper and add the asparagus and bread crumbs. You should obtain a fairly firm mixture—add more bread crumbs if it is not firm. • Spread the mixture over the meat. • Roll the meat up carefully and tie with kitchen string. • Roll out the bread dough then wrap it around the meat roll. • Place the roll seam-side down in an oiled baking dish. • Bake in the oven until the bread is golden brown and the meat is tender, about 1 hour. • Melt the butter in a medium saucepan and add the scallions. Sauté until very tender, 7–8 minutes. • Remove from the heat and chop finely with a sharp knife. • Return to the saucepan and stir in the flour, making sure no lumps form. • Season with salt and gradually stir in the milk. Simmer until the sauce thickens.
• Slice and serve hot with the sauce.

EGGS

EGGS

FRITTATA ROLL

Boil the peas in a small pan of lightly salted water. Drain well. • Beat the eggs in a large bowl. Add the bread crumbs, pecorino, and chives. Season with salt and pepper. • Heat 2 tablespoons of oil in a large frying pan over medium heat. Add the egg mixture and cook until golden brown underneath. • Remove from the heat and place a plate over the pan. Flip the pan so that the frittata is on the plate then slide it back into the pan, cooked side up. Cook until the other side is golden brown. • Heat the remaining oil in a small frying pan over high heat and sauté the peas, pine nuts, and thyme for 3–4 minutes. • When the frittata is cooked, place on a cutting board and spread with the pea and pine nut mixture. Sprinkle with the Parmesan and drizzle with the lemon juice. • Roll the frittata up carefully, slice, and serve hot.

Serves: 4

Preparation: 20 min.

Cooking: 15 min.

Level of difficulty: 2

• 1 cup (150 g) fresh or frozen peas
• 6 large eggs
• 1 cup (150 g) fine dry bread crumbs
• 2/3 cup (100 g) freshly grated pecorino cheese
• 2 tbsp chopped chives
• Salt and freshly ground black pepper
• 1/4 cup (60 ml) extra-virgin olive oil
• 2 tbsp pine nuts
• 1 tbsp finely chopped fresh thyme
• 4 tbsp freshly grated Parmesan cheese
• 1 tbsp freshly squeezed lemon juice

698

MINT AND PARSLEY FRITTATA

Serves: 4

Preparation: 10 min.

Cooking: 15 min.

Level of difficulty: 1

- 1 cup (150 g) fine dry bread crumbs
- 2/3 cup (100 g) freshly grated pecorino cheese
- 2 tbsp finely chopped parsley
- 2 tbsp finely chopped mint
- 6 large eggs
- Salt and freshly ground black pepper
- 2 tbsp extra-virgin olive oil

Beat the eggs in a large bowl. Add the bread crumbs, pecorino, and herbs. Season with salt and pepper. • Heat the oil in a large frying pan over medium heat. Add the frittata mixture and cook until golden brown underneath. • Remove from the heat and place a plate over the pan. Flip the pan so that the frittata is on the plate then slide it back into the pan, cooked side up. Cook until the other side is golden brown. • Serve hot.

BAKED VEGETABLE FRITTATA

Preheat the oven to 375°F (190°C/gas 5). • Boil the peas in a small pan of lightly salted water. Drain well. • Beat the eggs in a large bowl. Add the scarmoza, peas, lettuce, parsely, and oil. Season with salt and pepper. • Pour the frittata mixture into a 10-inch (25-cm) round earthenware baking dish. • Bake until puffed and golden brown, about 35 minutes. • Serve hot or at room temperature.

702

Serves: 4

Preparation: 15 min.

Cooking: 40 min.

Level of difficulty: 1

- 1 cup (150 g) fresh or frozen peas
- 6 large eggs
- $^2/_3$ cup (100 g) freshly grated scamorza cheese
- 1 small lettuce, coarsely chopped
- 1 tbsp finely chopped parsley
- 6 large eggs
- $^1/_4$ cup (60 ml) extra-virgin olive oil
- Salt and freshly ground black pepper

EGGS WITH POTATOES AND SPRING ONIONS

Put the potatoes into a medium saucepan and cover with water. Bring to a boil over medium heat. Simmer for 5 minutes. Drain well. • Heat the oil in a large frying pan over medium heat. Add the scallions and the potatoes. Sauté for 5 minutes, taking care not to break the potatoes. Season with salt. • Make space around the edges of the pan for the eggs using a spatula. Break the eggs into the pan and cook for 4 minutes, until the eggs are cooked and the potatoes are tender. Season the eggs with salt. • Dust with the paprika and serve hot.

Serves: 4

Preparation: 5 min.

Cooking: 15 min.

Level of difficulty: 1

- **4 large waxy potatoes, peeled and sliced $^1/_4$-inch (5-mm) thick**
- **$^1/_4$ cup (60 ml) extra-virgin olive oil**
- **6 scallions (spring onions), chopped**
- **Salt**
- **4 large eggs**
- **Pinch of hot paprika**

704

BAKED RADICCHIO FRITTATA

Serves: 4

Preparation: 10 min.

Cooking: 25 min.

Level of difficulty: 1

- **8 large eggs**
- **Salt and freshly ground black pepper**
- **$^1/_2$ cup (60 g) freshly grated Parmesan**
- **$^1/_3$ cup (90 ml) milk**
- **$^1/_4$ cup (60 ml) extra-virgin olive oil**
- **2 small heads radicchio, shredded**

Preheat the oven to 350°F (180°C/gas 4). • Beat the eggs in a large bowl. Season with salt and pepper. • Add the Parmesan and milk and beat well. • Heat the oil in a large frying pan over medium heat. Add the radicchio and sauté until tender, about 5 minutes. • Transfer to the bowl with the egg mixture and mix well. • Pour into an oiled baking dish. Bake until set and golden brown, about 20 minutes. • Run the blade of a knife around the edge of the dish and turn the frittata out onto a cutting board. • Cut it into squares and arrange on a serving dish.

POTATO FRITTATA WITH HAM AND PEAS

Serves: 4

Preparation: 10 min.

Cooking: 40 min.

Level of difficulty: 2

- 3 small onions
- $1/3$ cup (90 ml) extra-virgin olive oil
- $1^1/2$ lb (750 g) waxy potatoes, peeled and thinly sliced
- Salt and freshly ground black pepper
- 1 tbsp finely chopped fresh thyme
- 3 oz (90 g) cooked ham, chopped
- $1^1/4$ cups (200 g) fresh or frozen peas
- 4 large eggs
- $1/2$ cup (60 g) freshly grated Parmesan cheese

Slice 2 of the onions very finely. • Heat 2 tablespoons of the oil in a frying pan over low heat. Add the sliced onions and sauté for 3 minutes, until they begin to soften. • Add the potatoes and sauté for 10–15 minutes, until they are soft. Season with salt and pepper. • Add the thyme and mix well. Transfer to a bowl and let cool. • Chop the remaining onion. • Heat 2 tablespoons of the oil in a frying pan over moderate heat. Add the onion and sauté for 3 minutes, until it begins to soften. • Add the ham and the peas. Sauté for 5–7 minutes, until the peas are tender. • Season with salt and pepper. Remove from the heat. • Beat the eggs in a bowl. Add the Parmesan and season with salt and pepper. • Pour this mixture over the potatoes and mix well. Add the peas and ham and mix well. • Heat the remaining oil in a large nonstick frying pan over medium heat. Pour the frittata mixture into the pan and cook for 6–8 minutes, until the egg is almost set. • Slide the frittata onto a plate and then turn it back into the pan. Cook for 3–4 minutes, until it is golden brown all over. • Turn the frittata out onto a serving dish. Garnish with parsley and serve.

CRABMEAT OMELET

Lightly flour the crab meat. Heat 1/4 cup (60 ml) of oil in a medium frying pan and fry the crabmeat for 4–5 minutes. • Beat the eggs with the salt and pepper in a mixing bowl then add the prepared crabmeat and mix well. • Heat the remaining oil in the pan used to fry the crabmeat, and pour in the egg mixture. Cook for 4–5 minutes. • Turn the omelet carefully and cook for 4 minutes more. It should be firm and lightly browned on both sides. • Turn out onto a heated serving dish and serve hot.

Serves: 4

Preparation: 10 min.

Cooking: 15 min.

Level of difficulty: 1

- $1/2$ cup (75 g) all-purpose (plain) flour
- 14 oz (400 g) crabmeat, diced
- $1/2$ cup (125 ml) extra-virgin olive oil
- 8 large eggs
- Salt and freshly ground black pepper

BAKED CRÊPES WITH BROCCOLI

Prepare the batter for the crêpes. Let rest for 1 hour. • Cook the crêpes and set aside in a warm place. • Preheat the oven to 400°F (200°C/ gas 6). • Oil a baking dish. • Filling: Boil the broccoli in a medium saucepan of lightly salted water until just tender, about 5 minutes. Drain well. • Spread half the Béchamel on the crêpes. Fold them over and placed in the prepared baking dish. • Top with the broccoli and remaining Béchamel sauce. • Bake until golden brown, about 10 minutes. Serve hot.

Serves: 4–6

Preparation: 30 min. + time to make the crêpes

Cooking: 30 min.

Level of difficulty: 2

- 1 recipe crêpes (see page 713)

Filling
- 1 lb (500 g) broccoli, in florets
- 1 recipe Béchamel Sauce (see page 956)
- 8 oz (250 g) freshly grated Fontina cheese

ASPARAGUS AND ROBIOLA CRÊPES

Prepare the batter for the crêpes. Let rest for 1 hour. • Cook the crêpes and set aside in a warm place. • Preheat the oven to 400°F (200°C/gas 6). • Cook the asparagus in salted, boiling water until tender. Drain well, reserving the water. Cut off the tips and set aside. • Chop the stems in a food processor. • Combine with the robiola, Parmesan, and pancetta. Season with salt and pepper. • Spread a layer of this mixture on each crêpe, then fold it in half. • Place the crêpes in a large ovenproof dish and dot with butter. Prepare the Béchamel sauce, adding 1 cup (250 ml) of the reserved asparagus water. • Pour the sauce over the crêpes, sprinkle with the bread crumbs and the asparagus tips. • Bake until golden brown, about 10 minutes.

Serves: 4–6

Preparation: 30 min.
+ time to make the crêpes

Cooking: 45 min.

Level of difficulty: 1

- 1 recipe crêpes (see page 713)

Filling
- 2 lb (1 kg) asparagus
- 14 oz (400 g) robiola cheese
- 2 oz (60 g) Parmesan cheese
- 5 oz (150 g) pancetta, diced
- Salt and freshly ground black pepper
- 2 tbsp butter

- 1 recipe Béchamel Sauce (see page 956)

Topping
- 1 oz (30 g) fine dry dry bread crumbs
- 2 tbsp butter

Serves: 6–8

Preparation: 30 min. + time to make the crêpes

Cooking: 50 min.

Level of difficulty: 2

FLORENTINE CRÊPES

Crêpes

- 1 1/2 cups (325 ml) milk
- 1 cup (150 g) all-purpose (plain) flour
- 3 large eggs
- 1/4 tsp salt
- 4 tbsp water

Filling

- 1 clove garlic, finely chopped
- 3 tbsp extra-virgin olive oil
- 2 cups (500 g) boiled and chopped spinach
- Salt and freshly ground pepper
- Dash of nutmeg
- 5 oz (150 g) ricotta cheese
- 3 tbsp freshly grated Parmesan cheese

Sauce

- 4 tbsp extra-virgin olive oil
- 1/2 cup (75 g) flour
- 2 cups (500 ml) milk
- Salt and freshly ground black pepper
- Dash of nutmeg
- 3 tbsp freshly grated Parmesan cheese

Crêpes: Put the flour in a medium bowl and gradually add the milk, beating vigorously. Add the eggs, salt, and water and beat until smooth. Let rest for 1 hour. • Grease a small frying pan or crêpe pan over medium heat. • Pour in half a ladleful of batter and move the pan so that it spreads evenly over the bottom. As soon as the crêpe sets, flip it and cook the other side. Repeat, stacking the cooked crêpes in a pile. • Preheat the oven to 400°F (200°C/gas 6). • Filling: Sauté the garlic in the oil, add the spinach, salt, pepper, and nutmeg. Remove from the heat and mix with the ricotta and Parmesan. • Sauce: Heat the oil in a small saucepan. Add the flour, stirring constantly. Add the milk gradually, still stirring, until the mixture thickens. Stir in the salt, pepper, nutmeg, and Parmesan cheese. • Spread filling on each crêpe. Roll up and arrange in a baking dish. Pour the sauce over the top. • Bake until the top is golden.

BAKED CRÊPES WITH MEATBALLS

M eat Sauce: Heat the oil in a large saucepan over high heat. Add the beef, sausage, and ham and cook until browned all over, 5–7 minutes. • Pour in the wine and let it evaporate. • Stir in the tomatoes and season with salt and pepper. Simmer over low heat for 1 hour. • Prepare the batter for the crêpes. Let rest for 1 hour. • Meatballs: Mix the veal, eggs, and pecorino in a large bowl. Season with salt and pepper and form into balls the size of marbles. • Place the meatballs in the meat sauce and cook for 10 minutes. • Cook the crêpes. • Preheat the oven to 400°F (200°C/gas 6). • Grease a baking dish with oil and lay a crêpe on the bottom. Cover with a little of the meat sauce. Sprinkle with pieces of mozzarella, eggs, peas, and pecorino. Continue to layer until all the ingredients have been used. Dot with the butter and sprinkle with any remaining pecorino. • Bake until golden brown, 35–40 minutes. • Serve hot.

Serves: 4–6
Preparation: 30 min.
Cooking: 2 hr.
Level of difficulty: 3

Meat Sauce
- 8 oz (200 g) lean ground (minced) beef
- 3 oz (100 g) fatty and lean cooked ham, finely chopped
- 2 sausages, crumbled
- $1/3$ cup (90 ml) dry red wine
- 2 cups (500 ml) canned tomatoes, with juice
- 2 tbsp extra-virgin olive oil
- Salt and freshly ground black pepper

- 1 recipe crêpes (see page 713)

Meatballs
- 10 oz (300 g) lean ground (minced) beef
- 2 large eggs
- 2 tbsp freshly grated pecorino cheese

Filling
- 2 oz (60 g) mozzarella cheese, cut into cubes
- 2 hard-boiled eggs, thinly sliced
- $1/2$ cup (75 g) peas
- 1 cup (125 g) grated pecorino cheese
- $1/4$ cup (60 g) butter

SPINACH AND CHEESE SOUFFLE

Prepare the Béchamel sauce, adding the Gorgonzola as you cook it. It should melt completely into the sauce. • Preheat the oven to 400°F (200°C/gas 6). • Oil six 1-cup (250-ml) soufflé molds or one 6-cup (1.5-liter) large mold and sprinkle with bread crumbs. • Boil the spinach in lightly salted water until tender. • Drain and chop in a food processor until smooth. • Place in a bowl and stir in the ricotta, egg yolks, nutmeg, Parmesan, and Béchamel sauce. Season with salt and pepper. • Beat the egg whites until stiff peaks form. Fold them into the mixture. • Spoon the mixture into the prepared molds and bake until risen and golden brown, 15–20 minutes.
• Serve hot.

Serves: 4–6

Preparation: 20 min.

Cooking: 15–20 min.

Level of difficulty: 2

- $1/2$ recipe **Béchamel Sauce (see page 956)**
- 5 oz (150 g) **Gorgonzola cheese, in small cubes**
- $1/3$ cup (50 g) **fine dry bread crumbs**
- 2 lb (1 kg) **fresh spinach**
- $1/2$ cup (125 g) **fresh ricotta, drained**
- 3 large eggs, **separated**
- **Freshly grated nutmeg**
- 4 tbsp freshly **grated Parmesan cheese**
- **Salt and freshly ground white pepper**

716

VEGETABLES

EGGPLANT CAPONATA

Place the eggplant in a colander and sprinkle with the coarse sea salt. Let drain for 1 hour. • Heat the extra-virgin olive oil in a large saucepan over medium heat and sauté the onions until softened, about 5 minutes. • Season with salt and pepper. Add the tomatoes, celery, olives, and capers and simmer over low heat for 20 minutes. Set aside. • Rinse the eggplants under cold running water and dry with paper towels. • Heat the frying oil in a large frying pan and fry the eggplant in batches until tender, 5–7 minutes. Drain on paper towels. • Add the eggplant to the saucepan with the tomato sauce. Return to low heat and add the vinegar, sugar, pine nuts, golden raisins and pear, if using. Simmer until the vinegar has evaporated. • Remove from the heat. Stir in the basil and let cool to room temperature before serving.

Serves: 4–6

Preparation: 20 min. + 1 hr. to drain the eggplant

Cooking: 40 min.

Level of difficulty: 1

- 4 large eggplants (aubergines), peeled and cut in small cubes
- 2 tbsp coarse sea salt
- 2 tbsp extra-virgin olive oil
- 3 medium white onions, finely chopped
- Salt and freshly ground black pepper
- 1 lb (500 g) tomatoes, peeled and chopped
- 4 stalks celery, chopped
- 1 cup (100 g) green olives, pitted
- 2 tbsp salt-cured capers, rinsed
- 1 cup (250 ml) olive oil, for frying
- 1/4 cup (60 ml) white wine vinegar
- 1 tsp sugar
- 2 tbsp pine nuts
- 2 tbsp golden raisins (sultanas)
- 1 small ripe pear, peeled, cored, and cubed (optional)
- Fresh basil leaves

EGGPLANT STUFFED WITH HAM, CHICKEN, AND MORTADELLA

Serves: 4

Preparation: 30 min. +
1 hr. to drain
the eggplant

Cooking: 45 min.

Level of difficulty: 1

- **4 medium eggplants (aubergines), sliced ¹/₄-inch (5-mm) thick**
- **2 tbsp coarse sea salt**
- **12 oz (350 g) boneless skinless chicken breast**
- **4 oz (125 g) mortadella**
- **12 oz (350 g) ham**
- **1 cup (125 g) freshly grated Parmesan cheese**
- **1 large egg + 1 large egg yolk, beaten**
- **2 tbsp finely chopped fresh parsley**
- **3 cloves garlic, finely chopped**
- **Freshly ground black pepper**
- **2 cups (500 ml) oil, for frying**
- **¹/₄ cup (60 ml) extra-virgin olive oil**
- **1 medium onion, finely chopped**
- **1 (14-oz/400-g) can tomatoes, with juice**

Place the eggplant in layers in a colander. Sprinkle each layer with coarse sea salt. Let drain for 1 hour. • Preheat the oven to 350°F (180°C/gas 4). • Rinse the eggplants under cold running water and dry with paper towels. • Chop the chicken, mortadella, and ham finely in a food processor. • Place in a bowl with the Parmesan, eggs, garlic, pepper, and parsley and mix well. • Heat the frying oil in a large frying pan and fry the eggplant, turning the slices until they are golden brown. Drain on paper towels. • Arrange the slices on a clean work surface in pairs, crosswise one over the other. Place a little filling in the middle of each pair and fold the inner slice first, followed by the outer slice. Fasten with a toothpick. • Heat the oil in a large Dutch oven or casserole and sauté the onion until softened, about 5 minutes. • Add the tomatoes, season with salt and pepper and simmer for 5 more minutes. • Add the stuffed eggplant to the sauce. Bake for 30 minutes. Baste with the sauce from time to time. • Serve hot.

EGGPLANT AND PARMESAN BAKE

Place the eggplant in layers in a colander. Sprinkle each layer with coarse sea salt. Let drain for 1 hour. • Preheat the oven to 350°F (180°C/gas 4). • Rinse the eggplants under cold running water and dry with paper towels. Dust lightly with flour. • Heat the frying oil in a large frying pan and fry the eggplant, turning the slices until they are golden brown. Drain on paper towels. • Heat the extra-virgin oil in a large frying pan and sauté the onion until softened, about 5 minutes. • Add the tomatoes and basil, season with salt and pepper, and simmer over low heat for 20 minutes. • Place a layer of eggplant in an ovenproof dish. Sprinkle with Parmesan, cover with a layer of mozzarella, and top with tomato sauce. Repeat this layering process until all the ingredients are in the dish. • Bake until golden and bubbling, about 40 minutes. • Serve hot.

Serves: 4

Preparation: 30 min. + 1 hr. to drain the eggplant

Cooking: 75 min.

Level of difficulty: 1

- 4 medium eggplants (aubergines), sliced $^1/_4$-inch (5-mm) thick
- 2 tbsp coarse sea salt
- $^1/_2$ cup (75 g) all-purpose (plain) flour
- 2 cups (500 ml) oil, for frying
- 2 tbsp extra-virgin olive oil
- 1 small onion
- $1^1/_2$ lb (750 g) tomatoes, peeled and chopped
- 10 fresh basil leaves, torn
- Salt and freshly ground black pepper
- $1^1/_2$ cups (180 g) freshly grated Parmesan cheese
- 8 oz (250 g) fresh mozzarella cheese, thinly sliced

EGGPLANT COOKED WITH TOMATO AND GARLIC

Serves: 6

Preparation: 15 min.

Cooking: 20 min.

Level of difficulty: 1

- **4 medium eggplants (aubergines)**
- **4 cloves garlic, finely chopped**
- **5 tbsp extra-virgin olive oil**
- **Salt and freshly ground black pepper**
- **3 firm-ripe tomatoes, peeled and finely chopped**
- **2 tbsp finely chopped fresh parsley**

Slice the eggplants into 1-inch (2.5-cm) long pieces. • Sauté the garlic in the oil in a large frying pan for 2–3 minutes. • Add the eggplant and season with salt and pepper. Simmer over medium heat for 15 minutes. • Add the tomatoes and cook for 10 minutes more, or until the water released by the tomatoes has reduced. • Sprinkle with the parsley. • Serve hot.

727

GRILLED EGGPLANT

Heat a grill pan over medium-high heat. • Place the garlic in a small bowl. Season generously with salt and add the oil. Mix well. • Brush the oil mixture over the slices of eggplant then place in the grill pan. Grill in batches until tender and browned on both sides. • Drizzle the cooked eggplant with any remaining oil mixture and serve hot or at room temperature.

Serves: 4

Preparation: 10 min.

Cooking: 20 min.

Level of difficulty: 1

- **2 medium eggplant (aubergine), with peel, thinly sliced lengthwise**
- **1 clove garlic, finely chopped**
- **Salt**
- **$1/2$ cup (125 ml) extra-virgin olive oil**

GRILLED ZUCCHINI WITH SMOKED SCAMORZA

Preheat the oven to 400°F (200°C/gas 6).
• Arrange the zucchini in a well-oiled ovenproof baking dish. • In a bowl, whisk the oil with the vinegar, salt, and pepper until well blended.
• Pour over the zucchini then sprinkle with the mint.
• Bake for about 20 minutes, turning the slices frequently. Then, arrange the cheese slices in the center of the dish and bake for 5 more minutes, or until the cheese is melted and golden brown.
• Serve hot.

Serves: 2

Preparation: 10 min.

Cooking: 15 min.

Level of difficulty: 1

- **6 zucchini (courgettes), sliced thinly lengthwise**
- **3 tbsp extra-virgin olive oil**
- **1 tsp of apple cider vinegar**
- **Salt and freshly ground black pepper**
- **6 fresh mint leaves, torn**
- **3 oz (90 g) smoked Scamorza cheese, thinly sliced**

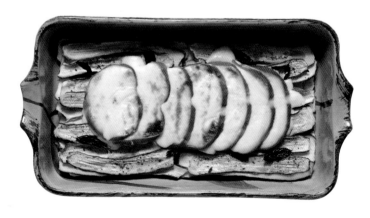

BAKED VEGETABLES WITH CACIOCAVALLO

Serves: 4

Preparation: 15 min.

Cooking: 25–30 min.

Level of difficulty: 1

- **1 eggplant (aubergine), thinly sliced**
- **2 large potatoes, thinly sliced**
- **2 large carrots, thinly sliced**
- **2 large zucchini (courgettes), thinly sliced**
- **1 bell pepper (capsicum), cut in strips**
- **2 bunches radicchio, shredded**
- **$^1/_4$ cup (60 ml) extra-virgin olive oil**
- **Salt and freshly ground black pepper**
- **2 tbsp finely chopped fresh oregano**
- **4 oz (125 g) Caciocavallo cheese, sliced**

Preheat the oven to 400°F (200°C/gas 6). • Place the prepared vegetables in an oiled ovenproof baking dish. • Drizzle with the oil, and sprinkle with salt, pepper, and oregano. • Bake for about 20 minutes. • Cover the vegetables with slices of cheese and return the dish to the oven for 5–10 minutes, or until the cheese melts.

BAKED ZUCCHINI
WITH MEAT SAUCE

Serves: 4–6

Preparation: 30 min.
+ 1 hr. to drain
the zucchini

Cooking: 45 min.

Level of difficulty: 1

- **1 recipe Meat Sauce (see page 950)**
- **6 large zucchini (courgettes)**
- **Salt**
- **$1/2$ cup (75 g) all-purpose (plain) flour**
- **2 large eggs, lightly beaten**
- **2 cups (500 ml) olive oil, for frying**
- **4 oz (125 g) mozzarella cheese, sliced**
- **1 cup (120 g) freshly grated Parmesan cheese**

Prepare the meat sauce. • Slice the zucchini lengthwise about ¼-inch (5 mm) thick. Place on a wire rack and sprinkle lightly with salt. Let rest for 1 hour. • Preheat the oven to 400°F (200°C/gas 6). • Rinse the zucchini and dry with a clean cloth. Dredge in the flour. Shake off any excess then dip in the egg. • Heat the oil in a frying pan to very hot. Fry the slices of zucchini in batches until golden brown on both sides. Drain on paper towels.

• Place a layer of zucchini in a baking dish. Cover with a layer of meat sauce and mozzarella cheese. Sprinkle with Parmesan. Repeat this layering process until all the ingredients are in the dish.

• Bake until bubbling and golden brown, 10–15 minutes. • Serve hot or at room temperature.

STUFFED ZUCCHINI

P reheat the oven to 400°F (200°C/gas 6).
• Blanch the zucchini in a large pan of salted boiling water for 5 minutes. Drain well and dry on a clean cloth. • Trim the bottom of each zucchini so that it will stand up in the pan. Cut a "hat" off the top of each zucchini and set aside. Use a teaspoon to scoop out the zucchini flesh.
• Chop the zucchini flesh and place in a bowl. Add the beef, garlic, walnuts, egg, Parmesan, milk, and nutmeg. Season with salt and pepper and mix well. • Stuff the zucchini with the filling and top each one with its "hat." • Place the filled zucchini in a baking dish. Drizzle with the oil and sprinkle with the bread crumbs. • Bake until tender and well cooked, 35–40 minutes.
• Serve hot or at room temperature.

734

Serves: 4

Preparation: 25 min.

Cooking: 40–45 min.

Level of difficulty: 1

- 8 round zucchini (courgettes) (tall about the same size)
- 1 lb (500 g) ground (minced) beef
- 1 clove garlic, finely chopped
- 1/2 cup (60 g) fairly finely chopped walnuts
- 1 large egg
- 1/2 cup (60 g) freshly grated Parmesan cheese
- 1/4 cup (60 ml) milk
- 1/4 tsp freshly grated nutmeg
- 2 tbsp extra-virgin olive oil
- 1/2 cup (75 g) fine dry bread crumbs
- Salt and freshly ground black pepper

ZUCCHINI STUFFED WITH AMARETTI COOKIES

Serves: 4

Preparation: 25 min.

Cooking: 30 min.

Level of difficulty: 1

- **6 zucchini (courgettes)**
- **Salt**
- **1 large egg + 1 large egg yolk, beaten**
- **4 tbsp freshly grated Parmesan cheese**
- **12 amaretti cookies, crushed**
- **2 tbsp finely chopped fresh parsley**
- **1 tbsp butter**
- **2 tbsp bread crumbs**
- **3 tbsp extra-virgin olive oil**

Preheat the oven to 350°F (180°C/gas 4). • Blanch the zucchini in a pot of salted, boiling water for 5 minutes. Drain well. • Cut in half lengthwise and, using a sharp knife, remove the pulp. • Place the amaretti cookies in a bowl with the eggs, chopped zucchini pulp, Parmesan, parsley, and salt. Blend well with a fork. • Fill the zucchini with this mixture and place in a buttered baking dish. • Sprinkle with the bread crumbs and drizzle with oil. • Bake for 25 minutes, until the topping is golden brown. • Serve hot or at room temperature.

BAKED ZUCCHINI

Preheat the oven to 400°F (200°C/gas 6).
• Heat the oil and butter in a large frying pan over medium heat and sauté the onion and garlic until softened, about 5 minutes. • Set a few slices of zucchini aside to decorate. Add the rest to the pan with the spinach, parsley, and thyme. Season with salt and simmer over low heat for 10–15 minutes. Remove from heat. • Add the ricotta, Emmental, and eggs and mix well. • Place the mixture in a baking dish and decorate the top with the reserved slices of zucchini. • Bake until the top is golden brown, 10–15 minutes. Serve hot.

Serves: 4

Preparation: 25 min.

Cooking: 30 min.

Level of difficulty: 1

- 3 tbsp extra-virgin olive oil
- 2 tbsp butter
- 1 onion, finely chopped
- 6 zucchini (courgettes), cut lengthwise in $^1/_4$-inch (5-mm) slices
- 2 cloves garlic, finely chopped
- 4 oz (125 g) spinach, coarsely chopped
- 2 tbsp finely chopped fresh parsley
- 2 tbsp finely chopped fresh thyme
- Salt
- $^1/_2$ cup (125 g) fresh ricotta cheese, drained
- $^1/_2$ cup (60 g) freshly grated Emmental or Swiss cheese
- 2 large eggs, beaten

FRIED ZUCCHINI FLOWERS

Remove the pistil (the bright yellow center) and calyx (the green leaflets at the base) from each flower. Wash quickly and gently pat dry with paper towels. • Put the flour in a bowl and make a well in the center. Add the salt and 1 tablespoon each of oil and water. Gradually mix into the flour, adding enough extra water to make a batter with a thick pouring consistency that will cling to the flowers.
• Heat the oil in a large frying pan until very hot.
• Dip the flowers in the batter and fry in batches until golden brown on both sides. • Drain on paper towels. • Serve immediately.

Serves: 4

Preparation: 10 min.

Cooking: 25 min.

Level of difficulty: 2

- **14 oz (400 g) very fresh zucchini (courgette) flowers**
- **1 cup (150 g) all-purpose (plain) flour**
- **Water**
- **1/2 tsp salt**
- **1 cup (250 ml) extra-virgin olive oil**
- **1–2 tbsp cold water**

ASPARAGUS MILAN-STYLE

Serves: 4

Preparation: 15 min.

Cooking: 25 min.

Level of difficulty: 1

- **2 lb (1 kg) fresh asparagus**
- **¹/₄ cup (60 g) butter**
- **¹/₂ cup (60 g) freshly grated Parmesan cheese**
- **Salt**

Trim the tough parts off the asparagus stalks and cut them all to the same length. • Starting halfway up the green stalks, use a sharp knife to scrape off the thin outer skin from the lower half of each stalk. • Place the asparagus upright, tips uppermost, in an asparagus steamer or a deep, narrow saucepan. Pour in sufficient boiling water to come two-thirds of the way up the stalks, leaving the very tender tips out of the water so that they steam cook. Cook for 10–15 minutes (depending on the thickness of the stalks), until tender. • Drain well and place on a heated serving dish. Sprinkle with the Parmesan. • Heat the butter in a heavy-bottomed pan until pale golden brown. Pour over the asparagus and serve.

STEWED ZUCCHINI WITH CHERRY TOMATOES

Heat the oil in a large frying pan and sauté the garlic and onion over medium heat until soft. • Add the butter, zucchini, and tomatoes, and simmer over high heat for 5 minutes. • Reduce heat to medium-low, cover, and simmer for 5 minutes. • Season with salt and pepper, uncover, and complete cooking. The zucchini should be firm, not mushy. • Remove from heat, add the parsley, toss well, and serve hot.

Serves: 4

Preparation: 10 min.

Cooking: 15 min.

Level of difficulty: 1

- $1/4$ cup (60 ml) **extra-virgin olive oil**
- 2 cloves garlic, **finely chopped**
- 1 small onion, **finely chopped**
- 2 tbsp **butter**
- $1^3/4$ lb (800 g) **small zucchini, sliced**
- 10 cherry **tomatoes, cut in half**
- Salt and freshly **ground black pepper**
- 2 tbsp finely **chopped fresh parsley**

TOMATOES PUGLIA-STYLE

Preheat the oven to 400°F (200°C/gas 6).
• Slice the tomatoes in half horizontally and use a teaspoon to remove the seeds and some of the flesh. Place the tomatoes in an oiled baking dish.
• Mix the bread crumbs, pecorino, parsley, basil, mint, salt, and pepper in a medium bowl. • Spoon this mixture into the tomatoes. Season again with salt and pepper and drizzle with the oil. • Bake until the tomatoes are tender, about 15 minutes.
• Serve hot or at room temperature.

744

Serves: 4

Preparation: 30 min.

Cooking: 40 min. + 2 days to marinate

Level of difficulty: 2

- **4 medium tomatoes, all the same size**
- **1 cup (150 g) fine dry bread crumbs**
- **$^1/_2$ cup (60 g) freshly grated pecorino cheese**
- **4 tbsp finely chopped fresh parsley**
- **2 tbsp finely chopped fresh basil**
- **1 tbsp finely chopped fresh mint**
- **2 tbsp extra-virgin olive oil**
- **Salt and freshly ground black pepper**

BAKED POTATOES, ONIONS, AND TOMATOES

Preheat the oven to 350°F (180°C/gas 4).
• Peel the potatoes and slice thinly. • Plunge the tomatoes into a pot of boiling water for 1 minute, then transfer to cold water. Slip off their skins. Cut in ½-inch (1-cm) slices. • Place the potatoes, onions, and tomatoes in a large mixing bowl. Add the Pecorino, salt, pepper, oil, and water and mix carefully. • Place in an ovenproof baking dish and sprinkle with the oregano. Bake in a preheated oven at 350°F for 1 hour. Serve hot or at room temperature.

Serves: 6

Preparation: 15 min.

Cooking: 1 hr.

Level of difficulty: 1

- **4 large red onions**
- **6 large ripe tomatoes**
- **Salt and freshly ground black pepper**
- **¹/₃ cup (90 ml) extra-virgin olive oil**
- **¹/₂ cup (125 ml) cold water**
- **¹/₃ cup (40 g) freshly grated pecorino cheese**
- **1 tsp dried oregano**

STUFFED ONIONS

Serves: 4

Preparation: 30 min.

Cooking: 40 min.

Level of difficulty: 2

- **4 medium white onions**
- **6 slices white sandwich bread, crusts removed, crumbled**
- **4 slices prosciutto (Parma ham), coarsely chopped**
- **2 large eggs**
- **$1/4$ cup (60 ml) heavy (double) cream**
- **4 oz (125 g) freshly grated Fontina cheese**
- **Salt and freshly ground black pepper**

Preheat the oven to 350°F (180°C/gas 4). • Peel the onions and boil in lightly salted water for 5 minutes. • Drain well and cut in half horizontally. Use a sharp knife to hollow out the insides of the onions. • Place the onion flesh, bread, prosciutto, eggs, cream, and half the cheese in a food processor and blend until smooth. • Fill the hollowed out onions with this mixture. • Bake in the oven for 30 minutes. • Top each onion with some of the remaining cheese and bake until golden brown, about 10 more minutes. • Serve hot or at room temperature.

PEAS AND EGGS PUGLIA-STYLE

Heat the oil in a large frying pan over medium heat. Add the onion and pancetta and sauté until the onion is softened, about 5 minutes. • Add the peas and sauté. Gradually add the water as the peas simmer and become tender; this will take 10–15 minutes depending on how fresh the peas are. • Just before the peas are ready, beat the eggs, bread crumbs, cheese, salt, and pepper in a medium bowl. • Pour this mixture into the pan with the peas and cook and stir until the egg is cooked. • Serve hot.

Serves: 6–8
Preparation: 10 min.
Cooking: 20 min.
Level of difficulty: 2

- 2 tbsp extra-virgin olive oil
- 1 medium white onion, finely chopped
- $^1/_2$ cup (75 g) pancetta, diced
- 2 lb (1 kg) fresh or frozen peas
- 1 cup (250 ml) boiling water
- $^1/_3$ cup (50 g) fine dry bread crumbs
- $^1/_2$ cup (60 g) freshly grated pecorino cheese
- 3 large eggs
- Salt

PEA MOUSSE

Bring 2 quarts (2 liters) of salted water to a boil in a pan and cook the peas and onion for 10–15 minutes. • Drain well and set aside to cool. • Place the goat cheese, peas, onion, and oil in a blender and blend until the mixture is creamy. Season with salt and pepper. • Line a 1-quart (1-liter) pudding mold with plastic wrap and pour the mixture in, pressing with a spoon to eliminate pockets of air. Knock the mold against the work bench to eliminate air bubbles. • Chill in the refrigerator for at least 2 hours. • Invert onto a round serving dish and, if liked, garnish with the cherry tomatoes and parsley.

Serves: 4

Preparation: 30 min. + 2 hr. to chill

Cooking: 15 min.

Level of difficulty: 2

- 1 lb (500 g) fresh or frozen peas
- 1 medium onion, cut in half
- 2 cups (500 g) soft creamy goat cheese (caprino)
- 3 tbsp extra-virgin olive oil
- Salt and freshly ground black pepper
- 8 cherry tomatoes, cut in quarters (optional)
- 8 tiny sprigs parsley (optional)

ONION, PEAS, POTATO, AND LETTUCE STEW

Serves: 4

Preparation: 10 min.

Cooking: 30 min.

Level of difficulty: 2

- **2 large potatoes, peeled and cut into bite-size chunks**
- **4 small onions**
- **2 tbsp extra virgin olive oil**
- **1 cup (150 g) fresh or frozen peas**
- **$1/3$ cup (90 ml) vegetable stock, boiling**
- **Salt and freshly ground black pepper**
- **1 head of lettuce, washed and dried**

Cook the potatoes in a large pot of salted boiling water for 10 minutes. • Add the onions and cook for 5 minutes, until the potatoes are almost tender. • Drain well. • Cut the onions into wedges. • Heat the oil in a large casserole over medium heat. • Add the potatoes and the onions. Sauté for 5 minutes, until the potatoes are lightly browned. • Add the peas and the stock. • Season with salt and pepper and cook over medium heat for 10 minutes, until all the vegetables are tender. • Remove from the heat and add the lettuce leaves. • Cover and let rest for 5 minutes. • Serve hot.

753

WARM FRIED POTATO SALAD

Serves: 4

Preparation: 20 min.

Cooking: 25 min.

Level of difficulty: 1

- 2 lb (1 kg) potatoes, peeled, cut in small cubes
- $^1/_2$ cup (125 ml) peanut oil
- 2 tbsp extra virgin olive oil
- 1 large onion, sliced
- 2 celery sticks, sliced
- $^1/_2$ cup (100 g) pine nuts
- $^1/_2$ cup (50 g) blanched almonds
- $^1/_2$ cup (100 g) golden raisins (sultanas)
- 1 cup (100 g) green olives, pitted
- 2 tbsp salt-cured capers, rinsed
- 1 tbsp sugar
- 2 tbsp white wine vinegar
- 2 tomatoes, peeled and chopped
- 1 tbsp freshly chopped oregano
- Pinch of red pepper flakes
- Salt and freshly ground black pepper

Place the potatoes in a bowl and cover with cold water. Soak for 10 minutes. Drain well.
• Heat the peanut oil in a large frying pan over medium heat. Add the potatoes and sauté until tender, 5–7 minutes. • Let drain on paper towels.
• Heat the olive oil in a large frying pan over medium heat. Add the onion and celery and sauté until softened, about 5 minutes. • Add the potatoes, pine nuts, almonds, sultanas, olives, capers, sugar, vinegar, tomato, oregano, and chile pepper. Season with salt and pepper and mix well.
• Simmer over low heat for 15 minutes. • Serve hot or at room temperature.

POTATO FRITTERS

Grate the potatoes, squeeze out the starchy moisture, and place in a large bowl. Add the pecorino, flour, and eggs. Season with salt and pepper and mix well. • Heat the oil in a deep-fryer or large frying pan until very hot. • Drop tablespoons of the batter into the hot oil and fry in batches until golden brown all over. Remove with a slotted spoon and drain on paper towels. • Serve hot.

Serves: 4-6

Preparation: 20 min.

Cooking: 30 min.

Level of difficulty: 1

- **1 lb (500 g) potatoes**
- **2 tbsp freshly grated pecorino cheese**
- **2–3 tbsp all-purpose (plain) flour**
- **2 large eggs, lightly beaten**
- **Salt and freshly ground black pepper**
- **2 cups (500 ml) olive oil, for frying**

BAKED POTATOES WITH CHEESE AND EGGS

Preheat the oven to 350°F (180°C/gas 4).
• Boil the potatoes in salted, boiling water for 12 minutes. Drain and slice. • Place a layer in an oiled baking dish. Sprinkle with cheese and thyme, drizzle with oil, and season with salt and pepper. Repeat this layering process until all the ingredients are in the dish. • Bake until golden brown, 20–25 minutes. • Place the potatoes in 4 serving dishes and keep warm. • Heat the butter in a large frying pan and fry the eggs until firm. • Place an egg on each serving of potatoes. Season with freshly ground black pepper and serve hot.

Serves: 4

Preparation: 15 min.

Cooking: 15 min

Level of difficulty: 1

- 1½ lb (750 g) potatoes, peeled
- 8 oz (250 g) freshly grated pecorino cheese
- 4 large eggs
- 2 tbsp finely chopped fresh thyme
- ⅓ cup (90 ml) extra-virgin olive oil
- 2 tbsp butter
- 1 clove garlic, whole but lightly crushed
- Salt and freshly ground black pepper

ARTICHOKE AND GOAT CHEESE BAKES

Serves: 4

Preparation: 10 min.

Cooking: 20 min

Level of difficulty: 1

- **12 oz (350 g) frozen artichoke hearts, thawed**
- **¼ cup (60 ml) extra-virgin olive oil**
- **Salt and freshly ground black pepper**
- **1 tbsp finely chopped fresh parsley**
- **1½ cups (90 g) fresh bread crumbs**
- **1¼ cups (300 ml) heavy (double) cream**
- **4 large eggs**
- **8 oz (250 g) soft goat cheese**
- **1 tbsp potato starch**

Preheat the oven to 350°F (180°C/gas 4). • Sauté the artichokes in the oil in a large frying pan over low heat for 5 minutes, or until tender. • Season with salt and pepper and add the parsley. Remove from the heat and let cool. • Mix the bread crumbs, cream, eggs, goat cheese, and potato starch in a large bowl. Season with salt and pepper and beat until smooth. • Arrange the artichokes in 4 individual ovenproof dishes. Pour the cheese mixture over the top. • Bake for 12–15 minutes, or until set and lightly browned. • Serve hot.

759

BAKED POTATOES WITH BELL PEPPERS AND OLIVES

Preheat the oven to 375°F (190°C/gas 5).
• Slice the tomatoes about ¼- inch (5 mm) thick. • Arrange the potatoes in a baking dish with slices of mozzarella and pieces of bell pepper between the slices. Sprinkle with the olives, Parmesan, and oregano. Season with salt and pepper. • Drizzle with the oil. • Bake until the potatoes are tender, about 45 minutes.
• Serve hot.

Serves: 4–6

Preparation: 25 min.

Cooking: 45 min.

Level of difficulty: 1

- 1 lb (500 g) potatoes, peeled
- 1 large red bell pepper (capsicum), cored and chopped
- 1 cup (100 g) pitted green olives
- 4 oz (125 g) mozzarella cheese, sliced
- 4 tbsp freshly grated Parmesan cheese
- 1 tsp dried oregano
- Salt and freshly ground white pepper
- ½ cup (125 ml) extra-virgin olive oil

ROAST POTATOES WITH ROSEMARY

Preheat the oven to 375°F (190°C/gas 5).
• Rinse the potatoes thoroughly under cold running water and dry well. • Drizzle ¼ cup (60 ml) of oil into a baking dish. • Arrange the potatoes in the dish in one layer. Season with salt and pepper and sprinkle with the rosemary and garlic, if using.
• Drizzle with the remaining oil and mix well.
• Bake for 30–35 minutes, or until the potatoes are tender, crisp, and golden brown all over, shaking the dish occasionally. • Season with extra salt, if liked. • Serve hot.

Serves: 4

Preparation: 10 min.

Cooking: 30–35 min.

Level of difficulty: 1

- **2 lb (1 kg) potatoes, peeled and cut into small chunks**
- **¹/₂ cup (125 ml) extra-virgin olive oil**
- **Salt and freshly ground black pepper**
- **2–3 bunches rosemary**
- **3 cloves garlic (optional)**

POTATOES VENETIAN-STYLE

Serves: 4

Preparation: 15 min.

Cooking: 30–35 min.

Level of difficulty: 1

- 1 onion, thinly sliced
- $1/3$ cup (90 ml) butter
- $1/3$ cup (90 ml) extra-virgin olive oil
- 2 lb (1 kg) yellow waxy potatoes, peeled and cut into small chunks
- Salt
- 2 tbsp finely chopped fresh parsley

Sauté the onion in the butter and oil in a large frying pan until lightly browned, about 5 minutes. • Add the potatoes and cook for 30–35 minutes, or until tender, stirring often. • Season with salt and sprinkle with the parsley. • Serve hot.

763

CARROTS IN CARAMEL SAUCE WITH PARSLEY

U se a peeler to scrape the carrots and rinse thoroughly under cold running water. • Cut the carrots into 2-inch (5-cm) sticks. • Place the carrots and water in a large deep frying pan. Add half the butter and cook over high heat until the water has evaporated. • Season with salt and pepper, add the remaining butter, and sprinkle with the sugar. • Sauté the carrots until caramelized. • Sprinkle with the parsley and serve hot.

Serves: 6–8

Preparation: 10 min.

Cooking: 20 min.

Level of difficulty: 1

- **3 lb (1.5 kg) carrots**
- **1 cup (250 ml) water**
- **$^1/_2$ cup (125 g) butter**
- **Salt and freshly ground black pepper**
- **2 tbsp sugar**
- **3 tbsp finely chopped fresh parsley**

BRAISED MUSHROOMS WITH EGG SAUCE

Serves: 4

Preparation: 15 min.

Cooking: 20 min.

Level of difficulty: 1

- $^1/_4$ cup (60 ml) extra-virgin olive oil
- 1 medium onion, finely chopped
- $1^3/_4$ lb (800 g) mixed fresh or frozen mushrooms (porcini, white, chanterelle, or Caesar's), trimmed
- Salt and freshly ground black pepper
- 3 egg yolks
- Freshly squeezed juice of 1 lemon
- 2 tbsp finely chopped fresh parsley

Heat the oil in a large frying pan and sauté the onion until softened, about 5 minutes. • Cut the larger mushrooms in thick slices and leave the smaller ones whole. • Add the mushrooms to the pan. Season with salt and pepper, cover, and cook for 15–20 minutes over medium-low heat. • While the mushrooms are cooking, beat the egg yolks in a bowl with the lemon juice and parsley. • Pour the egg sauce over the mushrooms and toss quickly so that the egg doesn't set but becomes a creamy sauce. • Serve hot.

MUSHROOM AND TOMATO STEW

Rinse the mushrooms thoroughly under cold running water and dry well. • Detach the stems from the caps. • Slice the caps and chop the stalks coarsely. • Sauté the garlic and parsley in the oil in a large frying pan for 3 minutes. Add the mushroom stems. Season with the salt and pepper and cook for 5 minutes. • Add the mushroom caps and mix well. Cook for 5 minutes. • Add enough water to moisten the mushrooms. • Stir in the tomatoes and mix well. Simmer for 15 minutes. • Serve hot.

Serves: 4

Preparation: 20 min.

Cooking: 30 min.

Level of difficulty: 1

- 2 lb (1 kg) fresh porcini or white mushrooms
- 2 cloves garlic, finely chopped
- 1 tbsp finely chopped fresh parsley
- $1/4$ cup (60 ml) extra-virgin olive oil
- Salt and freshly ground black pepper
- 1–2 tbsp hot water
- 1 cup (250 ml) tomatoes, peeled and chopped

FILLED BAKED ARTICHOKES

Preheat the oven to 350°F (180°C/gas 4).
• Clean the artichokes by removing the tough outer leaves. Trim the stalks so that the artichokes can stand upright in a dish. Place in a baking dish into which they fit snugly. Open the leaves out.
• Combine the bread crumbs, anchovies, parsley, garlic, pine nuts, pecorino, salt, and pepper in a small bowl. Mix well. • Press this mixture into the open leaves of the artichokes. • Drizzle with the oil. Half fill the baking dish with the wine.
• Bake until tender and well cooked, about 1 hour. • Serve hot or at room temperature.

Serves: 6

Preparation: 30 min.

Cooking: 1 hr.

Level of difficulty: 2

- 6 large artichokes
- $^1/_2$ cup (75 g) fine dry bread crumbs
- 3 anchovy fillets
- 2 tbsp finely chopped fresh parsley
- 2 cloves garlic, finely chopped
- 2 tbsp pine nuts
- 1 cup (120 g) freshly grated pecorino cheese
- 1 cup (250 ml) dry white wine
- $^1/_4$ cup (60 ml) extra-virgin olive oil
- Salt and freshly ground black pepper

GREEN BEANS, PIEDMONTESE-STYLE

Plunge the tomatoes into a pot of boiling water for 1 minute. Drain and place in cold water. Peel and cut in half. Squeeze out as many seeds as possible and chop coarsely. • Melt the lard in a large frying pan and add the garlic, basil, and parsley. Sauté over medium-high heat for 5 minutes. • Add the green beans, tomatoes, and wine, and season with salt and pepper. Cover and cook over medium-low heat for about 40 minutes, or until the beans are tender. • Serve hot or at room temperature.

Serves: 4

Preparation: 15 min.

Cooking: 45 min.

Level of difficulty: 1

- **1 lb (500 g) tomatoes**
- **2 tbsp lard (or butter)**
- **1 clove garlic, finely chopped**
- **8 leaves fresh basil, finely chopped**
- **2 tbsp finely chopped fresh parsley**
- **2 lb (1 kg) green beans, trimmed**
- **$1/2$ cup (125 ml) dry red wine**
- **Salt and freshly ground black pepper**

SPINACH SOUFFLÉ

Serves: 4

Preparation: 15 min.

Cooking: 40 min.

Level of difficulty: 2

- 1¹/₂ lb (750 g) spinach
- ¹/₃ cup (90 g) butter
- ¹/₄ cup (30 g) freshly grated Parmesan cheese
- 3 large eggs, separated
- Salt
- 3 tbsp fine dry bread crumbs
- 8 anchovy fillets

Preheat the oven to 350°F (180°C/gas 4).
• Rinse the spinach under cold running water. Do not drain. Cook over medium heat with just the water left clinging to the leaves. • Chop finely in a food processor. • Place in a small frying pan with ¹/₄ cup (60 g) of butter over medium heat and cook until all the butter has been absorbed . • In a mixing bowl, combine the spinach with the Parmesan and egg yolks. Mix until smooth. • Beat the egg whites with a pinch of salt until very stiff. Fold them into the spinach mixture. • Butter an 8-inch (20-cm) soufflé mold with 1 tablespoon of butter and sprinkle with the bread crumbs. • Place half the spinach mixture in the mold and cover with the anchovy fillets. Cover with the remaining spinach. • Chop the remaining butter and top the soufflé. • Bake for 30 minutes. Serve hot.

SPINACH SAUTÈED WITH GARLIC AND OIL

C ook the spinach in a pot of salted, boiling water for 8–10 minutes, or until tender. Drain, squeeze out excess moisture, and chop coarsely. • Sauté the garlic in the oil over high heat for 2–3 minutes. • Add the spinach and cook over medium-high heat for 3–4 minutes, tossing continually, so that the spinach absorbs the flavors of the garlic and oil. • Serve hot or at room temperature.

Serves: 6

Preparation: 10 min.

Cooking: 15 min.

Level of difficulty: 1

- 2 lb (1 kg) frozen spinach
- 2 large cloves garlic, finely chopped
- $^1/_3$ cup (90 ml) extra-virgin olive oil
- Salt

SWISS CHARD, ROMAN-STYLE

Clean the chard, chop coarsely, and rinse thoroughly under cold running water. • Boil in a pot of lightly salted water for about 10 minutes, or until tender. • Drain well and dry by wringing gently in a clean cotton cloth. • Heat the oil in a large skillet and sauté the garlic for 5 minutes. Discard the garlic. • Add the anchovy fillets to the flavored oil and mash with a fork until they dissolve in the oil. Add the tomatoes and cook for 15 minutes. • Add the chard and stir over medium heat for 5 minutes. • Serve hot.

Serves: 4

Preparation: 25 min.

Cooking: 55 min.

Level of difficulty: 1

- **2 lb (1 kg) Swiss chard (silverbeet)**
- **$^1/_4$ cup (60 ml) extra-virgin olive oil**
- **2 cloves garlic, finely chopped**
- **4 anchovy fillets**
- **6 medium tomatoes, peeled and diced**
- **Salt and freshly ground black pepper**

BAKED STUFFED BELL PEPPERS

Serves: 4

Preparation: 20 min.

Cooking: 35 min.

Level of difficulty: 1

- **4 large plump bell peppers (capsicums), mixed red and yellow**
- **8 slices day-old bread**
- **Salt and freshly ground black pepper**
- **2 tbsp salt-cured capers, rinsed**
- **14 oz (400 g) black olives, coarsely chopped**
- **4 cloves garlic, finely chopped**
- **¼ cup finely chopped parsley**
- **10 fresh basil leaves, torn**
- **8 anchovy fillets, crumbled**
- **12 oz (350 g) peeled and chopped fresh or canned tomatoes**
- **1½ cups (180 g) freshly grated Parmesan cheese**
- **1 cup (120 g) freshly grated pecorino cheese**
- **½ cup (125 ml) extra-virgin olive oil**
- **1 tbsp white wine vinegar**

Preheat the oven to 350°F (180°C/gas 4). • Trim the stalks of the bell peppers to about 1 inch (2.5 cm). Cut their tops off about ½ inch (1 cm) from the top and set aside. Remove the seeds and membranes. • Soak the bread in cold water for 10 minutes. Squeeze out excess moisture, crumble, and place in a bowl. Season with salt and pepper. • Add the capers, olives, garlic, parsley, basil, anchovies, tomatoes, Parmesan, and pecorino. Add the vinegar and half the oil and mix thoroughly. • Stuff the bell peppers with the filling, replace the tops, and stand them upright in an oiled roasting pan that is at least as tall as they are. Add the remaining oil and ½ cup (125 ml) of water. • Cook in a preheated oven at 350°F, basting often with liquid from the bottom of the pan. • After about 35 minutes, pierce a bell pepper with the point of a sharp knife; when done, the bell peppers will be soft. • Spoon the dark stock over the bell peppers and serve hot.

MIXED BRAISED BELL PEPPERS

Place the bell peppers, onions, and tomatoes in a large saucepan. Add the oil and garlic and season with salt and pepper. • Cover and cook over medium heat for 15 minutes. • Uncover and cook over high heat for 5 more minutes, to allow some of the cooking liquid to evaporate. Continue cooking for 5 minutes more, or until the bell peppers are tender. • Serve hot or at room temperature, garnished with the basil.

Serves: 4–6

Preparation: 15 min.

Cooking: 25 min.

Level of difficulty: 1

- **4–6 bell peppers (capsicums), mixed colors, cut into thin strips**
- **2 large onions, thinly sliced**
- **2 cups (500 g) tomatoes, peeled and chopped**
- **¹/₄ cup (60 ml) extra-virgin olive oil**
- **3 cloves garlic, finely chopped**
- **Salt and freshly ground black pepper**
- **6 leaves fresh basil, torn**

CAULIFLOWER MOLD WITH BLACK OLIVES

Preheat the oven to 350°F (180°C/gas 4).
• Divide the cauliflower into large florets and trim the stems. Cook in a pot of salted, boiling water for 5–7 minutes. Drain and set aside. • Prepare the Béchamel. • Mash the cauliflower until smooth. • Combine with the Béchamel, Parmesan, olives, eggs, salt, pepper, and nutmeg. • Grease a 12-inch (30-cm) ring mold with a little butter and sprinkle with bread crumbs. Pour the mixture into the mold and place in a larger container filled with water. • Bake for about 45 minutes. • Invert onto a platter while still hot. Serve hot or at room temperature.

Serves: 4

Preparation: 25 min.

Cooking: 55 min.

Level of difficulty: 2

- **2 lb (1 kg) cauliflower head**
- **1 recipe Béchamel Sauce (see page 956)**
- **$^1/_2$ cup (60 g) freshly grated Parmesan cheese**
- **20 black olives, pitted and chopped**
- **3 large eggs, beaten**
- **Salt and freshly ground black pepper**
- **$^1/_4$ tsp nutmeg**

GARBANZO BEANS COOKED WITH CHILE PEPPER

Serves: 4–6

Preparation: 25 min. + overnight to soak the garbanzo beans

Cooking: 2 hr. 20 min.

Level of difficulty: 2

- 2¹/₂ cups (250 g) dried garbanzo beans (chickpeas), soaked overnight
- Salt
- 3 tbsp extra-virgin olive oil
- 1 large onion, finely chopped
- 2 cloves garlic, lightly crushed but whole
- 1 or 2 dried chile peppers, crumbled
- 5 oz (150 g) peeled tomatoes, pushed through a fine mesh strainer
- 2 tbsp freshly chopped parsley

Put the garbanzo beans in a large saucepan and cover with salted water. Bring to a boil over medium heat and cook for about 2 hours, until tender. Drain well. • Heat the oil in a large saucepan over medium heat. Add the onion, garlic, and chile pepper. Sauté for 3 minutes, until the onion is transparent. • Add the garbanzo beans and sauté for 5 minutes. • Add the tomatoes and season with salt. Cook for 10 minutes over high heat, until the beans are tender and the sauce is slightly reduced. • Remove and discard the garlic. • Transfer to a serving dish. • Sprinkle with parsley and serve hot.

783

CABBAGE, RICE, AND TOMATO GRATIN

Preheat the oven to 350°F (180°C/gas 4).
• Cut the cabbage in half and then into strips.
Blanch in salted, boiling water, drain well, and
spread on a cloth to dry. • Heat the oil in a large
frying pan. Add the onion and garlic and sauté for
5 minutes. • Stir in the rice and season with salt
and pepper. Add the tomatoes and cook for 15
minutes, or until the rice is tender. • Prepare the
Béchamel, adding half the Gruyère. • Grease an
ovenproof dish and fill with alternate layers of
cabbage, rice, and tomatoes. • Cover with the
Béchamel and sprinkle with the remaining cheese.
• Bake until golden brown and bubbling, about
30 minutes.

Serves: 4

Preparation: 25 min.

Cooking: 55 min.

Level of difficulty: 1

- 1 medium Savoy cabbage
- 3 tbsp extra-virgin olive oil
- 2 onions, finely chopped
- 2 cloves garlic, finely chopped
- 1¹/₄ cups (250 g) parboiled rice
- 1 lb (500 g) tomatoes, peeled and chopped
- 1 recipe Béchamel Sauce (see page 956)
- 2 cups (250 g) Gruyère or Swiss cheese, grated
- 1 tbsp butter

VEGETABLES EN PAPILLOTE

Preheat the oven to 350°F (180°C/gas 4). • Put all the vegetables into a large bowl. Add the garlic, rosemary, parsley, thyme, and oregano. Season with salt and pepper and add the oil. Mix well. • Line a roasting pan with a very large sheet of waxed paper, large enough to contain all the vegetables. • Transfer the vegetable mixture to the paper and close the paper over it, folding to seal well. Secure the parcel with staples. • Bake for 45 minutes. • Remove from the oven and place on a large serving dish. Open the paper using a sharp knife and serve hot.

Serves:	4–6
Preparation:	15 min.
Cooking:	45 min.
Level of difficulty:	1

- **14 oz (400 g) Brussels sprouts, halved**
- **1 head broccoli, cut into florets**
- **5 oz (150 g) cherry tomatoes**
- **8 oz (250 g) baby carrots, tops removed**
- **2 celery sticks, tough outer ridges removed and discarded, sliced into 3/4-inch (2-cm) sections**
- **2 small leeks, sliced**
- **2 cloves garlic, finely chopped**
- **1 tbsp finely chopped fresh rosemary**
- **1 tbsp finely chopped fresh parsley**
- **1 tbsp finely chopped fresh thyme**
- **1 tbsp finely chopped fresh oregano**
- **Salt and freshly ground black pepper**
- **3 tbsp extra-virgin olive oil**

SALADS

CALABRIAN MIXED SALAD

Remove any discolored leaves from the fennel bulb. Cut it in quarters then slice finely. • Slice the carrots and zucchini into thin wheels. • Peel the cucumber (or leave the peel on, if preferred), and slice thinly. • Thinly slice the celery. • Place all the sliced vegetables in a salad bowl and season with salt. Drizzle with the oil, toss gently, and serve.

790

Serves: 4

Preparation: 10 min.

Level of difficulty: 1

- **1 small fennel bulb**
- **2 medium carrots**
- **2 medium zucchini (courgettes)**
- **1 small cucumber**
- **2 medium celery stalks**
- **Salt**
- **$1/3$ cup (90 ml) extra-virgin olive oil**

SICILIAN CARROT SALAD

Serves: 4

Preparation: 10 min.

Level of difficulty: 1

- **4 medium carrots**
- **1 tender celery heart**
- **Salt and freshly ground black pepper**
- **2–3 tbsp freshly squeezed lemon juice**
- **$1/3$ cup (90 ml) extra-virgin olive oil**
- **1 tsp sugar**

Scrape the carrots then grate them. Finely slice the celery. • Place the carrots and celery in a salad bowl, tossing gently to mix. • Mix the salt, pepper, lemon juice, and oil in a small bowl. Pour over the salad. Sprinkle with the sugar. • Toss again and serve.

TOMATO, ONION, AND CUCUMBER SALAD

Place the cherry tomatoes, onion, cucumber, and chile pepper in a salad bowl. • Season with the oregano, salt, and pepper and drizzle with the oil. Toss gently and serve.

Serves: 4

Preparation: 15 min.

Level of difficulty: 1

- **20–25 cherry tomatoes, cut in half**
- **1 medium white onion, thinly sliced**
- **1 medium cucumber, peeled and sliced**
- **1 fresh red chile pepper, thinly sliced**
- **1 tsp dried oregano**
- **Salt and freshly ground black pepper**
- **1/3 cup (90 ml) extra-virgin olive oil**

CALABRIAN POTATO SALAD

Preheat the oven to 400°F (200°C/gas 6).
• Wrap the potatoes individually in aluminum foil. Bake in the oven until tender, about 45 minutes. • Let cool a little then remove the foil and potato skins. Slice the potatoes. • Place in a salad bowl and let cool completely. • Add the onion and bell pepper. Season with salt and pepper and drizzle with the oil. • Toss gently and serve.

Serves: 4

Preparation: 15 min.

Cooking: 45 min.

Level of difficulty: 1

- **4 medium potatoes**
- **1 medium white onion, thinly sliced**
- **1–2 green bell peppers (capsicums), seeded and cut in short strips**
- **Salt and freshly ground black pepper**
- **$1/3$ cup (90 ml) extra-virgin olive oil**

RAW VEGETABLES WITH OIL, SALT, AND PEPPER DIP

Serves: 4–6

Preparation: 20 min.

Level of difficulty: 1

- **4 artichokes**
- **Freshly squeezed juice of 2 lemons**
- **4 carrots (or 8 baby spring carrots)**
- **4 celery hearts**
- **2 large fennel bulbs**
- **12 scallions**
- **12 radishes**
- **1¹/₂ cups (375 ml) extra-virgin olive oil**
- **Salt and freshly ground black pepper**

Wash all the vegetables thoroughly under cold running water. • Artichokes: Remove all but the pale inner leaves by pulling the outer ones down and snapping them off. Cut off the stem and the top third of the remaining leaves. Cut the artichokes in half lengthwise and scrape the fuzzy choke away with a knife. Cut each artichoke in wedges and soak in a bowl of cold water with the juice of 1 lemon for 15 minutes. • Carrots: Scrub with a brush or peel and soak in a bowl of cold water with the remaining lemon juice for 10 minutes. • Celery: Discard the stringy outer stalks and trim off the leafy tops. Keep the inner white stalks and the heart. • Fennel: Slice off the base, trim away the leafy tops, and discard the blemished outer leaves. Divide into 4 or more wedges, depending on size. • Scallions: Remove the roots and trim the tops. • Radishes: Cut the roots off and trim the tops. • For the dip: Whisk the oil with salt and pepper to taste. Pour into 4–6 small bowls.

SICILIAN ORANGE SALAD

Peel the oranges using a sharp knife, making sure that you remove all the white pith. Slice thinly. • Place the oranges in a large salad bowl. Add the onion and parsley and season with salt and pepper. Drizzle with the oil. • Toss gently and serve.

Serves: 4–6

Preparation: 20 min.

Level of difficulty: 1

- 4 oranges
- 1 small white onion, thinly sliced
- 1 tbsp finely chopped fresh parsley
- Salt and freshly ground black pepper
- $1/3$ cup (90 ml) extra-virgin olive oil

GREEN BEAN SALAD WITH FRIED BREAD

Top and tail the beans, cut in half, rinse well, and cook in a pot of boiling, salted water for 7–8 minutes, or until tender. Drain, dry on a cloth, and place in a large salad bowl. • Sauté the pancetta in a small frying pan with 1 tablespoon of oil until crisp. Drain and set aside. • Fry the bread in a frying pan with ¼ (cup (60 ml) of oil and the garlic until golden brown. Drain on paper towels.
• In a small bowl, dissolve a pinch of salt in the lemon juice, and add the pepper, oregano, parsley, scallions, and ¼ (cup (60 ml) of oil. Dress the salad, sprinkle with the capers, and toss with the diced bread. • Serve at once before the bread becomes soggy.

Serves: 4

Preparation: 20 min.

Cooking: 15 min.

Level of difficulty: 1

- **1 lb (500 g) green beans**
- **Salt and freshly ground black pepper**
- **2 bunches chives, finely chopped**
- **6 oz (180 g) pancetta, cut in strips**
- **¹/₂ cup (125 ml) extra-virgin olive oil**
- **5 thick slices firm-textured bread, diced**
- **1 large clove garlic, cut in quarters**
- **Freshly squeezed juice of 2 lemons**
- **1 tbsp finely chopped fresh parsley**
- **8 scallions (spring onions), finely chopped**
- **2 tbsp salt-cured capers, rinsed**

Serves: 4–6

Preparation: 10 min.

Cooking: 30 min.

Level of difficulty: 1

- 4 large floury (baking) potatoes, peeled
- 1¹/₂ lb (750 g) broccoli florets
- 1 small red onion, chopped
- ¹/₄ cup (60 ml) extra-virgin olive oil
- 3 tbsp white wine vinegar
- 1 clove garlic, finely chopped
- 2 tbsp finely chopped chives
- 1 tbsp capers preserved in brine
- 4 tbsp finely chopped fresh parsley
- Salt and freshly ground black pepper

POTATO AND BROCCOLI SALAD

Cook the potatoes in a large pot of salted boiling water for 20 minutes, or until tender. Drain and let cool slightly. • Cut the cooked potatoes into ¾-inch (2-cm) cubes. • Cook the broccoli in a large pot of salted boiling water for 5–7 minutes, until tender. Drain and transfer to a large salad bowl. • Add the potatoes and onion. • Beat together the oil, vinegar, garlic, chives, capers, and parsley in a bowl. Season with salt and pepper. • Drizzle the dressing over the salad. Mix well and serve.

ARUGULA SALAD WITH PARMESAN AND RED APPLE

Place the arugula a in a large salad bowl. Top with the Parmesan. • Cut the apple in half, remove the core, and cut into small dice. Drizzle with the lemon juice and add to the salad. Sprinkle with the walnuts. • Place the oil, vinegar, and mustard in a small bowl. season with salt and pepper and beat with a fork until well mixed. • Drizzle the dressing over the salad. Toss gently and serve at once.

Serves: 4

Preparation: 15 min.

Level of difficulty: 1

- **6 oz (180 g) arugula (rocket)**
- **4 oz (125 g) Parmesan, in flakes**
- **1 large Red Delicious apple**
- **Freshly squeezed juice of 1/2 lemon**
- **16 walnuts, coarsely chopped**
- **1/4 cup (60 ml) extra-virgin olive oil**
- **2 tbsp white wine vinegar**
- **1 tsp French mustard**
- **Salt and freshly ground black pepper**

Serves: 4–6

Preparation: 25 min.

Cooking: 50 min.

Level of difficulty: 2

- **2 large floury (baking) potatoes**
- **2 large carrots, cut into small cubes**
- **2 oz (60 g) green beans**
- **$1/4$ head cauliflower, cut into small florets**
- **3 oz (90 g) peas**
- **1 cup (250 ml) extra virgin olive oil**
- **1 tbsp white wine vinegar**
- **Salt and freshly ground black pepper**
- **3 pickled cucumbers (gherkins), cut into small cubes**
- **1 tsp salt-cured capers, rinsed**
- **4 anchovy fillets, chopped**
- **2 large egg yolks**
- **Freshly squeezed juice of $1/2$ lemon**
- **Fresh chives, to garnish**

RUSSIAN SALAD

Cook the potatoes in a large pot of salted boiling water for 25 minutes, until tender. • Drain and let cool. • Chop the potatoes into small cubes. • Cook the carrots in a large pot of salted boiling water for 7–8 minutes, until tender. Drain and let cool. • Cook the green beans in a large pot of salted boiling water for 5–7 minutes, until tender. Drain and let cool. • Chop the green beans. • Cook the cauliflower in a large pot of salted boiling water for 7–8 minutes, until tender. Drain and let cool. • Cook the peas in a large pot of salted boiling water for 5 minutes, until tender. Drain and let cool. • Put all the cooked vegetables into a large salad bowl and mix well. • Add 3 tablespoons of the oil and the vinegar. Season with salt and pepper. • Add the cucumbers, capers, and anchovies, followed by the mayonnaise to the salad. Mix well. • Garnish with chives and serve.

TUNA AND SPELT SALAD

Cook the spelt in a large pot of salted boiling water until tender, 35–40 minutes. Drain well and cool under cold running water. Drain again and transfer to a clean kitchen cloth. Dry well and place in a large salad bowl. • Add the tomatoes, onion, and tuna. Season with salt and pepper and toss well. • Drizzle with the oil, toss again, and serve.

Serves: 4–6
Preparation: 25 min.
Cooking: 35–40 min.
Level of difficulty: 1

- 1 lb (500 g) spelt (or pearl barley)
- 24 cherry tomatoes, cut in half
- 1 sweet red onion, finely chopped
- 8 oz (250 g) canned tuna, drained
- $^1/_4$ cup (60 ml) extra-virgin olive oil
- Salt and freshly ground black pepper

TUNA AND BEAN SALAD

Serves: 2–4

Preparation: 15 min.

Level of difficulty: 1

- **8 oz (250 g) canned tuna, drained**
- **1 (14-oz/400-g) can cannellini kidney beans, drained**
- **1 sweet red onion, sliced**
- **2 tbsp finely chopped fresh parsley**
- **1 tbsp finely chopped cilantro (coriander)**
- **1 small head lettuce**
- **$^1/_4$ cup (60 ml) extra-virgin olive oil**
- **2 tsp French mustard**
- **Juice of 1 lemon**
- **Salt and freshly ground black pepper**

Place the tuna in a medium bowl and break it up with a fork. • Add the beans, onion, parsley, and cilantro and toss well. • Arrange the lettuce leaves so that they line the base and sides of a medium salad bowl. Spoon the bean and tuna mixture into the lettuce leaves. • Place the oil, mustard, lemon juice, salt, and pepper in a small bowl and beat well with a fork. • Drizzle over the salad and serve at once.

MIXED SALAD WITH BASIL

P ut the tomatoes, bell peppers, cucumber, radishes, red onion, fava beans, olives, garlic, and celery in a large salad bowl. Mix well. • Beat together the basil, oil, vinegar, and salt in a small bowl. • Add the tuna. • Drizzle with the dressing and toss well. • Discard the garlic. • Arrange the eggs, artichokes, and anchovy fillets on top of the salad in a decorative manner.

Serves: 4

Preparation: 15 min.

Level of difficulty: 1

- **3 ripe tomatoes, cut into segments**
- **2 bell peppers, seeded and sliced**
- **1 cucumber, peeled and sliced**
- **10 radishes, cut into quarters**
- **1 small red onion, sliced**
- **14 oz (400 g) fresh fava (broad) beans, shelled**
- **20 black olives, pitted**
- **10 green olives, pitted**
- **2 cloves garlic, lightly crushed but whole**
- **1 stalk celery, finely chopped**
- **6 basil leaves, torn**
- **$^1/_4$ cup (60 ml) extra-virgin olive oil**
- **3 tbsp white wine vinegar**
- **Salt**
- **8 oz (250 g) cooked tuna fillet, broken into pieces**
- **3 hard-boiled eggs, cut into segments**
- **5 artichoke hearts preserved in oil, drained and cut into segments**
- **10 anchovy fillets**

DESSERTS

FROZEN GRAPEFRUITS

Cut the grapefruits in half. Hollow out the flesh with a sharp knife and a spoon, and place the shells in the freezer. • Stir the sugar and grapefruit zest and juice into the milk. • Beat the cream until just thickened and add to the milk mixture. • Pour into a metal bowl and place in the freezer. After 2 hours, remove from the freezer and stir with a fork. Freeze again and stir again after another 2 hours. • Spoon the mixture into the frozen grapefruit shells. Top with the extra zest.
• Freeze for 15 minutes before serving.

Serves: 4

Preparation: 20 min. + 4 hr. 15 min. to freeze

Level of difficulty: 1

- **2 large grapefruits**
- **¾ cup (150 g) sugar**
- **1 tbsp finely grated grapefruit zest, + extra, to decorate**
- **3 tbsp freshly squeezed grapefruit juice**
- **¾ cup (180 ml) milk**
- **½ cup (125 ml) heavy (double) cream**

STUFFED BAKED PEACHES

Serves: 4

Preparation: 20 min.

Cooking: 30 min.

Level of difficulty: 1

- **4 large ripe yellow peaches**
- **20 amaretti cookies, crushed**
- **²/₃ cup (125 g) sugar**
- **2 tbsp butter**
- **¹/₄ cup (60 ml) dark rum**

Preheat the oven to 350°F (180°C/gas 4).
• Rinse the peaches under cold running water and dry with paper towels. Cut them in half and remove the pits (stones). Use a teaspoon to make a hollow about the size of a golf ball in each peach half. Place the peach flesh in a bowl and add three-quarters of the amaretti cookies and all but ¼ cup (60 g) of sugar. Mix well and use to fill the peaches. • Use the butter to grease a baking pan large enough to hold all the peach halves snugly in a single layer. Arrange the peaches in the pan. • Drizzle with the rum and sprinkle with the remaining amaretti cookies and sugar. • Bake for 30 minutes. • Serve hot or at room temperature.

FRESH FRUIT SALAD

Rinse all the fruit thoroughly. • Peel the apples, kiwi fruit, oranges, and pineapple and cut into small cubes. • Hull the strawberries and cut into small pieces. • Peel the bananas and slice. • Pit the apricots or peaches and cut into small pieces. • Place all the fruit in a large salad bowl. Sprinkle with the sugar and drizzle with the lemon juice. Stir gently and let macerate 1 hour before serving. • Fresh fruit salad can be made throughout the year; vary the fruit according to the season and what you have in the garden or can buy at the supermarket.

818

Serves: 4–6

*Preparation: 30 min.
+ 1 hr. to macerate*

Level of difficulty: 1

- **2 tasty eating apples**
- **3 kiwi fruit**
- **2 oranges**
- **1 small pineapple**
- **5 oz (150 g) strawberries**
- **2 bananas**
- **4 apricots or 2 peaches**
- **2–4 tbsp sugar**
- **Freshly squeezed juice of 1 lemon**

FRUIT BASKETS WITH BALSAMIC VINEGAR

Serves: 6

Preparation: 25 min.

Cooking: 8–10 min.

Level of difficulty: 1

Preheat the oven to 400°F (200°C/gas 6). • Butter six small ovenproof ramekins. • Unroll or unfold the pastry on a lightly floured surface. Use a sharp knife to cut the pastry into 6 squares. • Line the bottom and sides of each prepared mold with a pastry square, trimming the edges to fit. Prick the pastry well with a fork. • Bake for 8–10 minutes, or until lightly browned. • Rinse the fruit thoroughly under cold running water and dry well. Cut into bite-sized pieces. • Place the fruit in a large bowl with the sugar and balsamic vinegar, mixing well. • Spoon the fruit into the baked pastry shells, decorate with the mint leaves, and serve immediately.

- 7 oz (200 g) frozen puff pastry, thawed
- 1 small cantaloupe (rock melon), about 1 lb (500 g)
- 4 apricots, pitted
- 6 oz (180 g) strawberries, hulled
- 2 peaches, pitted
- 2–4 red plums, pitted
- 1 watermelon, weighing about 12 oz (350 g)
- 2 tbsp sugar
- 2 tbsp balsamic vinegar
- 4 leaves fresh mint

- 1¹/₄ lb (600 g)
  fresh strawberries
- ¹/₃ cup (75 g)
  **superfine (caster)
  sugar**
- ¹/₂ cup (125 ml)
  dry white wine

STRAWBERRIES IN WHITE WINE

C lean the strawberries and rinse under cold running water. Drain well, then pat dry with paper towels. • Transfer the strawberries to a serving dish. Sprinkle with the sugar and drizzle with the wine. • Place in the refrigerator to rest for at least 1 hour before serving.

CREME BRULÉE

Preheat the oven to 375°F (190°C/gas 5).
• Spilt the vanilla pod lengthways and use a knife to scrape out the seeds. Combine the vanilla seeds in a bowl with the egg yolks and superfine sugar. Whisk until pale and creamy. • Gradually whisk in the cream and milk. Strain through a fine-mesh sieve into a pitcher (jug) and pour into a 9-inch (23-cm) round baking dish. • Place the baking dish in a larger baking pan. Pour enough boiling water into the baking pan to fill halfway up the sides of the dish. • Bake for 30 minutes, or until just set. Let cool to room temperature. Chill in the refrigerator for 4 hours. • Sprinkle the brown sugar evenly over the top, ensuring the cream is completely covered. • Light a chef's blowtorch or preheat the broiler (grill) until red-hot. Place the ramekins 3–4 inches (8-10 cm) below the heat and broil for 3–5 minutes, watching carefully, until the sugar begins to melt and turns to a golden caramel. • Serve at once or chill and serve later.

Serves: 4–6

Preparation: 15 min. + 4 hr. to chill

Cooking: 30 min.

Level of difficulty: 1

- 1 vanilla pod
- 3 large egg yolks
- ¼ cup (50 g) superfine (caster) sugar
- 1¼ cups (300 ml) light (single) or heavy (double) cream
- ¼ cup (60 ml) milk
- ½ cup (100 g) firmly packed light brown sugar

HONEY PARFAITS

Serves: 4

Preparation: 25 min.
  + 4 hr. to freeze

Cooking: 8–10 min.

Level of difficulty: 1

- 1 large egg
  + 4 large egg yolks
- 1 tbsp sugar
- $^1/_3$ cup (90 g)
  honey
- Finely grated zest
  of 1 small lemon
- 2 tbsp Grand
  Marnier
- 1 cup (250 ml)
  heavy (double)
  cream

Line 4 small ramekins with plastic wrap (cling film). • Place the egg, egg yolks, sugar, honey, and lemon zest in a double boiler over barely simmering water. Beat with a whisk until thick and frothy. Remove from the heat and stir in the Grand Marnier. Place the pan in a larger pan of iced water and beat until completely cool. • Beat the cream in a medium bowl with an electric mixer on high speed until thick. Fold the cream into the egg mixture. • Pour the mixture into the prepared ramekins and freeze for 4 hours. • Remove from the freezer and dip the base of the pan in boiling water for a few seconds. • Turn the parfaits out onto a serving dish.

PISTACHIO SPUMONE

Bring a small saucepan of water to a boil over high heat. Add the pistachios and boil for 1 minute. Drain well and dry on a clean cloth. Let cool a little then remove the skins with your hands. • Chop the pistachios with 2 tablespoons of sugar until smooth. • Place the remaining sugar in a small saucepan with the water and simmer for 10 minutes over low heat. • Meanwhile, beat the egg yolks and salt. Gradually pour the boiling sugar mixture into the egg yolk mixture, beating constantly. Keep beating until the mixture is cool, light, and foamy. Fold in the pistachios. • Beat the cream until thick. Fold into the mixture. • Spoon the mixture into 4 small ramekins and freeze for 3 hours. • Just before serving, dip the ramekins into hot water and turn out onto serving plates.

Serves: 4

Preparation: 20 min.
* + 3 hr. to freeze*

Cooking: 15 min.

Level of difficulty: 1

- 2 oz (60 g) pistachios
- $^1/_2$ cup (100 g) sugar
- $^1/_4$ cup (60 ml) water
- 3 large eggs
- Pinch of salt
- $^2/_3$ cup (150 ml) heavy (double) cream

COFFEE GRANITA

Place the sugar in a medium bowl. Pour the hot coffee in over the top and stir until the sugar has completely dissolved. Let cool to room temperature. • Pour the mixture into a plastic or stainless steel container about 10 inches (25 cm) square. Place in the freezer and leave for 1 hour. • Use a fork or hand blender to break the granita up into large crystals. • If using an ice cream machine, transfer to the machine at this point and follow the manufacturer's instructions. • To continue by hand, replace the container in the freezer for 30 minutes, then break up again with a fork. Repeat 3 or 4 times, until the crystals are completely frozen. • Scoop into 2–4 glasses or dessert bowls. Top with the whipped cream, if liked.

Serves: 2–4

Preparation: 20 min. + 3 hr. to freeze

Level of difficulty: 1

- $^1/_2$ cup (100 g) sugar
- $1^1/_2$ cups (375 ml) very hot strong black coffee
- $^1/_2$ cup (125 ml) whipped cream (optional)

LIMONCELLO CREAM WITH ALMONDS

Prepare the vanilla pastry cream. • Stir the Limoncello into the vanilla pastry cream. Place plastic wrap (cling film) on the surface to prevent a skin forming and set aside to cool. • Spoon into 4 individual bowls and chill for at least 1 hour. • Decorate with the candied peel and almonds and serve.

Serves: 4

Preparation: 15 min. + 1 hr. to chill

Cooking: 10 min.

Level of difficulty: 1

- **1 recipe Vanilla Pastry Cream made with 4 egg yolks (see page 962)**
- **1 cup (250 ml) Limoncello (sweet lemon liqueur)**
- **4 slices candied lemon peel**
- **2 oz (60 g) flaked almonds**

MANDARIN CREAM

Serves: 4–6

Preparation: 20 min.
+ 2 hr. to chill

Cooking: 10 min.

Level of difficulty: 1

- **3 large egg yolks**
- **¹/₄ cup (50 g) sugar**
- **¹/₃ cup (90 ml) freshly squeezed mandarin juice**
- **Finely grated zest of 1 mandarin**
- **1 tsp gelatin powder**
- **2 tbsp boiling water**
- **2 tbsp mandarin liqueur**
- **1¹/₂ cups (375 ml) heavy (double) cream**
- **2 mandarins, peeled and divided into segments**
- **Candied cherries, to garnish**
- **Fresh mint leaves, to garnish**

Beat the egg yolks and sugar in a medium bowl until pale and creamy. • Stir in the mandarin juice and zest. • Transfer the mixture to a double boiler over barely simmering water and simmer, beating constantly, until the mixture is thick and creamy, 7–10 minutes. • Dissolve the gelatin in a cup with 2 tablespoons of boiling water. • Stir the gelatin into the mandarin mixture. Add the mandarin liqueur and mix well. Let cool. • Whip the cream in a large bowl until stiff. Fold two-thirds of the cream into the mandarin mixture. • Spoon into individual serving dishes. Chill for 2 hours. • Decorate with the remaining cream, mandarin segments, cherries, and mint leaves just before serving.

AMARENE CHERRY GELATO

Serves: 4

Preparation: 20 min.
+ time to chill

Cooking: 10 min.

Level of difficulty: 1

- 1 oz (30 g) skim milk powder
- ³/₄ cup (150 g) sugar
- 1³/₄ cups (450 ml) milk
- 1¹/₃ cups (300 ml) heavy (double) cream
- ¹/₈ tsp salt
- 2 tbsp amarene cherry syrup
- 4 oz (120 g) canned amarene cherries (drained weight)

Mix the skim milk powder and sugar in a heavy-based saucepan and then add the milk, cream, and salt. • Place over high heat and, just before it begins to boil, turn the heat down to low and simmer for 2 minutes, stirring constantly.
• Remove from the heat, add the amarene cherry syrup, and beat with a whisk on medium speed until cool. Chill in the refrigerator for 30 minutes.
• Beat with a whisk for 2–3 minutes. Transfer the mixture to your ice cream machine and freeze following the manufacturer's instructions. • Cut the amarene cherries in half—leave a few whole to decorate—and add them to the ice cream machine one minute before you turn it off. Decorate with the whole cherries.

MALAGA GELATO

Rinse the raisins. Drain well and place in a small bowl. Cover with the Moscato or rum and let plump while you prepare the ice cream. • Place a large bowl in the freezer to chill. • Place the milk and cream in a heavy-based saucepan over medium heat and bring to a boil. • Beat the egg yolks and sugar in a medium bowl with an electric mixer on high speed until pale and creamy. • Pour the hot milk mixture into the bowl with the egg yolk mixture, beating constantly with a wooden spoon. Return to the saucepan and simmer over very low heat, beating constantly, until it just coats the back of the spoon. Do not let the mixture boil. • Remove from the heat and transfer to the chilled bowl. Let the mixture cool completely, stirring often. Chill in the refrigerator for 30 minutes. • Transfer the mixture to your ice cream machine and freeze following the manufacturer's instructions. Add the raisins and their liquid 1–2 minutes before the ice cream is ready.

Serves: 4

Preparation: 20 min.
  + time to chill

Cooking: 10 min.

Level of difficulty: 1

- $^1/_2$ cup (90 g) Malaga or other plump tasty raisins
- $^1/_4$ cup (60 ml) Moscato dessert wine (or rum)
- 2 cups (500 ml) milk
- $^3/_4$ cup (200 ml) heavy (double) cream
- 6 large egg yolks
- $^3/_4$ cup (150 g) sugar

CHOCOLATE HAZELNUT GELATO

Serves: 4

Preparation: 20 min.
+ time to chill

Cooking: 10 min.

Level of difficulty: 1

- 1/4 cup (30 g) toasted (unsalted) hazelnuts
- 2 tbsp confectioners' (icing) sugar
- 3 oz (90 g) bittersweet (dark) chocolate
- 4 large egg yolks
- 3/4 cup (150 g) sugar
- 2 1/2 cups (600 ml) milk
- 1/4 cup (125 ml) heavy (double) cream

Chop the hazelnuts and confectioners' sugar in a food processor until smooth. • Melt the chocolate in a double boiler over barely simmering water. • Stir the chocolate into the hazelnut mixture and set aside. • Beat the egg yolks and sugar in a medium bowl with an electric mixer on high speed until pale and creamy. • Place the milk and cream in a medium saucepan over medium heat and bring to a boil. • Pour the hot milk mixture over the egg mixture beating constantly with a whisk. • Return to low heat and beat constantly with the whisk until the mixture coats the back of a spoon. Make sure that the mixture does not boil at this stage. • Remove from the heat and pour a little of the hot milk mixture into the chocolate mixture. Stir well then pour the chocolate mixture into the hot milk. Beat with a whisk until cool. Chill in the refrigerator for 30 minutes. • Transfer the mixture to your ice cream machine and freeze following the manufacturer's instructions.

PUMPKIN AND AMARETTI COOKIE GELATO

Place a large bowl in the freezer to chill. • Peel the pumpkin, remove the seeds, and slice. Steam until just tender, 8–10 minutes. Let cool and then lightly squeeze with your hands to remove as much moisture as possible. • Weigh out 1 pound (500 g). Place in a food processor with the sugar and salt and chop until smooth. • Place the cream in a heavy-based saucepan over medium heat and bring to a boil. Remove from the heat and stir in the almond extract. • Pour into the chilled bowl. Let cool completely, stirring often. Chill in the refrigerator for 30 minutes. • Transfer the mixture to your ice cream machine and freeze following the manufacturer's instructions. Crumble half the amaretti cookies into serving bowls or glasses. Top with the ice cream and finish with an amaretti cookie.

Serves: 4

Preparation: 20 min.
+ time to chill

Cooking: 10 min.

Level of difficulty: 1

- 4 lb (2 kg) fresh pumpkin
- $^3/_4$ cup (150 g) sugar
- $^1/_8$ tsp salt
- $1^2/_3$ cups (400 ml) heavy (double) cream
- 2–3 drops bitter almond extract (essence)
- About 20 crisp amaretti cookies (biscuits)

COOKED CREAM WITH COFFEE

S prinkle the gelatin over the coffee in a bowl and leave to soften for 5 minutes. • Place 4 cups (1 liters) of the cream in a heavy saucepan with the sugar over low heat and bring to a boil. Remove from the heat. • Stir in the coffee and gelatin and mix until the gelatin is dissolved. • Pour the mixture into a loaf pan. When it begins to set (not before, otherwise the gelatin and cream will separate) refrigerate for at least 5 hours. • Whip the remaining cream and confectioners' sugar until stiff. Unmold the cooked cream and decorate with the coffee beans. • Serve with the whipped cream in a separate bowl.

Serves: 6

Preparation: 15 min. + 5 hr. to chill

Cooking: 5 min.

Level of difficulty: 2

- **1 packet unflavored gelatin**
- **$^2/_3$ cup (150 ml) strong espresso coffee**
- **5 cups (1.25 liters) heavy (double) cream**
- **$^3/_4$ cup (150 g) superfine (caster) sugar**
- **2 tablespoons confectioners' (icing) sugar**
- **Coffee beans to decorate**

Serves: 6

Preparation: 15 min.
+ 4 hr. to chill

Cooking: 10 min.

Level of difficulty: 2

- ²/₃ cup (150 ml) milk
- ¹/₂ cup (100 g) sugar
- 4 large egg yolks
- 4 oz (125 g) semisweet (dark) chocolate
- 1 tbsp gelatin powder
- 1 (9-inch/23-cm) store-bought sponge cake, about 1-inch (2.5-cm) high
- 2 tbsp rum
- 2 cups (500 ml) heavy (double) cream
- Grated semisweet (dark) and white chocolate, to garnish

CHOCOLATE BAVARIAN CREAM

B ring the milk to a boil in a small saucepan over low heat. • Beat the sugar and egg yolks in a medium bowl until pale and creamy. • Slowly pour the milk into the egg mixture, beating constantly. • Return to the saucepan and bring to a boil. Remove from the heat just before it boils. • Let cool for 5 minutes then add the chocolate and gelatin and stir until dissolved. • Let cool. • Place the sponge cake in 9-inch (23-cm) springform pan. • Brush with the rum. • Beat the cream until stiff and fold it into the chocolate mixture. • Spoon the mixture into the pan over the sponge. Chill in the refrigerator until set, about 4 hours. • Decorate with the grated chocolate just before serving.

MERINGUE CONES

Preheat the oven to 100°F (50°C). • Meringues: Beat the egg whites with ¼ cup (50 g) of sugar and the salt until soft peaks form. • Place the remaining sugar in a saucepan over medium-low heat and simmer until melted. • Pour the melted sugar in a thin trickle into the egg whites, beating constantly until thick and glossy. • take 16 cone-shaped molds and wrap the outside in parchment paper. • Place the meringue in a piping bag with a plain tip and pipe over the outside of the cones. • Cook for 3–4 hours, or until dry and crisp. • Let cool in the oven then carefully remove from the molds. • Filling: Beat the cream until thickened. Place in a piping bag and fill the cones. • Melt the chocolate in a double-boiler over barely simmering water. • Place in a piping bag and decorate the tops of the cones.

Serves: 6–8

Preparation: 45 min.

Cooking: 3–4 hr.

Level of difficulty: 3

Meringues
- **2 large egg whites**
- **1¹/₄ cups (250 g) sugar**
- **¹/₈ tsp salt**

Filling
- **1 cup (250 ml) heavy (double) cream**
- **2 oz (60 g) dark chocolate**

MERINGUE WITH CHOCOLATE AND CANDIED CHESTNUTS

Serves: 6-8

Preparation: 30 min.

Cooking: 90 min.

Level of difficulty: 2

- 1 cup (200 g) sugar
- 1/2 cup (100 g) confectioners' (icing) sugar
- 6 large egg whites
- 1/8 teaspoon salt
- 2 cups (500 ml) heavy (double) cream
- 1/2 tsp vanilla extract (essence)
- 6 tbsp dark chocolate chips
- 4 candied chestnuts, crumbled or coarsely chopped

Preheat the oven to 250°F (130°C/gas 1/2). • Cut four 8-inch (20-cm) rounds of parchment paper and place on two baking sheets. • Mix the sugar and confectioners' sugar in a medium bowl. • Beat the egg whites with half the sugar mixture and the salt in a large bowl with an electric mixer at medium speed until stiff, glossy peaks form. Gradually beat in the remaining sugar mixture. • Spread a third of the meringue onto each parchment round. • Bake for about 90 minutes, or until crisp and pale gold. • Turn the oven off and let cool. Carefully remove the paper. • Beat the cream and vanilla in a large bowl until stiff. • Fold in the chocolate chips and candied chestnuts. • Place one meringue round on a serving plate. Spread with one-third of the cream. Top with another meringue round and spread with one-third of the cream. Top with the last round and spread with the remaining cream. • Crumble the remaining meringue round over the cake.

STRAWBERRY THOUSAND LAYER CAKE

Preheat the oven to 400°F (200°C/gas 6).
• Roll out the pastry into three 10-inch (25-cm) disks. • Bake until golden brown, 15–20 minutes. Let cool on a wire rack. • Prepare the vanilla pastry cream and stir in the strawberry liqueur. • Place a layer of pastry on a serving dish and spread with half the pastry cream. Cover with another layer of pastry and top with the remaining pastry cream Top with the last layer of pastry. • Decorate with the whipped cream and strawberries.

Serves: 6–8

Preparation: 20 min.

Cooking: 15–20 min.

Level of difficulty: 1

- 12 oz (350 g) frozen puff pastry, thawed
- 1 recipe Vanilla Pastry Cream (see page 962)
- 2 tbsp strawberry liqueur
- $1/2$ cup (125 ml) whipped cream
- Fresh strawberries, to decorate

846

MILANESE CHARLOTTE

Preheat the oven to 350°F (180°C/gas 4).
• Place the golden raisins in a small bowl and cover with warm water. Let soak for 15 minutes.
• Peel and core the apples and cut into thin wedges. • Place the apples in a medium saucepan with all but 3 tablespoons of the sugar and the wine. Add enough water so that the apples are just covered. Bring to a gentle simmer over medium-low heat. Cook until just tender—do not let them get mushy—about 5 minutes. • Drain well and place the slices of apple on a clean kitchen towel.
• Mix the butter with the remaining sugar and use a part of this mixture to grease the sides of a 1-quart (1-liter) charlotte mold. • Line the mold with slices of bread. • Fill the center with layers of apples, raisins, and bread. Drizzle each layer with a little rum. Finish with a layer of bread. • Bake for 30 minutes, then cover with aluminum foil and bake for 20 more minutes. • Serve hot or warm.

Serves: 4-6

Preparation: 20 min.

Cooking: 1 hr.

Level of difficulty: 1

• 2 oz (60 g) golden raisins (sultanas)
• 14 oz (400 g) tart-tasting cooking apples (renette)
• $3/4$ cup (150 g) sugar
• 3 tbps pine nuts
• 2 tbsp butter
• 5 oz (150 g) day-old, firm-textured bread, thinly sliced, crusts removed
• $1/2$ cup (125 ml) dry white wine
• 2–4 tbsp rum

ZABAGLIONE WITH CREAM AND RASPBERRIES

Beat the egg yolks and sugar in a double boiler until pale and creamy • Add ¼ cup (60 ml) of Marsala and beat until smooth. • Place the double boiler over barely simmering water and beat with the whisk until doubled in volume, about 15 minutes. • Stir the remaining sugar and water in a saucepan over medium heat until the sugar is caramelized, about 10 minutes. • Let cool. • Beat the mascarpone in a medium bowl with half the cream. Add the remaining Marsala and whisk until light and creamy. • Fold the zabaglione carefully into this mixture. • Divide almost all the raspberries among four dessert bowls. Top with zabaglione and the remaining cream. • Decorate with the remaining raspberries and serve.

Serves: 4

Preparation: 10 min.

Cooking: 25 min.

Level of difficulty: 1

- **3 large egg yolks**
- **½ cup (100 g) sugar**
- **¾ cup (150 g) firmly pressed dark brown sugar**
- **¾ cup (180 ml) dry Marsala wine**
- **½ cup (125 g) mascarpone or cream cheese**
- **½ cup (125 ml) whipped cream, to decorate**
- **12 oz (350 g) fresh raspberries, to decorate**

COFFEE MOUSSE

Serves: 6

Preparation: 15 min.
+ 4 hr. to chill

Cooking: 1 hr.

Level of difficulty: 2

- 2 cups (500 ml) milk
- 2 tbsp instant coffee
- 1/4 cup (60 ml) coffee liqueur
- 3/4 cup (150 g) sugar
- 4 large eggs
- 4 large egg yolks
- 4 tbsp unsweetened cocoa powder
- 1/2 cup (125 ml) heavy (double) cream
- 1 tbsp confectioners' (icing) sugar
- 2 oz (60 g) semisweet (dark) chocolate, grated
- Coffee beans

Preheat the oven to 350°F (180°C/gas 4). • Oil a 4-cup (1-liter) pudding mold. • Heat the milk in a medium saucepan over low heat. Add the coffee and stir until dissolved. Remove from the heat and stir in the liqueur. • Beat the sugar, eggs, and egg yolks in a large bowl until pale and creamy. • Beat in the cocoa and, gradually, the milk mixture. • Pour the mixture into the prepared pudding mold. • Place the mold in a larger pan of cold water and bake in the oven until set, about 1 hour. • Let cool at room temperature then chill in the refrigerator for at least 4 hours. • Beat the cream with the confectioners' sugar until stiff. • Decorate the mousse with the cream, grated chocolate, and coffee beans just before serving.

851

NEAPOLITAN TRIFLE

Prepare the sponge cake in a 9-inch (23-cm) round cake pan. When cool, slice into three horizontally, then cut into thin strips. • Strain the ricotta through a fine sieve and place in a bowl. • Stir in the liqueur, 2 tablespoons of chocolate, and the vanilla. • Place the sugar and water in a heavy-based pan over medium-low heat and bring to a gentle boil. It should be smooth and slightly foamy. Simmer for 2 minutes then remove from the heat. • Gradually stir the sugar mixture into the ricotta. • Place a layer of sponge cake on a serving dish and drizzle with half the rum. Spread with a layer of cream. Cover with another layer of sponge cake drizzled with rum and spread with cream. Top with a final layer of spong and spread with the remaining cream. • Sprinkle with the remaining chocolate. • Place in the refrigerator for 1–2 hours before serving.

Serves: 6–8

Preparation: 30 min.
+ time to make the
sponge + 1–2 hr.
to cool

Cooking: 10 min.

Level of difficulty: 1

- **1 recipe Italian Sponge Cake (see page 961)**
- **1 lb (500 g) very fresh ricotta cheese, drained**
- **$^1/_2$ cup (125 ml) sweet dessert liqueur**
- **$3^1/_2$ oz (100 g) bittersweet (dark) chocolate, grated**
- **1 tsp vanilla extract (essence)**
- **$^3/_4$ cup (150 g) sugar**
- **2 tbsp water**
- **2 tbsp rum**

STRAWBERRY AMARETTO LADYFINGER CAKE

Serves: 6–8

Preparation: 30 min.

Cooking: 50 min.

Level of difficulty: 2

- 7 oz (200 g) ladyfingers
- ¼ cup (60 ml) amaretto (almond liqueur)
- 1 cup (250 g) strawberries, hulled
- 2 large eggs + 1 large egg yolk
- ½ cup (100 g) sugar
- 1 tsp vanilla extract (essence)
- ⅛ tsp salt
- ½ cup (125 ml) milk
- ¼ cup (60 g) cold butter, cut up
- 1 cup (250 ml) whipped cream, to serve
- Halved strawberries, to decorate

Preheat the oven to 350°F (180°C/gas 4.) • Butter and flour an 11 x 7-inch (28 x 18-cm) baking pan. • Arrange half the ladyfingers in the pan. Drizzle with 2 tablespoons of amaretto and top with the strawberries. Cover with the remaining ladyfingers and drizzle with the remaining amaretto. • Beat the eggs and egg yolk, sugar, vanilla, and salt in a large bowl with an electric mixer at medium speed until pale and thick. Add the milk. • Pour over the ladyfingers. Set aside for 5 minutes. • Dot with the butter. • Bake for 35 minutes. • Remove from the oven and cover with aluminum foil. Return to the oven and bake for 15 minutes more, or until lightly browned. • Cool completely in the pan. • Spread with the whipped cream and arrange the strawberries on top.

FROZEN TIRAMISU

Line the base and sides of a loaf pan with waxed paper or aluminum foil. • Beat the egg yolks and sugar with an electric mixer on high speed until pale and creamy. • Beat in the mascarpone. • Beat the egg whites and salt with an electric mixer on high speed until stiff peaks form. • Beat the cream until thickened. • Fold the egg whites and cream into the mascarpone mixture. • Mix the coffee and brandy, if using, in a bowl. • Place a layer of ladyfingers in the loaf pan. Brush with the coffee mixture and cover with a layer of the mascarpone mixture. Repeat this layering process until all the ingredients are in the pan. • Cover the pan with plastic wrap (cling film) and place in the freezer for 4 hours. • To serve, run a long sharp knife down the sides of the pan and turn out onto a serving plate. Let rest for 5 minutes before serving.

Serves: 6–8

Preparation: 30 min.

Cooking: 50 min.

Level of difficulty: 2

- **4 large eggs, separated**
- **$1/3$ cup (75 g) sugar**
- **1 cup (250 g) mascarpone cheese**
- **$1/8$ tsp salt**
- **$1/2$ cup (125 ml) heavy (double) cream**
- **4 oz (125 g) ladyfingers**
- **$1/2$ cup (125 ml) strong black coffee**
- **1 tbsp brandy (optional)**

FROZEN FLORENTINE TRIFLE

Serves: 10–12

Preparation: 45 min.
+ 5 hr. to chill

Level of difficulty: 2

- 1 cup (200 g) sugar
- 1 cup (250 ml) water
- 3 tbsp brandy
- 3 tbsp rum
- 1 recipe Italian Sponge Cake (see page 961), cut into ¼-inch (5-mm) thick slices
- ⅓ cup (50 g) confectioners' (icing) sugar
- ⅓ cup (50 g) almonds, finely ground
- ⅓ cup (50 g) hazelnuts, finely ground
- ¼ cup (50 g) mixed candied fruit, chopped
- 6 oz (180 g) semisweet (dark) chocolate, grated
- 1 quart (1 liter) whipped cream

Mix the sugar and water in a saucepan over medium heat until the sugar has dissolved and it comes to a boil. Boil for 5 minutes. Remove from the heat. Add the brandy and rum and let cool. • Moisten the edges of a domed 2-quart (2-liter) mold with a little syrup and line with half the cake slices. Brush with the syrup. • Gently fold the confectioners' sugar, nuts, candied fruit, and grated chocolate into the cream. Spoon the cream into the mold and top with the cake slices. • Refrigerate for 5 hours. • Dip the mold into cold water. Invert onto a serving plate.

CANDIED FRUIT AND MARSALA SEMIFREDDO

Place the Marsala and candied fruit in a bowl and let soak overnight. • Strain the ricotta through a fine mesh strainer and place in a bowl. • Stir in half the sugar, the egg yolk, and the lemon zest. Stir until smooth and well mixed. • Add the candied fruit along with the soaking liquid and mix well. • Beat the egg white and salt with an electric mixer on high speed until stiff peaks form. • Meanwhile, melt the remaining sugar with the water until caramelized. Beat into the egg whites and continue beating until the mixture is cool. • Beat the cream until thickened and fold it into the ricotta mixture. • Fold in the beaten egg white. • Pour the mixture into an 8-inch (20-cm) ring mold and place in the freezer for at least 4 hours. • Just before serving, dip the mold into boiling water and turn the semifreddo out onto a serving dish. Let stand for 5 minutes before serving.

Serves: 4

Preparation: 45 min.
 + 12 hr. to soak

Level of difficulty: 2

- 2 tbsp Marsala wine
- $1/2$ cup (125 g) mixed candied peel, cut in small cubes
- 1 cup (250 g) fresh ricotta cheese, drained
- 4 tbsp sugar
- 1 large egg, separated
- 1 tsp finely grated lemon zest
- 1 tbsp water
- Pinch of salt
- $1/3$ cup (90 ml) heavy (double) cream

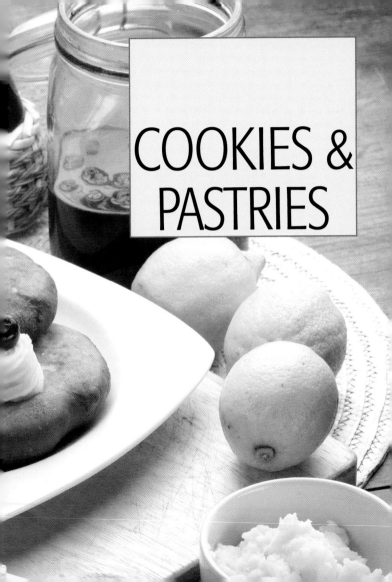

COOKIES &
PASTRIES

MILANESE COOKIES

Preheat the oven to 350°F (180°C/gas 4).
• Butter two cookie sheets. • Place the flour
and sugar in a large bowl and mix well. • Add the
egg yolks, water, lemon zest, and butter and beat
the mixture with a wooden spoon or with an
electric mixer on low speed until smooth and well
mixed. • Roll out the dough on a lightly floured
work surface to ¼-inch (5-mm) thick. • Use
differently shaped cookie cutters to cut out the
cookies. Gather the dough scraps, re-roll, and
continue cutting out cookies until all the dough
is used. • Transfer the cookies to the prepared
cookie sheets, placing them 1 inch (2.5 cm)
apart. • Bake until just golden, about 15 minutes.
• Transfer to racks and let cool completely.

Makes: about 50 cookies

Preparation: 20 min.

Cooking: 15 min.

Level of difficulty: 1

- 1²/₃ cups (250 g) all-purpose (plain) flour
- ²/₃ cup (120 g) sugar
- 3 tbsp butter
- 2 large egg yolks
- 3 tbsp water + extra, as required
- Finely grated zest of 1 lemon

SICILIAN PINE NUT CHEWIES

Plump the raisins in hot water to cover in a small bowl for 10 minutes. • Drain well and pat dry with paper towels. • Mix the flour, baking powder, and salt in a large bowl and make a well in the center. • Mix in the sugar, olive oil, and water to form a smooth dough. • Knead in the raisins and pine nuts. • Shape the dough into a ball, wrap in plastic wrap (cling film), and refrigerate for 30 minutes. • Preheat the oven to 350°F (180°C/gas 4). • Butter two cookie sheets. • Roll out the dough on a lightly floured work surface to ¼-inch (5 mm) thick. • Use a 2-inch (5-cm) cookie cutter to cut out the cookies. Gather the dough scraps, re-roll, and continue cutting out cookies until all the dough is used. • Transfer the cookies to the prepared cookie sheets, placing them 1 inch (2.5 cm) apart. • Bake for about 20 minutes, or until just golden. • Transfer to racks to cool completely.

Makes: about 30 cookies

Preparation: 40 min. + 30 min. to chill

Cooking: 20 min.

Level of difficulty: 1

- ¹/₃ cup (60 g) golden raisins (sultanas)
- 2²/₃ cups (400 g) all-purpose (plain) flour
- 2 tsp baking powder
- ¹/₈ tsp salt
- ¹/₂ cup (100 g) sugar
- ¹/₃ cup (90 ml) extra-virgin olive oil
- ¹/₃ cup (90 ml) water
- ¹/₃ cup (60 g) pine nuts

SIENNESE KISSES

Makes: about 8 kisses

Preparation: 30 min.

Cooking: 25–30 min.

Level of difficulty: 1

- 2 large eggs
  + 2 large egg yolks
- 1 1/3 cups (200 g) confectioners' (icing) sugar
- 1/2 tsp vanilla extract (essence)
- 2/3 cup (100 g) all-purpose (plain) flour
- 1/4 cup (60 g) butter, melted
- 1 tbsp honey
- 2/3 cup (180 ml) ricotta cheese
- 1/2 cup (50 g) diced candied peel
- 2 oz (60 g) dark chocolate, coarsely chopped

Preheat the oven to 350°F (180°C/gas 4). • Butter a baking sheet. • Beat the eggs, 2/3 cup (100 g) of confectioners' sugar, and vanilla in a large bowl until pale and thick. • Add the egg yolks and continue beating until thick. • Beat in the flour, melted butter, and honey. • Roll the dough out to 1/2-inch (1-cm) thick and cut into rounds using a plain cookie cutter or glass. • Place on the baking sheet, spacing well. • Bake until pale golden brown, 25–30 minutes. • Turn out onto racks and let cool completely. • Mix the ricotta, 1/3 cup (50 g) of confectioners' sugar, candied peel, and chocolate in a large bowl. Stick the rounds together in pairs with the ricotta mixture. Dust with the remaining confectioners' sugar.

SWEET TARALLI

Prepare the bread dough and set aside to rise.
• Preheat the oven to 400°F (200°C/gas 6).
• Oil three baking sheets. • When the bread dough is well risen, knead in the eggs, honey, and oil. The dough should be smooth and elastic. • Break off pieces of dough and shape into batons about ½-inch (1-cm) in diameter and 3 inches (8 cm) long. Shape the batons into rings or figure-8s. • Simmer the taralli in gently simmering water for 2–3 minutes. Remove with a slotted spoon and dry on a clean kitchen towel. • Place on the prepared baking sheets and bake until crisp and golden brown, 15–20 minutes. • Let cool on racks.

Makes: about 60 cookies

Preparation: 25 min. + time to prepare the bread dough

Cooking: 30 min.

Level of difficulty: 3

- 1 recipe Bread Dough (see page 952)
- 2 large eggs
- ⅓ cup (90 g) honey
- 2 tbsp extra-virgin olive oil

FILLED COOKIES, MANTUA-STYLE

Makes: about 15 cookies

Preparation: 30 min. + 30 min. to chill
Cooking: 35 min.

Level of difficulty: 2

Pastry
- 1²/₃ cups (250 g) all-purpose (plain) flour
- ¹/₃ cup (50 g) confectioners' (icing) sugar
- 2 large egg yolks
- ¹/₃ cup (90 g) butter

Filling
- ¹/₂ cup (75 g) all-purpose (plain) flour
- 2 tbsp cornstarch (cornflour)
- ²/₃ cup (100 g) confectioners' (icing) sugar
- 1 tbsp butter, melted and cooled slightly
- 2 large eggs, separated
- 1 large egg white, lightly beaten

Pastry: Mix the flour and confectioners' sugar in a large bowl. Make a well in the center and add the egg yolks and butter. Mix to make a smooth dough. Wrap in plastic wrap (cling film) and refrigerate for 30 minutes. • Preheat the oven to 350°F (180°C/gas 4). • Butter a large baking sheet. • Filling: Sift the flour and cornstarch into a medium bowl. Stir in the confectioners' sugar. • Add the butter and egg yolks. • Beat 2 egg whites in a large bowl with an electric mixer at high speed until stiff peaks form. Fold them into the mixture. • Roll the dough out on a lightly floured work surface to J inch (3 mm) thick. Cut into 3-inch (8-cm) rounds. • Brush each one with the remaining egg white. Spoon the filling into the center of each round. Fold in half and seal well. • Transfer to the prepared baking sheet. • Bake for 35 minutes. • Let cool completely. Dust with the confectioners' sugar just before serving.

SPIRALS WITH GOLDEN RAISINS

Preheat the oven to 350°F (180°C/gas 4). • Grease a large baking sheet. • Roll out the pastry on a lightly floured work surface to ¼ inch (5 mm) thick. • Spread with the pastry cream and sprinkle with the golden raisins. • Roll the pastry up into a log then cut into slices ½ inch (1 cm) thick. • Place the spirals on the prepared baking sheet and brush with some of the preserves. • Bake until golden brown, about 15 minutes. • Serve hot.

Serves: 8–10
Preparation: 30 min.
Cooking: 15 min.
Level of difficulty: 1

- 1 lb (500 g) frozen puff pastry, thawed
- ½ cup (125 g) golden raisins (sultanas)
- ½ recipe Vanilla Pastry Cream (see page 962)
- ¼ cup (60 g) apricot preserves (jam), warmed

GENOESE FRITTERS

Serves: 10–12

Preparation: 20 min.
+ 4 hr. to rise

Cooking: 20 min.

Level of difficulty: 2

- 1 oz (30 g) fresh yeast or 2 (¹/₄-oz/ 7-g) packets active dry yeast
- 2 cups (500 ml) warm water
- 3¹/₃ cups (500 g) all-purpose (plain) flour
- 1 cup (250 ml) milk
- Finely grated zest of 1 lemon
- ¹/₄ tsp salt
- 2 large eggs
- ³/₄ cup (150 g) sugar
- ¹/₂ cup (100 g) golden raisins (sultanas)
- 2 cups (500 ml) olive oil, for frying
- 2 tbsp confectioners' (icing) sugar, to dust

Mix the yeast and a little of the water in a cup. • Add enough flour to make a firm dough. • Cover and let rise for 2 hours. • Mix the remaining water, milk, lemon zest, salt, remaining flour, and the risen dough in a large bowl until smooth. Add the eggs and mix well. • Cover and let rise for about 2 hours. Add the sugar and the raisins and mix well. • Heat the oil in a deep fryer or large frying pan until very hot. Fry spoonfuls of the mixture in small batches until golden brown all over, about 5 minutes each batch. • Remove with a slotted spoon and drain on paper towels. • Dust with the confectioners' sugar and serve hot.

TUSCAN FALL TARTS

Serves: 6

Preparation: 30 min.
+ 1 hr. to chill
the pastry

Cooking: 20 min.

Level of difficulty: 2

Pastry
- 1 1/3 cups (200 g) all-purpose (plain) flour
- 1/3 cup (70 g) sugar
- 1/4 tsp salt
- Generous 1/3 cup (100 g) butter
- 2 large egg yolks

Filling
- 1 1/4 cups (400 g) fig preserves
- Fresh figs, cut into segments, to decorate

Pastry: Mix the flour, sugar, and salt in a large bowl. • Rub in the butter with your fingertips. • Add the egg yolks and mix to make a smooth dough. • Wrap in plastic wrap (cling film) and chill for 1 hour. • Preheat the oven to 375°F (190°C/gas 5). • Grease 12 tartlet pans. • Roll out the dough on a lightly floured work surface. Cut out rounds and use them to line the pans. • Fill each one with 2–3 tablespoons of preserves. • Bake for 20 minutes. • Remove from the oven and let cool. Transfer to serving dishes and decorate with the fresh figs.

SWEET RAVIOLI

Place the flour in a medium bowl. Add the eggs, ¼ cup (50 g) of sugar, 1 teaspoon of cinnamon, and ⅓ teaspoon of cloves and mix with a wooden spoon, adding enough water to obtain a fairly firm dough. • Transfer to a lightly floured work surface and knead until smooth and elastic, 10–15 minutes. • Roll out on a lightly floured work surface to about ⅛ inch (3 mm) thick. Use a plain 3-inch (7-cm) cookie cutter or glass to cut out disks of pasty. Re-roll the scraps and keep cutting out disks until all the pasty is used. • Place the ricotta in a medium bowl and stir in the remaining sugar, cinnamon, and cloves. • Place teaspoons of the ricotta mixture at the center of each disk of pastry. Fold the pastry over the top into half-moon shapes, pressing down on the edges with your fingertips to seal well. • Heat the oil in a deep-fryer or small deep frying pan to very hot. • Fry the ravioli in small batches until golden brown all over. Scoop out with a slotted spoon and drain on paper towels. repeat until all the ravioli are cooked.
• Sprinkle with extra sugar and serve hot.

Serves: 8

Preparation: 45 min.

Cooking: 30 min.

Level of difficulty: 2

- 1²/₃ cups (250 g) all-purpose (plain) flour
- 2 large eggs
- ³/₄ cup (150 g) sugar + extra, to sprinkle
- 1¹/₂ tsp ground cinnamon
- ¹/₂ tsp ground cloves
- ¹/₄ cup (60 ml) warm water + more, as required
- 14 oz (400 g) fresh ricotta cheese, drained
- 2 cups (500 ml) oil, for frying

FILLED BARI FRITTERS

P lace the yeast in a small bowl and pour in the water. Mix until dissolved and set aside for 10 minutes. • Place the flour in a large bowl. Pour in the yeast mixture and enough extra warm water to obtain and fairly soft dough. Mix well. • Shape the dough into a ball and place in a clean, lightly oiled bowl. Cover with a kitchen towel and set aside in a warm place to rise for about 1 hour. • Stir in the sugar, butter, eggs, and lemon zest, mixing well. • Lightly flour a clean work surface and place the dough on it. Knead for 2–3 minutes. • Break off pieces of dough about the size of an egg and shape into rings. Place the dough rings on a floured surface and let rise for 1 hour. • Heat the oil in a deep-fryer or deep frying pan to very hot. • Fry the fritters in batches until golden brown all over, 5–7 minutes per batch. Scoop out with a slotted spoon and drain on paper towels. • Fill the rings with vanilla custard and top each one with a cherry. • Serve warm.

Serves: 10–12

Preparation: 45 min. + 2 hr. to rise

Cooking: 30 min.

Level of difficulty: 2

Fritters

- 1 oz (30 g) fresh yeast or 2 (^{1}/4-oz/ 7-g) packages active dry yeast
- ^{1}/2 cup (125 ml) warm water + extra, as required
- 3^2/3 cups (550 g) all-purpose (plain) flour
- ^{3}/4 cup (150 g) sugar
- 5 tbsp butter, melted
- 2 large eggs, lightly beaten
- Finely grated zest of 1 lemon
- 2 cups (500 ml) oil, for frying

To Serve

- 1 recipe Vanilla Pastry Cream (see page 962)
- Canned cherries, drained, to decorate

SICILIAN RICE FRITTERS

Serves: 6–8

Preparation: 20 min.
+ 1 hr. to cool

Cooking: 50 min.

Level of difficulty: 2

- 2 cups (500 ml) water
- 1 1/2 cups (375 ml) milk
- 1/4 tsp salt
- 1 cup (200 g) short-grain rice
- 1/2 cup (50 g) sugar + extra, to sprinkle
- 1/2 cup (75 g) all-purpose (plain) flour
- 3/4 tsp baking powder
- 2 cups (500 ml) oil, for frying

Place the water, milk, and salt in a medium saucepan over high heat and bring to a boil.
• Add the rice, return to a boil, then turn the heat down to low. Simmer until the rice is very tender and the liquid is all absorbed. • Remove from the heat and stir in the sugar, flour, and baking powder. Set aside to cool for 1 hour. • Heat the oil in a deep-fryer or deep frying pan to very hot.
• Fry the fritters in batches until golden brown all over, 5–7 minutes per batch. Scoop out with a slotted spoon and drain on paper towels.
• Sprinkle with extra sugar and serve hot.

SWEET DIAMOND FRITTERS

Combine the water, extra-virgin olive oil, salt, and bay leaf in a medium saucepan. Bring to a boil then remove from the heat. • Add the flour and semolina all at once and beat rapidly with a wooden spoon. • Return the saucepan to the heat and continue to beat rapidly until the batter is smooth and well mixed. • Discard the bay leaf and spread the mixture out ½ inch (1 cm) thick on an oiled work surface. Let cool. • Cut the batter into diamond shapes and fry in batches in the oil until golden brown. Scoop out with a slotted spoon and drain on paper towels. • Dust with the confectioners' sugar and serve hot.

Serves: 8–10

Preparation: 40 min.

Cooking: 30 min.

Level of difficulty: 2

- **3 cups (750 ml) water**
- **3 tbsp extra-virgin olive oil**
- **¹/₃ tsp salt**
- **1 bay leaf**
- **2²/₃ cups (400 g) all-purpose (plain) flour**
- **3 tbsp semolina**
- **2 cups (500 ml) oil, for frying**
- **²/₃ cup (100 g) confectioners' (icing) sugar**

CHOCOLATE WALNUT CUPCAKES

Serves: 12

Preparation: 10 min.

Cooking: 30 min.

Level of difficulty: 1

Preheat the oven to 350°F (180°C/gas 4). • Set out 12 paper cupcake cases. • Melt the chocolate and butter in a double boiler over barely simmering water. • Add the sugar and egg yolks. Beat until smooth and glossy. Remove from the heat and let cool. • Beat the egg whites in a large bowl until stiff. • Fold the egg whites, flour, and baking powder into the chocolate mixture. • Divide the mixture among the cupcake cases. • Top each one with walnuts • Bake until well risen and springy to the touch, 15–20 minutes. • Serve warm.

8 oz (250 g) semisweet (dark) chocolate, broken into pieces

$1/3$ cup (90 g) butter

$1/2$ cup (100 g) sugar

3 large eggs, separated

$1/2$ cup (75 g) all-purpose (plain) flour

$1/2$ tsp baking powder

$1/2$ cup (60 g) walnuts, coarsely chopped

Serves: 10

Preparation: 30 min.
+ 2 hr. to cool

Cooking: 10 min.

Level of difficulty: 2

- ¹/₄ cup (60 g) butter, softened
- ¹/₃ cup (50 g) confectioners' (icing) sugar
- ¹/₃ cup (50 g) heavy (double) cream
- 1 tsp vanilla extract (essence)
- 12 oz (350 g) bittersweet (dark) chocolate, grated
- 3 tbsp unsweetened cocoa powder
- 3 tbsp shredded (dessicated) coconut
- 3 tbsp chopped hazelnuts

CHOCOLATE TRUFFLES

B eat the butter and confectioners' sugar in a medium bowl until pale and creamy. • Bring the cream to a boil. Remove from the heat and add the vanilla. • Pour the boiling cream into the butter mixture. Add the chocolate and stir until smooth and well mixed. • Let cool for at least 2 hours. • Shape into balls the size of small walnuts. • Roll one-third of the truffles in the cocoa, one-third in the coconut, and one-third in the nuts. • Chill in the refrigerator until ready to serve.

MINI RICOTTA CASSATAS

Blanch the almonds in boiling water for 2 minutes. Drain well and dry on a clean cloth. Rub off the inner skins. Chop finely in a food processor. • Combine the sugar and water in a small saucepan and place over medium-low heat until it caramelizes. • Line 8 small round molds with sponge cake and drizzle with the alchermes. • Place the ricotta, almonds, candied fruit, chocolate, caramelized sugar, lemon zest, and cinnamon in a medium bowl and mix well. • Fill the molds with this mixture and cover each one with a layer of sponge cake. • Chill in the refrigerator for 3–4 hours. • Roll the almond paste out thinly. Remove the mini cassatas from their molds and cover each one with a layer of almond pasta.

Serves: 8

Preparation: 30 min.
+ 3–4 hr. to chill

Cooking: 10 min.

Level of difficulty: 2

- 2 cups (200 g) almonds
- 1¹/₄ cups (250 g) superfine (caster) sugar
- ¹/₄ cup (60 ml) water
- 1 recipe Italian Sponge Cake (see page 961), thinly sliced
- ¹/₂ cup (125 ml) alchermes
- 12 oz (350 g) fresh ricotta cheese, drained
- ¹/₄ cup (50 g) candied fruit
- 2 oz (60 g) grated dark chocolate
- Finely grated zest of 1 lemon
- 1 tsp ground cinnamon
- 7 oz (200 g) almond paste

CANNOLI

Cannoli: Mix the flour and cocoa in a medium bowl. • Stir in the sugar, lard, eggs, and Marsala to make a smooth dough. • Roll the dough out on a lightly floured surface to ⅛ inch (3 mm) thick and cut into twelve 4-inch (10-cm) disks.
• Heat the oil in a deep-fryer over medium heat.
• Wrap a pastry disk around each cannoli mold, pressing the overlapping edges together to seal.
• Fry the cannoli, still on the mold, in small batches, for about 5 minutes, or until bubbly and golden brown. • Remove with a slotted spoon and drain on paper towels. Let cool slightly before carefully removing from the mold. • Filling: Beat the ricotta with the sugar and vanilla with a wooden spoon in a large bowl. Add the chocolate and candied fruit. • Just before serving, fill the pastry tubes with the filling and arrange on a serving dish.

Serves: 6

Preparation: 30 min.

Cooking: 15 min.

Level of difficulty: 3

Cannoli
- 1⅓ cups (200 g) all-purpose (plain) flour
- 1 tbsp unsweetened cocoa powder
- 2 tbsp sugar
- Generous 1 tbsp (20 g) lard, softened
- 2 large eggs, lightly beaten
- 2 tbsp dry Marsala wine
- 4 cups (1 liter) oil, for frying

Filling
- 2 cups (500 g) fresh ricotta cheese, drained
- 1½ cups (300 g) sugar
- 1 tsp vanilla extract (essence)
- 4 oz (125 g) semisweet (dark) chocolate, chopped
- 1 cup (200 g) chopped candied pumpkin, or other chopped candied fruit or peel

RUM BABA CAKES

Serves: 6–8

Preparation: 25 min.
 + 30 min. to rise

Cooking: 25 min.

Level of difficulty: 2

- 1 oz (30 g) fresh yeast or 2 (¹/₄-oz/ 7-g) packages active dry yeast
- ¹/₄ cup (60 ml) warm water
- 2 tbsp sugar
- 5 large eggs
- ¹/₂ cup (125 ml) extra-virgin olive oil
- ¹/₄ cup (60 g) butter, melted and cooled
- 2¹/₃ cups (350 g) all-purpose (plain) flour
- ¹/₄ tsp salt

Rum Syrup
- 2 cups (500 ml) water
- 1¹/₂ cups (300 g) sugar
- ¹/₂ cup (125 ml) rum
- 1 lemon, sliced

Butter twelve 2 x 3-inch (4 x 8-cm) baba molds. • Stir together the yeast, water, and 1 teaspoon sugar. Set aside for 10 minutes. • Beat the eggs and remaining sugar in a large bowl with an electric mixer at high speed until pale and thick. • Stir in the oil, butter, and yeast mixture. • Stir in the flour and salt. • Transfer to a lightly floured surface and knead until smooth. • Roll the dough into a fat sausage and cut into twelve equal pieces. Place in the prepared molds. Cover with plastic wrap (cling film) and let rise in a warm place until the dough has risen to just below the top of each mold, about 30 minutes. • Preheat the oven to 350°F (180°C/gas 4). • Bake for about 15 minutes, or until lightly browned. • Rum Syrup: Stir the water and sugar in a saucepan over medium heat until the mixture comes to a boil. Boil for about 10 minutes, or until syrupy and thick. • Stir in the rum and lemon. Let cool. • Cool the babas in the molds for 15 minutes. Soak in the rum syrup.

ALMOND BRITTLE

Cook the sugar and water in a large saucepan over low heat, stirring constantly with a wooden spoon, for about 10 minutes, or until golden brown. • Add the almonds and orange zest. Mix well and simmer for about 10 minutes, or until dark golden brown. Remove from the heat. • Oil a sheet of waxed paper with the sweet almond oil. • Pour the mixture out onto the prepared paper. Spread the brittle out on the paper; it should be about ½ inch (1 cm) thick. Let cool slightly. • While the mixture is still pliable, cut into squares with a sharp knife. Let cool completely.

Serves: 10–12

Preparation: 15 min.

Cooking: 25 min.

Level of difficulty: 2

- **2¹/₂ cups (500 g) sugar**
- **¹/₄ cup (60 ml) water**
- **Generous 3¹/₄ cups (500 g) blanched almonds**
- **Finely grated zest of 1 orange**
- **1 tbsp sweet almond oil**

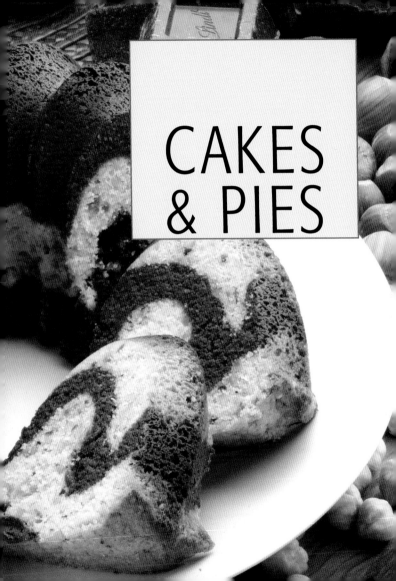

CAKES
& PIES

GRANDMOTHER'S PIE

Preheat the oven to 350°F (180°C/gas 4). • Butter a 10-inch (25-cm) pie pan. • Beat the butter and sugar with an electric mixer on medium speed until pale and creamy. Add the eggs one at a time, beating until just combined after each addition. • With mixer on low, gradually beat in the flour and baking powder. • Divide the dough in half and roll out into two rounds. • Place one in the prepared pie pan and cover with the pastry cream, piling it slightly higher in the center. • Cover with the other pastry round and seal the edges together. • Bake until pale golden brown, about 40 minutes. • Cool the pie in the pan on a wire rack. Sprinkle with the almonds and dust with the confectioners' sugar just before serving.

Serves:	8–10
Preparation:	30 min.
Cooking:	40 min.
Level of difficulty:	2

- $1/2$ cup (125 g) butter
- $3/4$ cup (150 g) sugar
- 2 large eggs
- $1 2/3$ cups (250 g) all-purpose (plain) flour
- 1 tsp baking powder
- $1/4$ tsp salt
- 1 recipe Vanilla Pastry Cream (see page 962)
- 2 tbsp almonds
- Confectioners' (icing) sugar, to dust

PINE NUT CAKE

Serves: 8–10

Preparation: 25 min.

Cooking: 40 min.

Level of difficulty: 1

- 1¹/₃ cups (200 g) all-purpose (plain) flour
- ¹/₂ teaspoon baking powder
- ¹/₈ teaspoon salt
- 2 large egg yolks + 1 large egg
- 1 cup (200 g) sugar
- 1 cup (250 g) butter
- 1 cup (150 g) pine nuts
- ¹/₃ cup (50 g) confectioners' (icing) sugar, to dust

Preheat the oven to 350°F (180°C/gas 4). • Butter a 9-inch (23-cm) springform pan. • Mix the flour, baking powder, and salt in a medium bowl. • Beat the egg yolks, whole egg, and sugar in a large bowl with an electric mixer at high speed until pale and thick. • Melt the butter and set aside to cool a little. • With mixer at low speed, gradually beat in the dry ingredients and half the pine nuts, followed by the butter. • Spoon the batter into the prepared pan. Sprinkle the remaining pine nuts over the top. • Bake for about 40 minutes, or until a toothpick inserted into the center comes out clean. • Cool in the pan for 10 minutes. Loosen and remove the pan sides and cool completely on a rack. • Dust with the confectioners' sugar just before serving.

LOMBARDY POLENTA CAKE

Preheat the oven to 400°F (200°C/gas 6).
• Butter a 9-inch (23-cm) round cake pan.
Sprinkle with a little extra polenta. • Bring a
medium saucepan of water to a boil and add the
almonds. Drain immediately and dry on a kitchen
towel. Remove the inner peels. • Chop finely in a
food processor. • Place the almonds, polenta, and
sugar in a large bowl and mix well. • Melt the
butter and pour into the bowl. Mix to obtain a thick,
crumbly batter. • Place the batter in the prepared
pan, spreading it in an even layer. • Bake until
golden brown, about 40 minutes. • Let cool in the
pan for 10 minutes. Turn out onto a rack and let
cool completely.

Serves: 6–8

Preparation: 30 min.

Cooking: 40 min.

Level of difficulty: 1

- **12 oz (300 g) almonds**
- **2 cups (300 g) polenta (finely ground yellow cornmeal)**
- **1 1/2 cups (300 g) sugar**
- **1 1/4 cups (300 g) butter**

POLENTA AND LEMON CAKE

Preheat the oven to 350°F (180°C/gas 4).
• Butter and flour a 9 x 3-inch (23 x 8-cm) fluted tube pan pan. • Melt the butter over very low heat and set aside to cool. • Beat the butter and sugar with an electric mixer on medium speed until pale and creamy. • Add the eggs and yolks one at a time, beating until just combined after each addition. • Stir in the lemon liqueur, almonds, polenta, flour, lemon zest, baking powder, and vanilla. • Spoon the batter into the prepared pan.
• Bake until risen and golden brown, 35–40 minutes. • Dust with confectioners' sugar just before serving.

Serves: 8–10

Preparation: 20 min.

Cooking: 35–40 min.

Level of difficulty: 1

- 1 cup (250 g) butter
- 2 1/2 cups (375 g) confectioners' (icing) sugar
- 3 large eggs + 6 large egg yolks
- 2 tbsp Limoncello (sweet lemon liqueur)
- 1 cup (150 g) finely ground almonds
- 1 3/4 cups (270 g) polenta (yellow cornmeal)
- 1 cup (150 g) all-purpose (plain) flour
- Finely grated zest of 1 lemon
- 1 teaspoon baking powder
- 1/2 teaspoon vanilla extract (essence)
- Confectioners' (icing) sugar, to dust

Serves: 8–10	
Preparation: 20 min.	
+ 3 hr. to rise	
Cooking: 30 min.	
Level of difficulty: 2	

- 1 oz (30 g) fresh yeast or 2 (^{1}/4-oz/ 7-g) packages active dry yeast
- 1 cup (250 ml) lukewarm water
- 4 cups (600 g) all-purpose (plain) flour
- 4 large eggs
- ^{3}/4 cup (150 g) sugar
- ^{1}/2 cup (125 g) butter, melted
- Finely grated zest of 1 orange
- Pinch of salt
- ^{1}/3 cup (50 g) confectioners' (icing) sugar, to dust

FLORENTINE CARNIVAL CAKE

Dissolve the yeast in a little of the warm water.
• Place the flour in a large bowl and pour in the yeast mixture. Mix until the flour has all been absorbed, adding enough of the remaining water to obtain a smooth dough. Transfer to a lightly floured work surface and knead for 5 minutes. Wrap in a clean cloth and leave in a warm place to rise for 1 hour. • Knead the dough again, adding the eggs, sugar, butter, orange zest, and salt. • Butter and flour a jelly-roll pan. Spread the dough out in the pan. Leave to rise for another 2 hours. • Preheat the oven to 350°F (180°C/gas 4). • Bake until risen and golden brown, about 30 minutes.
• Cool in the pan on a wire rack. Sprinkle with confectioners' sugar and serve.

CHOCOLATE HAZELNUT MARBLE CAKE

Preheat the oven to 325°F (170°C/gas 3).
• Butter a 9½-inch (23-cm) kugelhopf cake mold. • Place the flour, baking powder, and salt in a large bowl and mix well. • Melt the chocolate in a double boiler over barely simmering water. Set aside to cool. • Beat the butter and sugar in a large bowl with an electric mixer at high speed until pale and creamy. • Add the eggs one at a time, beating until just combined after each addition. • With mixer at low speed, gradually beat in the mixed dry ingredients. • Place half the batter in another bowl. Add the chocolate and stir until smooth and well mixed. • Stir the hazelnuts into the remaining plain batter. • Place alternate spoonfuls of the batter into the prepared pan.
• Bake until springy to the touch and a toothpick inserted in the center comes out clean, about 50 minutes. • Cool in the pan for 10 minutes then turn out onto a wire rack to cool completely.

Serves: 10–12

Preparation: 25 min.

Cooking 50 min.

Level of difficulty: 1

- 2 cups (300 g) all-purpose (plain) flour
- 2 tsp baking powder
- $^1/_4$ tsp salt
- 5 oz (150 g) bittersweet (dark) chocolate, chopped
- $1^1/_4$ cups (300 g) butter, softened
- $1^1/_2$ cups (300 g) sugar
- 5 large eggs
- 5 oz (150 g) coarsely chopped hazelnuts

ZABAGLIONE SPONGE CAKE WITH ORANGE

Serves: 8–10

Preparation: 10 min.

Cooking: 25 min.

Level of difficulty: 2

- $^1/_4$ cup (60 ml) orange liqueur
- 1 Italian Sponge Cake, 10 inches (25 cm) in diameter (see page 961)
- Freshly squeezed juice of 3 oranges, filtered
- 4 large egg yolks
- $^1/_2$ cup (100 g) sugar
- $^1/_4$ cup (30 g) confectioners' (icing) sugar
- $^1/_4$ cup (25 g) flaked almonds
- 1 orange, thinly sliced, to decorate
- Sprig of mint, to decorate

Preheat the oven to 425°F (220°C/gas 7). • Brush a 10-inch (25-cm) round ovenproof dish with a tablespoon of the liqueur. • Cut the sponge cake to the same size as the dish and then fit it to the dish. • Mix the orange juice and remaining liqueur in a small bowl. • Drizzle one-third of this mixture over the sponge cake. • Beat the egg yolks and sugar in a large bowl until pale and creamy. • Transfer to a double boiler over barely simmering water. Gradually add the liqueur mixture, beating constantly, until well thickened, about 10–15 minutes. • Pour the zabaglione over the sponge cake. Dust with the confectioners' sugar and sprinkle with almonds. • Bake until the top is golden brown, 5–10 minutes. • Remove from the oven. Decorate with orange zest and mint. • Serve hot.

ITALIAN PLUM CAKE

Plump the raisins in the rum in a small bowl for at least 30 minutes. Drain well and pat dry with paper towels. Sprinkle with the 2 tablespoons flour. • Preheat the oven to 350°F (180°C/gas 4). • Butter an 8½ x 4½-inch (21 x 9-cm) loaf pan. Line with aluminum foil, letting the edges overhang. Butter the foil. • Beat the eggs and sugar in a large bowl with an electric mixer at high speed until pale and thick. • With mixer at low speed, gradually beat in the remaining flour, baking powder, salt, candied fruit, butter, Marsala, raisins and lemon zest. • Spoon the batter into the prepared pan. • Bake for 45–55 minutes, or until a toothpick inserted into the center comes out clean. • Cool the loaf completely in the pan. Turn out onto a rack. Carefully remove the foil before serving.

Serves: 6–8

Preparation: 20 min. + 30 min. to soak

Cooking: 45–55 min.

Level of difficulty: 1

- ³/₄ cup (100 g) raisins
- 3 tbsp rum
- 1 cup (150 g) all-purpose (plain) flour
- 3 large eggs
- ¹/₂ cup (100 g) sugar
- 1 tsp baking powder
- ¹/₄ tsp salt
- ²/₃ cup (100 g) mixed candied fruit, chopped
- ¹/₃ cup (90 g) butter, melted
- 3 tbsp dry Marsala wine
- 2 tbsp finely grated lemon zest

PUGLIA-STYLE POTATO CAKE

Place the mashed potatoes in a large bowl and add ⅔ cup (120 g) of the sugar, the bread dough, eggs, butter, and as much as the flour as required to obtain a soft dough. • Shape the dough into a ball and sprinkle generously with flour. Wrap in a clean kitchen towel and set aside in a warm (not hot) place for 24 hours. • Unwrap the dough and knead briefly on a floured work surface.
• Shape the dough into a ring and place in an oiled 10-inch (25-cm) ring mold. • Set aside on a warm place for 1 hour. • Preheat the oven to 350°F (180°/gas 4). • Bake until golden brown and a toothpick inserted into the center comes out clean, 35–45 minutes. • Cool in the pan on a rack for 10 minutes. Turn out onto the rack and let cool completely. • Dust with confectioners' sugar just before serving.

Serves: 8–10

Preparation: 30 min.
+ time to make the
bread dough + 25
hr. to rest

Cooking: 35–45 min.

Level of difficulty: 3

- **4 oz (125 g)
  mashed potatoes**
- **¾ cup (150 g)
  sugar**
- **½ recipe
  Bread Dough
  (see page 952)**
- **5 large eggs**
- **¼ cup (60 g)
  butter, softened**
- **½ cup (75 g) all-
  purpose (plain)
  flour, as required**
- **4 tbsp
  confectioners'
  (icing) sugar,
  to dust**

TUSCAN HARVEST GRAPE BREAD

Serves: 10–12

Preparation: 15 min.
+ 3 hr. to rise

Cooking: 40–50 min.

Level of difficulty: 2

- 1 oz (25 g) fresh yeast or 2 ($^1/_4$-oz/ 7-g) packages active dry yeast
- $^2/_3$ cup (150 ml) lukewarm water
- 3 cups (450 g) all-purpose flour
- $^1/_2$ tsp salt
- $^1/_4$ cup (50 g) sugar
- 1 lb (500 g) black grapes
- $^3/_4$ cup (150 g) sugar

Butter a large baking sheet. Line with waxed paper. • Stir together the yeast and $^1/_3$ cup (90 ml) of water. Set aside for 10 minutes. • Stir together the flour, sugar, and salt in a large bowl and make a well in the center. Stir in the yeast mixture until the flour has all been absorbed, adding enough water to obtain a smooth dough. • Transfer to a lightly floured surface and knead until smooth. Shape into a ball. Cover with a clean tea towel and set aside to rise in a warm place for about 1 hour, or until doubled in bulk. • Divide the dough in two. Roll out the dough into two sheets about 1-inch (2.5-cm) thick. Place one sheet of dough in the prepared pan. Cover with half the grapes and half the sugar. Top with the remaining dough and seal the edges. • Spread the remaining grapes over the top, pressing them down into the dough. Sprinkle with the sugar and set aside to rise for 1 hour. • Preheat the oven to 350°F (180°C/ gas 4). • Bake until lightly browned, 40–50 minutes.

RICE CAKE

Prepare the pastry. • Put the milk and salt in a heavy-bottomed saucepan and bring to a boil. • Add the rice and simmer over low heat, stirring frequently, until very tender, about 30 minutes. Remove from the heat. • Stir in the sugar and lemon zest. Let cool. • Stir in the almonds, almond extract, and egg yolks. • Beat the egg whites and a pinch of salt until stiff, then fold them into the rice mixture. • Preheat the oven to 350°F (180°C/gas 4). • Butter a 10-inch (25-cm) springform pan. Roll out the pastry and use it to line the pan. Spoon in the rice mixture. • Bake until the pastry is cooked and the center is firm, 40–50 minutes. • Serve warm or at room temperature.

Serves: 6–8

Preparation: 45 min. + time to make the pastry

Cooking: 75 min.

Level of difficulty: 2

- **1 recipe Sweet Shortcrust Pastry (see page 959)**
- **4 cups (1 liter) milk**
- **$1/4$ tsp salt**
- **$1^1/4$ cups (250 g) short-grain rice**
- **$1/3$ cup (75 g) sugar**
- **Finely grated zest of 1 lemon (yellow part only)**
- **$3/4$ cup (120 g) finely chopped toasted almonds**
- **$1/8$ tsp almond extract (essence)**
- **4 large eggs, separated**

RICE CAKE WITH PEARS

Serves: 6–8

Preparation: 30 min.

Cooking: 75 min.

Level of difficulty: 2

- **4 cups (1 liter) milk**
- **1 cup (200 g) firmly packed brown sugar**
- **$^1/_4$ tsp salt**
- **1 cup (200 g) short-grain white rice**
- **3 tbsp butter**
- **4 large pears**
- **Freshly squeezed juice of $^1/_2$ lemon**
- **2 large eggs + 2 large egg yolks**
- **$^1/_2$ cup (75 g) fine dry bread crumbs**

Preheat the oven to 350°F (180°C/gas 4). • Bring the milk to a boil. Dissolve half the sugar and salt in the milk. Pour in the rice and simmer until the milk has been absorbed. • Remove from heat, stir in the butter and let cool. • Peel 3 of the pears, dice them, and cook with the lemon juice and all but 1 tablespoon of the remaining brown sugar until soft. • Add the whole eggs and yolks to the rice one at a time. • Pour half this mixture into the pan and sprinkle with bread crumbs. • Cover with two-thirds of the pear mixture, then add another layer of rice followed by the rest of the pear. • Peel the remaining pear, slice it thinly and arrange on top. • Sprinkle with the remaining brown sugar and bake until golden brown, 45 minutes. Serve warm.

SUMMER TART

Serves: 10–12

Preparation: 30 min.
+ 90 min. to chill

Cooking: 40 min.

Level of difficulty: 2

Pastry: Mix the flour and salt in a large bowl. Add the sugar and lemon zest. • Rub in the butter using your fingertips until the mixture resembles bread crumbs. • Add the egg and port and mix to make a smooth dough. • Wrap in plastic wrap (cling film) and refrigerate for 30 minutes.
• Preheat the oven to 400°F (200°C/gas 6).
• Butter a 10-inch (25-cm) pie plate. • Roll out the pastry on a floured work surface and use it to line the prepared pan. Cover with waxed paper and fill with dried beans. • Bake blind for 30 minutes.
• Let cool. Discard the beans and waxed paper. Transfer to a serving dish. • Filling: Bring the milk to a boil in a large saucepan. • Beat the egg yolks, flour, and sugar in a large bowl until pale and creamy. • Add the hot milk and beat well. Return the mixture to the saucepan and cook over low heat for 5–8 minutes, stirring constantly, until thickened. • Add the vanilla.Remove from the heat and let cool slightly. • Pour into the pastry case and refrigerate for 1 hour. • Arrange the strawberries on the top of the tart and brush with the apricot preserves.

Pastry
• 1¹⁄₃ cups (200 g) all-purpose (plain) flour
• ¹⁄₈ tsp salt
• ¹⁄₂ cup (100 g) sugar
• Finely grated zest of 1 lemon
• ¹⁄₃ cup (90 g) cold butter, cut into pieces
• 1 large egg, lightly beaten
• 2 tbsp port

Filling
• 1¹⁄₄ cups (310 ml) milk
• 2 large egg yolks
• 1 tbsp all-purpose (plain) flour
• ¹⁄₂ cup (100 g) sugar
• 1 tsp vanilla extract (essence)
• 10 oz (300 g) strawberries, hulled and sliced
• ¹⁄₂ cup (125 g) apricot preserves (jam), melted

FRESH FRUIT CROSTATA

Mix the flour, sugar, and salt in a large bowl. Cut in the butter with your fingertips until the mixture resembles coarse crumbs. • Add the egg yolk and water and mix to form a smooth dough. Shape into a ball, wrap in plastic wrap (cling film), and refrigerate for 30 minutes. • Roll the dough out on a lightly floured surface into a 12-inch (30-cm) round. Fit into a 9-inch (23-cm) tart pan, trimming the edges if needed. • Preheat the oven to 375°F (190°C/gas 5). • Line the pastry shell with a sheet of waxed paper and fill with dried beans or pie weights. • Bake for 15 minutes. Discard the paper and beans or pie weights. • Bake for about 15 minutes more, or until crisp. • Let cool completely. • Topping: Spoon the pastry cream into the pastry case. Arrange the fruit on top and brush with the preserves.

Serves: 6–8

Preparation: 40 min. + 30 min. to chill

Cooking: 30 min.

Level of difficulty: 2

Pastry
- 1 cup (150 g) all-purpose (plain) flour
- 2 tbsp sugar
- $1/4$ tsp salt
- $1/3$ cup (90 g) cold butter, cut up
- 1 large egg yolk
- 1 tbsp ice water

Topping
- 1 recipe Vanilla Pastry Cream (see page 962)
- 2 cups (500 g) sliced fresh fruit or whole berries
- $1/3$ cup (90 g) apricot preserves (jam), warmed

CHERRY PIE

Serves: 6–8

*Preparation: 20 min.
+ 2 hr. to soak*

Cooking: 40 min.

Level of difficulty: 2

- 1¹/₂ lb (750 g) ripe cherries, pitted
- Freshly squeezed juice of 2 lemons
- ³/₄ cup (150 g) sugar
- 4 cloves
- 1 cinnamon stick
- 1 recipe Sweet Shortcrust Pastry (see page 959)
- 1 cup (250 g) cherry jam
- 2 tbsp Kirsch (cherry liqueur)
- ²/₃ cup (150 g) butter

Place the cherries in a bowl with the lemon juice, sugar, cloves, and cinnamon. Stir gently and let stand for 2 hours. • Prepare the pastry. • Preheat the oven to 375°F (190°C/gas 5). • Put the cherry jam in a small heavy-bottomed saucepan with the liqueur and butter. Simmer for 5 minutes, then set aside to cool. • Break off two-thirds of the pastry dough and roll it out so that it is large enough to line an oiled 10-inch (25-cm) pie pan. Leave a narrow border of the pastry hanging over the sides. • Spread the cherry jam mixture over the bottom of the pastry and cover with the well-drained cherries. • Roll out the remaining pastry into a square sheet. Use a fluted pastry wheel to cut it into ¹/₂-inch (1-cm) wide strips. Place these over the cherries in a lattice pattern. Fold the overhanging pastry border over the ends of the lattice to form a rolled edge. • Bake until the pastry is golden brown, about 40 minutes. • Serve warm.

VANILLA CREAM PIE

Prepare the pastry. • Prepare the sponge cake. When cold, cut in half horizontally. • Prepare the pastry cream. • Preheat the oven to 375°F (190°C/gas 5). • Butter a 10-inch (25-cm) pie pan. • Roll out two-thirds of the dough on a lightly floured work surface. Line the pie pan with the pastry. • Place one layer of sponge cake in the bottom of the pan. Cover with half the pastry cream. Cover with the other layer of sponge cake and top with the remaining pastry cream. • Roll out the remaining pastry into a square sheet. Use a fluted pastry wheel to cut it into ½-inch (1-cm) wide strips. Place these over the pie in a lattice pattern. Fold the overhanging pastry border over the ends of the lattice to form a rolled edge. • Bake until the pastry is golden brown, about 40 minutes. • Decorate with the cherries and serve warm.

Serves: 6–8

Preparation: 1 hr.

Cooking: 30–40 min.

Level of difficulty: 2

- 1 recipe Sweet Shortcrust Pastry (see page 959)
- 1 Italian Sponge Cake, 10 inches (25 cm) in diameter (see page 961)
- 1 recipe Vanilla Pastry Cream (see page 962)
- 12–16 amarene cherries, to decorate

LEMON PIE

Prepare the pastry. • Preheat the oven to 350°F (180°C/gas 4). • Roll the pastry out so that it is large enough to line a 10-inch (25-cm) pie pan. Butter and flour the pan and line it with the pastry. Prick well with a fork. • Whisk the egg whites with the salt until stiff. • Beat the whole eggs with the sugar in a bowl, and add the almonds, egg whites, butter, and the lemon zest and juice. • Spread this mixture evenly over the dough. Bake until the pastry is golden brown, about 40 minutes.
• Decorate with the candied peel.

Serves: 6

Preparation: 15 min.
+ time to make
the pastry

Cooking: 40 min.

Level of difficulty: 2

- **1 recipe Sweet Shortcrust Pastry (see page 959)**
- **2 large eggs + 2 large egg whites**
- **$^1/_4$ tsp salt**
- **1 cup (200 g) sugar**
- **1$^1/_2$ cups (225 g) ground almonds**
- **$^1/_3$ cup (90 g) butter, melted**
- **Finely ground zest and juice of 2 lemons**
- **10 pieces candied lemon peel**

Serves: 4

Preparation: 15 min.

Cooking: 1 hr.

Level of difficulty: 1

- $^1/_4$ cup (60 g) butter
- $^1/_2$ cup (100 g) sugar
- $^1/_4$ tsp salt
- 2 large eggs, separated
- 8 oz (250 g) fresh ricotta cheese, drained
- $^1/_3$ cup (50 g) cornstarch (cornflour)
- Zest and juice of 1 lemon
- 2 tbsp toasted ground almonds
- 3 large peaches, pitted and sliced
- $^1/_4$ cup (30 g) bread crumbs

PEACH PIE

Preheat the oven to 350°F (180°C/gas 4).
• Beat the butter, sugar, and salt together until creamy. • Add the egg yolks one by one, followed by the ricotta. Mix in the cornstarch, lemon juice and zest, and almonds. • Beat the egg whites until stiff, and fold gently into the mixture. Stir in the peaches and pour the mixture into a greased 8-inch (20-cm) pie pan coated with the bread crumbs. • Bake until golden brown, about 45 minutes. • Serve warm.

CREAMY CHOCOLATE CROSTATA

Serves: 6–8

*Preparation: 30 min.
+ 30 min. to chill*

Cooking: 50 min.

Level of difficulty: 2

- 1 recipe Sweet
  Shortcrust Pastry
  (see page 959)
- 2–3 tbsp vanilla
  wafer crumbs

Chocolate Filling
- $^1/_2$ cup (125 g)
  butter
- 1 cup (200 g) sugar
- 6 oz (180 g)
  bittersweet (dark)
  chocolate,
  coarsely chopped
- 2 tbsp cornstarch
  (cornflour)
- 1 tsp vanilla extract
  (essence)
- $^1/_4$ cup (60 ml)
  milk
- 4 large eggs,
  separated
- 1 cup (250 ml)
  heavy (double)
  cream
- 2 tbsp unsweetened
  cocoa powder, to
  dust

P reheat the oven to 375°F (190°C/gas 5).
• Butter a 9-inch (23-cm) springform pan.
Sprinkle with the crumbs. • Roll the dough out on
a lightly floured work surface to line the base and
sides of the pan. Fit into the prepared pan.
Refrigerate for 30 minutes. • Chocolate Filling:
Melt the butter in a saucepan over low heat. Stir in
the sugar, chocolate, cornstarch, and vanilla. Add
the milk and egg yolks and simmer, stirring
constantly, for about 10 minutes, or until the filling
thickens. Remove from the heat and set aside to
cool. • Beat the egg whites in a large bowl with an
electric mixer at medium speed until stiff peaks
form. • Use a large rubber spatula to fold the
beaten whites and cream into the chocolate filling.
• Spoon into the pastry shell. • Bake for about 50
minutes, or until set. • Cool completely in the pan
on a rack. • Loosen and remove the pan sides.
Transfer to a serving plate. Dust with the cocoa.

ITALIAN CHOCOLATE GÂTEAU

Serves: 10–12

Preparation: 50 min.

Cooking: 20 min.

Level of difficulty: 2

Preheat the oven to 375°F (190°C/gas 5.)
• Butter two 9-inch (23-cm) round cake pans.
• Stir the almonds, flour, cocoa, baking powder, and salt in a large bowl. • Beat the egg yolks, 1 cup (200 g) sugar, and vanilla extract in a large bowl until pale and thick. • Gradually beat in the dry ingredients, alternating with the milk. • Beat the egg whites and remaining sugar in a large bowl until stiff, glossy peaks form. • Fold them into the batter. • Spoon half the batter into each of the prepared pans. • Bake for about 20 minutes, or until a toothpick inserted into the center comes out clean. • Cool in the pans for 10 minutes. Turn out onto racks and let cool completely. • Ricotta Filling: Beat the cream in a medium bowl until stiff. • Process the ricotta, confectioners' sugar, and candied peel in a food processor until smooth. Transfer to a large bowl. • Fold the cream into the ricotta mixture. • Split the cakes horizontally. Place one layer on a serving plate. Spread with one-third of the filling. Repeat with two more layers. Place the remaining layer on top. • Chocolate Frosting: Place the confectioners' sugar, cocoa, and butter in a bowl. Add enough boiling water to obtain a smooth frosting. Spread over the cake. • Decorate with the chocolate shavings.

- 1 1/2 cups (225 g) almonds, ground
- 2/3 cup (100 g) cake flour
- 2/3 cup (100 g) unsweetened cocoa powder
- 1 1/2 tsp baking powder
- 1/4 tsp salt
- 8 large eggs, separated
- 1 1/2 cups (300 g) sugar
- 2 tsp vanilla extract
- 1/2 cup (125 ml) milk

Ricotta Filling

- 1 cup (250 ml) heavy (double) cream
- 2 cups (500 g) ricotta cheese, drained
- 1/2 cup (75 g) confectioners' (icing) sugar
- 1/2 cup (50 g) chopped peel

Chocolate Frosting

- 2 cups (300 g) confectioners' (icing) sugar
- 1/2 cup (75 g) unsweetened cocoa
- 2 tbsp butter
- 2 tbsp boiling water
- Dark chocolate savings, to decorate

MOCHA CREAM CAKE

Serves: 6–8

Preparation: 30 min.

Cooking: 35 min.

Level of difficulty: 2

Preheat the oven to 350°F (180°C/gas 4).
• Beat the egg yolks and sugar until pale and creamy. • Stir in the milk, butter, cocoa powder, coffee, flour, and baking powder. Beat until smooth. • Whip the egg whites and salt until stiff and fold them into the mixture. • Butter and flour a 10-inch springform pan and pour in the mixture. Bake until a toothpick inserted into the center comes out clean, about 30 minutes. Place on a cake rack to cool. • Prepare the vanilla cream.
• Soften the gelatin in the cold water. Stir into the hot coffee until it dissolves. Combine the coffee mixture with the vanilla cream. • Cut the cake in half and fill with the vanilla cream. • Whip the heavy cream with the confectioners' sugar until stiff. Cover the cake with cream and coffee beans.

- **4 large eggs, separated**
- **1 cup (200 g) sugar**
- **¹/₃ cup milk**
- **1 cup (250 g) butter, melted and cooled**
- **¹/₄ cup (30 g) unsweetened cocoa powder**
- **2 tbsp instant coffee powder**
- **2 cups (300 g) all-purpose (plain) flour**
- **2 tsp baking powder**
- **Pinch of salt**
- **1 recipe Vanilla Pastry Cream (see page 962)**
- **2 tbsp unflavored gelatin**
- **2 tbsp cold water**
- **¹/₃ cup (90 ml) strong black coffee, boiling**
- **¹/₂ cup (125 ml) heavy (double) cream**
- **2 tbsp confectioners' (icing) sugar**
- **Coffee beans to garnish (optional)**

PANFORTE

Preheat the oven to 400°F (200°C/gas 6).
• Spread the almonds and walnuts out on baking sheets and bake 3–4 minutes. Allow to cool slightly and then chop finely. • Mix the nuts in a large bowl with the figs, candied peel, spices, and cocoa powder. • Dissolve the sugar in the honey and water in a double boiler. After about 8 minutes, test to see if it forms a thread when you lift a spoonful above the pan. If not, cook for a few minutes more. • Remove from heat and stir in the nut mixture. Line a a 9-inch (23-cm) pie plate with rice paper and place the mixture in it. • Bake until golden brown, about 40 minutes. • Place on a cake rack to cool. Dust with confectioners' sugar and serve.

934

- 2 cups (200 g) peeled whole almonds
- 1 cup (100 g) shelled walnuts
- 1/2 cup (60 g) dried figs, finely chopped
- 1 1/4 cups (120 g) candied peel (orange, citron, and melon), finely chopped
- 1 tbsp ground spice mixture (cinnamon, cloves, coriander seeds, white peppercorns, and nutmeg)
- 2/3 cup (100 g) unsweetened cocoa powder
- 1 1/4 cups (180 g) confectioners' (icing) sugar + extra to dust
- 1/2 cup (125 g) honey
- 1/2 cup (125 ml) water

CASTAGNACCIO

Serves: 8

Preparation: 15 min.

Cooking: 50 min.

Level of difficulty: 2

- 2²/₃ cups (400 g) chestnut flour
- 1¹/₂ cups (375 ml) water
- ²/₃ cup (150 ml) extra-virgin olive oil
- Pinch of salt
- ¹/₂ cup (60 g) small seedless white raisins, soaked in warm water for 15 minutes, drained and squeezed
- ¹/₃ cup (60 g) pine nuts
- Few young, tender rosemary leaves

Preheat the oven to 400°F (200°C/gas 6).
• Place the flour in a medium bowl, make a well in the center and pour in the water, 1 tablespoon of the oil, and the salt. Stir well to obtain a thick, lump-free, pouring batter. • Stir in the drained raisins and the nuts and then pour into a 9 x 13 inch baking pan greased with 2 tablespoons of the oil. • Sprinkle with the rosemary leaves and drizzle with the remaining oil. • Bake about 30 minutes, or until a thin crust has formed. • Serve hot or warm.

VERONA NOODLE CAKE

Preheat the oven to 400°F (200°C/gas 6).
• Place the flour into a large mixing bowl. Add the eggs, salt, and ¼ cup (60 g) of softened butter. Mix rapidly to form a smooth, elastic dough.
• Transfer to a floured work surface and roll out very thinly. • Grind the almonds in a food processor. Place in a bowl with the sugar and lemon zest and mix well. • Roll the sheet of dough up very loosely and cut it into thin strips or noodles. Lay them out on a clean cloth for 10 minutes. • Butter and flour a 10-inch springform pan. Cover the bottom with a layer of strips of dough. They should be scattered over the bottom, not carefully arranged. Sprinkle with part of the almond mixture. Repeat this process until all the dough and almond mixture are in the pan, finishing with a layer of noodles. • Melt the remaining butter. Pour the butter and liqueur over the noodles. Cover the cake with aluminum foil and bake for 1 hour.
• Remove the cake from the pan, drizzle with the lemon juice, and serve.

Serves: 6–8

Preparation: 20 min.

Cooking: 1 hr.

Level of difficulty: 2

- 2 cups (300 g) all-purpose (plain) flour
- 3 large eggs
- Pinch of salt
- 1 cup (250 g) butter, softened
- 1 cup (120 g) shelled almonds
- 1 cup (200 g) sugar
- Finely grated zest and the juice of 1 lemon
- 1 cup (250 ml) orange liqueur (Cointreau)

FILLED ITALIAN CHRISTMAS CAKE

Serves: 10–12

Preparation: 25 min.
+ 12 hr. to chill

Cooking: 5 min.

Level of difficulty: 1

- 1 panettone, weighing about 2 lb (1 kg)
- 2 tbsp butter, melted
- 2 tbsp slivered almonds
- 2 tbsp confectioners' (icing) sugar
- 1 cup (250 ml) heavy (double) cream
- $^1/_4$ cup (60 ml) rum
- 1 cup (250 g) sliced strawberries
- 6 slices pineapple, chopped

Preheat the oven to 400°F (200°C/gas 6). • Butter a baking sheet. • Use a knife to slice off the top third of the panettone horizontally. Use the knife to hollow out the base of the panettone, leaving a shell about H-inch (1-cm) thick. • Brush the top third of the panettone with the butter and place on the baking sheet. Sprinkle with the almonds and dust with 2 tablespoons of confectioners' sugar. • Bake for about 5 minutes, or until crisp and golden brown. • Beat the cream and remaining confectioners' sugar in a medium bowl with an electric mixer at high speed until stiff. • Brush the bottom and sides of the hollowed-out panettone with the rum. • Spread one-third of the cream inside the panettone. Cover with half the strawberries and pineapple. Repeat, then finish with cream. • Refrigerate for 12 hours. • Place the toasted lid on top just before serving.

NEAPOLITAN RICOTTA CHEESE CAKE

Stir the sugar and water in a saucepan over low heat until the mixture begins to boil. Continue cooking, without stirring, until the syrup is pale gold. Remove from the heat. • Place the ricotta in a large bowl and add the syrup, liqueur, and vanilla. • Split the cake horizontally. Place one layer on a serving plate. Drizzle with 2 tablespoons of rum. Spread with half the ricotta cream and sprinkle with half the chocolate. Top with the remaining layer. Drizzle with the remaining rum. Spread with the ricotta cream and sprinkle with the remaining chocolate. • Refrigerate for 2 hours.

Serves: 8–10

Preparation: 20 min.
  + time to make the sponge cake
  + 2 hr. to chill

Level of difficulty: 1

- $^3/_4$ cup (150 g) sugar
- $1^1/_2$ tbsp cold water
- 1 lb (500 g) ricotta cheese, pressed through a sieve
- 3 tbsp Galliano liqueur or brandy
- 1 tsp vanilla extract (essence)
- 1 Italian Sponge Cake (see page 961), baked in 9-inch (23-cm) square pan
- $^1/_4$ cup (60 ml) rum
- 5 oz (150 g) bittersweet (dark) chocolate, grated

BASIC
RECIPES

BLACK OLIVE SAUCE

Place the olives, parsley, capers, and garlic in a food processor and chop until smooth.
• By hand, stir in the egg yolk, vinegar, and pepper.
• Serve with this tasty sauce with poached fish, boiled meats, boiled or baked potatoes, or spread on slices of lightly toasted bread as a starter or snack.

Serves: 4

Preparation: 10 min.

Level of difficulty: 1

• **20 large black olives, pitted and chopped**
• **1/4 cup finely chopped fresh parsley**
• **1 tsp salt-cured capers, chopped**
• **1 clove garlic, finely chopped**
• **1 hard-boiled egg yolk**
• **1 tsp white vinegar**
• **Freshly ground black pepper**

PESTO

Serves: 4

Preparation: 10 min.

Level of difficulty: 1

- 2 oz (60 g) fresh basil leaves
- 2 tbsp pine nuts
- 2 cloves garlic
- $1/2$ cup (125 ml) extra-virgin olive oil
- Salt
- 2 tbsp freshly grated Parmesan cheese
- 2 tbsp freshly grated pecorino cheese

Place the basil, pine nuts, garlic, olive oil, and salt in a food processor and Chop until smooth. • Transfer the mixture to a medium serving bowl and stir in the cheeses. • This is a classic pasta sauce which is also delicious spooned over freshly boiled vegetables or rice; if serving with pasta add 1–2 spoonfuls of the cooking water.

945

BEEF STOCK

P ut all the vegetables, the meat, bones, and salt in a large pot with the water. • Bring to a boil over high heat. Lower heat to medium-low and simmer for about 2 hours. • Remove the bones and meat. Set the meat aside. • As the stock cools, fat will form on top and can be scooped off and discarded. • Use the stock as indicated in the recipes.

Makes: about 2 quarts (2 liters)

Preparation: 10 min.

Cooking: 2 hr.

Level of difficulty: 1

- **1 large carrot**
- **1 medium onion**
- **1 large stalk celery**
- **4 small tomatoes**
- **5 sprigs parsley**
- **10 leaves basil**
- **2 lb (1 kg) lean boiling beef + 2 lb (1 kg) beef bones**
- **1–2 tsp salt**
- **3 quarts (3 liters) water**

CHICKEN STOCK

P ut the chicken, whole, in a very large pot. Add the carrots, onion, celery, tomatoes, parsley, salt, and peppercorns. Cover with the cold water and simmer over medium-low heat for 3 hours. The water should barely move. • Strain the stock, discarding the vegetables. • To remove the fat, in part or completely, let the stock cool, then refrigerate for about 2 hours. The fat will solidify on the top and can easily be scooped off.

T hese stocks can be prepared in advance and frozen. Freeze in ice-cube trays so that you will always have fresh homemade stock on hand.

Makes: about 2 quarts (2 liters)

Preparation: 10 min. + 2 hr. to chill

Cooking: 3 hr.

Level of difficulty: 1

- **1 chicken (about 4 lb/2 kg)**
- **2 medium carrots**
- **1 onion, studded with 5 cloves**
- **1 large stalk celery**
- **4 small tomatoes**
- **5 sprigs parsley**
- **1–2 tsp salt**
- **5 peppercorns**
- **3 quarts (3 liters) water**

TOMATO SAUCE

Heat the oil in a large frying pan over medium heat. Add the onion, carrot, celery, and garlic and sauté until softened, about 5 minutes. • Add the tomatoes, parsley, basil, salt, pepper, and sugar. Partially cover the pan and simmer over low heat until the tomato and oil begin to separate, about 45 minutes. • For a smoother sauce, press the mixture through a food mill. • Serve with all kinds of fresh and dried pasta, and potato gnocchi.

Serves: 8

Preparation: 15 min.

Cooking: 50 min.

Level of difficulty: 1

- 4 lb (2 kg) fresh or canned tomatoes, peeled and chopped
- 1 large onion, coarsely chopped
- 1 large carrot, coarsely chopped
- 1 stalk celery, coarsely chopped
- 1 clove garlic, coarsely chopped
- 1 tbsp finely chopped fresh parsley
- 8 fresh basil leaves, torn
- $1/4$ cup (60 ml) extra-virgin olive oil
- 1 tsp sugar
- Salt and freshly ground black pepper

MEAT SAUCE

Serves: 4–6
Preparation: 20 min.
Cooking: 2 hr. 30 min.
Level of difficulty: 1

- 1/4 cup (60 g) butter
- 1/2 cup (60 g) diced pancetta
- 1 medium onion, finely chopped
- 1 stalk celery, finely chopped
- 1 carrot, finely chopped
- 12 oz (350 g) ground (minced) beef
- 4 oz (125 g) ground (minced) pork
- 4 oz (125 g) Italian pork sausage, peeled and crumbled
- 1 freshly ground clove
- Pinch of ground cinnamon
- 1 tsp freshly ground black pepper
- 1 (14-oz/400-g) can peeled and chopped tomatoes
- 1 cup (250 ml) milk
- Salt

Heat the butter in a large, heavy saucepan over medium heat and sauté the pancetta, onion, celery, and carrot in a sauté pan until softened, about 5 minutes. • Add the beef, pork, and sausage and sauté until browned, about 5 minutes. • Sprinkle with the clove, cinnamon, and pepper. Stir in the tomatoes and simmer over medium heat for 15 minutes. • Add the milk and season with salt. Turn the heat down to low and simmer for at least 2 hours, stirring frequently.

BREAD DOUGH

Place the yeast in a small bowl. Add the sugar and half the warm water and stir until dissolved. • Set aside for 15 minutes. • Place the flour and salt in a large bowl. • Pour in the yeast mixture and remaining water. Stir until the flour has been absorbed. • Kneading: Sprinkle a work surface, preferably made of wood, with a little flour. • Place the dough on the work surface. Curl your fingers around it and press together to form a compact ball. • Press down on the dough with your knuckles to spread it a little. Take the far end of the dough, fold it a short distance toward you, then push it away again with the heel of your palm. Flexing your wrist, fold it toward you again, give it a quarter turn, then push it away. Repeat, gently and with the lightest possible touch, for 8–10 minutes. When the dough is firm and no longer sticks to your hands or the work surface, lift it up and bang it down hard against the work surface a couple of times. This will develop the gluten. The dough should be smooth and elastic, show definite air bubbles beneath the surface, and spring back if you flatten it with your palm. • Place in a large, lightly oiled bowl and cover with a cloth. Set aside to rise. The dough should double in volume. • To test if ready, poke your finger gently into the dough; if the impression remains, then it is ready. Remember that yeast is a living ingredient, affected by temperature and humidity, among other things. Some days it will take longer to rise than others.

Preparation: 30 min.

Rising time: 90 min.

Level of difficulty: 1

Basic Focaccia
- 1 oz (25 g) fresh yeast or 2 (¹/₄-oz/ 7-g) packages active dry yeast
- 1 tsp sugar
- About ³/₄ cup (200 ml) warm water
- 3¹/₃ cups (500 g) all-purpose (plain) flour + ¹/₂ cup (75 g) to sprinkle work surface
- ³/₄ tsp salt

Basic Bread
- 1 oz (25 g) fresh yeast or 2 (¹/₄-oz/ 7-g) packages active dry yeast
- 1 tsp sugar
- About 1¹/₂ cups (350 ml) warm water
- 5 cups (750 g) all-purpose (plain) flour + ¹/₂ cup (75 g) to sprinkle work surface
- 1 tsp salt

PIZZA DOUGH

Place the fresh or active dry yeast in a small bowl. If using fresh yeast, crumble it with your fingertips. • Add half the warm water and stir until the yeast has dissolved. • Set the mixture aside for 15 minutes. It will look creamy when ready. Stir well. • Place the flour in a large bowl and sprinkle with the salt. • Make a hollow in the center and pour in the yeast mixture, the remaining water, and any other ingredients listed in the recipe. Use a wooden spoon to stir the mixture. Stir well until the flour has almost all been absorbed. • Knead the dough following the instructions for bread dough on the previous page (952). • To shape the pizza, place the dough in the pizza pan and use your fingertips to press it out, stretching it as you go, until it covers the pan. Set aside for 10 minutes before adding the topping. This will give the dough time to regain some volume and will make the crust lighter and more appetizing. • To make calzones, proceed as for pizza, giving the dough a round shape. Place the topping on one half of the disk only, leaving a 1-inch (2.5-cm) border around the edge. Fold the other half over the filling and press the edges together with your fingertips to seal.

Makes: one (12-inch/ 30-cm pizza)

Preparation: 30 min.

Rising time: 90 min.

Level of difficulty: 1

- 1 oz (25 g) fresh yeast or 2 ($1/4$-oz/ 7-g) packages active dry yeast
- About $2/3$ cup (150 ml) warm water
- 3 cups (450 g) all-purpose (plain) flour + $1/2$ cup (75 g) to sprinkle work surface
- $1/2$ tsp salt

BÉCHAMEL SAUCE

Melt the butter in a saucepan, add the flour and stir over medium heat until a light paste (or roux) is achieved. Pour in a dash of the milk to dissolve the roux. • Pour in the remaining milk and stir, making sure no lumps have formed. • Season with salt, white pepper, and freshly grated nutmeg to taste. Bring to a boil and simmer over low heat for 20 minutes. There is no need to stir continuously as the flour has already cooked through. If you are using the Béchamel in a baked dish, the cooking time of the sauce can be reduced to 10 minutes.

Makes: 2 cups
  (500 ml)

Preparation: 10 min.

Cooking: 10–20 min.

Level of difficulty: 2

- 3 tbsp butter, cut up
- 3 tbsp all-purpose (plain) flour
- 2 cups (500 ml) milk
- Salt and freshly ground white pepper
- Freshly grated nutmeg

SHORTCRUST PASTRY

959

Makes: pastry for a 9–10-inch (23–25-cm) pie pan

Preparation: 10 min. + 15 min. to chill

Level of difficulty: 1

- 2 cups (300 g) all-purpose (plain) flour
- $1/4$ tsp salt
- $1/2$ cup (125 g) butter, cut up
- 1 large egg + 1 large egg yolk
- About 2 tbsp cold water

Sweet Shortcrust Pastry
- $1/4$ (50 g) sugar

Mix the flour and salt in a large bowl. • Make a well in the center and add the butter, egg, egg yolk, and 1 tablespoon of water. Cut with a pastry blender until well mixed. The dough should be coarse and granular, but moist enough to stick together. Add the remaining water if it is too dry. • Place the dough on a lightly floured work surface and sprinkle with a little flour. Knead briefly by pushing the dough away from you using the heel of your hand. Fold back and repeat three or four times, or until the dough is smooth and does not stick to the work surface. Do not knead the dough too long or it will become tough and shrink during baking. • Shape into a disk, wrap in plastic wrap (cling film), and refrigerate for 15 minutes. • To make Sweet Shortcrust Pastry, add the sugar.

NEVER-FAIL QUICHE CRUST

Makes: pastry for a 9–10-inch (23–25-cm) pie pan

Preparation: 10 min. + 30 min. to chill

Level of difficulty: 1

- $1 2/3$ cups (250 g) all-purpose (plain) flour
- $1/4$ tsp salt
- $1/2$ cup (125 g) butter, cut up
- 2–4 tbsp cold water

Place the flour and salt in the bowl of a food processor with a metal blade. Add the butter and 2 tablespoons of water. Pulse until just amalgamated, adding more water if too crumbly. • Remove from the processor and press into a ball. • Wrap in plastic wrap (cling film) and refrigerate for 30 minutes.

ITALIAN SPONGE CAKE

Serves: 8–10

Preparation: 25 min.

Cooking: 40 min.

Level of difficulty: 2

- **6 large eggs**
- **1 cup (150 g) sugar**
- **2 tsp finely grated lemon zest**
- **1 cup (150 g) all-purpose (plain) flour**
- **$^1/_2$ cup (75 g) potato starch or cornstarch (cornflour)**
- **$^1/_4$ tsp salt**

Preheat the oven to 325°F (160°C/gas 3). • Butter and flour a 9-inch or 10-inch (23–25-cm) springform pan (depedning on the recipe you are preparing this cake for). • Place the eggs and sugar in the top part of a double boiler and whisk until frothy. • Remove from heat and add the lemon zest (yellow part only) and continue to whisk until cool. • Carefully fold in the flour, potato starch, and salt. • Spoon the dough into the prepared pan and bake until risen and golden brown, about 40 minutes.

VANILLA PASTRY CREAM

B eat the egg yolks and sugar until very pale and creamy. Stir in the flour. • Bring the milk to the boil, then remove from heat. • Stir the egg and flour mixture into the milk, then cook over very low heat, stirring constantly to prevent the mixture from becoming lumpy. • When thick, add the vanilla extract, and pour into a bowl. Cover with a layer of plastic wrap so that it touches the surface, to prevent a skin from forming.

Makes: about 2 cups (500 ml)

Preparation: 10 min.

Cooking: 15 min.

Level of difficulty: 1

- **5 large egg yolks**
- **$^3/_4$ cup (150 g) sugar**
- **$^1/_3$ cup (50 g) all-purpose (plain) flour**
- **2 cups (500 ml) whole milk**
- **$^1/_8$ tsp salt**
- **1 tsp vanilla extract**

Meringue with chocolate and candied chestnuts 845
Milanese charlotte 848
Milanese cookies 864
Mini ricotta cassatas 888
Mini sausage rolls 21
Mini seafood kebabs 493
Mint and parsley frittata 701
Mixed boiled meats 611
Mixed braised bell peppers 780
Mixed meat and vegetable skewers 588
Mixed salad with basil 810
Mocha cream cake 932
Mushroom and pumpkin risotto 266
Mushroom and sole risotto 286
Mushroom and tomato stew 768
Mushroom soup 192
Mussel fritters 34
Mussels with lemon and parsley 498

Neapolitan crostini 10
Neapolitan pork rolls 630
Neapolitan rice pie 297
Neapolitan ricotta cheese cake 940
Neapolitan trifle 852
Never-fail quiche crust 959

Octopus salad 58
Onion quiche 152
Onion, peas, potato, and lettuce stew 753
Orecchiette with broccoli 407
Orecchiette with potatoes and pecorino 408
Oregano bread sticks 88

Pan fried steak with green sauce 586
Pan roasted beef with beans and grapes 560
Pan roasted whole veal shanks 556
Panforte 934
Panzanella 59
Parmesan "ice cream" 49
Parmesan veal rolls 593
Pasta and peas in stock 199
Pasta salad with eggplant and pine nuts 351
Pasta salad with tuna 352
Pasta salad with tuna and olives 348
Pasta with leek and bell pepper crumble 327
Pea mousse 752
Peach pie 927
Pear and gorgonzola quiche 150

Potato Frittata with ham and peas 707
Potato fritters 756
Potato gnocchi with asparagus 213
Potato gnocchi with radicchio 212
Potato gnocchi with scampi and leek 209
Potato gnocchi with tomato and Parmesan 206
Potato ravioli with zucchini sauce 431
Potato tart 54
Potato tortelli with meat sauce 426
Potatoes Venetian-style 763
Prosciutto with cantaloupe 18
Prune gnocchi 223
Puff Pastry with creamy mushroom filling 155
Puglia-style beef parcels 596
Puglia-style potato cake 912

Quiche with cheese and peas 160
Quick gorgonzola focaccia 47
Quick mini pizzas 22

Ravioli with beet filling 452
Ravioli with zucchini in butter and rosemary sauce 445

Raw vegetables with oil, salt, and pepper dip 799
Rice and celery soup 176
Rice cake 916
Rice cake with pears 917
Rice Supplì 32
Rice with artichokes 260
Rice with eggplants 278
Rice with mussels 288
Rice with peas and beans 265
Rice with potatoes 272
Rice with sausage and rosemary 293
Rice with sundried tomato pesto and arugula 280
Ricotta gnocchi with meat sauce 228
Ricotta ravioli with tomato sauce 451
Ricotta tart 161
Rigatoni baked in pastry with meat sauce 369
Rigatoni with cauliflower, pine nuts, and raisins 334
Rigatoni with onion sauce 337
Rigatoni with peas and pesto 336
Rigatoni with roasted bell pepper sauce 328
Risotto with beans 262
Risotto with freshwater shrimp and peas 268

Veal cutlets with Parmesan cheese 580
Veal roll with potatoes 554
Veal shanks (Ossobuchi) with saffron rice 612
Vegetable mold 53
Vegetable soup with pesto 171
Vegetables en papillote 786
Vegetarian lasagne 411
Venetian-style liver 619
Venetian-style scallops 67
Verona noodle cake 936

Warm fried potato salad 755
Watercress tagliolini with basil sauce 380
Whole-wheat fusilli with onion and basil 340

Whole-wheat loaves 70
Whole-wheat penne with pumpkin and walnuts 354
Wild boar in red wine and tomato sauce 660
Winter cabbage soup 175

Zabaglione sponge cake with orange 909
Zabaglione with cream and raspberries 850
Zampone sausage with potatoes 648
Zite with cauliflower and tomato sauce 324
Zucchini and ham pie 142
Zucchini stuffed with amaretti cookies 737